NEW TEPS 완벽 반영

뉴텝스도 역시

KB136557

그냥 믿고 따라와 봐!

600점 만점!!

마스터편 실전 500+

독해 정일상, 넥서스TEPS연구소 지음 | 17,500원 **문법** 테스 김 지음 | 15,000원 **청해** 라보혜, 넥서스TEPS연구소 지음 | 18,000원

500점

실력편 실전 400+

독해 정일상, 넥서스TEPS연구소 지음 | 18,000원 **문법** 넥서스TEPS연구소 지음 | 15,000원 **청해** 라보혜, 넥서스TEPS연구소 지음 | 17,000원

400점

기본편 실전 300+

독해 정일상, 넥서스TEPS연구소 지음 | 19,000원 **문법** 장보금, 써니 박 지음 | 17,500원 **청해** 이기헌 지음 | 19,800원

300점

입문편 실전 250+

독해 넥서스TEPS연구소 지음 | 18,000원 **문법** 넥서스TEPS연구소 지음 | 15,000원 **청해** 넥서스TEPS연구소 지음 | 18,000원

MP3 듣기
모바일 단어장
온라인 받아쓰기
정답 자동 채점

넥서스
NEW TEPS 시리즈

목표 점수 달성을 위한
뉴텝스 기본서 + 실전서

뉴텝스 실전 완벽 대비
Actual Test 수록

고득점의 감을 확실하게 잡아 주는
상세한 해설 제공

모바일 단어장, 어휘 테스트 등
다양한 부가자료 제공

LEVEL CHART

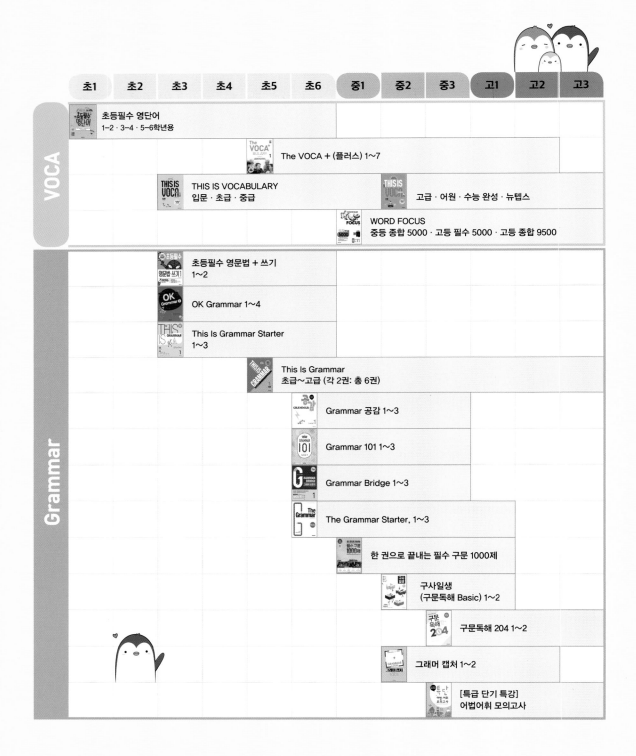

	초1	초2	초3	초4	초5	초6	중1	중2	중3	고1	고2	고3

VOCA

초등필수 영단어
1-2 · 3-4 · 5-6학년용

The VOCA + (플러스) 1~7

THIS IS VOCABULARY
입문 · 초급 · 중급

고급 · 어원 · 수능 완성 · 뉴텝스

WORD FOCUS
중등 종합 5000 · 고등 필수 5000 · 고등 종합 9500

Grammar

초등필수 영문법 + 쓰기
1~2

OK Grammar 1~4

This Is Grammar Starter
1~3

This Is Grammar
초급~고급 (각 2권: 총 6권)

Grammar 공감 1~3

Grammar 101 1~3

Grammar Bridge 1~3

The Grammar Starter, 1~3

한 권으로 끝내는 필수 구문 1000제

구사일생
(구문독해 Basic) 1~2

구문독해 204 1~2

그래머 캡처 1~2

[특급 단기 특강]
어법어휘 모의고사

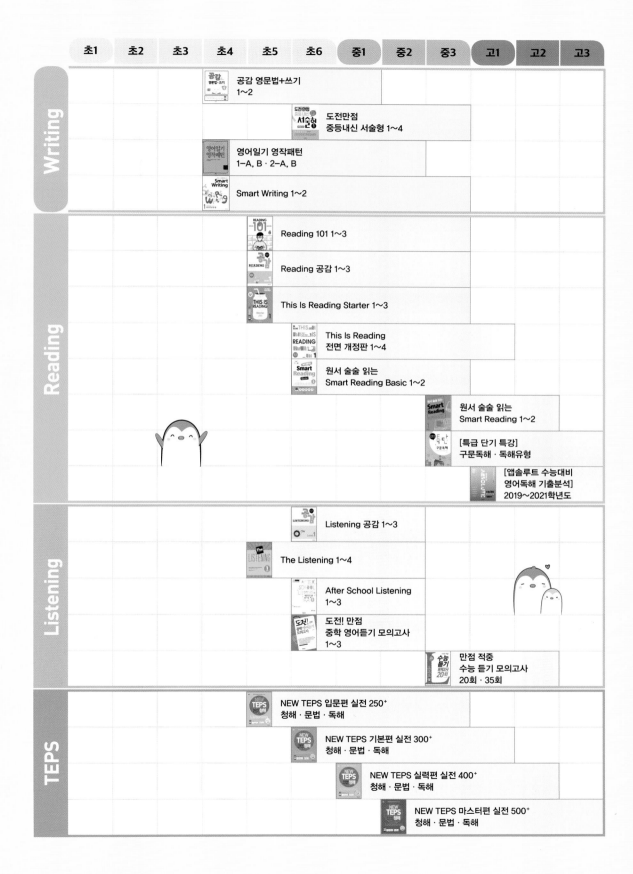

초1	초2	초3	초4	초5	초6	중1	중2	중3	고1	고2	고3

Writing

- 공감 영문법+쓰기 1~2
- 도전만점 중등내신 서술형 1~4
- 영어일기 영작패턴 1-A, B · 2-A, B
- Smart Writing 1~2

Reading

- Reading 101 1~3
- Reading 공감 1~3
- This Is Reading Starter 1~3
- This Is Reading 전면 개정판 1~4
- 원서 술술 읽는 Smart Reading Basic 1~2
- 원서 술술 읽는 Smart Reading 1~2
- [특급 단기 특강] 구문독해 · 독해유형
- [앱솔루트 수능대비 영어독해 기출분석] 2019~2021학년도

Listening

- Listening 공감 1~3
- The Listening 1~4
- After School Listening 1~3
- 도전! 만점 중학 영어듣기 모의고사 1~3
- 만점 적중 수능 듣기 모의고사 20회 · 35회

TEPS

- NEW TEPS 입문편 실전 250+ 청해 · 문법 · 독해
- NEW TEPS 기본편 실전 300+ 청해 · 문법 · 독해
- NEW TEPS 실력편 실전 400+ 청해 · 문법 · 독해
- NEW TEPS 마스터편 실전 500+ 청해 · 문법 · 독해

NEW
TEPS

실력편
실전 400+ 독해

NEW TEPS 실력편(실전 400+) 독해

지은이 정일상 · 넥서스TEPS연구소
펴낸이 임상진
펴낸곳 (주)넥서스

출판신고 1992년 4월 3일 제311-2002-2호 ⑫
10880 경기도 파주시 지목로 5
Tel (02)330-5500 Fax (02)330-5555
ISBN 979-11-964383-3-3 14740
         979-11-964383-2-6 14740 (SET)

www.nexusbook.com

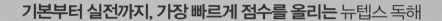

기본부터 실전까지, 가장 빠르게 점수를 올리는 뉴텝스 독해

NEW
TEPS

실력편
실전 400+ 독해

정일상·넥서스TEPS연구소 지음

Reading

NEXUS Edu

TEPS 점수 환산표 [TEPS → NEW TEPS]

TEPS	NEW TEPS	TEPS	NEW TEPS	TEPS	NEW TEPS	TEPS	NEW TEPS
981~990	590~600	771~780	433~437	561~570	303~308	351~360	185~189
971~980	579~589	761~770	426~432	551~560	298~303	341~350	181~184
961~970	570~578	751~760	419~426	541~550	292~297	331~340	177~180
951~960	564~569	741~750	414~419	531~540	286~291	321~330	173~177
941~950	556~563	731~740	406~413	521~530	281~285	311~320	169~173
931~940	547~555	721~730	399~405	511~520	275~280	301~310	163~168
921~930	538~546	711~720	392~399	501~510	268~274	291~300	154~163
911~920	532~538	701~710	387~392	491~500	263~268	281~290	151~154
901~910	526~532	691~700	381~386	481~490	258~262	271~280	146~150
891~900	515~525	681~690	374~380	471~480	252~257	261~270	140~146
881~890	509~515	671~680	369~374	461~470	247~252	251~260	135~139
871~880	502~509	661~670	361~368	451~460	241~247	241~250	130~134
861~870	495~501	651~660	355~361	441~450	236~241	231~240	128~130
851~860	488~495	641~650	350~355	431~440	229~235	221~230	123~127
841~850	483~488	631~640	343~350	421~430	223~229	211~220	119~123
831~840	473~481	621~630	338~342	411~420	217~223	201~210	111~118
821~830	467~472	611~620	332~337	401~410	212~216	191~200	105~110
811~820	458~465	601~610	327~331	391~400	206~211	181~190	102~105
801~810	453~458	591~600	321~327	381~390	201~206	171~180	100~102
791~800	445~452	581~590	315~320	371~380	196~200		
781~790	438~444	571~580	309~315	361~370	190~195		

※ 출처: 한국영어평가학회

보다 세분화된 환산표는
www.teps.or.kr에서
내려받을 수 있습니다.

어떠한 영어 시험이든 실제 그 사람이 가진 순수한 영어 실력만을 평가할 수는 없습니다. 시험마다 문제 구성, 난이도, 평가 체계 등이 다르기 때문에 그에 맞게 준비를 하고 시험장에 가야 합니다. 그러니 시험의 성격조차 파악하지 않고 단순히 지문을 읽고 문제를 푼다는 것은 어찌 보면 개인의 소중한 시간을 고스란히 내다 버리는 일이 됩니다.

특히 뉴텝스는 다른 공인 영어 시험과 차별화된 고유한 문제 스타일이 있습니다. 영어 실력이 주변 사람들보다 월등한데 실제 시험에서는 상대적으로 낮은 점수를 받는다면, 이는 뉴텝스 시험 자체를 제대로 파악하지 못했기 때문입니다. 뉴텝스의 4개 영역(청해, 어휘, 문법, 독해)이 어떻게 바뀌었는지, 각 파트별로는 어떤 차이가 있는지 문제 유형별로 분석하여 시험의 감을 잡는다면, 원하는 결과를 꼭 얻게 될 것입니다.

뉴텝스 독해는 지문 속 빈칸 채우기, 문맥상 어색한 내용 고르기, 지문을 읽고 가장 적절한 답 고르기(주제 찾기, 세부 내용 파악, 추론하기), 뉴텝스 신유형으로 등장하는 1지문 2문항 등 크게 4개의 파트로 이루어져 있습니다. 독해 지문은 편지나 광고 등 다양한 상황의 실용 지문과 과학, 문학, 예술, 철학, 역사 등을 다루는 학술 지문으로 나눌 수 있습니다.

〈NEW TEPS 실력편(실전 400+) 독해〉에는 뉴텝스 독해의 고유한 특성과 최신 기출 문제의 경향을 보여 주는 동시에 문제 유형별 전략까지 제시합니다. 독해에 꼭 필요한 문법 포인트와 문제 유형별 전략 및 주제별 독해 훈련을 통해 뉴텝스 독해의 기본을 다질 수 있으며, 뉴텝스 문제 유형을 가장 잘 반영한 실전 모의고사 5회분을 풀면서 실전 감각을 높일 수 있습니다.

탄탄한 기초 공사 없이 단기간에 원하는 점수를 받는 비법은 어느 시험에서도 없습니다. 하지만 효율적으로 원하는 점수를 얻고 전반적인 영어 실력까지 높이는 길은 우리가 찾을 수 있고, 없다면 만들어 낼 수도 있습니다. 아무쪼록 〈NEW TEPS 실력편(실전 400+) 독해〉를 통해 뉴텝스에 대한 이해를 높이고, 여러분 모두 실전에서 원하는 점수를 받을 수 있기를 바랍니다.

넥서스TEPS연구소

Contents

Ⅲ 주제별 독해 훈련

Ⅳ 실전 모의고사

정답 및 상세한 해설 (부록)

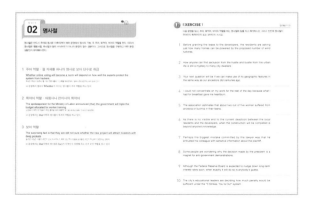

올바른 독해를 위한 문법

문장 구조 이해의 기본 바탕인 문법을 독해에
꼭 필요한 것만 선별해 5개 unit으로 정리
하였습니다.

유형별 독해 전략

뉴텝스 독해의 문제 유형을 8개 unit으로
나눠 각 유형에 맞는 독해 전략을 구사할
수 있도록 하였습니다.

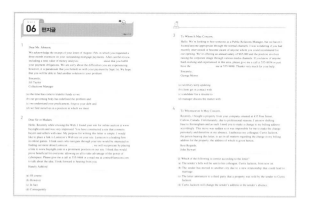

주제별 독해 훈련

뉴텝스 독해 지문에서 자주 나오는 주제를
세분화하여 시간 대비 효율적으로 공부할
수 있도록 정리하였습니다.

EXERCISE

실전 모의고사 5회분을 풀기 전에 몸풀기를 할 수 있도록 각 unit마다 연습 문제를 실었습니다. 문법과 독해 유형, 주제별 연습으로 실전의 감을 잡을 수 있도록 구성하였습니다.

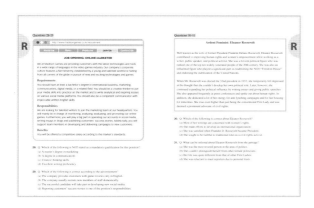

NEW TEPS 실전모의고사 5회분

뉴텝스에 맞춘 문제들로 구성된 ACTUAL TEST를 총 175문제, 5회분 모의고사로 준비하여 고득점에 다가갈 수 있도록 하였습니다.

상세한 해설 수록

알기 쉬운 해석과 어휘 정리는 물론, 상세하고 친절한 해설을 수록하여 혼자 공부해도 뉴텝스 독해에 만반의 준비를 할 수 있도록 구성하였습니다.

TEPS란?

TEPS는 Test of English Proficiency developed by Seoul National University의 약자로 서울대학교 언어교육원에서 개발하고, TEPS관리위원회에서 주관하는 국가공인 영어 시험입니다. 1999년 1월 처음 시행 이후 2018년 5월 12일부터 새롭게 바뀐 NEW TEPS가 시행되고 있습니다. TEPS는 정부기관 및 기업의 직원 채용이나 인사고과, 해외 파견 근무자 선발과 더불어 국내 유수의 대학과 특목고 입학 및 졸업 자격 요건, 국가고시 및 자격 시험의 영어 대체 시험으로 활용되고 있습니다.

1 / NEW TEPS는 종합적 지문 이해력 평가를 위한 시험으로, 실제 영어 사용 환경을 고려하여 평가 효율성을 높이고 시험 응시 피로도는 낮춰 수험자의 내재화된 영어 능력을 평가합니다.

2 / 편법이 없는 시험을 위해 청해(Listening)에서는 시험지에 선택지가 제시되어 있지 않아 눈으로 읽을 수 없고 오직 듣기 능력에만 의존해야 합니다. 청해나 독해(Reading)에서는 한 문제로 다음 문제의 답을 유추할 수 있는 가능성을 배제하기 위해 1지문 1문항을 고수해 왔지만 NEW TEPS부터 1지문 2문항 유형이 새롭게 추가되었습니다.

3 / 실생활에서 접할 수 있는 다양한 주제와 상황을 다룹니다. 일상생활과 비즈니스를 비롯해 문학, 과학, 역사 등 학술적인 소재도 출제됩니다.

4 / 청해, 어휘, 문법, 독해의 4영역으로 나뉘며, 총 135문항에 600점 만점입니다. 영역별 점수 산출이 가능하며, 점수 외에 5에서 1+까지 10등급으로 나뉩니다.

영역	문제 유형	문항수	제한 시간	점수 범위
청해 Listening Comprehension	**Part I** : 한 문장을 듣고 이어질 대화로 가장 적절한 답 고르기 (문장 1회 청취 후 선택지 1회 청취)	10	40분	0~240점
	Part II : 짧은 대화를 듣고 이어질 대화로 가장 적절한 답 고르기 (대화 1회 청취 후 선택지 1회 청취)	10		
	Part III : 긴 대화를 듣고 질문에 가장 적절한 답 고르기 (대화 및 질문 1회 청취 후 선택지 1회 청취)	10		
	Part IV : 담화를 듣고 질문에 가장 적절한 답 고르기 (1지문 1문항) (담화 및 질문 2회 청취 후 선택지 1회 청취)	6		
	Part V : 담화를 듣고 질문에 가장 적절한 답 고르기 (1지문 2문항) (담화 및 질문 2회 청취 후 선택지 1회 청취)	신유형 4		
어휘 Vocabulary	**Part I** : 대화문의 빈칸에 가장 적절한 어휘 고르기	10	통합 25분 변경	0~60점
	Part II : 단문의 빈칸에 가장 적절한 어휘 고르기	20		
문법 Grammar	**Part I** : 대화문의 빈칸에 가장 적절한 답 고르기	10		0~60점
	Part II : 단문의 빈칸에 가장 적절한 답 고르기	15		
	Part III : 대화 및 문단에서 문법상 틀리거나 어색한 부분 고르기	5		
독해 Reading Comprehension	**Part I** : 지문을 읽고 빈칸에 가장 적절한 답 고르기	10	40분	0~240점
	Part II : 지문을 읽고 문맥상 어색한 내용 고르기	2		
	Part III : 지문을 읽고 질문에 가장 적절한 답 고르기 (1지문 1문항)	13		
	Part IV : 지문을 읽고 질문에 가장 적절한 답 고르기 (1지문 2문항)	신유형 10		
총계	**14개 Parts**	135문항	105분	0~600점

청해 (Listening Comprehension) _40문항

정확한 청해 능력을 측정하기 위하여 문제와 보기 문항을 문제지에 인쇄하지 않고 들려줌으로써 자연스러운 의사소통의 인지 과정을 최대한 반영하였습니다. 다양한 의사소통 기능(Communicative Functions)의 대화와 다양한 상황(공고, 방송, 일상생활, 업무 상황, 대학 교양 수준의 강의 등)을 이해하는 데 필요한 전반적인 청해력을 측정하기 위해 대화문(dialogue)과 담화문(monologue)의 소재를 균형 있게 다루었습니다.

어휘 (Vocabulary) _30문항

문맥 없이 단순한 동의어 및 반의어를 선택하는 시험 유형을 배제하고 의미 있는 문맥을 근거로 가장 적절한 어휘를 선택하는 유형을 문어체와 구어체로 나누어 측정합니다.

문법 (Grammar) _30문항

밑줄 친 부분 중 오류를 식별하는 유형 등의 단편적이며 기계적인 문법 지식 학습을 조장할 우려가 있는 분리식 시험 유형을 배제하고, 의미 있는 문맥을 근거로 오류를 식별하는 유형을 통하여 진정한 의사소통 능력의 바탕이 되는 살아 있는 문법, 어법 능력을 문어체와 구어체를 통하여 측정합니다.

독해 (Reading Comprehension) _35문항

교양 있는 수준의 글(신문, 잡지, 대학 교양과목 개론 등)과 실용적인 글(서신, 광고, 홍보, 지시문, 설명문, 양식 등)을 이해하는 데 요구되는 총체적인 독해력을 측정하기 위해서 실용문 및 비전문적 학술문과 같은 독해 지문의 소재를 균형 있게 다루었습니다.

★ PART I (10문항)

두 사람의 질의응답 문제를 다루며, 한 번만 들려줍니다. 내용 자체는 단순하고 기본적인 수준의 생활 영어 표현으로 구성되어 있지만, 교과서적인 지식보다는 재빠른 상황 판단 능력이 필요합니다. Part I에서는 속도 적응 능력뿐만 아니라 순발력 있는 상황 판단 능력이 요구됩니다.

Choose the most appropriate response to the statement.

W I heard that it's going to be very hot tomorrow.

M _____

(a) It was the hottest day of the year.
(b) Be sure to dress warmly.
(c) Let's not sweat the details.
(d) It's going to be a real scorcher.

W 내일은 엄청 더운 날씨가 될 거래.

M _____

(a) 일 년 중 가장 더운 날이었어.
(b) 옷을 따뜻하게 입도록 해.
(c) 사소한 일에 신경 쓰지 말자.
(d) 엄청나게 더운 날이 될 거야.

정답 (d)

★ PART II (10문항)

짧은 대화 문제로, 두 사람이 A-B-A 순으로 보통의 속도로 대화하는 형식입니다. 소요 시간은 약 12초 전후로 짧습니다. Part I과 마찬가지로 한 번만 들려줍니다.

Choose the most appropriate response to complete the conversation.

M Would you like to join me to see a musical?
W Sorry no. I hate musicals.
M How could anyone possibly hate a musical?
W _____

(a) Different strokes for different folks.
(b) It's impossible to hate musicals.
(c) I agree with you.
(d) I'm not really musical.

M 나랑 같이 뮤지컬 보러 갈래?
W 미안하지만 안 갈래. 나 뮤지컬을 싫어하거든.
M 뮤지컬 싫어하는 사람도 있어?
W _____

(a) 사람마다 제각각이지 뭐.
(b) 뮤지컬을 싫어하는 것은 불가능해.
(c) 네 말에 동의해.
(d) 나는 그다지 음악에 재능이 없어.

정답 (a)

앞의 두 파트에 비해 다소 긴 대화를 들려줍니다. NEW TEPS에서는 대화와 질문 모두 한 번만 들려 줍니다. 대화의 주제나 주로 일어나고 있는 일, 화자가 갖고 있는 문제점, 세부 내용, 추론할 수 있는 것 등에 대해 묻습니다.

Choose the option that best answers the question.

W I just went to the dentist, and he said I need surgery.

M That sounds painful!

W Yeah, but that's not even the worst part. He said it will cost $5,000!

M Wow! That sounds too expensive. I think you should get a second opinion.

W Really? Do you know a good place?

M Sure. Let me recommend my guy I use. He's great.

Q: Which is correct according to the conversation?

(a) The man doesn't like his dentist.

(b) The woman believes that $5,000 sounds like a fair price.

(c) The man thinks that the dental surgery is too costly for her.

(d) The woman agrees that the dental treatment will be painless.

W 치과에 갔는데, 의사가 나보고 수술을 해야 한대.

M 아프겠다!

W 응, 하지만 더 심한 건 수술 비용이 5천 달러라는 거야!

M 와! 너무 비싸다. 다른 의사의 진단을 받아 보는 게 좋겠어.

W 그래? 어디 좋은 곳이라도 알고 있니?

M 물론이지. 내가 가는 곳을 추천해 줄게. 잘하시는 분이야.

Q 대화에 의하면 다음 중 옳은 것은?

(a) 남자는 담당 치과 의사를 좋아하지 않는다.

(b) 여자는 5천 달러가 적당한 가격이라고 생각한다.

(c) 남자는 치과 수술이 여자에게 너무 비싸다고 생각한다.

(d) 여자는 치과 시술이 아프지 않을 것이라는 점에 동의한다.

정답 (c)

14

★ PART IV (6문항)

이전 파트와 달리, 한 사람의 담화를 다룹니다. 방송이나 뉴스, 강의, 회의를 시작하면서 발제하는 것 등의 상황이 나옵니다. Part IV, Part V는 담화와 질문을 두 번씩 들려줍니다. 담화의 주제와 세부 내용, 추론할 수 있는 것 등에 대해 묻습니다.

Choose the option that best answers the question.

Tests confirmed that a 19-year-old woman recently died of the bird flu virus. This was the third such death in Indonesia. Cases such as this one have sparked panic in several Asian nations. Numerous countries have sought to discover a vaccine for this terrible illness. Officials from the Indonesian Ministry of Health examined the woman's house and neighborhood, but could not find the source of the virus. According to the ministry, the woman had fever for four days before arriving at the hospital.

Q: Which is correct according to the news report?
(a) There is an easy cure for the disease.
(b) Most nations are unconcerned with the virus.
(c) The woman caught the bird flu from an unknown source.
(d) The woman was sick for four days and then recovered.

최근 19세 여성이 조류 독감으로 사망한 것이 검사로 확인되었고, 인도네시아에서 이번이 세 번째이다. 이와 같은 사건들이 일부 아시아 국가들에게 극심한 공포를 불러 일으켰고, 많은 나라들이 이 끔찍한 병의 백신을 찾기 위해 힘쓰고 있다. 인도네시아 보건부의 직원들은 그녀의 집과 이웃을 조사했지만, 바이러스의 근원을 찾을 수 없었다. 보건부에 의하면, 그녀는 병원에 도착하기 전 나흘 동안 열이 있었다.

Q 뉴스 보도에 의하면 다음 중 옳은 것은?
(a) 이 병에는 간단한 치료법이 있다.
(b) 대부분의 나라들은 바이러스에 대해 관심이 없다.
(c) 여자는 알려지지 않은 원인에 의해 조류 독감에 걸렸다.
(d) 여자는 나흘 동안 앓고 나서 회복되었다.

정답 (c)

이번 NEW TEPS에 새롭게 추가된 유형으로 1지문 2문항 유형입니다. 2개의 지문이 나오므로 총 4문항을 풀어야 합니다. 주제와 세부 내용, 추론 문제가 섞여서 출제되며, 담화와 질문을 두 번씩 들려줍니다.

Choose the option that best answers each question.

Most of you have probably heard of the Tour de France, the most famous cycling race in the world. But you may not be familiar with its complex structure and award system. The annual race covers about 3,500 kilometers across 21 days of racing. It has a total of 198 riders split into 22 teams of 9. At the end of the tour, four riders are presented special jerseys.

The most prestigious of these is the yellow jerseys. This is given to the rider with the lowest overall time. The white jersey is awarded on the same criterion, but it's exclusive to participants under the age of 26. The green jersey and the polka-dot jersey are earned based on points awarded at every stage of the race. So what's the difference between these two jerseys? Well, the competitor with the most total points gets the green jersey, while the rider with the most points in just the mountain sections of the race receives the polka-dot one.

Q1: What is the talk mainly about?
(a) How the colors of the Tour de France jerseys were chosen.
(b) How the various Tour de France jerseys are won.
(c) Which Tour de France jerseys are the most coveted.
(d) Why riders in the Tour de France wear different colored jerseys.

Q2: Which jersey is given to the rider with the most points overall?
(a) The yellow jersey   (c) The green jersey
(b) The white jersey   (d) The polka-dot jersey

여러분은 아마도 세계에서 가장 유명한 사이클링 대회인 투르 드 프랑스에 대해 들어보셨을 것입니다. 하지만 여러분은 그 대회의 복잡한 구조와 수상 체계에 대해서는 잘 모를 것입니다. 매년 열리는 이 대회는 21일 동안 약 3,500킬로미터를 주행하게 되어있습니다. 이 대회에서 총 198명의 참가자가 각각 9명으로 구성된 22팀으로 나뉩니다. 대회 마지막에는 4명의 선수에게 특별한 저지를 수여합니다.

가장 영예로운 것은 노란색 저지입니다. 이것은 가장 단시간에 도착한 참가자에게 수여됩니다. 흰색 저지는 같은 기준에 의하여 수여되는데, 26세 미만의 참가자에게만 수여됩니다. 녹색 저지와 물방울무늬 저지는 대회의 매 단계의 점수에 기반하여 주어집니다. 그럼 이 두 저지의 차이점은 무엇일까요? 자, 가장 높은 총점을 딴 참가자는 녹색 저지를 받고, 산악 구간에서 가장 많은 점수를 딴 참가자는 물방울무늬 저지를 받습니다.

Q1 담화문의 주제는 무엇인가?

(a) 투르 드 프랑스 저지의 색깔은 어떻게 정해지는가
(b) 다양한 투르 드 프랑스 저지가 어떻게 수여되는가
(c) 어떤 투르 드 프랑스 저지가 가장 선망의 대상이 되는가
(d) 투르 드 프랑스의 선수들이 다양한 색의 저지를 입는 이유는 무엇인가   정답 (b)

Q2 가장 많은 총점을 획득한 선수에게 어떤 저지가 주어지는가?

(a) 노란색 저지   (c) 녹색 저지
(b) 흰색 저지   (d) 물방울무늬 저지   정답 (c)

어휘 Vocabulary

★ PART I (10문항)

구어체로 되어 있는 A와 B의 대화 중 빈칸에 가장 적절한 단어를 고르는 문제입니다. 단어의 단편적인 의미보다는 문맥에서 쓰인 의미가 더 중요합니다. 한 개의 단어로 된 선택지뿐만 아니라 두세 단어 이상의 구를 이루는 선택지도 있습니다.

Choose the option that best completes the dialogue.

A Congratulations on your _____ of the training course.

B Thank you. It was hard, but I managed to pull through.

(a) improvement
(b) resignation
(c) evacuation
(d) completion

A 훈련 과정을 완수한 거 축하해.

B 고마워. 어려웠지만 가까스로 끝낼 수 있었어.

(a) 개선
(b) 사임
(c) 철수
(d) 완료

정답 (d)

★ PART II (20문항)

하나 또는 두 개의 문장 속의 빈칸에 가장 적당한 단어를 고르는 문제입니다. 어휘력을 늘릴 때 한 개씩 단편적으로 암기하는 것보다는 하나의 표현으로, 즉 의미 단위로 알아 놓는 것이 제한된 시간 내에 어휘 시험을 정확히 푸는 데 많은 도움이 됩니다. 후반부로 갈수록 수준 높은 어휘가 출제되며, 단어 사이의 미묘한 의미의 차이를 묻는 문제도 출제됩니다.

Choose the option that best completes the sentence.

Brian was far ahead in the game and was certain to win, but his opponent refused to _____.

(a) yield
(b) agree
(c) waive
(d) forfeit

브라이언이 게임에 앞서 가고 있어서 승리가 확실했지만 그의 상대는 굴복하려 하지 않았다.

(a) 굴복하다
(b) 동의하다
(c) 포기하다
(d) 몰수당하다

정답 (a)

★ PART I (10문항)

A와 B 두 사람의 짧은 대화를 통해 구어체 관용 표현, 품사, 시제, 인칭, 어순 등 문법 전반에 대한 이해를 묻습니다. 대화 중에 빈칸이 있고, 그곳에 들어갈 적절한 표현을 고르는 형식입니다.

Choose the option that best completes the dialogue.

A   I can't attend the meeting, either.

B   Then we have no choice _____ the meeting.

(a) but canceling

(b) than to cancel

(c) than cancel

(d) but to cancel

A   저도 회의에 참석할 수 없어요.

B   그러면 회의를 <u>취소하는 수밖에요.</u>

(a) 그러나 취소하는

(b) 취소하는 것보다

(c) 취소하는 것보다

(d) 취소하는 수밖에

정답 (d)

★ PART II (15문항)

Part I에서 구어체의 대화를 나눴다면, Part II에서는 문어체의 문장이 나옵니다. 서술문 속의 빈칸을 채우는 문제로 수 일치, 태, 어순, 분사 등 문법 자체에 대한 이해도는 물론 구문에 대한 이해력이 중요합니다.

Choose the option that best completes the sentence.

_____ being pretty confident about it, Irene decided to check her facts.

(a) Nevertheless

(b) Because of

(c) Despite

(d) Instead of

그 일에 대해 매우 자신감이 있었음에도 불구하고 아이린은 사실을 확인하기로 했다.

(a) 그럼에도 불구하고

(b) 때문에

(c) 그럼에도 불구하고

(d) 대신에

정답 (c)

★ PART III (대화문: 2문항 / 지문: 3문항)

① A–B–A–B의 대화문에서 어법상 틀리거나 문맥상 어색한 부분이 있는 문장을 고르는 문제입니다. 이 영역 역시 문법 뿐만 아니라 정확한 구문 파악과 대화 내용을 이해하는 능력이 중요합니다.

Identify the option that contains a grammatical error.

(a) A: What are you doing this weekend?

(b) B: Going fishing as usual.

(c) A: Again? What's the fun in going fishing? Actually, I don't understand why people go fishing.

(d) B: For me, I like being alone, thinking deeply to me, being surrounded by nature.

(a) A 이번 주말에 뭐해?

(b) B 평소처럼 낚시 가.

(c) A 또 가? 낚시가 뭐 재미있니? 솔직히 난 사람들이 왜 낚시를 하러 가는지 모르겠어.

(d) B 내 경우엔 자연에 둘러 싸여서 혼자 깊이 생각해 볼 수 있다는 게 좋아.

정답 (d) me → myself

---

② 한 문단을 주고 그 가운데 문법적으로 틀리거나 어색한 문장을 고르는 문제입니다. 문법적으로 틀린 부분을 신속하게 골라야 하므로 독해 문제처럼 속독 능력도 중요합니다.

Identify the option that contains a grammatical error.

(a) The creators of a new video game hope to change the disturbing trend of using violence to enthrall young gamers. (b) Video game designers and experts on human development teamed up and designed a new computer game with the gameplay that helps young players overcome everyday school life situations. (c) The elements in the game resemble regular objects: pencils, erasers, and the like. (d) The players of the game "win" by choose peaceful solutions instead of violent ones.

(a) 새 비디오 게임 개발자들은 어린 게이머들의 흥미 유발을 위해 폭력적인 내용을 사용하는 불건전한 판도를 바꿔 놓을 수 있기를 바란다. (b) 비디오 게임 개발자들과 인간 발달 전문가들이 공동으로 개발한 새로운 컴퓨터 게임은 어린이들이 매일 학교에서 부딪히는 상황에 잘 대처할 수 있도록 도와준다. (c) 실제로 게임에는 연필과 지우개 같은 평범한 사물들이 나온다. (d) 폭력적인 해결책보다 비폭력적인 해결책을 선택하면 게임에서 이긴다.

정답 (d) by choose → by choosing

★ PART I (10문항)

지문 속 빈칸에 알맞은 것을 고르는 유형입니다. 글 전체의 흐름을 파악하여 문맥상 빈칸에 들어갈 내용을 찾아야 하는데, 주로 지문의 주제와 관련이 있습니다. 마지막 두 문제, 9번과 10번은 빈칸에 알맞은 연결어를 고르는 문제입니다. 문맥의 흐름을 논리적으로 파악할 수 있어야 합니다.

Read the passage and choose the option that best completes the passage.

Tech industry giants like Facebook, Google, Twitter, and Amazon have threatened to shut down their sites. They're protesting legislation that may regulate Internet content. The Stop Online Piracy Act, or SOPA, according to advocates, will make it easier for regulators to police intellectual property violations on the web, but the bill has drawn criticism from online activists who say SOPA will outlaw many common internet-based activities, like downloading copyrighted content. A boycott, or blackout, by the influential web companies acts to

_____.

(a) threaten lawmakers by halting all Internet access
(b) illustrate real-world effects of the proposed rule
(c) withdraw web activities the policy would prohibit
(d) laugh at the debate about what's allowed online

페이스북, 구글, 트위터, 아마존과 같은 거대 기술업체들이 그들의 사이트를 닫겠다고 위협했다. 그들은 인터넷 콘텐츠를 규제할지도 모르는 법령의 제정에 반대한다. 지지자들은 온라인 저작권 침해 금지 법안으로 인해 단속 기관들이 더 쉽게 웹상에서 지적 재산 침해 감시를 할 수 있다고 말한다. 그러나 온라인 활동가들은 저작권이 있는 콘텐츠를 다운로드하는 것과 같은 일반적인 인터넷 기반 활동들이 불법화될 것이라고 이 법안을 비판하고 있다. 영향력 있는 웹 기반 회사들에 의한 거부 운동 또는 보도 통제는 <u>발의된 법안이 현실에 미치는 영향을 보여 주기 위한</u> 것이다.

(a) 인터넷 접속을 금지시켜서 입법자들을 위협하기 위한
(b) 발의된 법안이 현실에 미치는 영향을 보여 주기 위한
(c) 그 정책이 금지하게 될 웹 활동들을 중단하기 위한
(d) 온라인에서 무엇이 허용될지에 대한 논쟁을 비웃기 위한

정답 (b)

★ PART II (2문항)

글의 흐름상 어색한 문장을 고르는 문제로, 전체 흐름을 파악하여 지문의 주제나 소재와 관계없는 내용을 고릅니다.

Read the passage and identify the option that does NOT belong.

For the next four months, major cities will experiment with new community awareness initiatives to decrease smoking in public places. (a) Anti-tobacco advertisements in recent years have relied on scare tactics to show how smokers hurt their own bodies. (b) But the new effort depicts the effects of second-hand smoke on children who breathe in adults' cigarette fumes. (c) Without these advertisements, few children would understand the effects of adults' hard-to-break habits. (d) Cities hope these messages will inspire people to think about others and cut back on their tobacco use.

향후 4개월 동안 주요 도시들은 공공장소에서의 흡연을 줄이기 위해 지역 사회의 의식을 촉구하는 새로운 계획을 시도할 것이다. (a) 최근에 금연 광고는 흡연자가 자신의 몸을 얼마나 해치고 있는지를 보여 주기 위해 겁을 주는 방식에 의존했다. (b) 그러나 이 새로운 시도는 어른들의 담배 연기를 마시는 아이들에게 미치는 간접흡연의 영향을 묘사한다. (c) 이러한 광고가 없다면, 아이들은 어른들의 끊기 힘든 습관이 미칠 영향을 모를 것이다. (d) 도시들은 이러한 메시지가 사람들에게 타인에 대해서 생각해 보고 담배 사용을 줄이는 마음이 생기게 할 것을 기대하고 있다.

정답 (c)

글의 내용 이해를 측정하는 문제로, 글의 주제나 대의 혹은 전반적 논조를 파악하는 문제, 세부 내용을 파악하는 문제, 추론하는 문제가 있습니다.

Read the passage, question, and options. Then, based on the given information, choose the option that best answers the question.

In theory, solar and wind energy farms could provide an alternative energy source and reduce our dependence on oil. But in reality, these methods face practical challenges no one has been able to solve. In Denmark, for example, a country with some of the world's largest wind farms, it turns out that winds blow most when people need electricity least. Because of this reduced demand, companies end up selling their power to other countries for little profit. In some cases, they pay customers to take the leftover energy.

Q: Which of the following is correct according to the passage?

(a) Energy companies can lose money on the power they produce.

(b) Research has expanded to balance supply and demand gaps.

(c) Solar and wind power are not viewed as possible options.

(d) Reliance on oil has led to political tensions in many countries.

이론상으로 태양과 풍력 에너지 발전 단지는 대체 에너지 자원을 제공하고 원유에 대한 의존을 낮출 수 있다. 그러나 사실상 이러한 방법들은 아무도 해결할 수 없었던 현실적인 문제에 부딪친다. 예를 들어 세계에서 가장 큰 풍력 에너지 발전 단지를 가진 덴마크에서 사람들이 전기를 가장 덜 필요로 할 때 가장 강한 바람이 분다는 것이 판명되었다. 이러한 낮은 수요 때문에 회사는 결국 그들의 전력을 적은 이윤으로 다른 나라에 팔게 되었다. 어떤 경우에는 남은 에너지를 가져가라고 고객에게 돈을 지불하기도 한다.

Q 이 글에 의하면 다음 중 옳은 것은?

(a) 에너지 회사는 그들이 생산한 전력으로 손해를 볼 수도 있다.

(b) 수요와 공급 격차를 조정하기 위해 연구가 확장되었다.

(c) 태양과 풍력 에너지는 가능한 대안으로 간주되지 않는다.

(d) 원유에 대한 의존은 많은 나라들 사이에 정치적 긴장감을 가져왔다.

정답 (a)

★ PART IV (5지문 10문항)

이번 NEW TEPS에 새롭게 추가된 유형으로 1지문 2문항 유형입니다. 5개의 지문이 나오므로 총 10문항을 풀어야 합니다. 주제와 세부 내용, 추론 문제가 섞여서 출제됩니다.

> **Read the passage, questions, and options. Then, based on the given information, choose the option that best answers each question.**
>
> You seem exasperated that the governor's proposed budget would triple the funding allocated to state parks. What's the problem? Such allocation hardly represents "profligate spending," as you put it. Don't forget that a third of all job positions at state parks were cut during the last recession. This left the parks badly understaffed, with a dearth of park rangers to serve the 33 million people who visit them annually. It also contributed to deterioration in the parks' natural beauty due to a decrease in maintenance work.
>
> These parks account for less than 1% of our state's recreational land, yet they attract more visitors than our top two largest national parks and national forests combined. They also perform a vital economic function, bringing wealth to nearby rural communities by attracting people to the area. The least we can do is to provide the minimum funding to help keep them in good condition.
>
> Q1: What is the writer mainly trying to do?
> (a) Justify the proposed spending on state parks
> (b) Draw attention to the popularity of state parks
> (c) Contest the annual number of state park visitors
> (d) Refute the governor's stance on the parks budget
>
> Q2: Which statement would the writer most likely agree with?
> (a) Low wages are behind the understaffing of the state parks.
> (b) State parks require more promotion than national parks.
> (c) The deterioration of state parks is due mainly to overuse.
> (d) The state parks' popularity is disproportionate to their size.

여러분은 주립 공원에 할당된 예산을 세배로 증가시키려는 주지사의 제안을 듣고 분노할지도 모른다. 무엇이 문제일까? 그와 같은 할당은 여러분들이 말하듯이 '낭비적인 지출'이라고 말하기 힘들다. 지난 경제 침체기 동안 주립 공원 일자리의 1/3이 삭감되었다는 사실을 잊지 말기 바란다. 이 때문에 공원은 부족한 관리인들이 매년 공원을 방문하는 3천3백만 명의 사람들을 처리해야 하는 인력 부족에 시달리고 있다. 또 그 때문에 관리 작업 부족으로 공원의 자연 경관이 망가지게 되었다.

이 공원들은 주의 여가지의 1%도 차지하지 않지만, 규모가 가장 큰 2개의 국립공원과 국립 숲을 합친 것보다 많은 방문객을 끌어들인다. 그들은 사람들을 그 지역으로 끌어들여 부를 주변의 공동체에게 가져다줌으로써 중요한 경제적 기능을 한다. 우리가 할 수 있는 최소한의 일은 공원이 잘 관리될 수 있도록 최소한의 자금을 조달하는 것이다.

Q1 작가가 주로 하고 있는 것은?

(a) 주립 공원 예산안을 정당화하기

(b) 주립 공원 인기에 대한 주의를 환기시키기

(c) 매년 주립 공원을 방문하는 사람 수에 대한 의문 제기하기

(d) 공원 예산에 대한 주지사의 입장에 대해 반박하기

정답 (a)

Q2 저자가 동의할 것 같은 내용은?

(a) 인력난에 시달리는 주립 공원의 배경에는 낮은 임금이 있다.

(b) 주립 공원은 국립공원보다 더 많은 지원이 필요하다.

(c) 주립 공원은 지나친 사용 때문에 망가지고 있다.

(d) 주립 공원의 인기는 그 규모와는 어울리지 않는다.

정답 (b)

※ 독해 Part 4 뉴텝스 샘플 문제는 서울대텝스관리위원회에서 제공한 문제입니다. (www.teps.or.kr)

NEW TEPS Q&A

1 / 시험 접수는 어떻게 해야 하나요?

정기 시험은 회차별로 지정된 접수 기간 중 인터넷(www.teps.or.kr) 또는 접수처를 방문하여 접수하실 수 있습니다. 정시 접수의 응시료는 42,000원입니다. 접수기간을 놓친 수험생의 응시편의를 위해 마련된 추가 접수도 있는데, 추가 접수 응시료는 45,000원입니다.

2 / 텝스관리위원회에서 인정하는 신분증은 무엇인가요?

아래 제시된 신분증 중 한 가지를 유효한 신분증으로 인정합니다.

일반인, 대학생	주민등록증, 운전면허증, 기간 만료전의 여권, 공무원증, 장애인 복지카드, 주민등록(재)발급 확인서 *대학(원)생 학생증은 사용할 수 없습니다.
중 · 고등학생	학생증(학생증 지참 시 유의 사항 참조), 기간 만료 전의 여권, 청소년증(발급 신청 확인서), 주민등록증(발급 신청 확인서), TEPS신분확인증명서
초등학생	기간 만료 전의 여권, 청소년증(발급신청확인서), TEPS신분확인증명서
군인	주민등록증(발급신청확인서), 운전면허증, 기간만료 전의 여권, 현역간부 신분증, 군무원증, TEPS신분확인증명서
외국인	외국인등록증, 기간 만료 전의 여권, 국내거소신고증(출입국 관리사무소 발행)

*시험 당일 신분증 미지참자 및 규정에 맞지 않는 신분증 소지자는 시험에 응시할 수 없습니다.

3 / TEPS 시험 볼 때 꼭 가져가야 하는 것은 무엇인가요?

신분증, 컴퓨터용 사인펜, 수정테이프(컴퓨터용 연필, 수정액은 사용 불가), 수험표입니다.

4 / TEPS 고사장에 도착해야 하는 시간은 언제인가요?

오전 9시 30분까지 입실을 완료해야 합니다. (토요일 시험의 경우 오후 2:30까지 입실 완료)

5 / 시험장의 시험 진행 일정은 어떻게 되나요?

	시험 진행 시간	내용	비고
시험 준비 단계 (입실 완료 후 30분)	10분	답안지 오리엔테이션	1차 신분확인
	5분	휴식	
	10분	신분확인 휴대폰 수거 (기타 통신전자기기 포함)	2차 신분확인
	5분	최종 방송 테스트 문제지 배부	
본 시험 (총 105분)	40분	청해	쉬는 시간 없이 시험 진행 각 영역별 제한시간 엄수
	25분	어휘/문법	
	40분	독해	

*시험 진행 시험 당일 고사장 사정에 따라 변동될 수 있습니다.
*영역별 제한 시간 내에 해당 영역의 문제 풀이 및 답안 마킹을 모두 완료해야 합니다.

6 / 시험 점수는 얼마 후에 알게 되나요?

TEPS 정기시험 성적 결과는 시험일 이후 2주차 화요일 17시에 TEPS 홈페이지를 통해 발표되며 우편 통보는 성적 발표일로부터 7~10일 가량 소요됩니다. 성적 확인을 위해서는 성적 확인용 비밀번호를 반드시 입력해야 합니다. 성적 확인 비밀번호는 가장 최근에 응시한 TEPS 정기 시험 답안지에 기재한 비밀번호 4자리입니다. 성적 발표일은 변경될 수 있으니 홈페이지 공지사항을 참고하시기 바랍니다. TEPS 성적은 2년간 유효합니다.

※자료 출처 : www.teps.or.kr

NEWTEPS 등급표

등급	점수	영역	능력검정기준(Description)
1+	526~600	전반	**외국인으로서 최상급 수준의 의사소통 능력** 교양 있는 원어민에 버금가는 정도로 의사소통이 가능하고 전문분야 업무에 대처할 수 있음 (Native Level of English Proficiency)
1	453~525	전반	**외국인으로서 최상급 수준에 근접한 의사소통능력** 단기간 집중 교육을 받으면 대부분의 의사소통이 가능하고 전문분야 업무에 별 무리 없이 대처할 수 있음 (Near-Native Level of Communicative Competence)
2+	387~452	전반	**외국인으로서 상급 수준의 의사소통능력** 단기간 집중 교육을 받으면 일반 분야업무를 큰 어려움 없이 수행할 수 있음 (Advanced Level of Communicative Competence)
2	327~386	전반	**외국인으로서 중상급 수준의 의사소통능력** 중장기간 집중 교육을 받으면 일반분야 업무를 큰 어려움 없이 수행할 수 있음 (High Intermediate Level of Communicative Competence)
3+	268~326	전반	**외국인으로서 중급 수준의 의사소통능력** 중장기간 집중 교육을 받으면 한정된 분야의 업무를 큰 어려움 없이 수행할 수 있음 (Mid Intermediate Level of Communicative Competence)
3	212~267	전반	**외국인으로서 중하급 수준의 의사소통능력** 중장기간 집중 교육을 받으면 한정된 분야의 업무를 다소 미흡하지만 큰 지장 없이 수행할 수 있음 (Low Intermediate Level of Communicative Competence)
4+	163~211	전반	**외국인으로서 하급수준의 의사소통능력** 장기간의 집중 교육을 받으면 한정된 분야의 업무를 대체로 어렵게 수행할 수 있음 (Novice Level of Communicative Competence)
4	111~162		
5+	55~110	전반	**외국인으로서 최하급 수준의 의사소통능력** 단편적인 지식만을 갖추고 있어 의사소통이 거의 불가능함 (Near-Zero Level of Communicative Competence)
5	0~54		

I

올바른 독해를 위한
문법

Unit 01 to부정사와 동명사

흔히 문장에서 to부정사와 동명사를 보면 동사로 착각하거나 수식어로 생각하지만 명사로 쓰이는 경우가 많다.
문장에서 명사로 쓰인다는 것은 곧 주어, 목적어, 보어의 역할을 한다는 뜻이다.

1 주어 역할

To mask the problem is not a wise way to deal with the situation.
문제를 감추는 것은 상황을 현명하게 다루는 방법이 아니다.

Figuring out the trends and habits of consumers takes a long time.
소비자들의 유행과 소비 습관을 알아내는 것은 시간이 오래 걸린다.

= To figure out the trends and habits of consumers takes a long time.

= It takes a long time to figure out the trends and habits of consumers.

⇨ to부정사가 주어일 때는 가주어 it을 문장 앞에 쓰고 진주어 to부정사를 뒤에 쓰는 것이 일반적이다.

2 목적어 역할

People need to stay as intellectually active as possible in order to prevent dementia.
사람들은 치매를 예방하기 위해서 가능한 한 지적 활동을 계속 해야 한다.

Not surprisingly, many couch potatoes reported working sedentary jobs.
놀랄 것 없이 텔레비전을 즐겨 보는 많은 사람들은 앉아서 일하는 직장을 가지고 있는 것으로 보고되었다.

3 보어 역할

A key to getting the job you want is to get dressed to the nines.
원하는 직장을 얻기 위한 비결은 멋있게 입는 것이다.

It says it's like lying on a cloud to sleep on this mattress.
이 매트리스에 자는 것은 구름에 누워 있는 것 같다고 한다.

다음 문장을 읽고, to부정사에 밑줄 치고 해석하시오. 그리고 빈칸에 to부정사가 주어인지 목적어인지 또는 보어인지 쓰시오.

1   To fly over ten hours to this corner of Indonesia's North Sulawesi province will not be a waste of time once you see the panoramic view of the Sulawesie Sea.

2   If it is a breathtaking picture of the sea that you want, the trick is to find the perfect time and place.

3   The mayor plans to attract more tourists this year to cover the losses coming from the city's falling real estate prices.

4   To lend a helping hand to the needy is not only rewarding but also comforting.

5   The job of the 15-member team is to feed, clean, and care for the orphaned animals.

6   For the first time in its 43-year-old history, the New Orleans Saints managed to reach the Super Bowl.

7   The proposed plan by the committee is to expand its niche in the lucrative market.

8   According to Doctor Holmes, to understand that book, which abounds with mysteries and ironies, will not be easy for his first-time readers.

9   As an administrator who swore to serve the country, the new secretary failed to resist getting involved in corruption.

10   To appease frantic investors, the new chief executive needs to articulate a clear and unified vision for the company.

다음 문장을 읽고, 동명사구에 밑줄 치고 해석하시오. 그리고 빈칸에 동명사가 주어인지 목적어인지 또는 보어인지 쓰시오.

1   Mr. Zhou, the zoo keeper, reports that the favorite activities of these furry creatures in this scorching season are slumbering in the shade and going for a dip in the water.

2   Escaping from the economic crisis gripping the entire continent will be on the top of the agenda at the summit meeting.

3   With another round of heavy rainfall anticipated, the immediate concern is housing the possible flood victims in school auditoriums and sports stadiums.

4   For a team who was widely expected to win the cup, getting eliminated in the preliminary round was more than a rude awakening.

5   The town residents favored relocating the landfill to the outskirts of the town in hopes of raising their real estate values.

6   Educators in this country must realize that the toughest part of the problem is weighing the merits and demerits of rewarding teachers for their performance.

7   Whenever the government proposes a new measure, the leftist critics love slamming it as unconstitutional and evocative of nationalist sentiments.

8   The president learned the hard way that pursuing domestic political objectives is more bureaucratic than achieving foreign-policy goals.

9   In order to preserve the essence of the original work, the artist suggested recreating fabric and upholstery based on the original designs.

10   The government has begun sending the refugees back to their war-stricken homeland, drawing criticism from the neighboring countries.

다음 글을 읽고 질문에 맞는 답을 고르시오.

In a 12-year-old study done by a team of scientists, it was discovered that intellectual brain activities can delay or even prevent the arrival of dementia, but at a price. For years, doctors have recommended keeping the brain intellectually stimulated by playing card games, reading books, and engaging in other mental exercises as ways of avoiding dementia. However, according to the new study, once dementia sets in, intellectually active people are more likely to show faster cognitive decline compared to the less active group. In fact, an experiment conducted on 1,157 men and women 65 years old or older showed that symptoms of dementia progressed 52% more rapidly among the subjects whose brains were intellectually exercised once the illness made its appearance.

Q: What is the passage mainly about?

(a) The symptoms of dementia and preventive measures

(b) Research study showing the dangers of physical exercise

(c) The relationship between mental activities and dementia

(d) The ways to exercise the mind to fight dementia

Unit 02 명사절

명사절은 반드시 주어와 동사로 이루어져야 하며 문장에서 명사의 기능, 즉 주어, 목적어, 보어의 역할을 한다. 따라서 명사절은 형용사절, 부사절과 달리 수식어구가 아니라 문장의 필수 성분이다. 그러므로 명사절을 구분하고 어떤 문장 성분인지 파악해야 한다.

1 주어 역할 – 절 자체를 하나의 명사로 보아 단수로 취급

<u>Whether online voting will become a norm</u> will depend on how well the experts protect the system from hackers.

온라인 투표가 표준이 될 지는 전문가들이 시스템을 해커로부터 얼마나 잘 보호하느냐에 달려 있다.

⇨ 문장에서 접속사 Whether가 이끄는 명사절이 주어 역할을 하고 있다.

2 목적어 역할 – 타동사나 전치사의 목적어

The spokesperson for the Ministry of Labor announced <u>(that) the government will triple the budget allocated for worker training</u>.

노동부의 대변인은 정부가 직업 훈련을 위해 배분한 예산을 세 배로 늘릴 것이라고 발표했다.

⇨ 문장에서는 that이하의 명사절이 타동사 announce의 목적어 역할을 하고 있다.

3 보어 역할

The surprising fact is <u>that they are still not sure whether the new project will attract investors with deep pockets</u>.

놀라운 사실은 그들이 여전히 신규 프로젝트가 재력 있는 투자자들을 끌어들일 것인지 확신하지 못한다는 점이다.

⇨ 문장에서는 that이하의 명사절은 fact가 무엇인지 설명해 주는 주격 보어 역할을 하고 있다.

다음 문장을 읽고, 주어, 목적어, 보어의 역할을 하는 명사절에 밑줄 치고 해석하시오. 그리고 빈칸에 명사절이 주어인지 목적어인지 또는 보어인지 쓰시오.

1   Before granting the lease to the developers, the residents are asking just how many homes can be powered by the proposed number of wind turbines.

2   How anyone can find seclusion from the hustle and bustle from this urban life is still a mystery to many city dwellers.

3   Your next question will be if we can make use of its geographic features in the same way as our ancestors did centuries ago.

4   I could not concentrate on my work for the rest of the day because what I had for breakfast gave me heartburn.

5   The association estimates that about two out of five women suffered from anorexia or bulimia in their teens.

6   As there is no visible end to the current deadlock between the local residents and the developers, when the construction will be completed is beyond anyone's knowledge.

7   Perhaps the biggest mistake committed by the lawyer was that he entrusted his colleague with sensitive information about the plaintiff.

8   Some people are wondering why the decision made by the president is a magnet for anti-government demonstrations.

9   Although the Federal Reserve Board is expected to nudge down long-term interest rates soon, when exactly it will do so is anybody's guess.

10 The city's educational leaders are deciding how much penalty would be sufficient under the "3 Strikes, You're Out" system.

다음 글을 읽고 질문에 맞는 답을 고르시오.

That overpopulation is conducive to environmental destruction and famine is in wide agreement among economists and demographers. However, Dr. Cohen, a demographer at the National Census Bureau, notes that the relationship between population growth and problems like poverty, starvation, and environmental degradation is not the whole story. According to Cohen, people ignore political factors that contribute to these problems. For example, when rich nations provide agricultural subsidies to the developing world, farming incomes are driven down, aggravating hunger in the developing countries. Furthermore, lack of funding for education, innovation, and health care is problems brought about by political corruption and abuse, not increase in population.

Q: Which of the following is correct according to the passage?

(a) Overpopulation is the most threatening cause of social and environmental problems.

(b) Political corruption is the most serious cause of social and environmental problems.

(c) The relationship between population increase and social problems is negative.

(d) There are problems that are brought about by political abuse, not overpopulation.

Unit 03 연결어

절과 절 또는 문장과 문장을 연결시키면서 서로의 관계를 보여주기 위해서 연결어를 사용할 수 있다. 연결하는 절과 절, 문장과 문장이 어떤 관계를 가지고 있는지 제대로 파악해야 한다.

1 접속 부사

1) 반대

> however   still   nonetheless   nevertheless   instead

In many situations, asking the right questions is important. **However**[; **however**]**,** at times it can be disrupting when rapport and trust are weak in a team.
많은 상황에서 옳은 질문을 하는 것은 중요하다. 그러나 때때로 화합과 신뢰가 약한 팀에서는 분열을 일으킬 수 있다.

2) 추가

> also   furthermore   moreover   similarly   besides   next

It has been discovered that women who smoke are more likely to develop ovarian cancer. **Moreover**[; **moreover**], the risk is even higher for those who has endometrial cancer.
흡연 여성이 난소암에 걸릴 위험이 더 높다고 밝혀졌다. 게다가 자궁암에 걸린 여성들은 그 위험이 훨씬 더 크다.

3) 확신

> indeed   certainly   undoubtedly

The region has been a hot spot for energy companies. **Indeed**[; **indeed**], the area is known to hold more than 15 percent of the world's oil reserves.
그 지역은 에너지 회사들에게는 인기 지역이었다. 실제로 그곳은 전 세계 석유 매장량의 15% 이상을 보유하고 있는 것으로 알려졌다.

4) 결과

> accordingly   hence   then   thereafter   therefore   consequently   thus   finally

Recent sit-in protest by the union has delayed the completion of the factory. **Thus**[; **thus**], the construction is rescheduled to be done in November.
최근 노동조합의 파업으로 공장 완공이 지연되었다. 따라서 공사완료는 11월로 재조정되었다.

5) 유사

> likewise   similarly

The Kenyan coffee growers have experienced substantial success with the introduction of new coffee seeds. **Likewise**[; **likewise**], their African rivals are attempting to test the new seeds.
케냐의 커피 재배자들은 새로운 커피 종자의 도입으로 상당한 성공을 거두었다. 이와 같이 아프리카의 경쟁자들도 그 새로운 종자를 시험하려 시도하고 있다.

2 기타 연결어구

1) 예

for example   for instance   to illustrate   in particular   as an illustration

The aging work force has been increasing recently. **For instance**, the proportion of the aged workers in service occupations has risen about 25 percent over five years.
고령화 인력이 최근 증가하고 있다. 예를 들어, 서비스 업종에서의 노령 노동자 비율이 지난 5년간 25% 증가했다.

2) 부연 설명

to elaborate   in other words   to be specific   to explain   to enumerate   in fact

The religious leaders will convene next week to work out their differences. **To be specific**, they will meet to draw a roadmap to harmony.
종교 지도자들이 의견 차이를 좁히기 위해 다음 주에 모일 것이다. 구체적으로 그들은 화합으로 가는 로드맵을 그릴 것이다.

3) 반박

on the contrary   in contrast   on one hand   on the other hand
at the same time   while this may be true

The heartless dictator expected the riot to subside under his force. **On the contrary**, the people have remained vigilant against his next political moves.
무자비한 독재자는 그의 세력 하에 폭동이 가라앉을 거라고 기대했다. 반대로 시민들은 그의 다음 정치적 움직임을 예의주시하고 있다.

4) 추가

in addition to   both … and   equally important   not only … but also
likewise   in fact   in the second place

There is much doubt about the environmental benefits of recycling. **In fact,** a study has revealed that recycling produces more carbon dioxide than new manufacturing.
재활용이 환경에 미치는 장점에 대한 의문이 많다. 실제로 한 연구에서 재활용이 새로운 제조품보다 더 많은 이산화탄소를 배출한다고 밝혀졌다.

5) 결과

as a result   in conclusion   with the result that   consequently   accordingly
due to   owing to   for this reason

The government has shown firm determination to keep all public places strictly smoke-free. **Consequently**, the smoking rates of Korean adults fell by more than 15 percent from last year.
정부는 모든 공공장소를 금연 구역으로 엄중하게 지키려는 강한 의지를 보였다. 그 결과 한국 성인의 흡연율이 작년보다 15% 줄었다.

다음 문장을 읽고 빈칸에 알맞은 연결어를 고르시오.

1   The authorities have failed to provide early warning about the hurricane to the coastal towns.
    _____, more than 200 people have lost their homes to the flood.

    (a) In contrast

    (b) To elaborate

    (c) Instead

    (d) As a result

2   Health officials have been working around the clock to vaccinate domesticated animals.
    _____, the movement of wild birds has been closely observed, but no outbreak of
    avian flu has been reported yet.

    (a) Specifically

    (b) In addition

    (c) Undoubtedly

    (d) Thus

3   Chilean agriculture products were able to make their way to Korean homes. _____,
    Korean manufactured goods have found a market in Chile.

    (a) Likewise

    (b) While this may be true

    (c) For this reason

    (d) In contrast

4   The symptoms of the disease are very subtle even years after contraction; _____,
    only 27 percent of cases are detected in the early stage, when the cure is most possible.

    (a) equally important

    (b) furthermore

    (c) in fact

    (d) however

5   With the local elections approaching, the administration has shown its will to appease the
    farmers. _____, the Agriculture Minister was removed from office for his aggressive
    attempt to liberalize the rice market, which infuriated the farmers.

    (a) Equally important

    (b) Hence

    (c) Therefore

    (d) For example

6   Many successful business moguls are known to start their day earlier than their competitors; _____, there are night-owls like me who just cannot be early birds.

(a) similarly

(b) however

(c) accordingly

(d) thereafter

7   Teens from seven different countries have learned to overcome their differences to achieve one purpose, which is to build a well in this drought-stricken village. _____, birds of different feathers do not flock together at first, but with the same objective, they eventually do.

(a) To illustrate

(b) In fact

(c) On the other hand

(d) In other words

8   The members of OPEC reached a consensus last week to expand their output. _____, the price of crude oil has dwindled to remove some burden from manufacturers.

(a) Then

(b) Indeed

(c) Certainly

(d) Accordingly

9   The retail industry has not fared so well in their best season. _____, the finance industry experienced a brisk fourth quarter despite the profit squeeze.

(a) In addition

(b) In contrast

(c) At the same time

(d) In other words

10   The public sentiment against further involvement in the war-torn region is higher than ever; _____, the president has given the green light to deployment of additional troops to Iraq.

(a) in fact

(b) also

(c) nevertheless

(d) undoubtedly

다음 글을 읽고 빈칸에 알맞은 답을 고르시오.

Why do people turn out the way they do? Is it their genes or is it their childhood environment? Some may think it is the choice in lifestyle people make as adults. _____, have you ever considered that it might be your life as a fetus? There is a provocative assertion that your nine months in your mother's womb may be the most critical period in your life. This period is when your brain is wired and vital organs such as the heart and the liver are formed. In addition to physical formation, development as a fetus may influence intelligence, temperament, and even sanity. The new discovery is expected to lead to an explosion of research in the subject. With further study of the fetal-stage, scientists are optimistic for a more accurate answer to where human qualities come from and when they begin to develop.

(a) Therefore

(b) In fact

(c) Specifically

(d) However

Unit 04 관계 대명사절과 관계 부사절

한 문장에 여러 개의 절이 있을 경우, 절이 각각 어디서 나누어지는지, 각각의 역할이 무엇인지 알면 문장을 이해하는 데 큰 도움이 된다. 문장 안에서 절은 명사, 부사, 형용사 등 여러 가지 역할을 하는데 관계 대명사, 관계 부사가 이끄는 절은 앞의 명사를 수식하는 형용사절 역할을 한다.

1 관계 대명사절

관계 대명사절은 관계 대명사로 시작하기 때문에, 생략되는 경우를 제외하고 관계 대명사를 보면 금방 알아볼 수 있다.

> **관계 대명사:** who   whom   which   that   whose

This is the perfect month for people **who** want to buy new cars at good prices.
이번 달은 좋은 가격에 새 차를 사고 싶어 하는 사람들에게는 완벽한 달이다.

My father told me that Mr. Park is an old friend of his **whom** he can trust.
아버지는 박 선생님은 신뢰할 수 있는 오랜 친구라고 말씀하셨다.

His essays reflect his love for all living things **which** he believes should be protected for coexistence and harmony.
그의 에세이는 공존과 화합을 위해서 보호해야 한다고 생각하는 모든 살아 있는 것에 대한 그의 사랑을 반영한다.

Having sold over 300,000 copies, Martin's new book is an instant hit **that** has brought him literary fame.
30만 부 이상 팔리면서 마틴의 새 책은 그에게 문학적 명성을 가져온 즉시 인기를 얻은 작품이다.

⇒ Having sold over 300,000 copies, Martin's new book is an instant hit **(that)** reviewers are hailing as his best work yet.
이 문장에서는 관계 대명사 that이 목적격이므로 (관계사절 안의 주어는 reviewers) hail의 목적어인 that은 생략 가능하다. 하지만 첫 번째 문장처럼 that이 주격이면 생략할 수 없다.

The Department of Education has reported that California is the state with the greatest number of students **whose** primary language is not English.
교육부는 영어가 주 언어가 아닌 학생들이 가장 많은 주는 캘리포니아라고 발표했다.

2 관계 부사절

> **관계 부사:** where   when   why

What you should never do on a first date is to take your date to a restaurant **where** you must use your bare hands to eat.
첫 번째 데이트에서 절대 하지 말아야 하는 것은 맨손으로 먹어야 하는 음식점에 데이트 상대를 데리고 가는 것이다.

This was a 10 percent jump from the previous year and the highest since November of 2017, **when** the company was first listed on the stock exchange.
작년보다 10% 높았으며 그 회사가 처음 거래소에 상장되었던 2017년 11월 이후로 가장 높았다.

The new striker is reputed to be overly prudent, which some critics claim is the reason **why** he is kept on the sidelines so long.
새로 영입한 스트라이커는 지나치게 신중하다고 알려져 있으며 일부 비평가들은 이런 점이 그가 너무 오랫동안 출전하지 못하는 이유라고 주장한다.

⇨ The new striker is reputed to be overly prudent, which some critics claim is the reason **(that)** he is kept on the sidelines so long.

관계 부사 why는 reason을 수식할 때 쓰지만 why 대신 관계 대명사 that도 쓸 수 있다. 이때 that은 생략할 수 있다.

다음 문장을 읽고 관계 대명사절 또는 관계 부사절에 밑줄 치고 해석하시오. 그리고 그 관계사절이 수식하는 명사를 빈칸에 쓰시오.

1　The movie, which premiered last week in New York, features new faces with no track record in the film industry.

_____ _____

2　The new controversial ad provides a few tips for guys who need to get out of hot water thereby helping them cheat on their wives.

_____ _____

3　The young artist made some changes to the Prime Minister's image from a picture taken in 1965 when the nation won its independence.

_____ _____

4　A recent series of bullying-related suicides is the reason why American moms are up in arms and determined to fight the problem.

_____ _____

5　Mr. Harris, who was admired among atheists as their role model, has been losing his followers after claiming that he believes in a spiritual being.

_____ _____

6　An economist and former executive at the World Bank, Mr. Hymer believes that the destitute country where there seemed to be no end to famine will finally find a ray of hope.

_____ _____

7　The ironic fact is that highly visible business people and celebrities that are recognized for lending a hand to the world's poor are not actively involved in the issue of domestic poverty.

_____ _____

8　With the New York Fashion Week finally over, the design house headed by Jesse Miller, whom the critics praised as a rising star in the industry, is busy filling orders from buyers.

_____ _____

9　More working moms are finding it nearly impossible to juggle work and house chores while trying to nurture their children right in a society where the term "housewife" has become anachronistic.

_____ _____

10　Wage disparities which discourage many female graduates from entering the corporate world will not be eradicated without a change in people's attitude.

_____ _____

다음 글을 읽고 질문에 맞는 답을 고르시오.

Through much of the nineteenth century, Great Britain managed to avoid the type of social uprisings that the European Continent had to suffer on and off between 1815 and 1870. Many British historians give credit for this success to the democracy adopted early by the British parliament. Although there is some truth to this claim, there is also some doubt. The Great Reform Bill of 1832, for example, was a landmark legislation that expanded voting rights to more men, but still only twenty percent of the male population had the right to vote. The following reform bill passed in 1867 again extended voting rights; nevertheless, the power remained with a minority such as property-owning elites with a common background, common education, and common perspective on domestic and foreign politics. England may have carried out its reform faster than its European neighbors, but it remained slow nonetheless.

Q: What is the main point of this passage?

(a) Britain's failed attempt to democratize the parliament

(b) Britain's success in democratizing the system

(c) Britain's gradual approach to democratize Europe

(d) Britain's early attempt to reform, but not quickly enough

Unit 05 분사 구문

분사 구문은 〈접속사 + 주어 + 동사〉에서 접속사와 주어를 생략하고 분사구로 줄여서 시간, 이유, 조건, 양보, 부대 상황 등을 나타내며 현재 분사 또는 과거 분사로 시작한다. 현재 분사로 시작하면 주체가 동사를 행하며 과거 분사면 주체가 동사의 대상이 된다.

1 현재 분사 구문을 만드는 방법

1) 현재 분사 구문은 종속절이 능동태일 때 가능하다. 현재 분사 구문을 만들기 위해서는 종속절에 있는 주어와 주절에 있는 주어가 같은 대상이어야 한다.

While **the president** told reporters how crucial the plan is, **he** reaffirmed his determination to push through with the bill.
대통령은 기자들에게 그 계획이 얼마나 중요한지 말하면서 법안을 밀고 나가기로 한 자신의 다짐을 다시 한 번 단언했다.

2) 종속절에 있는 접속사와 주어를 지운다.

~~While the president~~ **told** reporters how crucial the plan is, he reaffirmed his determination to push through the bill.
종속절에 있는 주어 the president를 지우면 주절에 있는 주어 he가 누구인지 모르므로 he를 the president로 바꾼다.

3) 종속절 안에 있는 동사가 능동태면 동사를 현재 분사(-ing)로 바꾸면 끝이다.

Telling reporters how crucial the plan is, **the president** reaffirmed his determination to push through the bill.
현재 분사 구문에서는 문장의 주어 the president가 앞의 현재 분사 telling을 하는 주체가 되어야 한다. 다음과 같은 문장은 자연스러워 보일 수 있으나 틀린 문장이다.

cf) **Telling** reporters how crucial the plan is, **the president's determination** to push through the bill was reaffirmed.
이 문장에서는 주어인 determination이 telling을 한다는 뜻이기 때문에 틀린 문장이다.

Other Examples

1. **Acknowledging** her failed attempt to build a multicultural nation, **the chancellor** announced her intention to step down.
   다국적 국가를 만들려던 시도가 실패했음을 인정하면서 총리는 직위를 포기한다는 의향을 알렸다.

   = **After** the chancellor acknowledged her failed attempt to build a multicultural nation, **she** announced her intention to step down.

2. **Building** a new casino against the background of ancient landmarks, **the city** will attract more tourists.
   역사적 고대 건물을 배경으로 새로운 카지노를 건설하면 도시는 더 많은 관광객을 끌어들일 것이다.

   = **If the city builds** a new casino against the background of ancient landmarks, **it** will attract more tourists.

2 과거 분사 구문을 만드는 방법

1) 과거 분사 구문으로 만드는 종속절이 수동태일 때 가능하다. 현재 분사 구문과 마찬가지로 과거 분사 구문을 만들기 위해서는 종속절에 있는 주어와 주절에 있는 주어가 같아야 한다.

Because **the children** were raised by parents who must toil in factories six days a week, **they** know how to take care of each other without a guardian.
아이들은 주 6일 동안 공장에서 노고를 하는 부모로부터 양육을 받았기 때문에 그들은 보호자 없이 서로를 돌보는 법을 안다.

2) Because에서 a week까지 종속절에 있는 접속사와 주어를 지운다.

~~Because the children~~ **were** raised by parents who must toil in factories six days a week, **the children** know how to take care of each other without a guardian.
종속절에 있는 주어 the children을 지우면 주절에 있는 주어 they가 누구인지 모르므로 they를 the children으로 바꾼다.

3) 과거 분사 앞에 있는 be동사도 지운다.

~~Being~~ **raised** by parents who must toil in factories six days a week, the children know how to take care of each other without a guardian.
과거 분사 구문에서는 문장의 주어 the children이 과거 분사 raised의 대상이 되어야 한다. 다시 말해서 아이들이 양육을 받는 것이다.
다음과 같은 문장은 자연스러워 보일 수 있으나 틀린 문장이다.

cf.) **Raised** by parents who must toil in factories six days a week, there was no **guardian** to take care of the children.
의미상의 주어 guardian이 과거 분사 raised를 받게 된다. 하지만 guardian이 양육되는 것이 아니므로 이 문장은 틀리다.

다음 문장을 읽고 분사 구문에 밑줄 치고 해석하시오. 그리고 분사 구문의 주체 또는 대상을 빈칸에 쓰시오.

1 Hailed as an extraordinary engineering achievement, the tunnel was completed by over 26,000 workers who had to battle dust and danger for 12 years.

2 Creating a super-fast rail-link under the sea, the two countries hope to boost trade and travel while cutting down cost and congestion.

3 Published last week in the *Parenthood*, the article introduces a study that suggests women's brains may actually grow bigger with motherhood.

4 Found to have violated the law, the insurance companies will be penalized for collaborating to fix the price.

5 Being extremely cautious not to spoil the trial, the official spoke on condition of anonymity because the investigation was just getting under way.

6 Possessing all the classic elements of successful internet start-ups, the new socializing website was never expected to sink.

7 Encouraged by rising incomes and red-hot growth attributing to exploding numbers of visitors, China has launched construction of new airports throughout the country.

8 Concerned about the stricter rules and harsher fines for dirty plays, the players are bemoaning that the new regulations will spoil the fun of the game.

9 Deprived of their helmets, football players would be less likely to use their heads as weapons, according to some experts.

10 Sitting through the entire movie for three hours, I realized that I had almost no memory of its content.

다음 글을 읽고 질문에 맞는 답을 고르시오.

With trips to space becoming longer and more frequent, a new concern has been raised regarding the health of astronauts. According to research conducted by Marquette University, spending more than 6 months in space can make astronauts as weak as 80-year-olds. Studies have revealed that the astronauts' muscles atrophy and lose their strength as their stays in space are prolonged. While claiming that the condition is only temporary, the head researcher Robert Fitts admits there are serious threats to be considered. What if a spacecraft makes an emergency landing and the astronauts are stranded? Also, what if astronauts must return immediately to space for an emergency repair after a very short visit to the Earth? These are only a couple of questions that must be answered to keep the astronauts physically young and strong even in space.

Q: Which of the following is correct according to the passage?

(a) Astronauts must exercise only if their trips to space are frequent.

(b) Trips to space should be made less often for astronauts to rest enough.

(c) Astronauts should not remain in space for more than half a year.

(d) Conditions in space make human muscles to wear out faster.

II

유형별
독해 전략

TEPS 독해에서 빈칸 채우기 문제들이 있는데 이중에서도 앞부분에 빈칸이 있는 지문들이 있다. 대부분의 경우 빈칸이 앞부분에 있을 경우 그 빈칸에는 글의 핵심, 즉 주제가 들어간다고 보면 된다. 따라서 빈칸 뒤에 오는 내용을 전체적으로 파악하고 그 내용을 한 문장으로 정리한 보기를 고르는 것이 바람직하다.

When it comes to battling global warming, people have concentrated far too much on electric cars and coal-burning power plants. But it turns out that there is a far more low-tech way to slow down global warming: _____. The poorer half of the world burns dung or wood in simple stoves or open hearths to cook, producing a component of black soot called black carbon, which is known to be more harmful per ton of emissions than carbon dioxide. In fact, 20 percent of the world's black carbon emissions come from cooking stoves and replacing the stoves in the poorer parts of the world would equal taking 130 million cars off the streets at only a fraction of the cost. However, obstacles do remain, perhaps the biggest one being that most of the poor cannot afford more environmentally friendly stoves.

(a) eating uncooked food

(b) installing better cook stoves

(c) using traditional stoves

(d) burning wood instead of cooking oil

해석   지구 온난화 해결에 관한 한, 사람들은 전기 자동차나 석탄을 동력으로 하는 화력 발전소에 너무 많이 치중한다. 하지만 지구 온난화 속도를 늦출 수 있는 훨씬 저차원적인 기술이 있는 것으로 밝혀졌다. 바로 좋은 요리용 스토브를 설치하는 것이다. 세계 인구의 빈곤한 절반은 요리하는 데 거름이나 장작을 태우는 스토브나 화덕을 사용하며 이는 이산화탄소보다 더욱 해로운 것으로 알려진 카본블랙이라 하는 검은 그을음의 성분을 만들어 낸다. 사실 세계의 카본블랙 배기가스의 20%는 요리용 스토브에서 나오는데 세계의 빈곤한 지역에서 이 스토브를 교체한다면 비용의 극히 일부만으로도 거리에서 1억 3천만대의 차를 없애는 효과와 맞먹는다. 하지만 장애물이 있는데, 아마 가장 큰 문제는 대부분의 빈곤자들이 보다 환경 친화적인 스토브를 살 여유가 없다는 것이다.

(a) 조리되지 않은 음식을 먹는 것
(b) 좋은 요리용 스토브를 설치하는 것
(c) 전통적인 스토브를 사용하는 것
(d) 조리용 기름 대신 나무를 태우는 것

어휘   global warming 지구 온난화   hearth 화덕   emission 배기   carbon dioxide 이산화탄소

해설   빈칸이 글 앞부분에 있고 보통 도입부에서 주제가 드러나는 경우가 많아서 빈칸 바로 뒤에 있는 내용을 파악하면 답을 쉽게 찾을 수 있다. 즉, 요리를 하기 위해 스토브나 화덕을 사용하지만 환경 문제가 발생하므로 환경친화적인, 다시 말해 좋은 요리용 스토브를 설치하는 것이 지구 온난화를 늦추는 일임을 알 수 있으므로 정답은 (b)가 된다.

1   To meet the growing demand for food supplies, farmers have resorted to fertilizers and genetically engineered food seeds. However, these practices have resulted in serious health hazards for consumers, which is the reason that more coffee consumers are starting to _____. The merits of using organic coffee beans include the fact that they taste better and coffee brewed with them has a richer flavor than the synthetically fertilized coffee beans. Their added advantage is that they are beneficial for the environment whereas inorganic coffee beans are cultivated through the usage of pesticides and chemical fertilizers. If farmers choose organic methods for growing coffee, they can help the environment and reduce the health hazards for animals and humans. One more benefit is that coffee drinkers can be sure about the quality of organic coffee beans as farmers must go through a strict process of certification by the government. So, the next time you pick up a bag of coffee beans from the store shelf, you might want to go organic.

(a) prefer organic coffee beans to inorganic coffee beans to reap the benefits
(b) cut down on coffee in the morning to improve their health and save the environment
(c) buy coffee from farmers who harvest inorganic coffee beans instead of organic ones
(d) care more about the quality and nutritious value of coffee than ever before

2   The Balance of Power in Europe was a system drawn with a purpose to preserve international order and peace by matching any rise in the power of one nation-state with a rise in power of the state's geographic or political rival. _____ is Europe's relations with the "sick man of Europe", otherwise known as the Ottoman Empire. At the height of its power, the Ottomans dominated the Middle East, parts of northern Africa, and regions to the north including Bosnia-Herzegovina. Because the Ottoman Empire had control over the Balkans despite the empire's weakening dominion, most of Europe helped the Ottoman Empire sustain itself in order to prevent any one European country from exerting power over the Balkan Peninsula. By helping the Ottoman capital Constantinople survive, the balance of power in Europe could be preserved. However, it was the volatile Balkan Peninsula that eventually shook the very foundation of the balance of power in Europe.

(a) One example that finds fault in this international system
(b) What scholars cannot explain through this theory
(c) A contradicting point to note about the balance of power
(d) One of the best illustrations of such balance of power

3   Freelancing.com is the country's _____. We have logged in thousands
of satisfied customers. We connect over 1.1 million employers with freelance workers
from over 270 regions. Companies can hire freelancers on our website to do work in
areas such as programming, data entry, sales, and accounting. We have created a safe
environment for employers via our secure payment system. We have thousands of
freelance writers, programmers, designers, marketers and more. Getting the best web
design, professional programming, custom writing or affordable marketing has never
been easier! Try outsourcing for free today! Don't forget to bookmark our homepage for
your next project or job.

(a) most popular website for jobseekers looking for a freelance position

(b) largest marketplace for businesses to hire freelance workers

(c) safest provider of secure online payment programs

(d) biggest site for locating the best job candidates for large firms

4   School is a place for gearing children up for test taking, so it is up to parents to find a variety of
ways to add to all of the lessons children learn in the classroom _____.
From theater and music to science and sports, parents can learn to supplement their
children's school activities in the aim of creating well-rounded children with diverse
interests. For example, there are many theater classes taught at art centers and studios,
and music lessons are offered by qualified private instructors who can be recommended
by the school music educator. Of course, not all children have an interest in theater or
music. Some children may want to explore the world of science a little more deeply. If
your child shows a heightened interest in biology or physics, look for local opportunities
to join science clubs or social clubs such as the Boy Scouts or the Girl Scouts. Adding
to childrens' education with arts or science will provide them with a well-rounded
experience and help them develop their interests and creativity.

(a) by participating as a teacher-for-a-day.

(b) through parent-teacher meetings.

(c) through experiences outside of the classroom.

(d) by helping their children with their assignments.

5　The wristwatch seems to have had its time, for a study has found that more and more people are _____ to keep them on track for appointments and meetings. The study by consumer analysts at McClann has revealed that one in seven people say mobile phones and computers have made traditional watches obsolete; it found 86 percent still own a wristwatch even though they no longer rely on it to know the correct time. The under-25s who have grown up carrying around mobile phones are half as likely to own a watch as the older generations, according to these analysts. Timothy Sanders, senior fashion analyst at McClann, said: "Many consumers have grown up with technology and are just as likely to associate the notion of checking the time with a mobile handset as with a watch." Mobile phone ownership is booming and increased usage by all ages could pose a threat to the demand for standard watches in the long-term.

(a) beginning to think wristwatches are fashion items

(b) starting to rely on newer technology

(c) using their desktops and notebook computers

(d) finding wristwatches uncomfortable

6　For many men who complain that car insurance companies are discriminatory in charging men much more than women for insurance policies, here is _____.
There are fewer women involved in fatal automobile accidents than men. In addition to that, there is a higher number of women that have never been involved in a car accident than men. Making sweeping generalizations may seem unfair, but the facts do not lie. Men statistically getting into more accidents means they have more money paid to them from the insurance companies. Of course, what an insurance company charges is heavily dictated by one's driving history. Nevertheless, men's car insurance rates will not come down unless they start being more careful behind the wheel.

(a) a helpful way to bring down the premium

(b) a reason to complain against the high cost

(c) an effective way to raise the premium

(d) a simple explanation for the higher premium

7 Using the Hubble Telescope, astronomers were able to discover that _____. So how do they know? Well, what they spotted through the telescope was a huge galactic cluster named Abell 1689, which distorts light from the stars in its direction. The galactic cluster acts as a magnifying glass that allows distant objects to be seen by bending light around it. Now how light bends around this cosmic lens is dependent upon three factors; the distance of the object, the mass of the cosmic cluster, and the distribution of dark energy in the vicinity. And it is the presence of the dark energy that reveals the likely fate of the universe: its incessant expansion. Scientists say dark energy is a mysterious force that expedites the expansion of the universe, causing it to ultimately become a cold, dead wasteland and, although it is completely invisible, we know it's there through indirect evidence such as Abell 1689.

(a) the universe will most likely expand forever

(b) the universe will expand even without dark energy

(c) the universe will disappear in the future

(d) the dark energy will always exist in the universe

8 In this fast-paced society, chronic fatigue is a common enemy faced by modern people. To help fight this illness, people must choose the right kind of diet. So, what is the right kind of diet? A more _____ is it. The human body is composed of about 75% water, and any human diet may be high either in acidity or alkalinity. Acidic foods break down in water, but leaves an "acidic residue" which can accumulate, causing body functions to slow down. However, alkaline foods dissolve easily in water and are absorbed quickly by the bloodstream thereby helping the human body achieve optimum performance. Unfortunately, the average diet of western society produces high levels of acid which causes various health problems including osteoporosis and heart attack. To maintain optimum balance between acid and alkaline, it is recommendable to increase the level of alkaline in people's diet.

(a) acid-rich diet

(b) western diet

(c) well-balanced diet

(d) alkaline diet

9 Leaders stand as models to follow and advisors to listen to. Then what are the qualities of a leader that entice people to follow him or her? A good leader _____ to meet the needs of his or her organization for success. Foremost, a leader should be competent at what others expect of him or her. Competence means doing a task well, inspiring people to follow. Another trait of leadership is the ability to communicate. A capable leader should not only transmit his or her ideas effectively so that his or her subordinates understand. A good leader should also have a strong purpose. Some leaders may seem cold and distant, but if their purpose is honest and true, people will still follow. There are many good people out there, but the ones with the above attributes will be fit to become talented leaders.

(a) must train his or her subordinates wisely

(b) must be careful in avoiding obstacles

(c) should possess the following features

(d) has to have lots of personal confidence

10 Preparing to compete in an Ironman race, you must keep a few things in mind lest the pre-race jitters make you _____. The final week is a time to remind yourself why you like this sport in the first place. You were probably drawn to the triathlon event because of the discipline it provides you; the physical training, the travel to places around the world, and the comradery that develops among athletes. Next, set your goals. Completing the race is always important. Then you have secondary goals such as beating your own personal record. Furthermore, maintaining consistency and focus in your training all the way up to the race is a must. The Ironman is all about overcoming obstacles and with your determination you will find a solution and make it to the finish line.

(a) injure yourself even before the race begins

(b) lose your sense of overall purpose

(c) perfectly fit to complete the Ironman successfully

(d) boost your motivation to compete in the race

02 중간 빈칸 채우기

빈칸 채우기 질문 중에서 중간에 빈칸이 있는 경우가 있는데 이런 경우는 주로 하나의 문장과 그 다음 문장의 흐름을 제대로 이해하는지를 묻는 문제이다.

After winning major battles in Gettysburg and Vicksburg in 1863, President Abraham Lincoln began to sketch a plan for Reconstruction to reunify the North and South with the war coming to a close. Lincoln never believed that the Confederate states had ever seceded from the Union legally, so his blueprint for Reconstruction was based on forgiveness. Therefore, he issued the Proclamation of Amnesty and Reconstruction in 1863 to convey his willingness to reunite the once-united states. _____, Lincoln hoped to win northern support and persuade weary Confederate troops to put down their guns. The Proclamation also promised to grant full pardon to all southern government officials except high-ranking Confederate army officers and protect the private property of southern soldiers, though not their slaves. Most moderate Union leaders supported the president's proposal for Reconstruction, for they wanted a quick end to the war.

(a) To illustrate the importance of the Proclamation
(b) Without passing the Proclamation
(c) Despite Lincoln's effort for reunification
(d) By passing the Proclamation

해석 1863년 게티스버그와 빅스버그의 대규모 전투에서 승리를 거둔 뒤, 에이브러햄 링컨 대통령은 종전이 가까워 오자 남과 북이 재통합을 할 수 있도록 재건 계획을 수립하기 시작하였다. 링컨은 남부 동맹이 북부 연합으로부터 합법적으로 분리 독립하지 않았다고 생각했다. 그래서 재건 계획의 청사진은 용서를 바탕으로 하였다. 그래서 그는 한때 합중국이던 남과 북을 재결합하려는 의지를 전하기 위해 1863년 사면과 재건 선언을 공표했다. 이 선언의 통과로 링컨은 전쟁의 발발 원인을 뒷받침하는 북의 지지를 얻고 지친 남부 동맹이 무기를 내려놓기를 기대했다. 이 선언은 또한 남부 동맹군의 고위 장교를 제외한 모든 남부 정부 관계자를 사면하고 남부군의 노예를 제외한 모든 사유 재산을 보호해 준다고 약속했다. 대부분의 온건한 북부 연합 지도자들은 전쟁의 빠른 종결을 원했으므로 재건에 대한 대통령의 제안을 지지했다.

(a) 선언의 중요성을 보여주기 위해
(b) 선언 통과 없이
(c) 링컨의 재결합 노력에도 불구하고
(d) 이 선언의 통과로

어휘 secede 탈퇴하다 blueprint 청사진 proclamation 선언서 persuade 설득하다 weary 지친

해설 빈칸이 글 중간 부분에 있다. 빈칸 전 문장은 링컨 대통령이 모든 주를 다시 통일하기 위해서 선언서를 냈다는 내용이며 그 다음 문장은 링컨 대통령이 북에 있는 주로부터는 전쟁을 시작한 이유에 대한 지지를 얻고 남부 동맹군이 항복하기를 희망했다는 내용이다. 따라서 빈칸 뒤에는 링컨이 선언서를 발표함으로써 성취하려고 했던 것이 나왔으므로 정답은 (d)이다.

1   Two contrasting ideologies about how to have immigrants acclimate to life in a foreign
    country have emerged, one called the "melting pot" and the other called the "mosaic." It
    has been said that the United States adheres to the melting pot; _____
    Canada follows the mosaic approach. By relinquishing distinctive ethnic customs and
    practices, including language, immigrants should attempt to blend into the mainstream
    of society according to the melting pot ideology. In contrast, the mosaic ideology
    encourages immigrants to maintain their ethnic identities, while integrating them with the
    other ethnicities in society.

    (a) notwithstanding
    (b) although
    (c) in effect
    (d) whereas

2   Manufactured in rugged 600D nylon, this new range of conference bags with added
    durability usually reserved for higher-priced products, feature tremendous functionality.
    _____ the velcro closures for the main compartment, additional
    zipper pockets as well as a sturdy carrying strap, this bag is sure to reflect your brand in a
    positive light as it is put to numerous uses. Join the ranks of the top notch firms offering
    these types of gifts today!

    (a) Without
    (b) Regarding
    (c) With respect to
    (d) On top of

3 Have you faced difficulties in choosing fresh and ripe pears in the market? If you have, you might want to pay attention to these useful tips when shopping for pears. First of all, pears are fruits which bruise easily and need to be harvested before they fully ripe on the tree. Hence you always need to remember to buy pears without any cuts, wounds, or bruises. Also, try to get pears which are not too heavily colored and with quite good firmness. _____, you need to keep them along with some fruits such as apple or orange in a box with some ventilation holes. The ethylene gas from the other fruits will assist the ripening process. The box can be kept at room temperature for a few days. Whether the pears are ready to be eaten will be indicated by the smoothness and tenderness near the stem area. Keeping these points in mind, you will be able to enjoy fresh pears in your home.

(a) Now if you want to mature the fruits at home

(b) Even if the pears are already ripe

(c) Because pears age fast after they are picked

(d) In order to protect the fruits from discoloring

4 In one of the most populous solar systems yet discovered, a new planet designated Gliese 581g has been discovered by astronomers. To begin with, the newly-discovered planet is about three or four times as massive as our home planet, which indicates that it is also likely to have a hard surface to support life. _____ is that the planet is situated right in the middle of the hospitable zone, meaning that it is orbiting at just the right distance from the star to allow water to stay in a liquid form rather than freezing or boiling away. As far as we know, that is the minimum requirement needed to sustain life. For centuries, scientists have been imagining the possible existence of another earth-like planet, and they have been inching closer to finding the possibility ever since. Evidently, they have finally reached a potential candidate.

(a) A contrasting point

(b) A more important fact

(c) A mysterious phenomenon

(d) The explanation for this

5 Whether people have been diagnosed with type 1 or type 2 diabetes, they must know the importance of finding ways to lower the blood sugar. Medications will help them reduce the level of sugar in their blood effectively. But the best way may be through natural methods and they are easy to perform. The most essential factor that greatly affects the blood sugar level is what people ingest. The foods people intake should contain high amounts of fiber, low saturated fats, and less sugar. The intervals between the meals and how much people eat also affect the sugar level. _____, it is better to eat small portions 5 to 6 times per day than larger portions 3 times per day. Eating in smaller servings within the day will help in regulating the digestive juices, which is a good way to lower blood sugar. Exercise is also an excellent way to reduce the level of blood sugar because it burns the fat and increases the sensitivity of the body to insulin. This means that the body will need less insulin to lower the sugar level. Battling diabetes is a long-term fight, and understanding the best methods will lead diabetes patients to a long, healthy life.

(a) To be specific

(b) In contrast

(c) Furthermore

(d) In light of these facts

6 With the First World War over, Americans' desire for economic and political conservatism was reflected in the election of President Warren G. Harding in 1920. After Harding was placed in office, Congress passed a tariff, which raised the average tariff on imports to a new high of nearly 40 percent. When it came to foreign policy, Harding held a very isolationist stance and tried to reduce America's influence abroad. _____, he oversaw the Five-Power Naval Treaty in 1922 to place limits on the number of American, British, and Japanese naval ships in the Pacific. The US also signed the Four-Power Treaty that year which worked to maintain the status quo in the Pacific. Harding's domestic and foreign policies did much to sweep away the remnants of progressive legislation made by the previous administration.

(a) However

(b) Also

(c) For example

(d) Doubtlessly

7

To All Staff Members,

Beginning this January 9th, Aldus will implement the following amendment
in our company policy with regard to annual leave: every year one employee
from each department will be awarded an annual bonus holiday for outstanding
work performance. These employees will receive an additional 5 days of annual
leave credited on January 9th. The bonus leave will remain available until used,
_____ any other limitation on the total number of days of annual
leave. We will have a meeting on December 15 at 10 a.m. to discuss the results of
this year's performance evaluation and announce the final list of employees eligible
for the bonus. If you have any questions or comments, please let me know before the
meeting.

Gerald Evans,
Executive Manager

(a) in addition to

(b) notwithstanding

(c) resulting in

(d) except

8 High resolution images from the Lunar Reconnaissance Orbiter Camera revealed a series
of fault lines induced by geological pressure exerted across the Moon's surface. The
images captured 14 fault lines, also known as lobate scarps. The structure of the lines
evidently proves that the Moon is subject to geological pressures associated with its
shrinking, according to experts at the Australian Institute of Planetary Science. The lunar
lobate scarps can be understood as a painted balloon that is gradually deflated after the
paint dries. _____, the dried paint cracks and the balloon shrivels.
This is what is happening with the scarps. The shrinking phenomenon of the moon can be
attributed to the Moon's slow cooling since its molten birth more that 4 billion years ago.

(a) When the balloon pops

(b) Before the paint dries completely

(c) When the air is let out

(d) As the balloon becomes smaller

9 Some people suffer from anxiety and panic attacks for years and most likely their first one came out of the blue with little or no warning, leaving them wondering what happened to them. To fight the disorder, people need to find out what causes these anxiety attacks and understand the symptoms leading up to them. One definite cause is perhaps the mother of all causes, stress. People face varying degrees of stresses daily and _____ a little stress is actually good but major stressors, such as a dead-end job or the death of someone close could trigger a panic attack. Some medications such as steroids and antidepressants have been known to lead to attacks, so people should consult a physician before taking these medications. Some common symptoms of anxiety attacks include rapid increase of heart and respiratory rates, pupil dilation, panting, and shaking of the body. There are other causes and symptoms, but the important thing is to recognize what is happening in the moments leading up to the attack and during the attack itself.

(a) in fact

(b) henceforth

(c) though

(d) albeit

10 Ho Chi Minh, a socialist and nationalist, grabbed the opportunity in World War Two to establish Viet Minh, or the League for Vietnamese Independence. During the war, when Germany invaded France, Japan occupied Vietnam from 1940 to 1945. That is when Ho decided to use the Japanese invasion as a chance to build up a new nationalist force which would appeal to all of Vietnamese society. _____, Ho founded the Viet Minh in 1941. At the time because Americans opposed the Japanese in World War Two, Ho was able to convince the U.S. leaders to secretly equip the Viet Minh with weapons to drive out the new Japanese oppressors. This is when Ho advised his general Vo Nguyen Giap to adopt guerilla tactics to fight successfully against the Japanese forces. Throughout the war, the Viet Minh successfully expanded its power base in Tonkin and Annam and won immense popularity with the Vietnamese people.

(a) Nevertheless

(b) Surprisingly

(c) As a result

(d) For example

글의 마지막 부분은 앞에서 언급했던 핵심 내용을 다시 한번 더 정리해서 말하는 경우가 많기 때문에 앞에서 글의 핵심 내용을 파악하되 만약 핵심 내용이 앞에서 보이지 않는다면 글을 전체적으로 읽어가면서 마지막에 결론을 맺는 문장을 골라야 한다.

In many societies, when disposing dead bodies, it comes down to making two choices: bury or cremate. However, although both of these are natural processes, they both damage the environment. In order to solve that problem, an aquamation company has devised a cheaper and more carbon-neutral way to dispose of corpses, alkaline hydrolysis. In this process, a body is placed in a stainless-steel container filled with 93-degree Celsius potassium hydroxide and water solution for four hours until all that is left is the skeleton. At that point, the bones are soft enough to crush into small pieces to hand over to the family of the deceased. The residual liquid has no trace of DNA and the entire process takes only 5% to 10% of the energy that is used in cremation. Hence, aquamation may be _____.

(a) the way to lower the cost of disposing the dead for the poor
(b) an alternative method for cremating corpses in the future
(c) the answer to finding the most eco-friendly way to take care of the dead
(d) a revolutionary way of burying the dead without harming the environment

해석   많은 사회에서는 시체를 처리할 때 묻거나 화장하거나 둘 중 하나를 선택하게 된다. 그러나 비록 가장 자연적인 절차라고 할지라도 두 방법은 자연을 파괴한다. 이 문제를 해결하기 위해 수장을 전문으로 하는 한 회사가 보다 저렴하고 탄소 중립적인 시신 처리 방법인 알카리 가수분해법을 고안해냈다. 이 과정에서 시신은 뼈만 남을 때까지 4시간 동안 섭씨 93도의 수산화칼륨과 물을 넣은 용액으로 채워진 스테인리스강 용기에 놓여진다. 그 시점에 뼈는 유가족에게 넘겨질 수 있게 작은 조각으로 빻아질 수 있을 만큼 부드러워진다. 남은 액체는 DNA의 흔적도 없고 전 과정은 화장할 때 사용되는 에너지의 5%에서 10%정도 밖에 소모되지 않는다. 따라서 수장은 고인을 모시는 가장 환경친화적인 방법을 찾는 것에 대한 답이 될 수 있을 것이다.

(a) 가난한 사람들을 위한 보다 저렴한 시체 처리 방법
(b) 미래에 시체를 화장하는 것을 대체할 방법
(c) 고인을 모시는 가장 환경친화적인 방법을 찾는 것에 대한 답
(d) 자연환경을 손상하지 않고 고인을 묻는 획기적인 방법

어휘   cremate 화장시키다   corpse 시체   solution 용액   residual 잔여의   trace 흔적

해설   윗글에서는 빈칸이 글 끝 부분에 있기 때문에 글 전체의 핵심 내용을 정리하는 문장이라는 것을 알 수 있다. 이 글의 핵심 내용은 aquamation이라는 시체를 처리하는 획기적인 방법을 소개하는 것이다. aquamation이라는 방법을 이해했다면 이 방법은 매장을 하는 것도 아니고 불로 화장을 하는 것도 아니라는 것을 알 수가 있다. 그리고 돈이 없는 사람들을 위해 저렴한 방법이라는 점은 언급되지 않았기 때문에 답은 (c)라는 것을 알 수 있다.

1   The candy industry, despite an economy in recession, is increasing in sales and
    popularity. The economy might have worked against the confectionery industry but in
    fact is allowing for increased profits. Chocolate sales in 2017 came in at just below 80
    billion dollars. While all types of chocolate have seen an increase in sales from 2016 to
    2017, this is expected to again increase in the future. The non-chocolate candy industry
    in 2016 had sales of 45 billion dollars, while 2017 saw close to 49 billion dollars. This
    rising trend is only expected to continue in the coming years. Without a doubt, the
    confectionery industry can be expected to be successful for years to come. Wholesale
    candy and candy store sales should stay strong _____.

    (a) because there are new players in the market
    (b) after the new players enter the market
    (c) despite new players coming into the market
    (d) as long as the new players are in the market

2   The very incident that sparked the First World War was the result of a chance happening.
    June 28, 1914, the archduke of Austria, Franz Ferdinand, and his wife were on their
    way the city of Sarajevo in Bosnia-Herzegovina on an official visit. During the visit,
    Serbian militants who were fighting for independence from Austria-Hungary planned
    to assassinate the archduke. The militants threw a bomb at his car after he arrived in
    Sarajevo, but the plan failed when the bomb bounced off the car. Later that day, while
    the archduke was on his way to the hospital to visit a wounded officer from the earlier
    attack, Gavrilo Princip, a nineteen-year-old militant Bosnian Serb who had been part of
    the assassination attempt that morning, happened to be there. Grabbing the opportunity,
    Princip approached the car and shot both the archduke and his wife at point-blank range.
    It is very interesting and unfortunate at the same time to see that perhaps one of the most
    tragic events in history _____.

    (a) could have been avoided with a little luck
    (b) came about through careful planning
    (c) had to happen because of human greed
    (d) was caused by a misled struggle for freedom

3 Expressing thankfulness is a defining characteristic of successful individuals worldwide. So, why is this so important? People who appreciate things in life, both big and small, focus on what is right regarding their life rather than what is wrong. After all, people become what they think about all day. In other words, the things that people tend to dwell on mentally are what they tend to attract in their lives. Therefore, when people learn to consciously focus on the items that they are thankful for, they get a lot of them. Furthermore, thankful people understand the needs of others and extend their help with a smile, so their blessings become their neighbors' blessings. Abraham Lincoln said that "It's not possible to lift the burden of another while not conjointly lifting your own." Successful and joyous people are _____, which attracts more of them into their lives.

(a) unappreciative of great things in life

(b) very skilled at counting their blessings

(c) grateful to themselves only

(d) oblivious to what they have in life

4 A new paper by biodiversity researchers explores the possibilities of a future where algae could be supplying us with energy. Algae have a great potential in being harvested as fuel according to these experts. They generally grow at lower densities than bacteria or yeast, but their growth rates are far superior to either of them. This feature enhances the organism's capability to produce oil. Moreover, algae yields oil at least 10 times more than standard oil seed crops. In addition, they can grow by feeding on environmental waste such as carbon dioxide and waste water. Once the process for algal fuel production is developed, _____.

(a) algae will become the most widely used eco-friendly energy source

(b) oil will become depleted in most parts of the world

(c) the world will have to worry about fighting algal pollutants

(d) demand for algae will soar the most in non-oil producing countries

5 It is important to know the signs of heart disease in women, especially if you're a
husband with a wife suffering from a heart problem. The challenge is that the signs
of heart disease in women are different from that in men. The most observed heart
attack symptom in both sexes is the discomfort experienced within the chest area.
This symptom, however, does not always indicate a serious heart condition, especially
in women. Besides chest pain, other symptoms commonly experienced by women
before a heart attack include dizziness, difficulty in breathing, vomiting or nausea,
fatigue, sweating, or pain in body parts including the shoulder, neck, abdomen, or
upper back. These signs of heart disease in women, however, are more restrained than
stabbing chest pain. This may be due to women having blockages in the smaller arteries
and not just in the major ones. By knowing these signs of heart disease, you could
_____ any serious heart problem such as a heart attack or stroke.

(a) treat and cure

(b) avoid the symptoms of

(c) spot the consequences of

(d) prevent the incidence of

6 In 1947, State Department analyst George F. Kennan helped sketch a cohesive foreign
policy which eventually became the basis of America's "containment" policy to ward off
the Soviet Union's expansion of communism. According to Kennan, the Soviet Union
would take the opportunity to spread communism into all corners of the world, either
by conquering neighboring countries or by secretly aiding communist revolutionaries in
politically turbulent countries. To prevent the global domination of communism, America
could adopt the strategy of "containment." To maintain the status quo, America had to
thwart communist aggression abroad, according to Kennan. Kennan's idea quickly caught
on and it was used as strategy to _____ until the Cold War ended in
the early 1990s.

(a) educate the world about democracy

(b) keep communism in check

(c) convert communist revolutionaries

(d) contain politically unstable countries

7   In an article called "The Role of Higher Education in Social Mobility", the authors state that while most Americans believe the notion that anyone with strong motivation and sufficient ability should successfully gain entry into America's universities, this simply isn't what the research is conveying. Income related gaps in terms of access to and success in higher education are ballooning. The pool of qualified youth is far greater than the number admitted and enrolled, meaning that it would be possible for universities to increase enrollment without _____.

(a) blemishing their affirmative action records

(b) targeting protected groups

(c) reducing the quality of the student body

(d) creating a diluted brand

8   Speed reading is the ability to read and understand an entire text when only some of the text is read. It is generally recommended that someone wanting to become a speed reader should first practice the following strategies. First the reader learns how to recognize a word from just a few letters in the word. For example, control could be cntrl and expert would be exprt; reader could be rdr, and so forth. Another method involves ignoring the words that join the sentence together. To provide an example: words such as but, the, and which can be ignored without altering the context or comprehension. Reading comprehension is important in any kind of reading and speed reading is no exception. Therefore, it's crucial that as the speed of reading increases, a speed reader retains more information. The strategies aforementioned will _____ the expertise of speed reading and reading comprehension.

(a) help you teach a novice reader about

(b) assist in understanding the importance of

(c) prevent an amateur reader from making

(d) start a brand-new reader off on attaining

9 A street lighting system is one of essential parts of urban lighting. It's said that traditional street lamps are going to be replaced by LED lights in some big cities in China, for LED lighting has many advantages compared with traditional ones. First, LED light has a very long lifetime. Its lifetime can reach 25,000 hours, compared with metallic halide lamps at 6,000 to 12,000 hours. Second, LED light is durable since its structure is designed to protect the internal components from strong external shocks. Third, LED light is highly efficient and will not cause pollution to the environment. LED light is called "cool light", which means it will produce little heat with the same degree of brightness as traditional light. Last but not least, LED power consumption is quite low. It saves 80% more electricity than traditional light sources. With traditional energy sources being depleted and with restrictions on pollution, the demand for LED lighting is growing _____ .

(a) for its low-consuming and non-harmful features

(b) because of its affordability and durability

(c) despite its environmentally friendly qualities

(d) with the rising price of energy throughout the world

10 Babies of 4 to 6 months of age need to be provided with rich fruits like pears. When it is time for you to start feeding your baby with more solid food rather than liquid ones, fruits like pears can be a good option. These hypo allergic (fruits with no negative effects or allergies) are recommended by physicians and child care specialists. Another reason for selecting pears is that the fruit can be easily be cooked or steamed before feeding the baby. Also a nice puree can be made out of it either from the cooked form or from the fresh fruit. If the baby is of more than eight months, it is recommended to feed it steamed fruits. These will assist the infant in the breakdown of the sugars and fiber contents present in the fruit. The fruit is also a rich hub of minerals such as potassium, magnesium and calcium along with good provisions of vitamin A and C. In general, pears can be _____ for babies.

(a) a nutritious alternative for vegetables and milk

(b) a good, healthy and nutritive solid food

(c) good supplemental food to provide protein

(d) food that is easily swallowed and digested

Unit 04 불필요한 문장 고르기

Part 2에 나오는 문제로 지문을 읽고 문맥상 어색한 문장을 골라야 한다. 지문의 핵심 내용을 벗어나는 문장을 파악하기 위해서는 지문 앞부분에 나오는 주제를 파악하고 보기들 중 주제와 전혀 관계가 없거나 글의 흐름을 방해하는 문장이 있는지 확인하면 된다.

Often, you send messages to others through your posture, gestures, and facial expressions without even knowing what the messages are. (a) Therefore, wrong body language can be the reason for many strains in relationships. (b) For example, if you stand with your chest slumped forward and your eyes avoiding everyone else, people are likely to think you are completely lacking in confidence. (c) If you are holding your breath or breathing in a shallow, jerky manner, this is a sign of anxiety. (d) When it comes to facial expressions, a gentle, pleasant smile should do the trick most of the time, but too much smiling that never lets up can look forced and nervous.

해석 흔히 상대방에게 자세, 몸짓, 표정으로 메시지가 무엇인지 모르면서도 보낸다. (a) 그러므로 잘못된 보디랭귀지는 관계에서 긴장을 초래하는 이유가 될 수 있다. (b) 예를 들어 가슴이 앞으로 구부정하고 다른 사람들의 눈을 피해 서 있으면 사람들은 당신이 자신감이 완전히 결여되어 있다고 판단할 수 있다. (c) 만약 당신이 숨을 죽이고 있거나 얕고 거칠게 호흡을 하면 이것은 불안하다는 표시이다. (d) 얼굴 표정에 있어서는 부드럽고 유쾌한 미소가 대부분 성공할 것이지만, 너무 지나친 미소는 억지로 하는 것으로 보여 불안해 보일 수 있다.

어휘 posture 자세   slump 구부정해지다   hold one's breath 숨을 죽이다   shallow 얕은   anxiety 불안감   let up 누그러지다

해설 몸의 자세, 행동이나 표정이 전하는 메시지를 설명해 준다. 여러 가지 예시를 주는데 (a)는 잘못된 몸동작이 관계를 악화 시킬 수 있다는 이야기를 하기 때문에 글에 흐름에서 벗어난다.

1   To be filed under the category of a lifestyle hazard, stress is indeed the root cause of many physical and mental ailments. (a) One of the physical manifestations of stress on the body may come in the form of headaches. (b) Or maybe you are just feeling that your mind and body are simply not performing at their optimal levels. (c) Although stress may be the cause of these symptoms as well as others, there are many simple ways to vent your stress such as talking it out with someone or getting some physical exercise to refresh yourself. (d) Stress not only wears down an individual who suffers it but often rubs off to family members and close friends as well.

2   Chronobiologists study humans' internal body clocks and the effects of light and sleep on our health. (a) They've found that exposure to artificial light during nighttime hours can leave people more susceptible to cancer. (b) At the same time, people aren't spending as much time outdoors, robbing the body of the sunlight that helps regulate healthy biorhythms. (c) These problems are compounded by new technologies that allow people to work and play during all hours of the day and night, further interrupting sleep patterns. (d) Similar innovations allow chronobiologists to research and assess modern lifestyles and their impact on quality of life.

3   The use of the atomic bomb in World War II has long been the subject of debate and controversy around the world. (a) Critics claim that Japan was already ready to surrender by the summer of 1945 and that the atomic bombs inhumanely killed hundreds of thousands of innocent civilians. (b) On the other hand, supporters of the bombings say that the invasions of Iwo Jima and Okinawa showed that the Japanese army was unwilling to surrender and that the atomic bomb ended the war while preventing enormous casualties. (c) The first bomb was dropped on Hiroshima and the second on Nagasaki. (d) The only other option to the bombings was a ground invasion of Japan which could have been tremendously wasteful in both American and Japanese lives.

4   The population of American cities exploded drastically during the 1920s because of rapid industrialization and urbanization. (a) Rural areas and suburbs were not popular destinations for immigrants as they did not offer the jobs and services of the urban centers. (b) First, the decade saw millions of people flock to the cities from country farmlands; in particular, African-Americans fled the South for northern cities in the post-World War I black migration. (c) Immigrants, especially eastern Europeans, also flooded the cities for diverse types of employment and proximity to fellow countrymen. (d) As a result of these changes, the number of American city dwellers came to outnumber those who lived in rural areas for the first time in U.S. history.

5   T-shirts are great for several reasons, including the fact that they are comfortable to wear and also that they can be customized to fit your exact tastes. (a) Another great thing about t-shirts is that they are extremely easy to have made just the way you want them. (b) But you must be careful when washing customized t-shirts as the designs may fade if you wash in an inappropriate manner. (c) You can pay somebody else to design and make shirts for you or you can easily come up with your own design. (d) The possibilities are endless and they only stop with your imagination for what you want to express to the world on your t-shirt.

6   The water tap in my kitchen was leaking so that I brought it up with my building manager on Sunday, April 12, and he promised he would fix it that week. (a) It is now almost three months later and the problem still hasn't been corrected. (b) It isn't a big danger but the wasted water is raising my water bills. (c) I would be grateful if you could install a new towel rack, too. (d) Also, the constant sound of the drip is starting to become irritating so I would appreciate it if you could speak to the manager about this problem.

7 Developmental education understands that students learn in different ways and teachers need to be sensitive to these differences. (a) There are early childhood developmental programs and developmental programs designed for high school students. (b) The early childhood programs start at around 3 months and continue until the child is ready for kindergarten. (c) The program for high school students begins after middle school and are designed for older students between the ages of 14 and 18. (d) Students who go through early childhood developmental programs are more likely to do better in high school and go onto college.

8 The cosmetic dental industry has evolved two main procedures called teeth bleaching and teeth whitening. (a) Teeth whitening is a process which restores the natural color of the teeth by getting rid of the dirt and grime that has accumulated on them over the years. (b) On the other hand, teeth bleaching is done to whiten teeth beyond their natural color for a bright and shiny white gloss. (c) In other words, the teeth whitening procedure has the aim to turn yellow teeth back to their prior state, and bleaching is done with the purpose of achieving a white smile. (d) Teeth bleaching and whitening are equally popular methods among celebrities, for the teeth do become whiter.

9   Due to the development of an enormous number of synthetic compounds that are carcinogenic, increasing numbers of people are contracting cancer. (a) Carcinogens are even detected in low concentrations in air fresheners and detergents. (b) These compounds are used in the food industry as flavor compounds, pigments, and preservatives. (c) Synthetic chemicals that are used in the food industry are especially suspected of causing many cases of liver and kidney cancer. (d) This is so because the liver is the site of food metabolism, and the kidney is the site where these compounds are cleared from the body.

10   The roaring twenties in America not only displayed a cultural blossoming but also more rights and freedoms for women. (a) The 19th Amendment of 1920 gave women in the US the right to vote. (b) Just as significantly, many women acquired financial independence as they entered the workforce in great numbers. (c) It was not possible for them to be promoted due to the glass ceiling in most companies. (d) As women's rights and independence flourished, so did their social freedoms as seen in the flapper girl phenomenon with their bobbed hair, short skirts, and liberal attitudes.

모든 독해 문제에서 가장 자주 출제되는 것이 주제를 찾는 문제이다. 주제는 글의 앞부분만 읽어도 바로 알 수 있거나 전체적으로 끝까지 읽고 이해해야 파악할 수 있는 경우가 있다. 그러므로 주제와 관련된 세부 내용들을 가지치기하면서 빠르게 읽어내는 일이 가장 중요하다.

Drivers with blood alcohol content (BAC) of .08 grams per deciliters (g/dL) are 11 times more likely to be in a fatal accident than sober drivers. To reach a BAC level of .08 g/dL, a man weighing approximately 170 pounds needs to consume four drinks in one hour on an empty stomach and a woman weighing about 140 pounds needs to consume three drinks in one hour. People require approximately six hours after their last drink to completely rid themselves of alcohol after reaching a BAC level of .08 g/dL. Finally, even at BAC levels as low as .02 g/dL, alcohol can affect a person's response time and driving ability.

Q: What is the main idea of the passage above?

(a) Even a few drinks can impair driving.

(b) Men can drink a little and still drive well.

(c) It is better to eat while drinking.

(d) One can drive several hours after drinking.

해석 혈중 알코올 농도(BAC)가 .08g/dL인 운전자들은 술 취하지 않은 운전사들보다 치명적인 사고를 당할 위험이 11배나 더 높다. 혈중 알코올 농도가 .08g/dL이 되려면, 몸무게가 약 170파운드(77kg)인 남성이 빈속에 1시간 동안 4잔을 마셔야 하고, 몸무게가 약 140파운드(63kg)인 여성은 1시간 동안 3잔을 마셔야 한다. 사람들이 혈중 알코올 농도 .08g/dL에 도달하고 나서 술에서 완전히 깨려면 마지막 잔을 마신 후로 6시간 정도가 필요하다. 마지막으로, 혈중 알코올 농도가 .02g/dL로 낮더라도, 술은 사람의 반응 시간과 운전 능력에 영향을 미칠 수 있다.

Q: 이 글의 주제는 무엇인가?
(a) 겨우 몇 잔이라도 운전에 지장을 준다.
(b) 남자들이 술을 조금 마시고 운전도 잘 한다.
(c) 술을 마실 땐 뭘 좀 먹는 게 좋다.
(d) 음주 후 몇 시간 운전할 수 있다.

어휘 blood alcohol content (BAC) 혈중 알코올 농도 grams per deciliters (g/dL) 데시리터 당 그램 fatal 치명적인 sober 술 취하지 않은 consume 마시다 rid of alcohol 술에서 깨다 impair 손상시키다

해설 1시간 동안 3~4잔의 술을 마시면 혈중 알코올 농도가 사고의 위험성을 11배 정도 높일 수 있는 단계에 이를 수 있다고 했으므로 정답은 (a)이다.

1 Currently we are going through global warming and to fight the harmful impact of global warming, there is an urgent need to conserve energy. The surprising thing is that we can find ways of energy conservation while saving ourselves some money. We can begin in our homes by unplugging any electric devices such as TVs, DVD players, and such when they are not being used. These types of electrical home devices are energy consuming even if they are turned off but still plugged in. Changing small practices such as hanging the laundry for air drying instead of using the dryer saves energy, and walking or bicycling to nearby places rather than using the car is another energy-saving habit. We must understand the fact that energy conservation is within our reach if we only participate and do the right thing to conserve energy.

Q: What is the passage mainly about?
(a) Conserving energy not only saves money but also the environment.
(b) Our failure to conserve energy is the major reason behind global warming.
(c) There are serious environmental consequences to our energy policies.
(d) Electronic devices should be designed to waste less energy.

2 An accomplice to a crime faces legal punishment for either direct or indirect involvement in executing the crime. A person who knowingly supplies weapons for a robbery, for example, will be named an accomplice. To help define an accomplice in crime, the law provides the following definitions. An accomplice must be aware of the criminal intent of the main actor in a crime. An accomplice must also be a willing participant in the crime either directly or indirectly. Someone who helped plan the crime but was not present at the scene is also an accomplice. In sum, any person who provides assistance to the crime in any form with awareness can be just as guilty as the principal criminal.

Q: Which of the following best describes the purpose of the passage?
(a) To explain what defines an accomplice in a crime
(b) To clarify the difference between an accomplice and a criminal
(c) To explain why an accomplice should be guilty
(d) To show why an accomplice should not be guilty

3

Dear Mr. Davidson,

We have reviewed your application for our position as Assistant Accountant. We are pleased to say that your resume was most impressive in its work experience. Our wish is to meet with you personally to discuss the possibility of your working here. I will be available on the 2nd through 4th of this month. If you would kindly contact my secretary Anna Dwight at 555-1473, she can help arrange a time for us to meet. Please direct any of your questions with her. Then I look forward to our meeting. Have a good day.

Yours sincerely,
Danielle Avila

Q: Which of the following best describes the purpose of the letter?

(a) To set up an appointment for a job interview with a prospective employer

(b) To schedule a meeting with a job hunter to locate an Assistant Manager

(c) To schedule an interview with a job applicant

(d) To make an appointment for helping an applicant write a resume

4 Losing your hair could finally be a thing of the past as a new stem cell treatment that successfully treats male-pattern baldness has become available. A little known British company has successfully brought such a treatment out to a market of well over 100 million hair loss sufferers worldwide. Working for the past few years in a high tech laboratory, the company has finally been able to successfully re-grow hair on patients' scalps using stem cell technology. The company has been perfecting its autologous approach, that is, using stem cells taken from the patients' own bodies in regenerating hair. For many men, the revolutionary treatment will allow them to wake up in the morning and see hair growing back day after day, as opposed to getting used to seeing hair shed slowly day by day.

Q: What is the main topic of the passage?

(a) Various treatment options for baldness

(b) Using stem cells to regain hair

(c) A natural remedy against baldness

(d) Regenerating tissues by using stem cells

5 You know you're the best at what you do. You'd urge anyone to turn their home or office cleaning over to your company. With your magical touch, everything is spic and span in the end. If that's the case, shouldn't you do the same thing and turn your company advertising over to the best? What's the point of being the best if no one knows how good you really are? HousekeepingandCleaners.com provides the best quality cleaning service advertisements you'll find anywhere. In today's troubled economy, individuals and families have less time than ever to spend on cleaning. They've also gotten used to having the world at their fingertips via the Internet. Cleaning service advertising is only effective if the right people see it. At HousekeepingandCleaners.com, we make that happen, providing you with quality advertisements every time and placing them in perfect places for your customers to see.

Q: Which of the following best describes the purpose of the passage?

(a) To introduce a website that teaches how to clean offices

(b) To introduce a website for customers looking for good cleaners

(c) To advertise a website that helps cleaners find customers

(d) To advertise a professional cleaning company

6

Dear Mr. Clellan,

The first shipment of equipment from your company has arrived before the estimated arrival date, and we would like to thank you for the prompt shipment. We are delighted with every piece. Therefore, we decided to make another purchase. I am attaching our purchase order No. 3422 for additional goods totaling $700,000. I hope you will continue to provide us with the same quality service and products. Since you already have a copy of our Procurement Guidelines, I shall not attach them to this order. As before, we will establish a letter of credit. Please inform me of shipping dates. Thank you for your consideration.

Best wishes,
Robert Williams

Q: Which of the following best describes the purpose of the letter?

(a) To complain about early shipment

(b) To make an order of additional purchase

(c) To cancel an order that was previously made

(d) To inquire about the arrival of ordered product

7 As the world continues to progress, many scientists are looking for ways to develop alternative green energy which is pollution-free. One of the many green sources of electricity is solar energy. Solar energy is produced by the sun which will continue to supply its energy for millions of years. Another green power source is plant power, better known as biomass. This energy source uses biological material that come from living organisms, biodegradable products, or garbage. Wind power is another good example of a green energy source that actually works effectively in breezy places. It involves using wind mills, wind turbines, and wind pumps to turn on an electric power generator. Although a lot of money is needed to build infrastructure to utilize these sources, there are lots of individuals who engage in protecting our planet by means of harnessing these green power sources.

Q: What is the passage mainly about?

(a) The benefits of using wind power and solar Energy

(b) The urgent need to develop new energy sources

(c) The need to exploit solar energy

(d) Exploring diverse green energy sources

8 Understanding what dehydration is and how it affects our bodies will help us prevent damage to the body and promote a healthy metabolism. Dehydration means a lack of water in the body or excessive loss of water in the body. The serious effects of dehydration include damage to the organs and in the most serious case, death. In most individuals, the total weight in a human body is 70% water. Thus, people are encouraged to drink more than 2 liters of water per day for proper metabolism in the body. Consumption of adequate water will help keep the body strong and healthy. On the other hand, a lack of water can lead to drastic changes to the body. For instance, the body needs water to flush out toxins through breathing, urination, stool, and sweating. Therefore, it is recommended that sufficient water is consumed for promoting rejuvenation of cells and for prolonged longevity.

Q: What is the main idea of the passage?

(a) Keeping healthy with plenty of water

(b) How clean water can help the body

(c) How to assess drinking water

(d) Food that can replace water

9   The meaning of offshoring has been familiar to us for over a decade now, but the increasing usage of yet another term 'inshoring' is now gaining prominence. Dictionaries define inshoring as a term used to mean the opposite of offshoring, when a firm relocates a part of its productive activity into the domestic economy. As countries are starting to recognize the merits of inshoring, governments are building a business environment friendlier to it. Through inshoring, a company can enjoy more control over their business. Inshoring also empowers a company to maximize cost-effective operational benefits. Furthermore, a company can minimize cultural and time-zone differences. Best yet, a company can develop local talents in the country. Domestic inshoring uses local labor, resources and technologies, adds value to the business, and ensures economic and social gains for the country.

Q: What is the main topic of the passage?

(a) Benefits of offshoring and inshoring

(b) Understanding the advantages of inshoring

(c) How to inshore in the global world

(d) Why inshoring is a waning global trend

10   In the midst of the many laudable achievements of President Kennedy, there is one failure that many people remember him by: the Bay of Pigs. In an attempt to overthrow the communist leader of Cuba, Fidel Castro, Kennedy had the CIA train and arm pro-democracy Cuban exiles to mount an invasion of Cuba in 1961. The US government hoped that the trained army of exiles, with US Air Force support, could defeat Castro's forces and spark a popular uprising. Shortly before the attempt coup, however, Kennedy decided not to provide air support for the ground troops. The storming of the Bay of Pigs turned out to be less than successful without the air cover. Castro's army thwarted the would-be coup d'état and declared victory against America. The invasion was an utter disaster and Kennedy accepted full responsibility for the fiasco.

Q: What is the passage mainly about?

(a) Kennedy's failure to settle differences with Castro

(b) Kennedy's failure to remove Castro from power

(c) Different mistakes made by the Kennedy administration

(d) America's successful effort to overthrow Castro

독해 문제에서 가장 꼼꼼하게 풀어야 하면서도 의외로 쉽게 답을 찾을 수 있는 문제가 구체적인 사실을 묻는 질문이다.

Mahogany Apartments is a new exclusive apartment located in the best spot in Acapulco, the northern shore overlooking the Pacific. The exquisite residence offers, 2, 3, and 4 bedroom apartments in various sizes from 950 to 1800 square feet. Mahogany offers excellent facilities such as a club house, swimming pool, kiddy's pool, party lawn, amphitheater, jogging track, tennis court, adventure park, and many more. Our apartment is constructed by highly experienced engineers who have worked in the industry for over 20 years. Mahogany is the result of one of the biggest projects by Mahogun, a company with an unblemished record of building luxury apartments with a relaxing environment. The company always strives to provide optimal specifications thereby adding more value and cost benefit for the customers.

Q: Which of the following is correct according to the passage?
(a) Mahogany Apartments has a great view of the mountains.
(b) Mahogany Apartments offers five bedroom apartments.
(c) Mahogany Apartments does not have any musical facilities.
(d) Mahogany Apartments was constructed by Mahogun.

해석   마호가니 아파트는 태평양이 내려다보이는 북쪽 해안에 있는 아카풀코의 가장 좋은 자리에 위치한 새로운 고급 아파트입니다. 매우 아름다운 이 아파트는 950평방피트에서 1800평방피트까지 다양한 크기에 2개, 3개, 4개의 침실을 갖추고 있습니다. 마호가니 아파트는 클럽 하우스, 수영장, 어린이 전용 수영장, 파티용 잔디, 원형 극장, 조깅 트랙, 테니스 코트, 놀이 공원 등 훌륭한 시설을 제공합니다. 저희 아파트는 업계에서 20년 이상 근무해온 상당한 경력을 가진 기술자들이 건설하였습니다. 마호가니 아파트는 편안한 분위기의 고급 아파트를 건설하는 데 흠집을 데 없는 기록을 보유한 회사인 마호군의 가장 큰 프로젝트 중 하나의 결과입니다. 이 회사는 언제나 최적의 사양을 제공하려고 노력하여 고객에게 더 많은 가치를 부여하고 비용적인 혜택을 주고자 합니다.
Q: 지문에 따르면 다음 중 옳은 것은?
(a) 마호가니 아파트는 산의 멋진 전망을 보여준다.
(b) 마호가니 아파트는 2개에서 5개의 침실을 갖추고 있다.
(c) 마호가니 아파트는 어떠한 음악적 시설도 갖추지 않았다.
(d) 마호가니 아파트는 마호군이 건설했다.

어휘   exclusive 독점적인 exquisite 매우 아름다운 unblemished 흠집 없는 optimal 최적의 kiddy pool 아이들용 수영장

해설   옳은 답을 고르는 것도 중요하지만 틀린 답을 소거하는 방법도 도움이 된다. (a)는 첫 문장에 아파트가 바다를 바라본다고 하기 때문에 틀렸으며 (b)는 침실이 4개까지만 있다고 나오기 때문에 답이 될 수 없으며 (c)는 여러 시설 중 amphitheater가 언급되었기에 음악 시설을 갖추고 있다는 것을 알 수 있으므로 정답은 (d)이다.

1 When parents take their children to a mountain for a hike, they should be sure to do some "homework". Before anything, parents should prepare a contact card with the names of the guardian and the children and phone numbers. They should place the card in the children's pockets or backpacks. Next, they ought to let the children put on light, breathable, and comfortable clothes to protect them against heat stroke. It is also recommended that the children put on a visor to block ultraviolet rays. When putting on a good sunscreen, parents should pay special attention to the face, hands, and legs which are easily exposed to sunlight. Parents should also prepare some high-calorie food and a first-aid kit. Following these simple steps can keep children safe in the woods even when they are met with danger.

Q: Which of the following is correct according to the passage?
(a) Children should put on sunscreen only on the face.
(b) Parents should place their business cards in their pockets or backpacks.
(c) Parents need to wear sunglasses for protection against the sun.
(d) Children need to take some food high in calories when hiking.

2 How do you remove particles wedged in chains, engines, or conveyor belts which pile up and disrupt their functioning? Well, the answer is an air knife. An air knife is a tool used to blow off liquid or solid debris from chains and belts. Air knives are normally used in manufacturing, maintaining, and cleaning machine parts. The knife consists of a high intensity, uniform air flow sometimes known as a streamline flow. The impact from the compressed air can range from a gentle breeze to a Mach 0.6 in order to clean a surface without physical contact. Air knives can also be used to dry or cool down surfaces. Air knives are the most efficient method of removing unwanted or foreign substances on any surface.

Q: Which of the following is correct about the air knife?
(a) An air knife shoots high-velocity wind to dry and clean.
(b) An air knife is powerful enough to cut through plastic.
(c) An air knife can be used not only in manufacturing but also in the home.
(d) An air knife is a very portable tool used in manufacturing machine parts.

3

Dear Ms. Foster,

We regret that the furniture set you ordered from us last week is no longer manufactured by us due to low demand. Though we've discontinued that line, we hope that you might find something else to meet your needs in our new catalog enclosed here for your consideration. The items on page 7 of our catalog may offer some of the features you were looking for in your order. Please let us know if you find any of these items of interest to you.

Best Regards,
Joyce Wilders

Q: Which of the following is correct according to the letter?
(a) New furniture will be delivered to replace the old one.
(b) Originally ordered furniture is all sold out.
(c) The furniture arranged to be delivered will arrive late.
(d) Previously requested furniture is out of production.

4 Language skills are the way children learn to understand and communicate at an early age. However, as the child gets older, language learning becomes more difficult. In fact, most language skills are learned in the first three years of life when the brain is still developing. Some believe language skills start as early as when the child is a fetus and can recognize its mother's voice and speech patterns. Language skills start out with simple babbling and mimicry. By 9 months, a baby is usually able to understand simple words and commands, and may even be able to say a few words. As the child gets older, he starts to combine words and form simple sentences. At age five, the child's language skills should be similar to that of an adult. That is why many parents opt to practice communicating with their children through active interaction from infancy.

Q: Which of the following is correct according to the passage?
(a) A baby first starts to understand words three years after birth.
(b) The first three years are the most important for language learning.
(c) Language development stops only in late adulthood.
(d) Language learning starts only after the child is born.

5   Besides its application in providing a navigational system for everyday driving, GPS also have several other useful applications. As a satellite network that scans the entire globe, GPS is able to track information about the land itself, not just the roads found on it. In other words, GPS can actually analyze the composition of the soil. This can help farmers decide on how best to manage their farmland. It can also be used to keep track of people who need such assistance. Alzheimer's patients can carry a GPS unit on them and be located by others in case they get lost. These are only a few of the applications of GPS today and it is sure to find others in the future.

Q: Which of the following is correct according to the passage?
(a) GPS indicates the location of the Earth.
(b) GPS is a useful device for finding missing belongings.
(c) GPS helps patients look up good doctors.
(d) GPS is used by farmers to find good farming land.

6   The lives of Renaissance women were mostly characterized by restriction and subjugation. A girl was controlled by her parents throughout her childhood and then handed directly into the hands of a husband whom she most likely had not chosen herself and who would exercise control over her until her death or his. Women who did not marry for whatever reason were granted no independence of thought and action, living in the home of a male relative or in a convent where a woman could become a nun, the only career accessible to females. Women were frequently discouraged from participating in the arts and sciences and thus the age never knew the full literary and artistic potential of women. The times did not allow a woman to distinguish and express herself.

Q: Which of the following were women allowed to do during the Renaissance?
(a) Become a member of a female religious group
(b) Write scripts for plays
(c) Perform scientific experiments
(d) Paint portraits and landscapes

7

Dear Mrs. Dent,

Please accept this letter of application for the Assistant Manager position currently available with Speedway Travel, as advertised in the *Chicago Times* (Sunday, November 1). My resume is enclosed for review and consideration. My history reflects a solid office background and education, as well as extensive practical experience in office automation. My experience includes monthly reporting and administrative management. I am confident that with my abilities I can make an immediate and valuable contribution to Speedway Travel. Thank you for your time. I look forward to hearing from you in the near future to schedule an interview at your convenience.

Sincerely,
Hellen Dempsey

Q: Which of the following is correct according to the letter?
(a) The writer of the letter is a prospective employer.
(b) The writer read about the position in the newspaper.
(c) The writer is going to send the resume separately.
(d) The writer is a recent college graduate.

8 By 1811, Napoleon exerted a dominant control over Europe. However, though Napoleon's empire looked strong, it was becoming increasingly riddled with weaknesses. French dominance inspired local nationalism in Germany and Spain, and Napoleon's more established enemies bided their time to strike the French army when it was weak. In Russia, Alexander I, who wanted dominion over Poland, had soured on Napoleon since Napoleon had insulted the czar by acknowledging an independent Poland and calling it The Grand Duchy of Warsaw. Furthermore, the exiled Prussian Baron Stein was now in Alexander's court, whispering in Alexander's ear to turn on his former ally Napoleon. These unfavorable circumstances and turn of events paved the road for the eventual fall of Napoleon's empire.

Q: Which of the following is correct according to the passage?
(a) Napoleon did not accept Poland's independence.
(b) Russia was Napoleon's greatest enemy.
(c) Germany and Spain were enemies of Prussia.
(d) Russia did not approve of Poland's independence.

9 Is your room always the last in the house to be cooled by the air conditioner? If it is, a split air conditioner can cool your temper and your room. A split air-conditioning unit is one that has the two main components separate from each other, with one being inside the building and the other being outside. The two main components of a split air-conditioning system have different functions. The unit situated outdoors, called a compressor, cools the air and handles condensation. This saves the trouble of having to find a way to drain the water created from the air-conditioning process indoors. The inside unit, called the blower, is responsible for distributing the air to the rest of the house. Remember, when you choose an air conditioner unit, make sure you are choosing a unit capable of handling the needs of every member of the household in the most efficient way.

Q: Which of the following is correct according to the passage?

(a) The air conditioner unit used indoors is called a compressor.

(b) The blower handles the condensation that builds up indoors.

(c) The two units of a split air conditioner have separate functions.

(d) A split air conditioner costs more than a regular air conditioner.

10
Dear Ms. Turner,

The Fairway Art Center is pleased to announce that tickets for next season will be going on sale next week. We value you as a season ticket holder and hope that you continue your patronage of our performances. We regret to inform you however, that next season's rates will be going up as a result of rising costs and rental fees. The ticket prices will be increasing from its current $265 to $292. Single performance prices will also see an increase as well. Despite this necessary rate hike, we sincerely hope that you will continue to join us for another exciting year of celebrating the arts.

Our Fairway symphony orchestra especially is observing its 24th year together and depends on season ticket customers for filling a fourth of its seats. Without such loyal patrons such as you, the fate of our acclaimed orchestra falls into uncertainty. We look forward to having you at our functions again this coming season.

Theresa Hanley

Q: Which of the following is correct according to the letter?

(a) The price of the tickets rose due to a lack of audience.

(b) The price of single-viewing tickets will remain the same.

(c) The Fairway Symphony was founded twenty-five years ago.

(d) About one-fourth of the audience is season-ticket holders.

Unit
07 추론하기

지문 내용을 이해하고 논리적인 추론으로 올바른 답을 골라야 하는 유형이다. 이때 주의해야 할 점은 답이 세부 내용 찾기처럼 명백히 지문에 나와 있지 않고 지문의 내용을 이해해야만 답을 고를 수 있다는 것이다. 주로 직접적으로 유추를 하라고 물어보지만 가끔은 글을 쓴 사람이 어느 주장에 동의할 것 같은지를 묻기도 하므로 글의 논리를 정확하게 이해하는 것이 중요하다.

Dear Mr. Scott,

As you know, our company is currently looking for talented, dynamic and motivated individuals to become part of our creative team. After assessing your application for a position in our organization, we are pleased to inform you that we are considering you for the position of copywriter. As part of the initial screening process, we would like you to come to our office on January 25 at 2 p.m. for testing and a preliminary interview. Look for Mr. Sam Richman in Suite 452. Please bring your résumé and a portfolio of your past work with you to the interview. If you cannot make it on the above date, please call Ms. Sheila Johnson at 050-555-1458 to reschedule the interview. We look forward to meeting you!

Yours sincerely,
Sam Richman

Q: What can be inferred about the writer of the letter?
(a) The writer has not read the application.
(b) The writer is looking for a job.
(c) The writer has never met the receiver of the letter.
(d) The writer lost the résumé.

해석　스캇 씨께
　　　아시다시피 저희 회사는 현재 창작팀의 구성원이 될 재능 있고 열정적이며 동기 부여가 된 인재를 찾고 있습니다. 저희 조직의 직무에 지원해 주신 귀하의 지원서를 평가한 뒤, 저희는 카피라이터 자리에 귀하를 고려하고 있음을 알려드립니다. 첫 심사 과정의 일부로 1월 25일 2시에 저희 사무실에 오셔서 테스트와 사전 면접을 받으셨으면 합니다. 452호의 샘 리치맨을 찾으세요. 면접에 오실 때 이력서와 이전 업무의 포트폴리오를 지참하십시오. 위에서 말씀 드린 날짜에 오실 수 없다면, 쉘라 존슨 씨에게 050-555-1458번으로 전화를 걸어 면접 일정을 변경하여 주세요. 만나 뵙기를 기대하겠습니다.
　　　샘 리치맨
　　　Q: 편지를 쓴 사람에 대해 유추할 수 있는 것은?
　　　(a) 지원서를 읽지 않았다.
　　　(b) 직업을 구하고 있다.
　　　(c) 이 편지의 수신인을 만난 적이 없다.
　　　(d) 이력서를 잃어버렸다.

어휘　dynamic 활동적인　motivated 동기 부여된　assess 평가하다　preliminary 예비적인　copywriter 카피라이터, 광고 문안 작성자

해설　편지 내용을 보면 입사 지원서를 통과한 후 지원자에게 면접 날짜를 알려주는 편지라는 것을 알 수 있다. 따라서 (a)와 (b)는 답이 될 수 없다. (d)는 추론이기는 하나 편지 끝에 글쓴이가 이력서를 가지고 오라는 이유가 이력서를 잃어버려서인지 편지 내용만으로는 알 수 없다. 심지어 지원서 외에 이력서를 따로 미리 받았다고도 추측할 수도 없다. 따라서 면접 날짜를 잡는 편지이기 때문에 편지를 쓴 사람과 받는 사람이 서로 모른다고 유추할 수 있으므로 정답은 (c)가 되겠다.

1   Medicinal herbs can play such an important role when it comes to boosting your immune
    system. One herb is Astragalus, a popular herb mainly used in China, and it has been
    known to strengthen the lungs considerably. Ganoderma is another one that can be quite
    beneficial. Ganoderma helps you gain more energy and is used to purify the blood. This
    herb is supposed to increase the number of white blood cells in the body while inhibiting
    the growth of bacteria and viruses. There are numerous medicinal herbs out there that
    are great for your body and provide a holistic and natural way of increasing the body's
    natural defense systems against invasion.

    Q: What can be inferred about medicinal herbs?
    (a) Ganoderma is a popular herb in China for preventing the cold.
    (b) Astragalus has many diverse medical applications.
    (c) Medicinal herbs are not known to have a good scent.
    (d) Astragalus is recommended for people who have trouble breathing.

2   Among the public health issues the world faces, one easily overlooked concern is the
    bacterium known as FNB-3. This type of bacteria is known to suppress and resist the
    attack of most antibiotics, thus becoming antibiotic-resistive bacteria. The bacteria
    can easily develop resistance to antibiotics by altering their genetic makeup through
    mutation. These mutant strains may then spread and make up another new colony that is
    resistant to the antibiotics presently available in the market. Currently, the best way we
    can defend ourselves against infection is to regularly wash our hands and maintain our
    hygiene.

    Q: What can be inferred about FNB-3?
    (a) It is vulnerable to antibiotics.
    (b) It always maintains its correct form.
    (c) It infects through the air.
    (d) There is no sure vaccine against it.

3 Human resource developers these days are speaking more and more of the so-called soft skills that successful workers seem to capitalize on. To fortify the soft skills of their employees, organizations must know what soft skills are. Soft skills are qualities, personality traits, and social skills that everyone possesses to a certain degree. Success at work largely depends on an employee's skills in good communication, the sharing of information, decision-making ability, flexibility, integrity, and a good sense of humor. An employee's positive outlook on life and friendliness are also soft skills needed to build a good rapport with other team members. The best way for employees to enhance their soft skills is to attend seminars, workshops, and company events where they can gather to share their insights.

Q: What opinion would the writer most likely agree with?

(a) Graduating from a prestigious university is a soft skill.

(b) Good mathematical skills are a soft skill.

(c) Listening attentively to others is a soft skill.

(d) Having good computer skills is a soft skill.

4

Dear Mr. McAvity,

This letter is in regard to your September 20 shipment to us, which we ordered from you on September 5. If you will recall, the order we made was for 250,000 units of Boshe earphones and 60,000 units of Denk speakers. However, upon examination at our warehouse, the shipment of earphones was found to be in excess of 50,000 units. The brand of speakers sent to us was also not the brand that we had requested.
We assume this is merely an oversight on your part; therefore, we are returning the erroneous shipment. We are also enclosing, for your information, a copy of the original sales invoice showing our correct order. We would appreciate receiving the corrected order by September 25 at the latest.

Thank you for your prompt action,
Sandy Lockhart

Q: What can be inferred from the letter?

(a) Both earphones and speakers will be returned.

(b) The letter was sent before September 20.

(c) 60,000 units of Denk speakers were delivered.

(d) Only 200,000 units of earphones arrived.

5 Although some historians cite Germany's invasion of Poland in World War II as a simple military tactic, many historians see it as a sinister attempt to wipe out the Polish population. For instance, rather than heading directly to the capital Warsaw, Germany's forces moved through the countryside, destroying targets that were neither military nor political. They worked not just to defeat the Polish military but also to crush the resistance of the Polish people. Both Jewish and non-Jewish civilians were persecuted regardless of their surrendering or resisting. Whole towns were razed and any survivors were ruthlessly hunted down. Though these atrocities would be dwarfed by what was to come, Hitler's invasion of Poland was a gruesome demonstration of the German war machine's capabilities and intentions.

Q: What opinion would the writer most likely agree with?

(a) Germany's sole purpose in invading Poland was to overthrow the government.

(b) The invasion of Poland was the worst atrocity committed by Germany.

(c) Civilians are not legitimate military targets in a war.

(d) It was necessary for Hitler to wipe out the Polish population to win the war.

6 In the 150 years of its glorious history, Alpha has been playing the role of technology innovation leader. With perseverance and pioneering spirit, our wristwear travels to different areas from the vastness of space to the depths of the ocean to challenge the elements. Alpha is also the leader in sports timing. Known for its unsurpassed technical expertise, Alpha is the authority for a number of international events requiring timing services. The international swimming time board is a proud product of Alpha, and Alpha provides timing services for the Nordic Winter Games. Alpha is a brand of high quality products and pioneering spirit. Since its foundation in 1849, Alpha has been dedicated to creating a glorious history in the industry.

Q: What can be inferred from the passage?

(a) Alpha has international branches in over 150 countries.

(b) Alpha has been a major sponsor of the Olympics since 1849.

(c) Alpha has recently begun to manufacture winter sports equipment.

(d) Alpha strives to develop products that work normally under extreme circumstances.

7 To understand and predict the decisions of countries, many politicians look through the lens of international relations theories. One very popular school of international relations theory is liberalism. Liberalism claims the world is a harsh and dangerous place, but the consequences of using military power often outweigh the benefits. International cooperation is therefore in the interest of every state. Also, military power is not the only form of power. Economic and social power matter a great deal too. Exercising economic power has proven more effective than exercising military power. Furthermore, international rules and organizations can help foster cooperation, trust, and prosperity. With rapid globalization and a rise in communications technology, liberalism has gained much favor in understanding the actions of states.

Q: What can be inferred about liberalism according to the passage?
(a) War is the way to solve international conflicts.
(b) A country has to build as many relationships as it can.
(c) There are many friendly countries in the world.
(d) World peace can be bought with money.

8 Computer systems not only provide us with tremendous utility and convenience but they also open up the possibility of a cyber-attack that can be quite debilitating. Not to fall a victim of such threats, there are several things that you need to keep in mind. First, you should first be able to familiarize yourself with the actual threats by consulting the Internet and using your favorite search engine. Another thing that you can do to avoid the loss of data is to create a back-up of the important files that you have on your computer. You can save them on portable storage devices such as USB flash drives or external hard disks. Alternatively, you can also use online storage sites for creating a back-up of your important files. It is also recommended that you install dependable anti-virus software to help you protect your system against viruses. Protecting your data will ultimately depend on how ready and alert you are against external threats.

Q: What can be inferred from the passage?
(a) Portable storage devices are the only places to store data externally.
(b) The Internet has much information about computer viruses.
(c) Anti-virus software must be constantly updated to be effective.
(d) Saving data on an internal hard disk is a way to make a back-up.

9 An outsider might look at a group of teenagers and see only an apparently random grouping of individuals. This interpretation, however, would be misleading, just as misleading as it would be to describe a colony of herring gulls as a mere bunch of birds. A gullery is, in reality, a highly structured society with leaders and followers, and this is the same with the group of teenagers. Everybody in the group knows who is their leader, and a careful observer may spot them by the particular confidence in the way that they walk or stand.

Q: What can be inferred from the passage?

(a) A group of teenagers is as highly structured as a gullery.

(b) Teenagers are as randomly grouped as a gullery is.

(c) A gullery is more structured than a group of teenagers.

(d) People can easily identify a leader in a group of teenagers.

10 Irrespective of the place you work or study, essay writing is an indispensable skill to cultivate. To facilitate your writing skills, you might want to consider these easy-to-follow instructions. First, ascertain the required essay lengths. If your professor or boss requires a specific amount of writing, you must comply with it. Next, observe the 3S's of good writing. In other words, write with succinctness, simplicity, and specificity. This means write a short, comprehensible, yet thorough analysis that provides ample data on your topic. Third, conduct adequate research. The information in your essay should be derived from a balanced variety of sources. Through constant practice using these principles, you could significantly improve your writing proficiency to assist you in your career or in academics.

Q: What can be inferred about writing skills?

(a) Writing more than the assigned amount will get you a good grade.

(b) Long and detailed writing is appreciated by all readers.

(c) It is possible to write succinctly and thoroughly at the same time.

(d) Good writing skill is not necessary after graduating from college.

NEW TEPS 독해의 새로운 유형으로서, 26번부터 35번까지 총 5개 지문에서 각 2문항씩, 총 10문항이 출제된다. 세부 사항, 주제, 내용 일치, 그리고 내용 추론 문제들이 출제된다. 최소 15분 정도의 시간 확보가 필요하므로, 1~25번까지 최 대한 빠른 시간 내에 문제를 풀고, 15분을 남기고 장문 지문에 접근하는 것이 중요하다.

📝 문제유형

1. **신문 기사** News Article

   발생한 사건 사고를 다루는 신문 기사가 출제된다. 특정한 사건 및 사고의 발생원인, 현황, 그리고 결과에 대해 파악하는 것이 중요하다.

2. **독자 투고** Opinion

   특정한 사설 및 신문기사에 대해 평가하고 의견을 제시하는 독자 투고가 출제된다. 내용을 파악한 이후, 이에 대한 글쓴이의 입장을 파악해야 한다.

3. **사설** Editorial

   특정한 주제에 대하여 편집자가 쓰는 사설이 출제된다. 정부 정책, 사회적 이슈 등에 대한 내용이며, 편집자의 입장에서 비판적인 접근이 주로 제시된다.

4. **채팅 메시지** Chat Messages

   두 사람 사이의 채팅 메시지가 출제된다. 첫 번째 메시지에서는 메시지를 보내는 이유를 파악해야 하며, 두 번째 메시지에서는 그에 대한 답장으로 내용을 파악한다.

5. **편지글** Letter

   편지글에서는 주로 일정 확인, 불만 및 요구 사항의 내용을 다룬다. 발신인이 글을 쓴 목적과 이유를 정확히 파악해야 하며 수취인이 취해야 할 행동 등을 예측할 수 있어야 한다.

6. **구인 광고** Wanted

   특정한 분야에서 사람을 찾는 구인 광고이다. 직책, 자격 요건, 업무, 지원 절차 등에 대한 세부 사항을 파악해야 한다.

7. **리뷰** Review **– 도서, 연극, 영화 등**

   새로운 도서, 연극, 그리고 영화 등에 대한 리뷰가 출제된다. 각 작품의 특징에 대해 파악해야 하며, 사회적 영향력까지 파악해야 한다.

8. **전문적인 주제**

   다양한 주제의 전문적인 내용을 다루는 지문이 출제된다. 제목과 함께 제시되며 세부적인 사항을 제시하므로, 구체적인 내용을 파악하는 것이 중요하다.

핵심

1. 전체 내용을 이해하여 세부사항, 주제, 내용 일치, 내용 추론 문제를 풀어가야 하므로 속독이 요구된다.

2. 세부사항은 시간, 날짜, 장소 등의 구체적인 사항을 물어볼 수 있으므로 특정한 사항에 집중한다.

3. 주제 찾기 유형의 문제는 두 개의 문단을 모두 파악해야 한다. 첫 번째 문단을 정확히 파악하고, 두 번째 문단의 도입 부분을 파악하여 정답을 찾는다.

4. 내용 일치 유형의 문제는 두 개의 문단에서 동시에 출제될 수 있으므로, 첫 번째 문단에서 두 개의 선택지를 파악하고, 두 번째 문단에서 나머지 두 개의 선택지를 파악하는 연습을 한다.

5. 내용 추론 유형의 문제는 첫 번째 문단에서 전체 흐름을 제시하고, 두 번째 문단에서 추론에 해당하는 정답의 근거를 제시할 가능성이 높으므로 두 번째 문단에서 정답을 추론한다.

문제풀이 전략

1. **지문 유형에 대해 파악한다.**
   신문 기사 – 독자 투고 – 사설 – 채팅 메시지 – 편지글 – 구인 광고 – 리뷰 – 전문적인 주제

2. **문제 유형을 파악한다.**
   구체적 내용 – 주제 찾기 – 내용 일치 – 내용 추론

3. **문제 및 선택지 파악하기**
   문제 및 선택지를 먼저 읽고, 핵심적인 사항에 밑줄을 긋거나 형광펜으로 표시하여 중요 사항을 파악해 두어야 한다.

4. **본문과 비교하면서 풀기**
   긴 지문 속에서 정답을 찾아야 하므로, 속독 연습을 통하여 빠르게 읽고 문제 및 선택지와 비교하는 훈련이 필요하다.

다음 글을 읽고 질문에 맞는 답을 고르시오.

☰ THE EASTERN POST 🔍

Recalling Asthma Inhalers

by Daniel Hoffman

Dozens of kinds of asthma inhalers have recently been recalled due to potential defects that might pose a threat to patients' lives. Around 8,000 sorts of inhalers are being used by asthma patients on the market only in the United States. Among them, more than 200 types of inhalers are reported to be affected adversely and need to be returned. The recall comes after officials at the Public Healthcare Products Review Agency (PHPRA) urged asthma patients to return their inhalers, used for the emergency relief of asthmatic symptoms, since they were discovered not to deliver the full dose required.

Jessica McLaine, manager at the product assessment unit at the PHPRA Inspection Division, said patients using asthma inhalers should check whether their inhalers are subject to recall. She said patients and their families should often check whether their treatment devices will be safe and effective. She told reporters in an interview that those with faulty inhalers could be put at risk. They might experience aggravating asthma symptoms such as a cough, breathlessness, wheezing or a tight chest. Those who are using asthma inhalers should check the serial number on the bottom of their inhaler. If the number is on the recall list, they should get medical advice and return to their pharmacist for a replacement.

Q1. What is the writer mainly trying to do?

(a) To report the recall of faulty asthma inhalers detrimental to health

(b) To notify patients of the role of the Public Healthcare Products Review Agency

(c) To promote safe and effective treatment devices to ameliorate asthma symptoms

(d) To complain about the negligence of pharmaceutical companies

Q2. Which statement would the writer most likely agree with?

(a) Most of the asthma inhalers on the market can be refunded at the request of patients.

(b) Patients themselves should confirm whether their inhalers will be recalled.

(c) Only a small amount of dose can be effective in treating asthmatic symptoms.

(d) The recall list should be posted on the website of the Public Healthcare Products Review Agency.

다음 글을 읽고 질문에 맞는 답을 고르시오.

Questions 3-4

Dear Colleague Researchers,

On behalf of the organizing committee, I'm pleased to inform you that the 20th International Conference on Civil Engineering will take place from May 16 to 20. This prestigious long-established international conference has played an important role as an academic platform for researchers to learn about the latest research findings in the field. We have sought to contribute to presenting and sharing novel research results in all aspects of civil engineering.

The conference has been committed to bringing together leading academic scholars and researchers to exchange and share their experiences and latest research results. It has consistently offered experts the opportunity to experience the premier interdisciplinary forum among scientists, engineers, and practitioners from around the world.

During the conference period, several subdivision discussion sessions will be held at a few assigned meeting rooms. The programs will focus on various current advances in the research, production, and use of civil engineering. The goal of the conference and detailed discussion sessions is to provide forums for prestigious scholars from around the world and promote the interactive exchange of state-of-the-art knowledge. If you are interested, please let me know if you will attend by April 10 at the latest.

Best regards,

Prof. Alice McDowell

Indiana State Technical University

Dept. of Civil Engineering

Q3. Why did Prof. McDowell send the letter?

    (a) To inform researchers about the accomplishments of a prestigious conference

    (b) To ask researchers in a certain field to attend an international conference

    (c) To share among civil engineering scholars the latest research results

    (d) To ask for innovative ideas to organize a conventional international conference

Q4. Which of the following is correct according to the letter?

    (a) The conference will deal with domestic issues on civil engineering.

    (b) The organizing committee is asking that research papers be contributed in advance.

    (c) Researchers from other academic fields cannot attend the conference.

    (d) Those who attend the conference can obtain the latest information in their field.

다음 글을 읽고 질문에 맞는 답을 고르시오.

Questions 5-6

Segway, one of the leading providers of the latest electric personal transportation in the world, is pleased to announce that we are going to expand our personal transportation line by releasing two new electric scooters: Segscooter 1 and Segscooter 2. While riding the Segscooters, consumers can leverage smartphone applications and use other convenient features as they ride along. Developers who participated in the whole process from designing to producing are confident that our electric Segscooters will be excellent.

Segscooter 1

Segscooter 1 has a maximum speed of 6 mph (10 km/h) with a range of approximately 15 miles (24 km) out of a single charge. It also features a self-balancing device, LED digital display, and anti-lock brake system.

Segscooter 2

Segscooter 2 model can reach a maximum speed of about 12 mph (20 km/h) with a maximum range of up to 15 miles (24 km) out of a single charge. Besides all the features found in Segscooter 1, it is equipped with a rear shock-absorption function to ensure a comfortable ride.

Availability

All products are currently available at major retailers throughout the U.S.

For years, Segway has been known as the world leader in commercial-grade, electric, self-balancing personal transportation. We're applying our intellectual property to consumer products to help lifestyle and recreational riders. For more information, please visit www. segscooter.com.

Q5. How far can consumers run the Segscooters once the battery is fully charged?
  (a) 6 miles   (b) 10 miles
  (c) 12 miles   (d) 15 miles

Q6. What can be inferred from the advertisement?
  (a) Segscooter 2 has more features than Segscooter 1.
  (b) The anti-lock brake system has been widely used in most scooters on the market.
  (c) Both of the new Segscooters are equipped with shock-absorbing devices.
  (d) Segway has local distributors all over the country which customers can contact.

다음 글을 읽고 질문에 맞는 답을 고르시오.

Questions 7-8

Jonathan Swift: Gulliver's Travels

Many literary critics assert that Irish writer Jonathan Swift described human nature through a misanthropic lens and parodied the changes and situations of English society. His representative novel *Gulliver's Travels* depicts the journey of an Englishman Lemuel Gulliver and his peculiar experiences. This work has caused a myriad of controversies because of satirical comments on human nature as well as political and social issues of England in the 18th century. Gulliver talks of the selfishness of human beings and a profusion of instances showing human vanities.

Actually it seems that in *Gulliver's Travels*, Swift no doubt shares Gulliver's perspective on the hopelessness of humanity. Especially, Gulliver's fourth travel is ostensibly understood as an attack on human nature due to the vivid attack on the Yahoos. However, a careful reading on the novel suggests that Swift is just satirical toward Gulliver and the Yahoos. He doesn't target humanity on a large scale but clearly finds humanity flawed. In an essay, he expresses a similar sense of indignation about humans, but within that indignation he still expresses hope that humans can improve their nature by rectifying their defects. For all of the flaws inherent in humanity, he actually cared for his fellow men and wished only for their improvement.

Q7. What is the main point of the passage?

(a) To criticize Jonathan Swift's satirical and misanthropic writing style

(b) To refute the misconception that Jonathan Swift was a misanthrope

(c) To highlight the inevitable aspects of human selfishness in England

(d) To inform readers of the flaws of characters in *Gulliver's Travels*

Q8. Which of the following is correct about Jonathan Swift?

(a) He was in favor of the political changes and situations in English society.

(b) He didn't make himself sufficiently clear about human nature in *Gulliver's Travels*.

(c) He conceived of the Yahoos as having a similar nature to human beings.

(d) He was indignant with human beings for not trying to improve their flaws.

다음 글을 읽고 질문에 맞는 답을 고르시오.

Questions 9-10

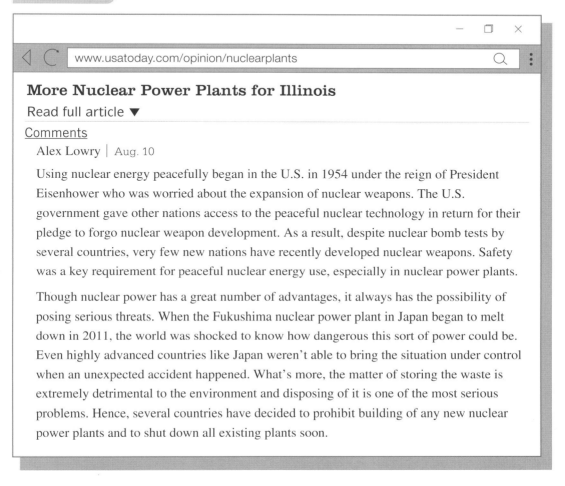

More Nuclear Power Plants for Illinois
Read full article ▼

Comments

Alex Lowry | Aug. 10

Using nuclear energy peacefully began in the U.S. in 1954 under the reign of President Eisenhower who was worried about the expansion of nuclear weapons. The U.S. government gave other nations access to the peaceful nuclear technology in return for their pledge to forgo nuclear weapon development. As a result, despite nuclear bomb tests by several countries, very few new nations have recently developed nuclear weapons. Safety was a key requirement for peaceful nuclear energy use, especially in nuclear power plants.

Though nuclear power has a great number of advantages, it always has the possibility of posing serious threats. When the Fukushima nuclear power plant in Japan began to melt down in 2011, the world was shocked to know how dangerous this sort of power could be. Even highly advanced countries like Japan weren't able to bring the situation under control when an unexpected accident happened. What's more, the matter of storing the waste is extremely detrimental to the environment and disposing of it is one of the most serious problems. Hence, several countries have decided to prohibit building of any new nuclear power plants and to shut down all existing plants soon.

Q9. What is the main idea of the passage?

(a) Peaceful nuclear technology is likely to solve many current problems.

(b) In spite of many merits, nuclear energy leaves much to be desired.

(c) Most advanced countries keep nuclear power plants under control.

(d) Some nations have already solved the problem of storing nuclear waste.

Q10. Which of the following is correct according to the passage?

(a) The U.S. government once hailed the expansion of nuclear weapons.

(b) Thanks to the U.S. government's efforts, all countries forsook nuclear technology.

(c) Most people didn't recognize the danger of nuclear energy before the meltdown in Fukushima.

(d) Efforts to eliminate nuclear power plants have been made, but with little or no effect.

III

주제별
독해 훈련

1 Ozone exists _____ the stratosphere and the troposphere. Since the late 70s, the stratospheric ozone above Antarctica has been depleting. This "ozone hole" is approximately the size of North America and is analogous to an infection that is spreading throughout the world. The main issue arising from the depletion of the ozone is the Earth's increased exposure to ultraviolet radiation which leads to a host of problems such as skin cancer, eye damage, global warming, crop damage and more. Tropospheric ozone is actually 'bad ozone' and is seen in smog around highly populated areas.

(a) together with uranium creating

(b) in two atmospheric layers called

(c) for the purposes of light in

(d) for most planets orbiting the sun in

2 It hasn't been so long ago that we had discovered the crucial role that an ozone layer plays in our atmosphere. But reversing the dangerous destruction of it would require lifestyle and political changes in countries worldwide. Ozone depleting substances, or ODS, are synthetic chemicals that extinguish ozone molecules and reducing the manufacture of these chemicals would help reverse the destruction of the ozone. When no ODS is manufactured, natural ozone production is expected to reverse the damage that has been done to the ozone for approximately 50 years. _____, there is a worldwide effort to stop the use of ozone depleting chemicals. Unfortunately, this opportunity will not be here forever because at a certain point, the damage will be so severe that the effects of the sun's ultraviolet rays will cause so much damage that we may experience permanent environmental problems.

(a) In light of this fact

(b) Nevertheless

(c) Previously

(d) For instance

3   A new type of gel promises to offer the chance of reversing brain damage due to physical trauma such as sudden impacts or even gunshots. This breakthrough invention is injected in liquid form at the site of the injury and stimulates the growth of stem cells there. Scientists have previously experimented with donor brain cells placed in the wound to repair damaged tissue. But this has proved to be only partially effective in treating brain injuries. The donor cells may not repair the injury because of inflammation and scarring. The new gel, however, can lead to more success for the donor cells by creating a better environment for them to grow in. In research done on rats, the use of the gel helped re-establish the blood supply at the site of the brain injury. With further development, the new gel can help open doors to a safer and surer way to _____.

(a) further stem cell research on the brain
(b) achieve successful brain transplantation
(c) treat physical damage to the brain
(d) help mental patients recover

4   With the outbreak of dengue fever and malaria in many countries, the world again turns its attention to the danger posed by mosquitoes. Most people are calling for the complete eradication of these creatures, but this might not be a practical solution. Thus, some scientists are playing with the idea of changing the mosquitoes' genetics; however, we must answer these questions first before giving a green light to the genetic modification of mosquitoes. If the mosquitoes are genetically altered not to live long or even properly fly, what will arise to take their niche in the ecosystem? Is there any chance of mutation and transmission to other species? While the reduction in human suffering associated with better control of mosquitoes and the diseases they spread will be immense, we need to have a thorough handle on the downstream effects that these changes could cause.

Q: What is the main topic of the passage?
(a) Concerns over wiping out mosquitoes
(b) A sure way to exterminate mosquitoes
(c) How to protect against mosquitoes
(d) A dangerous and unwanted insect

5   Scientists from the University of Oxford have found a new and interesting side effect from passing electricity through the brain. Researchers tested subjects who were treated with mild electric currents for a few minutes and found that their abilities in mathematical skills were actually heightened. This result was not completely unexpected as the electric stimulation was directed at the parietal lobe where cognitive functions with numbers are thought to take place. But a rather surprising finding was that the perceivable improvement in math ability was observed even six months after the treatment. The Oxford team is entertaining the idea of offering this kind of mental enhancement service to the public. Whether such a service will ever catch on, the potential for helping those of us with severe mathematical handicaps seems there.

Q: What is the passage mainly about?

(a) Practicing math raises brain capacity.

(b) Electrical current can improve memory.

(c) The majority of population needs TDCS.

(d) An electrical current improves math ability.

6   Scientists and engineers have come up with a latest generation underwater submersible for scientific research. This new class of autonomous underwater vehicle (AUV) features the long-distance capability of underwater gliders with the short-distance maneuverability of propeller vehicles. The prototype, named Tethys by its creator, is capable of traveling for hundreds of miles at great velocity or simply glide with the water currents for weeks. And with its advanced arsenal of scientific instruments on board, Tethys promises to open up more of the ocean for extensive study. The prototype currently costs about the same as a glider at around $150,000 but loaded with the latest high-tech equipment.

Q: Which of the following is correct according to the passage?

(a) Tethys can travel long distances but lacks scientific instruments.

(b) Tethys is equipped with many scientific equipments but cannot travel long distances.

(c) Tethys can travel long distances and is equipped with many scientific equipments.

(d) Tethys cannot travel long distances and is not equipped with many scientific equipments.

7 A man in Finland is the focus of a revolutionary new treatment for blindness. A new experimental chip uses the eye's own lens to feed the optic nerve instead of using mechanical cameras or synthetic lenses. The Finnish man fitted with this device was able to make out letters, shades of gray, and even some everyday objects such as clock faces. Subsequent clinical trials with other patients confirmed that people with this device could see well enough to recognize objects and navigate around a room. Devices like this could one day help patients with other forms of retinal blindness including macular degeneration.

Q: What can be inferred from the passage?
(a) A blind person using the special chip can tell the color of a flower.
(b) A blind person using the special chip can see a table in front of him.
(c) The special chip is inserted in a pair of glasses and worn over the eyes.
(d) A blind person using the special chip does not need light to see.

8 Read the passage and identify the option that does NOT belong.

A new type of medicine created by a team of molecular biologists can get rid of a virus from within the cell while leaving the cell intact. (a) You can kill the cell, which will destroy the virus, but doing that too often is harmful to the body's health. (b) But this new medicine developed by the team could boost the cells' own defenses and give them the ability to kill viruses even after they've entered. (c) The creation of the medicine was possible through the funding of two major pharmaceutical companies. (d) Assisting the cell's natural defenses allows the cell to remain functional after it has destroyed the virus.

1   Good news for chocolate lovers. It has been shown that the decadently delectable
    treat _____. The Journal of Heart Association published the result of an
    experiment conducted on 34,000 Swedish women aged between 40 and 82 over the
    span of eight years. The study points out that one or two 20 to 30 gram servings of dark
    chocolate a week reduced the risk of heart failure by 30%. The percentage fell to 26%
    when one to three servings were consumed per month. The study confutes the warning
    given by dieticians that eating chocolate frequently can be damaging to health. However,
    before ripping open another chocolate bar, be sure to keep two points in mind. First,
    to reap the benefit, you must eat only dark chocolate in moderation. Second, the same
    health benefits can also be enjoyed by eating alternatives such as fruits and vegetables.

    (a) should not be consumed too frequently
    (b) may be beneficial to your health
    (c) increases the risk of heart attack
    (d) can be helpful to people suffering from diabetes

2   It is widely known that men are more susceptible to obesity-related illnesses like heart
    attack and diabetes than women. Interestingly enough, it costs women more to be
    overweight than men by nearly fifty percent after factoring in diverse variables including
    number of sick days from work, grocery bills, medical bills, and even gasoline costs (the
    more weight you add to your car, the more gasoline you guzzle). _____,
    women must pay about $4,500 per year while men must pay $2,500. When the cost of
    premature death due to obesity is calculated, the cost hikes up to $8,300 for women and
    $6,500 for men per year. One important thing to note is that medical spending had little
    to do with the cost differential; it was the impact on salary that had more influence.
    Obese women were found to be paid less than their normal-weight counterparts while for
    men the salary was relatively the same regardless of weight.

    (a) Based on that science
    (b) Contrary to the result
    (c) As proven
    (d) As a result

3 A recent report published in the Journal of Public Health suggests that people's engagement in 'active travel' using bicycles or walking rather than driving depends more on the physical environment of the city than on personal will. After studying the population, landscape, and infrastructure of 15 different cities in the United States, researchers compiled data noting that the availability of public transit, street connectivity, housing density, and mixed land use were the major factors that made an area conducive to walking and cycling and discouraged people from getting behind the wheel. However, to optimize this trend, the city should also place restrictions on cars such as _____ and more expensive car parking.

(a) higher fine for jaywalkers

(b) easier access to public parking lots

(c) installation of more traffic lanes

(d) reductions in motor vehicle speeds

4 To study the differences between learned and inherited behaviors, identical twins are a great lab subject. Thanks to their matching genetics, scientists are able to study them to conclude if product preferences are more acquired or more innate behavior. In a journal published by Consumer Research, the product preferences of pairs of identical twins were compared with pairs of fraternal twins who are no more genetically similar than any other pair of siblings. The study revealed that identical twins were more likely to exhibit the same tastes across a wide range of items such as chocolate, cars, movies, and music. Of course, we can count on the fact that identical twins are subject to the social expectation to think and behave similarly which may contribute to their similar preferences. Nevertheless, the results should help marketers understand why certain customers favor certain products while not others.

Q: What is the passage mainly about?

(a) The diverging shopping habits of twins

(b) Identical and unidentical twins

(c) A study on genetic influence on preferences

(d) Product preference and marketing

5   Got ginger? A popular home remedy for ailing pregnant women, patients undergoing chemotherapy, and travelers who use the root to soothe their weak stomachs, ginger has been discovered to act as an analgesic. A group of scientists at the University of Georgia tested 74 healthy adults who took 2 grams of either cooked or raw ginger or a placebo every day for two weeks. Then the subjects all participated in exercises that induced inflammation and muscle pain around the elbows. The purpose of the study was to see the effectiveness of ginger in treating muscle pain. The findings showed that the raw ginger group lowered their muscle pain by 23% more than the placebo group 24 hours after finishing the exercises. Similarly, the cooked ginger group reported reduced pain level by 21% compared with the placebo group.

Q: What is the passage mainly about?
(a) The pain-killing effects of ginger
(b) The diverse uses of ginger as home medicine
(c) The benefits of ginger for enhancing athletic performance
(d) The side-effects of eating too much ginger

6   In recent years, there have been ungrounded stories that Hawaiians die earlier than their white and black counterparts, but a new piece of evidence based on research confirms the stories to be true. Researchers have discovered that Hawaiians are at greater risk of premature death than white Americans and those 65 years or older were more likely to die earlier than black Americans. The speculation covers various factors such as diabetes, obesity, substance abuse, and the lack of good prenatal care leading to higher infant mortality rate. The study should help initiate targeted health and behavioral programs to help Hawaiians enjoy the benefits of longevity which Americans have enjoyed in recent years.

Q: Which of the following is correct according to the passage?
(a) Hawaiians generally die at an earlier age than white and black Americans.
(b) Black Americans who are 65 or older die earlier than their Hawaiian counterparts.
(c) The causes of Hawaiians' premature death has been determined to be diet.
(d) It is unknown whether Hawaiians have similar health statistics as other Americans.

7 The winter months are when people and viruses come into close contact with each other, rendering children more vulnerable to colds. Usually children will shake off the sniffles after a few days, but the bad news is that battling the cold may lead to obesity. This new link between the common cold and obesity has been established after studying 120 children aged 8 to 17. Those with a trace of an antibody for the common cold virus were about three times more likely to be overweight than children without the antibody. In fact, those who possessed the antibody were about 35 pounds heavier than those without it. The study has shown that the cold virus revs up the cell's development cycle, inducing immature fat cells to mature faster and expand in number. The study also points out the significance of preventive health measures such as washing hands before eating and covering sneezes.

Q: What opinion would the writer most likely agree with?

(a) Children will lose weight if they catch colds.

(b) As antibodies to the common cold grow in a child, the child is likely to grow obese.

(c) Obese children tend to be more susceptible to catch cold.

(d) The number of antibodies in a child starts to decrease once the child loses weight.

8 Read the passage and identify the option that does NOT belong.

After giving daily doses of vitamin C to acute care patients, doctors now have a new piece of evidence that backs up previous claims that vitamin C improves people's mood and even sexual activity. (a) Lack of vitamin C is a characteristic generally found in acute care patients, and the experiment showed that a controlled group of 80 patients displayed a boost in their mood after taking regular doses of vitamin C. (b) The bottom line is that sufficient amounts of vitamins in your diet may help you start your day brighter than usual. (c) In contrast, there was no change in mood when the same patients consumed normal daily portions of vitamin D. (d) The result should help explain the relationship between deficiencies of vitamins C and D and psychological well-being.

1   General MacArthur, a celebrated war hero from the Pacific War, had to relinquish his
command during the Korean War due to _____. When China entered the
war to help the communist North Korea, the general pressured President Truman to
use the atomic bomb on China. He reasoned that this would allow him not only to win
the war in Korea but also force the collapse of the communist government in Beijing.
Truman and his military advisors, however, didn't believe that America at the time could
take on fighting China while it was busy in its Cold War with the Soviet Union in both
Europe and Asia. Bypassing the leadership's opinion, MacArthur took his case to the
American public, criticizing the president in the process. Feeling this was tantamount to
insubordination, Truman relieved him of his duties in 1951, even with the Korean War
ongoing.

(a) his disloyalty to his country

(b) his desire to run for presidency

(c) his clash with President Truman

(d) his failure to stop the Chinese forces

2   The North Atlantic Treaty Organization (NATO) is a remnant of the Cold War which is
still active today. As communism was spreading quickly in eastern Europe, the American
president Truman used the NATO alliance to secure western Europe from Soviet
infiltration. The multi-national agreement signed in 1949 allied the major European
countries of Italy, Norway, France, and Britain with the US and Canada in a mutual
defense treaty. _____, an attack on any one of the member countries was
considered an attack on all of the members. Greece and Turkey joined in 1952, followed
by West Germany in 1955. The greatest legacy of NATO was that it pledged the United
States to defend western Europe and prevented the conservative voices from again
isolating America from the world as they had after World War I.

(a) Contrary to the NATO charter

(b) According to the NATO charter

(c) Before the charter was written

(d) Even thought the charter was made

3 Although Americans did not invent the car, they certainly expanded its production and use, and much of the credit for this feat went to Henry Ford and his assembly-line method. Thanks to Ford, the car was transformed from a luxury item into a necessity for modern living. By the mid-1920s, even many working-class families could afford a brand-new Model T Ford, priced at just over $250. Increasing demand for the automobile in turn trickled down to many other industries. The demand for oil, for example, boomed, and oil prospectors set up new wells in Texas and the Southwest practically overnight. Newer and smoother roads were constructed across America, dotted with new service stations. _____, almost one in three Americans drove cars by 1930.

(a) Ignited by the falling price of oil

(b) Owing to the expansion of American highways

(c) Sparked by the success of the Model T

(d) Despite Henry Ford's assembly line

4 Although many critics lamented that the New Deal by Frankiln D. Roosevelt involved too much government in the daily lives of the American people, the New Deal did in fact help millions of Americans survive the Great Depression. Unlike his predecessor, Herbert Hoover, President Roosevelt tried to directly help as many people as the conservatives in Congress and the Supreme Court would allow him to. His New Deal legislation helped create new jobs, build houses and shelters for the homeless, and distribute food to the hungry. New Deal policy also raised agricultural commodity prices, put banks back on solid footing, and greatly improved the national infrastructure. Despite the increased budget deficit and national debt, the New Deal did help America survive the worst financial debacle in its history.

Q: What is the main topic of the passage?

(a) The New Deal which kept America alive through the depression

(b) How the New Deal changed American politics

(c) Controversy regarding the benefits of the New Deal

(d) New Deal, a poison, not a cure for the depression

5   In the 1970s and 1980s, multinational corporations bought up and merged many American movie studios, ending a period of artistic experimentation in Hollywood and opening the road to mass production of spectacular films to attract the masses. Owing to the multinational companies, the industry has returned to financial success and global dominance through the development of blockbuster franchises, large-scale marketing campaigns, and content aimed at children. The corporate investors also placed increasing emphasis on spectacular special effects in order to draw audiences into movie theaters. Even independent film-makers were able to receive funding as long as their scenarios showed potential to lure millions of viewers. The final result of this transition was the production of films of various genres appealing to a wide spectrum of moviegoers.

Q: What is the passage mainly about?

(a) How multinational companies destroyed the artistic value of movies

(b) How independent film-makers were able to succeed in Hollywood

(c) How Hollywood movies were able to succeed in foreign markets

(d) How multinational firms helped Hollywood movies become popular

6   Since the end of World War II, the global balance of power has been shifted a couple of times. After the war, only two great world powers remained: the United States and the Soviet Union. Although some other important states existed, almost all states were understood within the context of their relations with the two superpowers. This global system was called bipolar because the system centered on two great powers. Since the end of the Cold War and the fall of the Soviet Union, the geopolitics of the world has changed again. Only one superpower remains, leading some scholars to label the new international system unipolar. However, others point to the increasing economic power of some European and Asian states and label the new system multipolar. To some extent, both terms are accurate, as the world witnesses China rising as a rapidly growing superpower.

Q: Which of the following is correct according to the passage?

(a) After the Cold War, the world became bipolar.

(b) A unipolar geopolitical system is inherently unstable.

(c) War is when the world behaves as if multipolar.

(d) The current world can be seen as unipolar or multipolar.

7 The age of revolutions in Europe saw a heyday in the mid-1800s. Spurred by ideals of equality and liberty, the people of Europe rose up to do away with the old regimes and bring about a new era of freedom. To those directly affected, the winds of revolution may have been harsh. But looking at the overall state of the continent, historians can point to some signs of the approaching storms. A widespread famine in 1846, perhaps the last such food crisis in European history, drove food prices to skyrocket and the population unable to afford to feed itself. Because wages did not rise along with rising prices, people bought fewer things and so profit margins fell. A negative spiral ensued and the economies shrank, leading to mass unemployment. This was the background to revolt and revolution. The chain of events that ignited the revolutionary fervor was clearly ripening, and there was nothing to stop it.

Q: What opinion would the writer most likely agree with?

(a) If people had seen the signs of revolution, it could have been stopped.

(b) People could not have seen the signs of revolution.

(c) If wages had been increased, the profit margin would have risen.

(d) Because food prices were high, there was a great profit margin.

8 Read the passage and identify the option that does NOT belong.

In terms of international relations, the Crimean War marked the end of Russian military dominance in the European continent. (a) Russia's economy was critically damaged by its long involvement in the war. (b) It was Russia who guaranteed to maintain order in Europe after the defeat of Napoleon, but after the war, that power was effectively eliminated; therefore, the power shifted to other European states. (c) On the national side, the Crimean War marked the beginning of the road to the Russian Revolution of 1917. (d) Ever since the Crimean War, many Russians, especially military personnel who had served abroad, were inspired by growing democratic movements in Europe.

1   As attested by experienced educators, _____ is a skill well worth tuning by all collegiate for improving their thinking abilities as well as their written reports. Researchers would tell you that the act of writing papers and essays can go a long way in improving a college student's grasp of a subject and analytical ability. Students who write papers learn the material at a deeper level and are capable of viewing matters from several angles. Even a survey by the Board of Education at 250 college campuses showed that writing facilitated a greater interaction and engagement among students and professors. Assigning writing in the college classroom is evidently very conducive to the whole educational and learning process.

(a) doing written research

(b) teaching writing in college

(c) college level writing

(d) conducting writing surveys

2   Working while attending college is not for the faint of heart. Even part time jobs intrude on the busy schedules of college students. In addition to academics, the whole college experience of socializing on campus may diminish from the mental and physical demands of holding down a job. Among the daily time constraints of the average student, there are the classes to attend. _____, studying and working would take up almost all of the student's remaining time and energy. It may take some trials for some college students to realize that they have to focus on study more than on working, at least while they are in college.

(a) In addition

(b) On the other hand

(c) Otherwise

(d) As a result

3 Most students know how important choosing a college is to their future. And they probably have their own opinion on which school is the best. So, how do you pick the right school? The first step is to set your own priorities: what is important to you? Ask yourself what you would like to study. What do you do well? Once you narrow down what you would like to study, you can zero in on schools that offer it as a major. Make a list of what's important to you, and ask yourself more questions. Do you want to commute or live on campus? Do you prefer a large campus or a small one? Other factors to consider include the total student experience. Is the faculty well respected? Are recreation opportunities nearby? How many graduates are hired? Choosing a college is important but it can also be exciting. And higher education can make your dreams come true, so _____ wisely and early.

(a) set your goals

(b) choose your major

(c) begin researching

(d) start studying

4 For many parents of multiracial children, the thought of sending their kids to a school for the first time causes fear and anxiety so they tend to be very careful when choosing the right school. Making an informed school choice requires parents to first educate themselves about how sensitive the school is to cultural diversity. Parents of multiracial students should determine whether the school has a strong curriculum that uses role-playing and discussion to teach students about multiculturalism. Parents should also find out whether teachers and administrators welcome parents' input on issues of multiculturalism and support students' multiracial identity. Parents can be encouraged to visit the classroom to share their culture, celebrations, and history to build an environment that is friendly to multiracial children. By knowing where they are sending their children, parents of multiracial children can enroll their kids in a safe haven where the student's full potential can be realized.

Q: What is the passage mainly about?

(a) Understanding multicultural children

(b) Finding a school friendly to multiculturalism

(c) Teaching multicultural children

(d) Overcoming cultural conflicts in schools

5   A college interview can be nerve-wracking for teenagers, but not all interviews are the same. The actual interview varies from school to school and is generally tied to how selective a school is. Regardless of the type of interview or the person conducting the interview, there are some basic rules to remember. First, dress to impress. You don't have to wear a blazer and tie to every interview but sweats are not a good idea either. Research about the school and dress appropriately. Second, a refresher course on manners is a plus. Address your interviewer as "Mr." or "Ms." unless instructed otherwise. Sit up straight and speak when you're spoken to. Third, no cell phones! In our technology-based world, we need to remember that cell phones must be turned off and put away. Last but not least, be on time. If you present yourself in the best way possible at an interview, you can truly show that you fit the school and the school fits you.

Q: What is the passage mainly about?
(a) What college interviewers look for in a student
(b) Types of questions asked at a college interview
(c) Things to avoid when conducting a college interview
(d) Important tips to remember about college interview

6   Many child psychiatrists believe that a child's personality development is immensely influenced by music. This is why kids' songs can help children learn more regardless of their different learning styles. One of the specialized features of kids' educational music is that the CDs containing the customized songs are developed with the child's name being mentioned several times. Also, when lyrics and rhymes in kids' songs are selected, the writers keep in mind the interest of the kids who are going to explore the world through the knowledge that they gain from the songs. Using rhymes as a form of learning is one of the most meaningful processes of teaching kids. In the view of modern science, music can enhance the creativity as well as the memory of an individual. Hence, various pre-schools and primary schools are paying greater attention to teaching students through songs for their effectiveness.

Q: How do children's songs help kids learn?
(a) By repeating difficult words in lyrics
(b) By telling a story in a song
(c) By having kids sing alone
(d) By promoting creativity

7 People committed to single-sex education believe that a women's college can prepare young women for the real world in a better way with the following benefits. To begin, they are more engaged in their schoolwork than their peers at coeducation institutions. Also, they are more likely to experience high levels of academic challenge. They engage in more active and collaborative learning in their classes. Additionally, students at a women's college take part in activities that integrate both their classroom and outside experiences more than their counterparts at coeducational institutions. Most importantly, they are more likely to graduate and more than twice as likely as female graduates of coeducational colleges to earn doctoral degrees and to enter medical school. All colleges offer various opportunities to women, but women's colleges seem to offer more opportunity to women.

Q: What opinion would the writer most likely agree with?

(a) Female students at women's colleges get better grades than male students.

(b) Graduates of women's colleges earn higher salaries than female graduates of co-ed colleges.

(c) Professors at women's colleges are stricter than those in co-ed colleges.

(d) Classes at women's colleges are probably more difficult than those of co-ed colleges.

8 Read the passage and identify the option that does NOT belong.

Motivation comes in two broad categories, intrinsic and extrinsic motivation. (a) The intrinsic type originates from interest and enjoyment in a task and forms within the person. (b) This type of motivation is correlated with advanced educational attainment according to studies. (c) On the other hand, extrinsic forms of motivation include things such as money or other kinds of rewards as well as negative factors such as force or threats. (d) When people are internally motivated, it is more likely that they are pursuing their own values, interests, and goals.

1 Flexeril is a medication that relaxes the muscles. It is used together with rest and physical therapy to _____ associated with strains, sprains or other muscle injuries. Flexeril Drug is also called Cyclobenzaprine; it does not impair muscle function. Flexeril is a tablet to take orally usually two to four times a day. Do not take this medicine for more than 3 weeks without talking to your doctor. Follow the directions on your prescription label and ask your doctor or pharmacist to explain any part you do not understand. Take Flexeril as directed by your doctor. If you want to take Flexeril without going to the local pharmacy, make use of online pharmacies to get this product.

(a) alleviate joint pain and inflammation

(b) reduce pain and muscle spasms

(c) boost muscle strength and endurance

(d) enhance physical performance

2 If you are looking to buy a quality pair of warm sheepskin boots, you really need to try the Outlander classic tall boots. Because of the quality of the finish, Outlander boots are guaranteed to last 4 or 5 times longer than the cheaper brands and the level of comfort they provide to the wearer is much higher. Don't let the cost of buying Outlander knitted boots put you off _____ they can be purchased much cheaper than you would expect. The price of our regular pair of boots ranges from $80 to $120. With this price, you can enjoy the extreme comfort of Outlander boots enhanced by a molded EVA outsole which not only makes this part of the boot more flexible but also lightweight. So when it comes to finding a pair of boots that will match any outfit in your wardrobe, then it is worth considering investing your money in a pair of classic Outlander boots this winter.

(a) because

(b) although

(c) before

(d) even if

3 Elmhurst Furniture offers a wide range of choice in high-end home furnishings. Our pieces come in a variety of styles from English country to urban contemporary. We feature items for every room in the house. Our Estates leather sofa creates a comfortable experience for your friends and family to share. The Estates night table has gracious curves and is made of solid hardwood with a redwood veneer which gives it a unique sense of style. The Estates dining table is a dream piece for your dining room. The marble top gives this item a sophisticated and luxurious appearance. It is made of traditional English materials and finishes. The next time you need to decorate your home, visit Elmhurst Furniture for _____.

(a) a beautiful and comfortable apartment

(b) luxury and elegant furnishing

(c) state-of-the-art home appliances

(d) gracious and traditional home decorations

4 Since a company logo is a visual representation of your company, any organization which is serious about its image would be careful in getting its logo made. Although there are a number of design agencies, not all could be said to have the needed skill for creating exceptional designs. If you are looking for a top-notch designer, consider iBrand for creating your company logo. We at iBrand have an exceptional designing team with skill and dedication in their work. And we know that time is an important factor so we value punctuality and keep to a strict deadline. The quality of work provided by our designers is the best in the market and comes at a reasonable price. Our designers will work with you to find a design that sends out the perfect image for your company.

Q: What is the purpose of the passage?

(a) To decide on a brand name

(b) To advertise a business to potential clients

(c) To ask for opinions about some logo designs

(d) To advertise a job opening at a design company

5   When you are planning your next ski trip, remember to take your Spyder Wear 2 with you. The insulated Spyder Wear 2 is an ideal jacket for all types of weather including cold, rain, snow, high winds, and hail conditions. There are many different designs and functions so it will allow you to adjust to any weather changes. The Thermax fleece linings and Thermacore insulation will preserve your body temperature even in below-zero temperatures. In addition, our line of jackets are light for easy movement and they control the moisture that builds up inside and outside the jacket so you can keep dry at all times. For high-end ski clothing, make Spyder your next choice.

Q: What is the main purpose of the advertisement?
(a) To explain skiwear thermodynamics
(b) To advertise the company's ski jackets
(c) To advise on fashions when skiing
(d) To talk about clothing technology

6   Within just a few days, the Christmas season will once again be upon us and it will be time for fun and celebration. Especially for kids, Christmas is all about excitement, entertainment, gifts from Santa, and perhaps most importantly, Christmas costumes they will be showing off to their friends. At Costume4me, you can find a variety of costumes for your little ones. We carry costumes of various classic characters such as Rudolph, Frosty the snowman, angels, and elves as well as costumes that are inspired by Hollywood movies. We have a great selection of Christmas costumes that are offered online as well as offline in our local stores. Our costumes are guaranteed to make your child look festive for the holiday season. You can check us out at www.costume4me.com before paying us a visit and find the perfect costume for your child this Christmas.

Q: Which of the following is correct according to the passage?
(a) Costumes can only be ordered through the Internet.
(b) Costume4me sells only costumes of traditional characters.
(c) Costume4me sells costumes of movie characters.
(d) Costume4me sells Christmas costumes for adults.

7   How many times a day do you open and close the door to your house? When you do, do you ever wonder how burglar-proof your home is? Living in this peaceful area with its beautiful beaches and scenery can give you a false sense of security. While we want to believe that people are honest and nothing bad will happen, sometimes it does, and sadly there are people out there who look for vulnerabilities in others and prey on them. This is why it makes sense to invest in a good quality Lock & Key home security lock for your house. Installing a Lock & Key security lock will ensure you are never a victim of crime and give you a wonderful feeling of security. Lock & Key home security locks will give your mind peace in knowing that all your home security needs will be met with commitment, understanding, and dedication.

Q: What can be inferred from the advertisement?

(a) Beaches and beautiful scenery increase the perception of crime in an area.

(b) The readers likely live in relatively dangerous neighborhoods.

(c) Lock & Key sells a product fundamentally different from other brands.

(d) The company promises to provide relief from concerns of home burglary.

8   Read the passage and identify the option that does NOT belong.

The Sea House Beach Resort is a tranquil place situated in Lupe Beach, perfect for people who want to rejuvenate themselves or get away from their hectic lives. (a) It is only a 30-minutes drive from the nearby Krabi International Airport on the beautiful beaches of the Pacific. (b) The airport was constructed eleven years ago to serve the local region. (c) Lupe Beach is a new area of development that is still naturally unspoiled and provides ample opportunity for outdoor activities such as hiking or sailing. (d) While staying with us, you can also visit the famous Abdan Mountain which is approximately 50 minutes away by car.

1

Dear Ms. Johnson,

We acknowledge the receipt of your letter of August 15th, in which you requested a three month extension on your outstanding mortgage payments. After careful review, including a time value of money analysis, _____ insist that you fulfill your payment obligations. We are sorry about the difficulties you are experiencing; however, it is paramount that you furnish us with your payment by Sept 1st. We hope that you will be able to find another solution to your problem.

Sincerely,
Jill Taylor
Collections Manager

(a) the time has come to transfer funds so we

(b) our governing body has redefined the problem and

(c) we understand your predicament, forgive your debt and

(d) we find ourselves in a position in which we must

2

Dear Sir or Madam,

Hello. Recently while cruising the Web, I found your site for online auction at www. buyright.com and was very impressed. You have constructed a site that connects buyers and sellers with ease. My purpose for writing this letter is simple: I would like to place a link to Lumicon's Web site on your site. Lumicon is a leading firm in online games. I think users who navigate through your site would be interested in finding out more about Lumicon. _____, we will reciprocate by placing a link to www.buyright.com in a prominent position on our site. I think this would prove beneficial for everyone, allowing us all to take advantage of the power of cyberspace. Please give me a call at 555-9484 or e-mail me at contra@lumicon.com to talk about the idea. I look forward to hearing from you.

Hanely Ashford

(a) Of course

(b) However

(c) In fact

(d) Consequently

3

To Whom It May Concern,

Hello. We're looking to hire someone as a Public Relations Manager, but we haven't located anyone appropriate through the normal channels. I was wondering if you had recently interviewed or become aware of anyone whom you could recommend for our opening. We're offering an annual salary of $65,000 and the position involves raising the corporate image through various media channels. If you know of anyone hard-working and experienced in this area, please give me a call at 555-8934 or just have the _____ me at 555-9898. Thanks very much for your help.

Sincerely,
George Morris

(a) secretary keep updating

(b) client get in contact with

(c) candidate fax a résumé to

(d) manager discuss the matter with

4

To Whomsoever It May Concern,

Recently, I bought a property from your company situated at 435 Fine Street, Callow, Canada. Unfortunately, due to professional reasons, I am now shifting base to Birmingham and as such I need you to make a change to my billing address accordingly. This move was sudden so it was impossible for me to make the change personally and therefore in my absence, I authorize my colleague, Curtis Jackson, the person bearing this letter, to act in all matters regarding the change in my billing address for the property, the address of which is given herein.

Best Regards,
John Stewart

Q: Which of the following is correct according to the letter?

(a) The sender's bills will be sent to his colleague, Curtis Jackson, from now on.

(b) The sender has moved to another city due to a new relationship that could lead to marriage.

(c) The letter announces to a third party that a property was sold by the sender to Curtis Jackson.

(d) Curtis Jackson will change the sender's address in the sender's absence.

5

Dear Mr. Davis,

Our records show that you have an outstanding balance dating back to January of this year. Your January invoice was for $445 and we have yet to receive this payment. Please find a copy of the invoice enclosed. If this amount has already been paid, please disregard this notice. Otherwise, please forward us the amount owed in full by March 1st. As our contract indicates, we begin charging 5% interest for any outstanding balances after 30 days. Thank you in advance for your cooperation. We hope to continue doing business with you in the future.

Sincerely,
Mary Leighton

Q: What is the main purpose of the letter?

(a) To confirm an amount on the invoice

(b) To remind of a changed interest rate

(c) To return an overpaid payment

(d) To collect an unpaid invoice amount

6

Dear Adrienne,

Welcome to our Team! It is a pleasure to welcome you to the staff of Silo Electronics. We are excited to have you join our team and we hope that you will enjoy working with our company. On the first Monday of each month, we hold a special staff lunch to welcome any new employees. Please be sure to come next week to meet all of our senior staff and any other new staff members who have joined us this month. Alice Peters will e-mail you with further details. If you have any questions during your training period, please do not hesitate to contact me. You can reach me at my email address or on my office line at 555-2222.

Yours truly,
Vicky Evans

Q: Which of the following is correct according to the letter?

(a) Adrienne will start working for the company Tuesday.

(b) Monday's lunch will only be attended by the new employees.

(c) Adrienne and the writer of the letter will work on the same team.

(d) The writer of the letter has already met Adrienne.

7

Dear Fred,

Kindly accept my heart-filled congratulations on becoming a grandfather! I was thrilled for you upon hearing the news of your daughter in law giving birth to a beautiful baby girl. I can just imagine how you must be doting over your new family member, knowing you as I do. I don't blame you at all; they grow up so fast! Before you know it she will be standing up, walking and calling you grandpa. Grace and I would love to see your grandchild. Please let us know a suitable time we can meet up with you and greet the darling little girl.

Best Wishes,
Peter and Grace

Q: What can be inferred about Fred?

(a) He is the baby's maternal grandfather.

(b) He is known to be warm and friendly.

(c) His son will be having a baby girl quite soon.

(d) Peter thinks Fred will not be an affectionate grandparent.

8

Dear Mrs. Waters,

I am writing to provide formal notice of my resignation from Ridgefield Pharmacy. I started working for Ridgefield in 2013. My last day will be November 14th. I trust that two weeks is sufficient notice for you to find a replacement for my position. I would be pleased to help train the individual you choose to take my place. Thank you for employing me for the past years. My experience as clerk, supervisor, and floor manager has been very positive and I'm confident that I will use many of the skills I have learned at Fielders in the future. If you have any concerns, please contact me at my personal email address.

Sincerely,
Thomas Manns

Q: What can be inferred from this letter?

(a) Thomas Manns will work for Fielders in the future.

(b) Mrs. Waters is the owner of Ridgefield Pharmacy.

(c) A new replacement must be trained before Thomas quits.

(d) Mr. Manns worked as a pharmacist at Ridgefield.

1 Perhaps shockingly, Game Theory has become _____ governmental public resource auctions, encompassing such things as the airwave spectrum, timber rights, pollution reduction credits, etc. Game Theory, first contemplated in 1940s, as a method to research poker strategy, determines a player's action based on the likely rewards for performing that action, in concert with the likelihood of their opponents also performing the same action or an alternate one and their potential rewards. Using this method to forecast expected results and plan has greatly improved governmental and commercial strategies.

(a) an obsolete method for

(b) a calculated deception in

(c) a dehumanizing force in

(d) a standardized practice for

2 These days, there are conflicting views on the most appropriate teaching methods to employ for recent immigrants. One view contends that total immersion is useless and that a student's native language should be leveraged to improve learning. _____, there is a view postulating that immersion offers a superior method in that it forces students to learn the necessary vocabulary and grammar to communicate their needs. Perhaps a hybrid of these two schools of thought may offer the most viable solution.

(a) In contrast

(b) Furthermore

(c) Moreover

(d) In concert

3 In her book, *The Androgynous Manager*, Alice Sargent posited that an effective manager espoused aspects of both masculine and feminine traits. To investigate this hypothesis, she conducted in-depth interviews with a multitude of managers; however, one stood out from the crowd. Buford Macklin, an outspoken critic of this concept, stated that employing a conciliatory and homogenized style of management would render a person invisible and ineffective. He went on to say that apt managers are in a constant uphill battle to convince others that they are competent and deserving of their position, _____.

(a) emphasizing a positive environment

(b) utilizing a strong, rational style

(c) portraying a calm, helpful demeanor

(d) possessing depth and moral focus

4 Students of architecture gain essential tools and develop techniques for successfully designing and building commercial and residential structures, but before jumping into this field, students should have a good grasp of the profession of architects. Today's architects are innovative and creative thinkers. To be a good architect, understanding the needs of clients is a must, and having patience and insight will serve well. Architects work with CEOs, landscapers, and engineers in order to draft building plans that satisfy the needs of all involved parties. A love of art and the aesthetic beauty found in everyday objects is another trait of a successful architect. The profession often requires keeping irregular and lengthy work hours and is therefore a labor of love. Creative individuals with a passion for design and a drive to create, therefore, have much to gain from this lucrative career.

Q: What is the main topic of the passage?

(a) The definiton of architecture

(b) Building great architecture

(c) The job of an architect

(d) Great architects in history

5   If you have a friend or family member who is elderly and desire to live alone, you may want to pay him a visit and have a look around the living quarters for safety. First, you should check the smoke detectors to make sure that they are working properly and that the batteries are fully charged. Also, take a look at the rugs and carpets to assure that there are no uneven areas that would be easy to trip on. Make sure that there is nothing flammable such as towels near the heating appliances. Judge if handrails or grip bars might be necessary in certain areas of the house, especially in the bathroom. Finally, make sure that the dwelling is well-lit, and replace any burned-out light bulbs. Remember that nothing is ever 100 percent certain in our world, especially when it comes to accident prevention in the homes of seniors and the elderly.

Q: What is the passage mainly about?

(a) Remodeling the house for senior citizens

(b) Training the elderly about the dangers at home

(c) Protecting senior citizens from fire hazards

(d) Keeping the home safe for the elderly

6   November marks the start of the skiing calendar in many areas of the world, and if you choose your resort wisely, you will be able to get in some skiing action right at the start of the season. Val Thorens in France is a good bet for a November skiing holiday. It is much cheaper than it would be to visit during the height of the season. You can also head further afield to America and try skiing in the Lake Tahoe area. This area sits high in the Sierra Nevada Mountains, on the boundary between California and Nevada, so you can expect great scenery and plenty of opportunities to strap those skis on. Back in Europe, you might want to consider Finland if you are keen to try somewhere a bit different. Levi is a superb choice since the snow generally starts in October. Even if you book a last minute skiing holiday, you should always know your options to enjoy the best early experiences in skiing in the world.

Q: Which of the following is correct according to the passage?

(a) It is cheaper to ski in Val Thorens in the peak season.

(b) Lake Tahoe is located in Finland.

(c) It is possible to ski in Finland in October.

(d) Skiing starts as early as October in the Lake Tahoe area.

7 India has hiked interest rates for the sixth time this year in a bid to tackle high inflation. A huge hike in food prices has emerged as the toughest problem for the government to solve as India copes with persistently high inflation. Although overall inflation is down to about 8.5 percent, food inflation is hovering around 15 percent. Citing inflation as an overriding concern, the Central Bank raised interest rates by a quarter percentage point. Policy makers say the rising interest rates will not disrupt the momentum of growth in the economy. However, the return to growth of around 8.5 percent is straining the pockets of the middle class. Nevertheless, this is a necessary step as millions of poor people in the country who are marginalized by the growing economy are finding it particularly hard to cope with the higher food prices.

Q: What can be inferred from the passage?

(a) The middle class suffer the most from high inflation.

(b) Raising the interest rate leads to lower prices of goods and services.

(c) Food inflation is always higher than average inflation.

(d) Lowering the interest rate slows the growth of the economy.

8 Read the passage and identify the option that does NOT belong.

Living a lifestyle that is environmentally friendly has become the thing to do and so here are some tips on how to go about it. (a) For starters, only use appliances such as dishwashers and washers when they are filled to capacity. (b) Also, you can use cold water when hot water is not necessary and take a shorter and cooler shower. (c) Attempt to shorten your showers by a minute or two while using water at a slightly lower but comfortable temperature. (d) This way you can leave your skin moist and soft in the dry weather, thereby not only helping the environment and conserving resources but staying healthy also.

IV

NEW TEPS
실전 모의고사

ACTUAL TEST

1

Reading
Comprehension

DIRECTIONS

This section tests your ability to comprehend reading passages. You will have 40 minutes to complete 35 questions. Be sure to follow the directions given by the proctor.

R

Read the passage and choose the option that best completes the passage.

1. In order to succeed in setting up a profitable home business through NetBuy auction site, you must take heed of the following tips. First, describe the offerings that you are promoting with as much detail as possible. Use the keywords that make the description accurate. Also, include a good image of the item that you are selling so people can have a feel of what you are selling. In addition, it is important that you state your refund policy very precisely. Finally, have your customers write feedback about the service you provide. Follow these tips for your auction site and you will achieve your goals of _____.

   (a) buying the best items
   (b) earning cash on the net
   (c) locating the best auction site
   (d) selling the cheapest products

2. Scientists have perfected a new technique for producing biodiesel from combining animal fats with methanol. The chemical bonded to the end of the chains of fatty acids in the lard, turning them into 76 gallons of fatty-acid methyl esters which could then be processed into biodiesel that can be burned in most diesel engines. The technique can be applied to other dirty solid grease. Many restaurants have their used frying oil converted into biofuel but plenty of grease washes down kitchen drains and solidifies in sewers. The new process can convert the gunk into diesel at about $2.50 a gallon. The scientists next hope to install a facility to power a city's bus fleet using biodiesel _____.

   (a) present in wastewater
   (b) refined into solid grease
   (c) produced from fatty waste
   (d) added with methanol

3. Understanding different types of treatments available for rheumatoid arthritis joint pain and choosing the right one can _____. One effective way to alleviate the pain is through acupuncture. In this process, needles are inserted to specific points in your body in order to alleviate the pain. Another natural treatment is consuming probiotics which is a type of bacteria present in every yogurt that you find in stores. An herb called the devil's claw is also proven to achieve effective results in treatment. A correct form of remedy will improve your pain management caused by rheumatoid arthritis.

(a) get rid of arthritis once and for all
(b) soothe muscle pain of patients
(c) stimulate joints to become stronger
(d) help patients reduce their suffering

4. Why was there no revolutionary uprising in Victorian Great Britain even when the country was ruled by an aristocratic class that excluded liberal voices and workers? The answer may be because its ruling elites were able to change and adapt to the shifting needs and opinions of the times. The Liberals represented the economic and political wishes of the British bourgeoisie and the Conservatives represented the conservative elements of society. Granted, everyone else in society was excluded from voting; however, in many cases, both parties responded to the needs of workers and the poor. As a result, the English ruling class was faster to _____ and respond to them with gradual change.

(a) understand liberal demands
(b) suppress the peasants
(c) reject the needs of the commoners
(d) satisfy the needs of the bourgeois

5. A 40-inch digital menu board is one of the most popular sizes of digital posters on the market for several reasons. One of the chief benefits of a digital menu board is that it will surely create a stir with passers-by, so the bigger the monitor is, the greater the impact, turning demand into profit. This panel can display movies, pictures, PowerPoint presentations, and full digital advertisements. When installed, the unit can be placed on a stand or hung from a window or a door. Next time a company wants to display jaw-dropping advertisements or give an impressive presentation, it will do well to consider _____.

(a) marketing digital menu boards to potential clients
(b) improving upon the problems of the old digital menu boards
(c) advertising its digital menu boards to attract customers
(d) setting up a digital menu board to reap the benefits

6.

Entertainment News

The Wonders, a funky new rock band from the US, will start their European tour next month. As soon as their long-awaited second album "Life in a Box" was released last week, it debuted at number 4 on the European Albums Chart. The Wonders skyrocketed to stardom with their debut album "Diamond" which shot to the top in Europe. Their tour will kick off from France on November 26 and move on to Belgium, Germany, Italy, and Sweden before arriving in Ireland and the UK for a Christmas concert. Tickets will go on sale on October 20. Now is the perfect time to _____ so you don't miss a single show!

(a) reserve their newest album
(b) get the best tickets available
(c) reserve a seat at their American concert
(d) download their hit album

136

7. For undergraduate students looking for an internship, the first thing to know about writing a résumé is _____. There are several parts to a résumé, with the first being the objective. This simple line lets a potential employer know just exactly what the applicant's intentions are. Next is the applicant's educational background. This should include the name and location of the applicant's school, current GPA based on a 4.0 scale, and the degree a student is pursuing. The third part is where an applicant would list relevant experience. If students keep this résumé format in mind, they will know how to create a résumé that looks professional and accurately represents them.

(a) reflecting on your goals
(b) where to find appropriate help
(c) researching about yourself
(d) what to write and in what order

8. Dark circles underneath the eyes are the absolute tell-tale sign of old age and here are some tips to help you understand _____ so that you can make them go away. Dark circles often appear on people who have gluten intolerance, which is an allergic reaction to wheat or flour. People who do not get adequate sleep are often seen with black bags under their eyes. Different skin allergies can also cause dark circles as they cause discoloration of the skin. Last is something you have no control over. It is heredity. Determining why you have your unwanted dark eye circles will help you look into just what you can do to treat them.

(a) how dark circles affect your appearance
(b) what makes dark circles so hazardous
(c) how to treat your dark circles
(d) where your dark circles originate from

9.

Dear Sir or Madam,

In August you sent me a check for $250 with regard to my motor insurance. The check was issued in my maiden name Smith. However, in June of this year, I got married and changed my surname to Jones. _____, this means that my bank will not accept your check. My bank account is now in my married name. I return the check herewith and request that a payment be re-issued in the name of Mrs. Sarah Jones. I also enclose a copy of my marriage certificate so that you may amend my name on your records. My address details remain the same. Thank you for your assistance.

Regards,
Sarah Jones

(a) On the other hand
(b) Fortunately
(c) Without a doubt
(d) Regrettably

10. No matter what area of life, having a positive outlook makes things better so here are a couple of tips. We should not look at problems as problems but as challenges. The word "problem" itself gives the impression of something that is unconquerable. Another way to ease negative feelings is to make your situations positive and add a time frame to them. _____, instead of saying you can't stand a person or a condition, you can say that you can tolerate a person or a situation for a certain length of time. You mentally accept that the time will pass and the uncomfortable event will end. With this attitude, your overall aggravation and irritation will decrease.

(a) As a rule
(b) To expatiate
(c) As an illustration
(d) Subsequently

Part II **Questions 11—12**
Read the passage and identify the option that does NOT belong.

R

11. Forget the recession, immigration, and the mortgage industry collapse—when it comes to the loss of American jobs, robots are to blame. (a) Some claim that manufacturing is still strong in this country; it's just that robots, not humans, are the ones manning the factories. (b) If automation becomes the future of manufacturing, medicine and other fields, less-educated Americans could be left in the dust. (c) To add to the list, secretaries, bank tellers, and other clerks perform work that is highly routine and thus are vulnerable to automation. (d) Automation, however, drives down manufacturing cost and saves millions of dollars for companies.

12. When talking about European imperialism, there are some dark consequences that must be acknowledged. (a) Imperialism led to the dislocation of thousands of small societies when the Europeans drew haphazard and illogical lines on their colonial maps. (b) Industrial development disturbed the pristine environment of the colonies and the traditional societies were dissolved by Europeans. (c) Now there is a strong effort to return to the traditional days and recover lost customs of the past. (d) While slavery had gone out of favor some time ago, African and Asian men and women were viewed as cheap labor for European factories.

Part III **Questions 13—25**

Read the passage, question, and options. Then, based on the given information, choose the option that best answers each question.

13. Most countries in the world adopt a "jus sanguinis" ideology to citizenship, meaning that children automatically possess the citizenship of their parents. Conversely, "jus soli," the right to citizenship in the country of birth, is mostly a New World phenomenon, dating from a time when the underpopulated Western Hemisphere countries were desperate for new residents and when assimilation was enforced as a cultural norm or in some cases, by law. Nowadays we live in a different world, one in which a multicultural ideology discourages assimilation and travel has made it easy to cross borders.

Q: What is the main point of the passage?

(a) Immigrants should be allowed to choose the country of their children's citizenship.
(b) Gaining the citizenship of a birth country is an outdated practice.
(c) Illegal immigration is an epidemic.
(d) Citizenship should be granted to those willing to assimilate a country's cultural norms.

14. Lately, juicing fruit and vegetables has turned out to be quite common even though it takes a great deal of effort. However, the rewards of juicing are definitely worth the work put into it. Many fruits and veggies provide fantastic vitamins and minerals that guard the body from difficulties like heart sickness and selected cancers. There are also enzymes in many fruits and vegetables that your body needs to perform properly. In addition, if you were to acquire the same amount of nutrients from a single glass of carrot juice, you would have to take the time to chew and eat the equivalent amount of carrots. If you transform your lifestyle to include juicing every morning, you will reap the many advantages.

Q: What is the passage mainly about?

(a) How to buy the best juicers for your home
(b) Why fruit juice is better than solid fruits
(c) How to juice your fruits and vegetables
(d) Why it is good to juice fruits and vegetables

15.

American College of Art and Design

Multimedia, an enormous field, merges images, animation, graphics, audio and video for creating virtual magic. One very exciting field in multimedia is animation. To become a professional in animation, an individual must receive training from a top institute and the American College of Art and Design (ACAD) can help you on your way to become the best in the industry. If you have basic sketching skills and a passion for animation, you can start your career in this field. For earning a degree in animation, the minimum educational qualification is 110 credit hours. At our institute, you are sure to get the best training from the most qualified professionals in the field.

Q: What is being advertised in the passage?

(a) Animation school

(b) Multimedia institute

(c) Animation course

(d) Animation job

16. The weeks before a college entrance exam day can be a very stressful period for both parents and students. There are, however, things that parents can do to vent their stress. Parents must not put too much pressure on themselves. They should remember that they have done their best to support their children academically. Moreover, it is wrong to view exam success as the only measure of children's future career prospects. More importantly, parents ought to take some quality time for themselves because parents' stress levels affect those of their children. By helping themselves, parents can make a home atmosphere that is congenial to children awaiting a very important test day.

Q: What is the main topic of the passage?

(a) Notifying parents about the must-dos prior to a big test

(b) Taking steps to help students achieve high scores

(c) Helping parents let out stress before their kids' test

(d) Teaching parents to help their kids reduce exam pressure

17. Vehicle wrapping is a very effective form of advertising. It first became popular for use on buses but it is now frequently used on smaller cars and vans for its visual impact. It is relatively cheap compared to other forms of advertising as well as eye-catching. Also, the types of people who see your advertisement are diverse so you give your company a broad public identity. Lastly, these 3D billboards on wheels are easily removed and changed. This innovative and highly visible form of mobile advertisement has become very popular for business promotion and the positive effect it has will likely expand your business.

Q: Which of the following is correct according to the passage?

(a) Using a vehicle for advertising is effective but expensive.

(b) Advertising all over a vehicle gets the message out loud and clear.

(c) Vehicle wrapping is only available on vans and buses.

(d) Advertisement becomes permanently attached to the car once wrapped.

18. Different theories of international relations express different notions of how nations interact with each other in the world. One major theory is realism which states that countries only seek to grow more powerful compared to other countries. In this sense, realism sees the world as a hostile and competitive place. In addition, a state's primary interest is self-preservation. Therefore, the state must always seek power and protect itself. And moral behavior is risky because it can undermine a state's ability to protect itself. Politicians have practiced realism as long as states have existed. Especially during the Cold War, scholars and policy makers used its tenets extensively.

Q: Which of the following is correct about realism?

(a) It is justified for a state to be unethical.

(b) Surprise attack is the best defense for survival.

(c) Collaboration among states must be achieved.

(d) Self-sustainment of a country is of secondary interest.

19. The late 1800s saw the rise of two revolutionary new trends of thought, evolutionism and Marxism. In his work *The Origin of Species*, Charles Darwin argued that life perpetuated itself through a selection process in which the successful forms adapted themselves to changing circumstances and survived while those that did not change died out. In 1848, Karl Marx claimed in his *Communist Manifesto* that any society based on class division held the key to its own undoing because that division would eventually lead to a dissatisfaction and revolution on the part of the suppressed class, in this case the proletariat class.

Q: Which of the following is correct according to the passage?

(a) Darwin supported Marx's criticism of capitalism.
(b) Marx believed capitalistic society enjoyed solidarity.
(c) Darwin maintained change was essential for survival.
(d) Marx asserted that proletariats were suppressive.

20. Asbestos is all around us for it has been used in just about everything from fire insulation to roofing. Sadly, this substance is a big industrial hazard. Just what makes this once useful material so lethal? A serious problem with asbestos is that once these fibers penetrate your lungs, they are stuck there and continue to cause harm. Symptoms include a severe form of asthma, a thickening of the lung lining, and even lung cancer. Normally, symptoms show themselves between 10 to 40 or more years after exposure. Similarly, there is no safe limit to exposure. To fight this silent killer, people must be aware of its deadly properties of this material and ban its use.

Q: Which of the following is correct about asbestos?

(a) It causes signs of illness to show immediately.
(b) Once it enters the body, it does not come out.
(c) The body's digestive system is vulnerable to asbestos.
(d) Asbestos is not easy to come in contact with.

21. As is the case with the other great cuisines of the world such as French or Chinese, Thai food also has its international face apart from its domestic roots. Whereas there may exist a degree of diversity in the regional food of Thailand proper, one could be hard pressed to find some of these subtle variations reflected in the menus at their local Thai restaurant. To better accommodate global taste, restaurants sometimes attempt to strike a cosmopolitan balance in taste. Some of the more extreme flavors and spice levels are often toned down. The results of these efforts to please a wide audience might be called a kind of standardization of dishes. Fusion restaurants take it one step further and meld different cuisines to produce ever more universal appeal.

Q: What is correct according to the passage?

(a) Thai food outside of Thailand is usually not authentic.
(b) Few foreigners can handle the spiciness of Thai food.
(c) World cuisines are somewhat moderated and consistent.
(d) Dishes taste the best in their own country of origin.

22. The risk for developing heart diseases is higher in people with high levels of LDL (Low-Density Lipoprotein) cholesterol, also referred to as bad cholesterol. To lower LDL cholesterol levels, the following four steps should be followed. First is to modify diet. A diet low in saturated fat but high in fiber and vitamins is recommended. Second, because obesity is associated with high levels of LDL cholesterol, aiming for an ideal weight is a must. Third, exercising lowers the levels of LDL cholesterol. Fourth, taking cholesterol supplements helps make up for the healthy cholesterol needed in your body along with other nutrients. It is important to know how lifestyle plays an essential role in determining the blood cholesterol level.

Q: Which of the following is correct according to the passage?

(a) Weight reduction can lower LDL cholesterol levels.
(b) The liver produces much of the cholesterol in a body.
(c) Saturated fat is good for the body.
(d) A diet high in fiber causes heart problems.

23.

Dear Ms. Nickols,

Thank you for ordering 15 cases of premium paper from Imperial Stationery. Your order has been processed and shipped Thursday morning and should reach you within the next five business days. Please find enclosed your total bill for the order amounting to $800 and the check for $40 is your refund. Because you paid in advance, we are giving you 5% discount and we also are paying for shipping and handling since your order exceeds $500. Imperial Stationery is pleased to add you to its list of customers. We look forward to your next order.

With Regards,
Ronald Tillman

Q: What can be inferred from the letter?

(a) The order will arrive on Monday at the latest.
(b) Shipping and handling will be free if the order totals $500.
(c) Ms. Nickols will get 5% discount on $760.
(d) This was the customer's first order with the company.

24. The "space race" between the United States and the Soviet Union started when Soviet scientists successfully launched the first man-made satellite Sputnik I into orbit in 1957. Although the satellite itself posed no danger to the US, Americans feared that the Soviet Union had the ability to control space and attack American soil with nuclear-tipped intercontinental ballistic missiles. The event urged the US to create the National Aeronautics and Space Administration (NASA) in 1958. Congress, meanwhile, increased defense spending and passed the National Defense Education Act in 1958 to fund more science classes in public schools. The fear that the USSR would win the space race spurred the US not to fall behind in space exploration.

Q: What can be inferred from the passage?

(a) Investment in space exploration would not have been made without the launch of Sputnik.
(b) The satellite was launched by the Soviet Union to test a long range missile.
(c) The Soviet Union did not have the technology to fire intercontinental ballistic missiles.
(d) America did not care as much as the Soviet Union about space exploration before 1957.

25.

Bad Eating Habits for Your Brain

Did you know some eating habits can actually slow the brain down? Then, how can you change your eating habits to boost your brain power?

- Eating too much is obviously a no-no. Your body will need to concentrate on digesting so there won't be enough energy left for thinking.
- You might suppose sugar offers you energy and it will but solely in short sharp bursts so it isn't what the brain needs.
- White flour is so processed that the brain cannot get the nutrients from it.
- Caffeine might be a nice little pick-me-up in the morning but too much will make you feel uptight and jittery.
- An excessive amount of alcohol promotes forgetfulness so it can't be good for the brain.

Q: What can be inferred from the passage?

(a) A large breakfast on exam day will get you a good score.

(b) Processed food has many types of nutrients.

(c) The brain needs a stable and lasting supply of energy.

(d) Coffee is good for the brain if you add sugar.

Read the passage, questions, and options. Then, based on the given information, choose the option that best answers each question.

R

Questions 26-27

Mothers' Agony

Henry Stevenson

We Americans are living in a society that usually seeks to conceal the realities or miseries of war — especially the disastrous violence, the irreparable destruction, and the traumatic toll it takes on those who survive. Therefore, a dancing performance, *Mothers' Agony*, presented by Kate Dancing Team (KDT) will tackle the narrative of American mothers whose adult children have been dispatched to some areas with violent conflicts. Attention to this show has been paid by the media.

Its world premiere performance will be held on Friday, June 15th and Saturday, June 16th at the Greenwood Theater. Its director commented that ordinary women are facing different challenges while living in a period of aggression and militarization. It is expected to function as a platform for all mothers to tell their own inner stories and those of their children.

26. Q: What is the passage mainly about?
   (a) A performance representing women's anguish
   (b) A demonstration against wars around the world
   (c) Conflicts among soldiers dispatched to various areas
   (d) Various challenges ordinary women encounter

27. Q: What can be inferred from the passage?
   (a) The dancing performance was designed to remedy soldiers' trauma.
   (b) Realities of war have been made public by the media.
   (c) The performance will be held only in the United States.
   (d) Performances like *Mother's Agony* often speak for the inner world of people.

R

<u>Early Childhood Educator Wanted</u>

- Dedicated Early Childhood Teacher -

Salem Preschool is an award-winning preschool celebrating 50 years of excellence in early childhood education. We are seeking a preschool teacher to start in January next year. For more information on our school, please visit our website at www.salemprep.or.us.

Qualifications:
- Early Childhood Education Certificate
- Valid First Aid License
- Criminal Record Check
- Experience working with preschoolers preferred
- Tryout in the classroom prior to hiring

Benefits:
- Competitive remuneration
- Two weeks' paid break in a year
- Paid professional development days
- Paid sick days
- Overtime work not required (counseling with parents is held during class times)
- Some weekend work required

---

28. Q: What requirement is mentioned in the job opening announcement?

(a) License of emergency surgery

(b) Record of criminal history

(c) Mandatory experience with preschoolers

(d) Preliminary classes after hiring

29. Which of the following is correct about the job in the passage?

(a) The successful candidate should start the job by the end of the year.

(b) Years of training with early children are necessary for the job.

(c) A generous wage is guaranteed for the successful candidate.

(d) The new teacher should often work overtime if necessary.

Questions 30-31

NATIONAL >SOCIETY *The Weekly News*

Editorial: Solutions to Grocery Store Food Waste

Maire Patterson | Aug. 20

Read full article ▼

The economic impact of food waste in grocery stores has become a major problem, as it is estimated that 45 percent of produce goes to landfill uneaten, according to a report written by the National Center for Food and Nutrition. While some of it is thrown away by consumers, some of it is also dumped by retailers. The produce losses totaled about 38 billion pounds last year, equivalent to 12 percent of the nation's total food supply at the retail level.

Some U.S. states have unsuccessfully sought to come up with a profusion of solutions to curtail produce waste triggered by grocery stores. Last year, however, some European countries passed a law to ban their grocery stores from throwing away unsold edible produce. To keep up with them, several states should plan to take action by implementing further restrictions. The states need to encourage grocery stores to donate or re-purpose usable produce.

30. Q: What is the main purpose of the editorial?

(a) To call for state governments to curtail the number of grocery stores

(b) To explain the reasons retailers discard lots of unsold produce

(c) To advise grocery stores to donate edible food to charities

(d) To urge state governments to set up measures to reduce food waste

31. Q: Which of the following is correct according to the editorial?

(a) Food waste is the most serious issue in the United States.

(b) Most of the edible produce is thrown away by retail stores.

(c) Some U.S. states have failed to find measures to reduce food waste.

(d) Several U.S. states are already taking steps to impose legal controls.

R

Local News

Portland Mayor Proposes $20 Million Business Tax Hike

Portland Mayor Tim Tyler is expected to propose a $20 million increase in the city's business taxes, according to the city government. The upsurge is expected to solidify the city budget, which has been in a deficit despite increasing tax revenues. A tax raise of that scale would represent approximately a 12 percent increase, which will especially affect the city's highest-grossing businesses.

The city's revenue officials expect the business tax to be used for their discretionary budget to pay for police officers, firefighters and upkeep of parks, as the costs for them have continued to increase at a surprising rate. Additionally, the revenue from the tax increase will fund specific additional services for the homeless. Officials hope that the increase will help them better address one of the city's top priorities: the homeless crisis.

Nevertheless, the proposal still must overcome some challenges. Former Mayor Charles McDonald attempted to raise the business tax five years ago, only to be faced with public opposition to the proposal. Most citizens called the proposed tax increase a gratuitous one. His plan turned out to be impractical since he didn't earn the city council's support.

32. Q: Which of the following will not be financed from the tax increase?
   (a) Police officers
   (b) Firefighters
   (c) The homeless
   (d) City officials

33. Q: What can be inferred from the news article?
   (a) Increasing tax revenues have been solving the budget deficit in the city.
   (b) The proposed tax increase is expected to be allotted for next year's budget.
   (c) Mayor Tyler's proposal is likely to fail unless it is supported by the city council.
   (d) The homeless crisis has been the most serious issue among city officials.

Pablo Picasso's *Guernica*

Pablo Picasso's *Guernica*, which was inspired by the German planes' bombing in 1937 on a Spanish city with the same name, is estimated to be his most powerful political statement. Tackling the tragedies of war and the anguish it inflicts on innocent civilians, this work gained a perpetual status as an anti-war symbol. Upon completion, the work was displayed at a throng of art galleries around the world, becoming famous and widely acclaimed. The exhibitions helped bring the disastrous scenes of the Spanish Civil War to the world's attention.

Over the years, however, interpretations of *Guernica* have varied widely and contradicted one another. For example, the painting's two dominant elements, the bull and the horse, have been controversial ones. Some critics pointed out that Picasso certainly used these characters to play several different roles throughout his career since they are important animals in Spanish culture. But other critics claim that the bull probably represents the onslaught of Fascism and the horse symbolizes the innocent people of Guernica.

34. Q: What is the main topic of the passage?

(a) Why *Guernica* gained popularity among Spanish people

(b) How Picasso painted *Guernica* and spurred controversies

(c) How the Spanish Civil War damaged the artistic establishment

(d) Why critics initially did not acclaim Picasso's works

35. Q: What can be inferred about *Guernica*?

(a) It minimized the tragedies of war to hide its realities.

(b) It created momentum for other countries to enter the Spanish Civil War.

(c) The animals in it were derived from other cultures to gain sympathy.

(d) The bull and horse in it have multifaceted meanings.

ACTUAL TEST

2

Reading
Comprehension

Part I **Questions 1—10**

Read the passage and choose the option that best completes the passage.

R

1. Bipolar disorder is a condition which can cause mood swings that go from depression to elation or vice-versa in a matter of minutes. Fortunately, there are simple ways to protect against the disorder with regards to diet. First, increasing intake of folic acid commonly found in cabbage can assist with the problem. Second, food with low-fat proteins like fish and poultry is essential, as proteins improve moods. Fresh fruit can be eaten in moderation daily, and all the saturated fats that people normally consume should be replaced with healthy fats like olive oil and fish oil. Remember to _____ needed to help with this disorder.

(a) limit the daily intake of various nutrients
(b) boost your daily consumption of the essential nutrients
(c) take the recommended amount of medicine
(d) consume various types of healthy fruits and vegetables

2.

> **Spend Christmas in Dublin!**
>
> This year, take a break in the amazing city of Dublin during Christmas. The place to be in Dublin for an enchanting Christmas shopping experience is the Docklands Christmas Market. This market will be brought to Ireland's capital by a German organization offering authentic Germanic Christmas magic; think beautiful decorations, chalets and handmade arts and crafts — not to be missed! After a long day of shopping, relax in one of the many great Dublin hotels which are brilliantly comfortable for anyone wanting to do their Christmas shopping in Ireland's capital. Three-star Best Sheldon Park Hotel is only 15 minutes away from Dublin's city center. So, what are you waiting for, _____!

(a) give yourself a break now
(b) enjoy your long-waited break
(c) book that break now
(d) make a break for it now

3. Cameras have _____ since their creation. Cameras in the nineteenth century were large and based on very primitive techniques. For example, they required photographic plates and a long time for exposure. Subjects in portraits would have to sit for minutes. Now, many film photographers are beginning to explore the new capabilities made possible with digital cameras. The most compelling part of digital photography is the idea of showing pictures to people wherever they are, as long as they are in front of a computer connected to the Web. The evolution of cameras has been amazing and their continued development will achieve perfect confluence of chance, observation, and memory.

(a) gone through major improvements
(b) endured many hardships in development
(c) started to become obsolete
(d) fallen back in development

4. Loans for the unemployed are divided into two types: secured loans and unsecured loans. Secured loans will be given if you are able to put any of your valuable assets as collateral against the loan. Through these secured loans, you can attain a larger loan amount at a lower interest rate. However, unsecured loans do not come with a requirement of placing any collateral against the loan, but you obtain less money than secured loans. You will have to pay comparatively more interest due to their collateral-free nature. With the help of these two types of loans, jobless people don't need to hesitate anymore to

_____.

(a) look for a new job
(b) apply for financial funding
(c) register for welfare benefits
(d) ask for financial advice

5. Since the dawn of man, to exist meant to survive. Ancient man had to obtain four basic survival needs—water, fire, shelter, and food. First, to secure drinking water, ancient man had to locate a source. Fire was a morale booster and gave a good defense from potential predators, not to mention a means for food preparation as well as disinfecting. For shelter, early men would likely search out a haven within elevated caverns intended for protection from potential predators and bad weather. A spear and a crude survival knife afforded early man fresh game, and eventually trapping skills had been learned. Everything was primarily based upon these four factors to _____.

(a) survive on a deserted island
(b) protect against adverse weather
(c) assure wilderness survival
(d) fight against predators

6.

Dear Ms. Wolff,

We are pleased to inform you that the new SoftEZ text editing program is ready. You can _____ free of charge and without any conditions from our website www.softez.com and test it for 30 days. If you are not satisfied with the performance, all you need to do is uninstall it which should take a couple of minutes. The new editing program is compatible with Invoice 3.0 and Addresses 2.0 so you can start revising your invoices and address lists with speed and comfort. Now it is easy to create your business letters and mailing lists without any mistakes. Please feel free to contact me for further help. Thank you.

Best wishes,
Mark Owen

(a) install the vaccine program
(b) download the document correcting program
(c) uninstall the editing program
(d) upload your word processor

7. One of the most basic advantages of being bilingual is a purely linguistic one where people can be _____. People who can speak more than one language can communicate with more people. They do not have to rely on others to know their own language or resort to an interpreter to get their message across. Their message can be heard and understood without the aid of others. In contrast, people who are monolingual must put all their trust in others in order to make communication happen. In fact, there is no disadvantage to speaking more than one language, and more people should put the effort in learning another language.

(a) independent and self-reliant
(b) sociable and outspoken
(c) reliable and communicative
(d) linguistic and dependent

8. The hyoid bone, found suspended in the muscles of the neck, is exclusive to humans, and is _____. This small horseshoe-shaped bone's position in the body allows it to work in conjunction with the larynx and tongue to give humans the capability of forming complex sounds. In addition to the presence of the hyoid bone, one other important development is necessary for speech — the larynx drop. An infant's larynx is positioned high in the nasal cavity so that babies can drink and breathe at the same time, but preventing the infant from speaking. At around three months, the larynx drops much lower in the throat, putting it in the proper position to make speech possible.

(a) the same shape as found in horse skeletons
(b) found in most animals that can make sounds
(c) what gives people the ability for speech
(d) formed only months later after we are born

9. In British Columbia, restrictions are in place on open fires in all of the coastal and interior areas of the province though campfires and forest use are permitted in all regions. _____, in the prairies, prevention notices or bans continue to be in effect in several high risk districts. Finally, the North Slave region of the Northwest Territories is still described as critically dry; authorized personnel only are permitted to set controlled burns.

(a) Nevertheless
(b) Consequently
(c) Beyond that
(d) In sharp contrast

10. Business development is vital in any organization, and to pursue the optimal development, there are some key characteristics that an organization must possess. Good communication is an essential skill required in any business. In addition, a management style that best suits the nature of the company will determine how well an organization will grow. _____, factories and businesses which require meeting weekly productivity goals might do better to adopt an autocratic style since orders come from the management. On the other hand, an organization such as an advertising firm might fare better with a more democratic management. These are only a couple of necessary variables to factor in to establish a prosperous business.

(a) For instance
(b) In addition
(c) Without doubt
(d) Nevertheless

Part II **Questions 11—12**
Read the passage and identify the option that does NOT belong.

R

11. Aspen trees are appreciated for their wood which offer many different uses. (a) One notable use is for making matches, where the wood's low flammability makes it easy to blow out compared to other woods. (b) Shredded aspen wood is also popular animal bedding as it lacks phenols, natural chemicals thought to cause respiratory ailments in some animals. (c) On the other hand, phenols are found in high quantities in pine and juniper which make them less suitable as choices for furniture wood. (d) Aspen log furniture adds a great deal of character to many households as it adds environmentally-friendly beauty to everyday life.

12. Scientists have been studying the topic of intelligence for many years and they suggest that there are different forms of intelligence. (a) People who have a strong linguistic intelligence will respond in a profound way to the construction and sound of language. (b) People with logical-mathematical intelligence can become successful mathematicians, computer programmers, and scientists. (c) Other forms of intelligence include bodily-kinetic, social-interpersonal intelligence, and intra-personal intelligence. (d) Musical intelligence is an ability to understand and respond to music, not just as background noise but with a capacity to get deep meaning from the interaction of melodies, textures, and rhythms.

Part III **Questions 13—25**

Read the passage, question, and options. Then, based on the given information, choose the option that best answers each question.

13. To shop wisely, consumers need to know that the terms biodegradable and compostable are different. A compostable item must possess three attributes: biodegradability, disintegration, and eco-toxicity. Biodegradability signifies that 60 to 90 percent of an item will break down within 180 days when placed in an industrial composting facility. Disintegration means that 90% of an item will break down into little pieces that are 2mm in diameter or smaller. Eco-Toxicity indicates that when an item degrades in an industrial facility, it won't leave heavy poisonous metals. The term biodegradable, on the other hand, just means that the product is going to degrade over a period of time by natural occurrences which could mean tens to thousands of years.

Q: What is the passage mainly about?

(a) Differences between biodegradable and compostable products
(b) The harmful properties of biodegradable and compostable items
(c) The reasons to use biodegradable products instead of compostable ones
(d) The environmental benefits of using compostable products

14. The art of sculpting has been considered important in the art world, and it has gone through many changes to become what it is today. Sculptures can be witnesses to the ancient past. For example, relics discovered from ancient ruins depict life during the ancient Greek civilization. These sculptures help us understand the evolution of art through the ages. Starting from the classical Hellenistic era, sculptures have evolved to romantic styles and even the abstract styles preferred today. Traditionally regarded as a form of art, sculptures will never lose their function and effectiveness as a medium of expression.

Q: What is the main topic of the passage?

(a) Prominent sculptors in history
(b) Development of the art of sculpting
(c) The artistic value of sculptures
(d) Contemporary sculpting techniques

15.

McDowell and Douglass Inc.

Company brands need to be visually appealing in order to stand out and catch the attention of a lot of people. Therefore, we here at McDowell and Douglass Inc. are dedicated to offering exceptional graphic and brand designs that can make your products sell. Our design firm creates marvelous concepts meant for a business to inspire clientele to buy what the company sells. We continue to seize the hearts of millions of people, locally and worldwide, by means of elegant ideas in business art. We have been in business for over 50 years, which is more than enough experience and know-how to help your company stand out and reach your business goals.

Q: Which of the following best describes the purpose of the advertisement?

(a) To advertise a web design company
(b) To advertise a consulting company
(c) To advertise a brand naming company
(d) To advertise a brand designing company

16. Antibiotics are substances that kill bacteria or inhibit their growth, but overprescribing them has resulted in the development of bacteria that don't respond to antibiotics anymore. People overuse antibiotics even when bacteria are not causing much trouble in their bodies. The problem is that they are hurting the healthy bacteria in the process. Naturally, the healthy bacteria begin to fight back and they find ways to defend themselves from the antibiotics. It is only a matter of time before these antibiotic-resistant, healthy bacteria become antibiotic-resistant unhealthy bacteria. The result is a disease-causing bug that cannot be treated with available medications.

Q: What is the passage mainly about?

(a) The need for new antibiotics for new bacteria
(b) The benefits of antibiotics in fighting bacteria
(c) The danger of overdependence on antibiotics
(d) The differences between healthy and unhealthy bacteria

17. Seasonal Affective Disorder (SAD) sufferers have been known to increase sharply especially during the long, cold winter months. And the reason for this? Well, a lack of sun, of course, and perhaps the best remedy is to embark on a winter escape to places on Earth that experience year-round good weather. One popular destination is Florida, a peninsula with over a thousand miles of coastline with fantastic beaches to enjoy the warm weather. If you prefer the bright lights of a big city, then you can head to the entertainment capital of the world — Las Vegas, where the first thing you'll notice is the plethora of casinos, bars and hotels. Other warm destinations include Barcelona, Cyprus, or Lisbon.

Q: Which of the following is correct according to the passage?

(a) SAD patients are not affected by the weather.

(b) Florida is well-known for its big cities.

(c) Barcelona has many casinos and bars.

(d) Cyprus is warm most days throughout the year.

18.

Dear Mr. Thrall,

I just wanted to make sure that you have not overlooked your first membership renewal notice. We look forward to your continuing membership at the Hardaway Fitness Club for another year. There are several payment options:

• Monthly automatic withdrawal: We will continue your membership indefinitely. Should you wish to cancel at a later date, let us know prior to the first of the month.

• A discount for cash: Paying in cash, you will receive the lowest rate possible.

• Master Card and Visa are both accepted: All credit card payments are not subject to discounts.

We thank you for your patronage and look forward to seeing you again.

Best wishes,
David Caruso

Q: Which of the following is correct according to the letter?

(a) It is possible to get a discount when using a Visa.

(b) Paying cash is the cheapest way to pay for membership.

(c) Automatic withdrawal cannot be cancelled in the middle of the year.

(d) It is possible to pay in installations by using credit cards.

19. To help people understand about jazz, here are brief descriptions of a few styles of jazz. More popularly called 'New Orleans jazz' because of its origins, classic jazz originated in the late 1800's to early 1900's with brass bands performing for dances and parties using an assortment of musical instruments. Hot Jazz was pioneered by Louis Armstrong. It was characterized by improvised solos that built up to an emotional and 'hot' crescendo that was supported by bass, drums and guitar or banjo. If New Orleans was the birth place of jazz, Chicago was the breeding ground. Several young, dynamic performers significantly furthered jazz improvisations with a combination of high technical ability and harmonic arrangements to create Chicago-style jazz.

Q: Which of the following is correct according to the passage?

(a) Hot jazz did not originate from New Orleans.

(b) Chicago jazz was created by brass bands.

(c) A characteristic of classic jazz is the crescendo.

(d) Chicago jazz was improvised by young musicians.

20.

THE SOUTHVILLE TIMES

Food > Local Restaurants

Berlin's cuisine is constantly evolving. Close to many Berlin hotels lie some unusual restaurants where guests are treated to a rather unique experience. One of Germany's most popular restaurants has been serving guests toilet-themed food and drink for 40 years. Guests are served traditional German sausages and sauerkraut in enamel potties, and beer comes delivered in urine sample bottles. In another well-known restaurant, Nocti Vagus, half the fun will come from the experience of being literally kept in the dark. However, this is more than just a gimmick; diners have found that by taking away sight, all the other senses are heightened. Therefore, guests can fully concentrate on the taste of the food rather than other stimulus.

Q: Which of the following is correct according to the passage?

(a) Eating in the dark enhances the sense of taste.

(b) In Nocti Vagus, diners can try dishes with a bathroom theme.

(c) In Nocti Vagus, diners are blindfolded when they eat.

(d) In a toilet-themed restaurant, urine is served in beer mugs.

21. Plastic bags bring a lot of convenience but they also bring long-term problems. First, plastic bags hinder agricultural development. When waste plastic products mix in the soil, they will affect the absorption of nutrients and water by the crops. Secondly, if animals mistakenly swallow some plastic products as food, they can die. Thirdly, waste plastics are difficult to dispose. Waste plastics not only take up a lot of land, but the land occupied will not recover for a long time. If the waste plastic products are buried in the ground, it will take 200 years for the degradation. In order to decrease the damage from using plastic bags, the replacement of plastics with other degradable materials is extremely urgent.

Q: Which of the following is correct about plastic bags?

(a) Plastic bags only harm the soil and crops.
(b) Waste plastics pollute the soil.
(c) Waste plastics disappear relatively fast.
(d) Waste plastics do not occupy much space.

22. In recent years, people have noticed the trend of using natural stones such as the marble and granite in construction. So, what is so special about these stones? Marble specifically adds elegance to entrance halls and lanais. There is a multitude of marble that one may fall in love with. Marble usually fits right into the home or office while naturally enhancing its beauty. Granite is one of nature's most versatile and wonderful gems. When granite is cut and polished, it then becomes resistant to scratches, weathering, staining, and heat. The overwhelming interest in employing natural stones to new or remodeled construction shows the value people place on the beauty and versatility of Mother Nature's treasures.

Q: Which of the following is correct according to the passage?

(a) Granite can endure hot temperatures.
(b) Marble is scratch-proof.
(c) Marble is used mostly in offices.
(d) Granite is popular for its beauty.

23. For many reasons, health professionals have been recommending heart-healthy Mediterranean eating habits to people who have cardiovascular illnesses or who just want to shore up their defenses. Mediterranean diets are large on olive oil, vegetables and fish, and light on red meat and dairy fat. Hence, they have a good deal of fatty fish like salmon in them compared to other diet programs. As a result, Mediterranean diet programs are high in omega 3 fatty acids, vital nutrients identified in salmon oil. Omega 3 fatty acids are not just great for your heart but they also can decrease your threat of diabetes, fortify your immune system, diminish allergic responses and ease muscle aches and joint pains.

R

Q: What opinion would the writer most likely agree with?

(a) Olive oil is dangerous for people with heart problems.
(b) The Mediterranean diet contains much cheese.
(c) Omega 3 is found in all types of fish.
(d) Beef is not used very much in Mediterranean cooking.

24.

> Attention: to all our valued clients,
>
> Material costs rising as they are, we are forced to also incrementally raise our merchandise prices to meet the pressures. Although we have tried to avoid doing so, we are faced with the stark economic necessity. Enclosed is a price list which will be effective until August 2nd. Any orders made up until that date shall be under the current price structure. We thank you again for your loyalty with us and trust that you understand our circumstances. If you have any questions, please do not hesitate to contact us.
>
> Thank you.
> Jacob Gibson

Q: What can be inferred from the letter?

(a) The price of merchandise will be raised before August 2nd.
(b) All merchandise is subject to a discount before August 2nd.
(c) It is cheaper to order merchandise before August 2nd.
(d) As the cost of raw material rises, the price of merchandise falls.

25. When discussing the onion-like nature of the Earth, it is important to know what layers constitute the planet. First, the lithosphere is the rocky ground which upon we live. It is comprised of the crust of the planet and the mantle below the crust. The mantle consists of hot, molten rock and is the birthplace of new crust and the recycling point for old crust. The outer core lies a few thousand miles below the crust. At the very center of the planet is the inner core. The core is believed to be primarily iron and massively dense. Due to gravity and extremely high pressures, the inner core is believed to be solid.

Q: What opinion would the writer most likely agree with?

(a) The mantle is created from the core of the Earth.

(b) The core is between the mantle and the crust.

(c) The mantle below the crust is in a liquid state.

(d) The pressure in the mantle is stronger than that in the core.

Read the passage, questions, and options. Then, based on the given information, choose the option that best answers each question.

Questions 26-27

WANTED: Writer/Editor in Communications Division

We at the Public Information Center are seeking a junior writer/editor who can work in our Communications Division. He or she will edit content across all branches within the company. His or her responsibility is to ensure that the content is regularly updated, perform research, and develop a variety of written materials.

Duties: The essential duties for this job include assisting in developing information and educational programs, coordinating personnel to research subject materials, maintaining publication deadlines, researching and producing written materials for publication, reviewing and analyzing incoming materials from personnel, and performing other job-related duties as assigned.

Requirements: The required qualifications for this job include complete knowledge of publishing processes, considerable understanding of writing strategies to develop informational materials, effective working relationships with individuals and groups, and proficiency in personal computers and applicable programs.

Education: A bachelor's degree in Communications, Public Relations, Business or related disciplines is required.

Work Experience: Experience in the related fields is preferred, but no supervisory experience is required.

---

26. Q: What responsibility will the applicant have?

(a) Development of information and educational programs

(b) Maintenance of copyrights in the publication process

(c) Outsourcing of written materials to experts

(d) Analysis of a variety of materials from other agencies

27. Q: Which of the following is stated as a mandatory qualification for this position?

(a) Knowledge about management

(b) Proficiency in developing applications

(c) Degree in specific disciplines

(d) Any supervisory experience

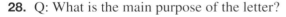

Request for More Supplies

Requested by: Clara Harris, Grade 3 Math, Road Hill Elementary School
Sent to: Martin Luther, Procurement Department of Road Hill School District

This year my class is 12 percent larger than last year, but I only received 12 textbooks in good condition for my 25 students. Even though you already said that students can share these books in class, half of the students aren't able to study at home. I have been printing extra workbook pages for homework, which has already caused me to squander this semester's copy paper allowance. I myself have no choice but to buy either new textbooks or more copy paper.

I calculated that even if all pages are printed error-free, I will need another 30 reams of copy paper for the rest of this semester. At bulk rates, I was quoted $5 per ream, for a total of $150. As all of the parents already pay $50 per semester in school fees, I think it would be another burden to ask them to pay for copies when their children should have their own textbooks. I will purchase the paper myself, provided that the school district reimburses me later. For comparison, I will be enclosing quotes from several retailers.

28. Q: What is the main purpose of the letter?
   (a) To confirm receipt of reimbursement for work-related payment
   (b) To ask the department to cover all the costs of a class
   (c) To petition for funds to purchase new textbooks for students
   (d) To ask for payment for copy paper for students

29. Q: Which of the following is correct according to the passage?
   (a) The number of students has decreased by 12 percent this year.
   (b) The teacher couldn't hand over homework to her students.
   (c) The teacher doesn't want to ask parents to pay for copy paper.
   (d) The teacher will purchase new textbooks if reimbursed for the costs.

The First Female Astronaut: Valentina Tereshkova

Soviet cosmonaut Valentina Tereshkova became the first woman to travel into space on June 16, 1963, having spent more time in space than any other astronaut to that date. Having made her first parachute jump at age 22, she extended her enthusiasm for skydiving to the Soviet space program. The Soviet government sought to dispatch a female pilot into space as a means of accomplishing another "space first" before the U.S. Eventually, on that fateful day, spacecraft Vostok 6, with Tereshkova aboard, was launched into space and she successfully returned to earth three days later.

Three years after her historic space flight, Tereshkova became a member of the Supreme Soviet, the USSR's national parliament. Since she was a world-renowned pioneer, she served as a representative to a profusion of international women's organizations. While she never entered space again, her pioneering work strongly influenced other possible astronaut training programs around the world—especially regarding women.

30. Q: Which of the following is correct about Valentina Tereshkova?

(a) She had experienced parachute jumping before becoming an astronaut.

(b) She didn't have qualifications to match the Soviet government's new program.

(c) She was elected a representative in the national parliament right after her flight.

(d) She limited her political activities to domestic obligations in the USSR.

31. Q: What can be inferred about Valentina Tereshkova from the passage?

(a) She had an influence on international communities other than space programs.

(b) She tried parachute jumping so as to become the first female cosmonaut.

(c) She returned to the ground earlier than expected because of technical limitations.

(d) Although her space mission wasn't successful, she was appointed a member in the national assembly.

R

U.S. States with Income Inequality

By Margaret Moore

Income inequality is a growing issue in the U.S. as well as across the globe. A recent report issued by the Oxford Committee for Famine Relief (Oxfam) found that only a few wealthiest people control nearly 80% of the total wealth in the world. The problem of income inequality can also be discussed on a local scale. The U.S. Census showed that inequality in the U.S. varies from state to state according to each state's Gini coefficient, a commonly used metric that quantifies income inequality on a scale from one to 100. The issue continues to be a topic of discussion as a growing bother among economic experts.

Under these circumstances, some economic leaders have proposed solutions to alleviate the problem. Some of them have suggested levying a progressive tax on capital rather than income, which is likely to prevent or slow the spread of inequality. In the meantime, some business owners are in favor of a progressive tax on consumption. They stated that each state needs policies that can return the economy to full employment, reduce income inequality, and return purchasing power to workers.

32. Q: What is the main topic of the passage?
    (a) A variety of effects of income inequality in each state of the U.S.
    (b) The importance of a progressive tax in addressing income inequality
    (c) The problem of income imbalance and proposed alternatives
    (d) The consequences of increased income imbalance in the U.S.

33. Q: Which of the following is correct about income inequality in the passage?
    (a) It is a serious problem only in the U.S.
    (b) It is determined by the Gini coefficient.
    (c) It fails to be alleviated by a progressive tax in the U.S.
    (d) It is one of the major concerns among business owners.

⚡ THE ENERGY TIMES

| Home | National | International | Editorials | Contact Us |

In Need of Eco-Friendly Energy Sources

By James Renwick

Generating power has become a major cause of air pollution and one of the largest sources of global warming emissions around the world. As a fuel source, coal is reported to be the worst offender, producing less than half the total electricity but causing nearly 80 percent of all power plant carbon emissions.

Fortunately, the good news is that the use of coal is on the decline in the U.S. The number of power plants burning coal is gradually shrinking, and no new coal plants are being designed or approved in the U.S.

Rather, we are moving toward a natural gas-dominated electricity system, but hinging on natural gas is not a long-term solution to our energy needs. Like petroleum and coal, it is just a fossil fuel, which will trigger considerable global warming emissions.

By contrast, scientists are looking for better, clearer, and more sustainable ways to meet our energy needs. Alternative energy sources like wind and solar power can produce electricity with less pollution and lower global warming emissions.

The government should support practical, cost-effective policies that can promote renewable energy sources. They can be reliable, affordable, and beneficial for our health and our planet.

34. Q: What is the main purpose of the article?

(a) To criticize the overuse of coal burning power plants

(b) To highlight the necessity of using alternative energy sources

(c) To ask for greater action from electric power companies

(d) To underline the government's air pollution initiative

35. Q: Which statement would the writer most likely agree with?

(a) Coal is reported to be the most cost-effective in producing electricity.

(b) Natural gas, unlike other fossil fuels, can be an alternative energy source.

(c) The government should not evade responsibility for finding renewable energy sources.

(d) Global warming emissions have recently become an issue among environmentalists.

ACTUAL TEST

3

TEPS

Reading
Comprehension

DIRECTIONS

This section tests your ability to comprehend reading passages. You will have 40 minutes to complete 35 questions. Be sure to follow the directions given by the proctor.

Part I **Questions 1—10**

Read the passage and choose the option that best completes the passage.

1. In the 1960s and 1970s, the Korean government was much stricter about the country's morality. Many Latin dances, such as the tango and salsa, were _____ and fell under the laws on immorality that existed in Korea at the time. Those who had a passion for Latin dance had to frequent secret clubs, using pseudonyms to protect their identity from the intrusive morality police. Today, Korea has evolved past these antiquated views of dance, with clubs specializing in different forms of Latin dance found in most of its major cities. There are even high-society dance clubs that meet on a regular basis to celebrate their affection for all different forms of dance, but especially the sultry Latin dances.

   (a) socially inept
   (b) labeled indecent
   (c) discretely banned
   (d) proclaimed oppressive

2. Earthworms help to keep the soil in proper condition. As they crawl about underground, they loosen the soil. In their search for food, some of the earth enters their mouths and passes straight through their bodies. In this way, the soil is ground up and _____. Air and water enter the ground through the tiny holes made by earthworms, and loose leaves and seeds that the earthworms pull into the ground decay, enriching the soil. Many thousands of earthworms at work in an acre of land can greatly benefit the soil. Because of this, in places where there aren't many earthworms, farmers will buy them to add to their soil, hoping they will enrich their farmland.

   (a) not fortified with nutrients
   (b) kept from getting compact
   (c) prepared to be harvested
   (d) prevented from aerating

3. Every two years (with the winter and summer games alternating with each other), the best athletes from around the world gather at the Olympic Games, with over 200 countries and 11,000 athletes coming to vie in this international competition. The modern Olympic Games was the idea of French baron, Pierre de Coubertin, in an effort to promote peace among the world's nations. While de Coubertin's vision for the Olympics as a symbol of peace and cooperation has come true, the Olympic Games have also been used to _____ recently when many people called for a boycott of the Beijing Games due to China's past human rights record.

(a) display some real political muscle
(b) protest against some hosting nations
(c) showcase the process of democracy
(d) bargain with hostile enemy states

4. The Black Death has been _____ of 25-60% of the European population from 1348 through 1351. Many people thought it was the result of a punishment from God for the sins of the people. Others believed it was caused by the bad air released from earthquakes or some astronomical event with the misalignment of Saturn, Jupiter, and Mars. It was believed that bathing also spread the disease because the skin's pores opened more when in hot water. Medieval doctors recommended that people should maintain a positive attitude, drink good wine, avoid eating fruit, not abuse the poor, and eat and drink in moderation.

(a) vaguely blamed for the disruption
(b) the catalyst for the movement
(c) plaguing the normal daily lives
(d) estimated to have claimed the lives

5. Connecting the city of London with its suburbs of Essex, Hertfordshire, and Buckinghamshire, the London Underground is one of the world's premier rapid transit systems. It is also the world's oldest subway system, having opened in 1863, and was the first to use electric trains in 1890. Some of the deep tunnels being of rather narrow breadth, the nickname "The Tube" has stuck over the years. Today it has the fifth largest number of stations in the world at 270 and is third in length with 400km of track. Its 1.38 billion annual passengers make it the third busiest subway system in Europe after the ones in the capitals of France and Russia. And yet more than half of its network is actually above ground, _____ "Underground."

(a) disguising as themselves
(b) belying any trend toward
(c) repudiating the moniker
(d) circumventing any direct accusation

6.

Dear Mr. Mohammad,

As per our telephone conversation yesterday, we have ceased production of the A123 Videx as it no longer fits the image of our company. Officially, the last shipment of this product will go out our door at the end of this month. If you still desire this product, we would suggest that you contact Jameson Security, _____ a reasonable price. We wish to thank your patronage as it is always a pleasure assisting you with your security camera needs. Should your company wish to upgrade its cameras to our new B123 Videtron camera, do not hesitate to call on us as we are more than willing to install them free of charge.

Regards,
Raj Mohan

(a) a company that offers the same products at
(b) a second-hand jeweller that can offer
(c) a security company with inventory at
(d) a telephone directory service that is offered at

7. Many of us have been entranced by the waves on the ocean at sunset. We might be forgiven for thinking that these waves are due to the ocean water traveling for many miles. But as author Megan Watts tells us in her new book *The Ocean Ecology*, water in the ocean actually only travels short distances. A molecule of water is only subject to movement through contact with its surrounding molecules. And though the waves travel long distances, the water molecules only bounce back and forth. An analogy can be drawn with fields of wheat blowing in the wind. Though the wind _____, the stalks of grain remain in their rooted positions.

(a) is in the air and the plants are on the ground
(b) may be relatively quick compared to ocean waves
(c) is the ocean and the wheat is the wave
(d) travels far and produce waves in the field

8.

Dear Sam,

_____ for you as you head off to your new workplace. We will always remember our days of working with you as both an honor and a pleasure for us all. I suppose it is now time to say farewell to you in an official capacity. You can be sure that your presence will be missed, even as you've accomplished so much for the company over the years. We can only hope that whoever takes your place here will try very hard to fill your shoes.

We wish you only the best for your future ahead. Your new employment seems to promise much success and development for your career. And we would be ever so glad to hear from you from time to time.

Yours sincerely,
Lisa Bremen

(a) We at the office only have the fondest of wishes
(b) I am writing this letter in lieu of goodbyes
(c) We would like to take this opportunity in extending
(d) All the best departures and most wonderful memories

9. In 14th century Europe, the Medici family rose to power in Florence, Italy _____ the riches that it had earned through its businesses. In those days, artisans could only survive by being sponsored by someone of wealth. The Medici family had a fervent interest in promoting culture, and by commissioning works by the great minds of the time (such as Michelangelo, Raphael, Brunelleschi, da Vinci, Galileo, and Botticelli), the Medici family enabled colossal works in art, science, and culture to be constructed. Their efforts pushed the city of Florence to the forefront of the Renaissance that spread throughout Europe, and brought the Western World out of the Dark Ages.

(a) through
(b) while
(c) over
(d) because

10. The Vatican is the world's smallest independent city-state and has population of 800 people living on 44 hectares of land. The city is an enclave being surrounded completely by Rome and is divided into 2 areas, the Holy See and the Vatican City. Different forms of passports are issued to residents of the 2 areas, for the residents in the Holy See, diplomatic and service passports are issued; whereas outside the Holy See, but still in Vatican City, regular Vatican passports are issued. _____, the Vatican has its own guards, about 450 automotive license plates, its own national anthem (Pontifical Hymn) and finally its own legal tender that is accepted throughout the EU. While a group of cardinals appointed by the Pope have authority for legislative and judicial purposes, the Pope has absolute power.

(a) Nonetheless
(b) Accordingly
(c) Equally
(d) Additionally

Part II **Questions 11—12**

Read the passage and identify the option that does NOT belong.

11. William Henry Harrison did many remarkable acts as the ninth president of the United States. (a) He was the only president to study to become a doctor although he did not finish medical school. (b) He was the youngest of seven children and also served in the army before becoming President. (c) On March 4, 1841, he made the longest inaugural speech by any president. (d) Thirty-two days later, he caught a cold that developed into pneumonia and on April 4, 1841, he became the first president to die in office after having served the shortest term of any president in US history.

12. According to a survey of American high school students, they do not know very much about world geography. (a) A surprisingly large number of students did not know the capital of the state in which they live. (b) Many could not find Mexico on a map, even though it is one of only two countries that border the United States, the other being Canada. (c) Canadian students in comparison fared much worse in knowing who their geographic neighbors were. (d) Some educators blame this lack of geographic knowledge on the move away from memorization of material that has taken place in recent years in US schools.

Part III Questions 13—25

Read the passage, question, and options. Then, based on the given information, choose the option that best answers each question.

R

13. Uncontrollable wildfires in wilderness areas can be started by lightning, volcanoes, even sparks from rock falls. In a sense, they can be considered an inevitable part of the ecology. But what's inevitable in nature is sought to be controlled by man. In managing wildfires, people drop water from helicopters or airplanes. Sometimes they literally fight fire with fire. A spot of land deliberately cleared by a small controlled fire blocks the spread of a wildfire by depriving it of fuel. This is a delicate task as these prescribed fires can turn into wildfires themselves.

    Q: What is the main point of the passage?

    (a) Men should not set controlled fires to stop wildfires.

    (b) People manage wildfires as best they can.

    (c) Wildfires should be left to burn on their own.

    (d) Dropping water on wildfires is safer than using fire.

14. Twice a year, two astronomical phenomena, a solstice and an equinox, occur at regular intervals. A solstice occurs when the sun reaches a position in the sky in which it appears to stop and reverse its course. For example, in North America, the summer solstice is June 21st as it is the longest day of the year. In contrast, on December 22nd, the winter solstice, North America experiences its shortest day. The equinox occurs when day and night are equal in length as the sun passes the equator. There is the vernal or spring equinox which occurs on March 21st and the autumnal equinox on September 22nd.

    Q: What is main topic of the passage?

    (a) Where to view a solstice or equinox

    (b) Predicting the day and night cycle

    (c) The sun and the amount of daylight

    (d) Annual solstice and equinox occurrences

15. In fishing villages across China, one can still see an ancient technique in operation. When fishermen in this village in Suzhou set out in the mornings, they bring with them a bird. No, these are not simply pet birds that they keep for company. These are working birds, cormorants to be exact. These long-necked feathered friends assist the fisherman in their quest to grab their daily catch. But how, you might ask? Simply put, the birds are trained to do it. Harnessing their instinct for swooping up fish, fishermen have literally put these birds on a lease. In addition, a ring on the neck ensures that the swallowed fish are still available at the fisherman's request. Unfair to the cormorants, you say? At the end of their shift, they have been known to take in a few catches for their own.

Q: What is this passage mainly about?

(a) An example of domestication
(b) An ancient fisherman's rite
(c) Fishing using trained animals
(d) A vanishing way of life

16. People either deliberately or accidently switching the consonants of words are said to be making a 'Spoonerism' or a 'Marrowsky'. These two terms came from two people, Reverend William Archibald Spooner of New College, Oxford and a Polish count named Marrowsky. They were famously known to pronounce phrases with the consonants all mixed up, oftentimes resulting in some amusing utterances. Examples of these types of utterances are "sale of two titties" which means "Tale of two cities" or "chewing the doors" which means "doing the chores." Many comedians have used this type of speech for their routines in which they are acting drunk. The humor comes when the audience figures out that the improper sounds also have their own meanings.

Q: What is the main topic of the passage above?

(a) Spooner and Marrowsky invented a new type of joke.
(b) Groups of words create difficulty in speaking.
(c) Comedians commit many speech errors.
(d) Consonants are switched in Spoonerisms.

17.

R

> To Whom It May Concern:
>
> This is to verify that I can wholeheartedly recommend Frank Aaron for admission to a Doctoral program in the field of Chemical Engineering. I have acted as his graduate academic advisor here at Cullman College for two years and have full confidence that he is ready and worthy of pursuing a PhD degree in this area of study. He was a very conscientious graduate student who performed his duties with utmost care and excellence. Before coming to me, he was also an outstanding undergraduate student, being on the Dean's List several years.
>
> He is very much the kind of student who would succeed in pursuit of a Doctoral Degree. I would certainly hope that you would appreciate his past accomplishments and admit him as a student with great potential in his further studies.
>
> Terrance Wellington, PhD

Q: Which of the following is correct according to the letter?

(a) The student is applying to study with the professor.
(b) The letter advises the student to pursue a doctorate.
(c) Cullman College does not have a graduate school.
(d) The professor was the student's advisor for two years.

18. Before cities were established, most people had to learn how to be self-sufficient, supplying all the necessities of life by themselves. Soon people found it was easier to concentrate on producing one or just a few goods, and trade the surplus to other villagers for the other items they needed to live. People were willing to travel farther and farther to exchange goods with other people, and in this way, "trade" was the catalyst for exploration and cross-cultural interaction. "Trade" was also the cause for many cities to grow in wealth and power, as merchants from all over flocked to their marketplaces. This also raised the demand for improved ways to carry goods over long distances.

Q: Which of the following is correct according to the passage?

(a) Traders were unwilling to journey very far from their base.
(b) People should produce all the things they needed to survive.
(c) Expeditions were initiated in order to learn about culture.
(d) Transportation advanced to accommodate commerce.

19.

How to Take Care of Your Skin

Take care of your skin so your complexion will always be beautiful and you will not only have good skin but preserve younger-looking skin for longer!

- You must avoid too much sun exposure as it can cause skin cancer, faster aging, and wrinkles.
- If you are a smoker, cut down on cigarettes. Cigarettes lower the blood flow, thereby depriving the skin of oxygen and vitamin A which are essential for healthy skin.
- Having daily hot showers or baths can remove important oils from your skin, so enjoy less time in the bath and reduce the bath temperature.
- Stop utilizing very strong scented soaps; instead use mild unperfumed cleansers.

Q: Which of the following is recommended for better skin?

(a) Not taking a shower every day

(b) Using perfumed cleansers

(c) Staying out in the sun

(d) Spending more time in the bath

20. The fossils of a dinosaur, which are the first remains of a horned dinosaur to be found on the Korean peninsula, have recently been uncovered. Koreaceratops hwaseongensis, a reptile from the late Early Cretaceous related to the Triceratops, was a relatively small dinosaur, measuring two meters long and weighing between 27 to 45 kilograms. Its parrot-like beak points to the likelihood that the dinosaur was an herbivore and an examination of its hind feet gives evidence that it was a fast-moving, bipedal animal. Its tail was unique in that it was short in comparison to other dinosaurs, and contained a column of spikes that was the base for a large frill-like structure the dinosaur probably used for communication.

Q: Which of the following is correct according to the passage?

(a) This dinosaur's only distinguishing feature is the column of spikes on its tail.

(b) Before this find, Korea was unknown to have dinosaurs like the Triceratops.

(c) The overall appearance was very much like that of a large bird.

(d) Speed was used to prey on other smaller animals.

21. The World Series of baseball is considered by many fans and sport writers to be a 'de facto' world athletic challenge though it only consists of teams from the US and Canada. The popularity of the game in North America draws crowds large enough to support such a contest. Major League Baseball is divided into two divisions, the American League and the National League. In the play-offs, the top three teams and a wild card team play each other in a best-of-five series until there is only one team left for each division. Those two teams play each other for the commissioner's trophy which is given to the championship team along with rings for each player and team management.

Q: Which is correct according to the passage?

(a) Many consider the World Series to be the world's premier baseball contest.

(b) Each team in the play-offs plays one game against each other with the loser declared 'out'.

(c) Teams from the National League play teams from the American League until only one remains.

(d) The winning team in each division receives a championship trophy and rings.

22.

Unforgettable Holiday in Paris

There are several ways you might enjoy a romantic vacation in Paris. A lot of travelers just stroll through the magnificent Champs-Elysees shopping at the excellent array of high-end shops. If you like to skip the shopping part, then maybe you should pay a visit to one of the numerous parks in the city. If you are in the mood to take a cruise, there's the river Seine and its innumerable sights. Why not go to the Moulin Rouge for some cabaret and a taste of old-time music and dance? In truth, many couples want to go to see Paris at least once in their lifetimes, so why don't you pay a visit and find out why?

Q: Which of the following is correct according to the passage?

(a) The Moulin Rouge is not located in Paris.

(b) Paris is not recommended for shopping.

(c) Champs-Elysees is famous for fancy shops.

(d) The River Seine flows around Paris.

23. Scholars over the centuries have often considered pi to be the most recognized and intriguing mathematical constant in the world. It is defined as the irrational ratio of a circle's circumference to its diameter. One of the earliest known records of pi was written by an Egyptian scribe named Ahmes in 1650 B.C. on what is now known as the Rhind Papyrus. His calculation varied by less than 1% of the modern approximation of 3.141592. The Rhind Papyrus was the first attempt to calculate pi by "squaring the circle," which is to measure the diameter of a circle by building a square inside of it.

Q: What can be inferred by the passage?

(a) The value of pi can be approximated using geometry.
(b) Mathematicians today have the exact number for pi.
(c) An ancient scribe completely solved the mystery of pi.
(d) This constant is widely known thanks to a papyrus.

24. Architecture has embraced concepts from mathematics, science, art, history, politics and philosophy in its development over thousands of years. To create and implement an architectural design, architects must strike an acceptable balance between artistry and pragmatism. For example, some of the most beautiful designs aren't feasible in terms of engineering, falling victim to the laws of physics. Other designs are rejected on politic grounds. Building an artistic but costly convention center during a time of economic crisis would be a politically risky decision and would most likely be rejected.

Q: What can be inferred from the passage?

(a) A politician needs to know physics to wisely review potential building projects.
(b) Engineering considerations are less restrictive than the art of designing a building.
(c) Architects need to be both creative and practical in their designs to achieve success.
(d) What gets built often has to do with which political party is in power at the time.

25. If you ever find yourself in the extreme southern latitudes, be aware of the lights in the sky peculiar to that area of the world. The aurora australis or southern lights is the Southern Hemisphere's equivalent to the aurora borealis or northern lights of the northern Arctic. Whether in the north or south, these auroras have a singular cause. This would be the so-called solar wind, electrons from the sun, coming into contact with the Earth's magnetic field which is inside the atmosphere. The magnetic field lies within the atmosphere at the poles and consequently those are where the aurora lights can be seen.

Q: What can be inferred from the passage?

(a) Aurora australis can be seen in Russia only.

(b) The causes of aurora borealis and australis are different.

(c) The color of the aurora is not white in the southern hemisphere.

(d) The Earth's magnetic field is partially responsible for the auroras.

Part IV **Questions 26—35**

Read the passage, questions, and options. Then, based on the given information, choose the option that best answers each question.

R

Questions 26-27

Dear Ms. Gardner:

Please accept this letter as an appeal to Spirit Insurance Company's decision to reject coverage for the recent gastroscopy procedure. You notified me that reimbursement has been denied since a gastroscopy is not approved more than once a year without the presence of cancerous cells. However, I was diagnosed as developing gastric cancer at the end of last year and underwent a resection of my stomach. The recent gastroscopy procedure was conducted to identify the current state, which was recommended by Dr. Richard Donaldson.

I believe that you didn't have all the necessary information when making your initial review. Please find attached a follow-up letter from Dr. Donaldson at Oregon Medical Center. He was in charge of my operation and is one of the top ranking specialists in his field. His letter discusses in more detail why the procedure was necessary and inevitable. Also attached are my medical records, which explain why the additional procedure was necessary. Based on the information, I am requesting that your company cover my gastroscopy procedure.

Sincerely,
Stella Smith
Policy Number : 878230 - 987632

26. Q: What is the main purpose of the letter?
   (a) To reject the offer to subscribe to an insurance policy
   (b) To notify the insurance company of the writer's gastroscopy procedure
   (c) To ask the insurance company to cover the writer's medical expense
   (d) To review the diagnosis from a medical center

27. Q: Which of the following is correct according to the letter?
   (a) The insurance company never reimburses for the gastroscopy procedure.
   (b) The writer had surgery for gastric cancer at the end of last year.
   (c) The insurance company reviewed a letter from Dr. Donaldson at first.
   (d) The writer is upset with the overtreatment conducted by Dr. Donaldson.

JOB OPENING: ONLINE MARKETER

We at Madison Games are providing customers with the latest technologies and tools in a wide range of languages in the video games industry. Our company's corporate culture features a flat hierarchy, established by a young and talented workforce hailing from all corners of the globe in pursuit of new and exciting technologies and games.

Requirements

You should have at least a bachelor's degree in international business, marketing, communications, digital media, or a related field. You should be a creative thinker to put your media skills into practice on the market and to write analytical and inspiring essays on various social media platforms. You should also be a competent communicator with impeccable written English skills.

Responsibilities

We are looking for talented writers to join the marketing team at our headquarters. You will mainly be in charge of monitoring, analyzing, evaluating, and promoting our online games. Furthermore, you will play a big part in operating our accounts in social media, writing essays in blogs and publishing customers' success stories. Additionally, you will support team members in developing and delivering campaigns to new customers.

Benefits

You will be offered a competitive salary according to the market's standards.

---

28. Q: Which of the following is NOT stated as a mandatory qualification for this position?

    (a) A master's degree in marketing

    (b) A degree in communications

    (c) Creative thinking skills

    (d) Excellent writing proficiency

29. Q: Which of the following is correct according to the advertisement?

    (a) The company provides customers with game reviews only in English.

    (b) The company usually recruits new members of staff domestically.

    (c) The successful candidate will take part in developing new social media.

    (d) Reporting customers' success stories is one of the position's responsibilities.

Ardent Feminist: Eleanor Roosevelt

Well known as the wife of former President Franklin Delano Roosevelt, Eleanor Roosevelt contributed to improving human rights and women's empowerment while working as a writer, public speaker, and political activist. She was a fervent political figure who was ranked one of the top ten widely venerated people of the 20th century. She was also an influential figure who played a significant part in establishing the NGO "Freedom House" and endorsing the stabilization of the United Nations.

When Mr. Roosevelt was elected the 32nd president in 1933, she temporarily felt depressed at the thought that she couldn't develop her own political role. Later, however, she continued expanding her political influence by writing essays and giving public speeches. She also appeared frequently at press conferences and spoke out about human rights. In addition, she dedicated a lot of her energy for anti-lynching campaigns and for fair housing for minorities. She rose even higher than just being the conventional First Lady and was deemed a prominent advocate of civil rights.

30. Q: Which of the following is correct about Eleanor Roosevelt?
   (a) Most of her writings are concerned with women's rights.
   (b) She made efforts to develop an international organization.
   (c) She was satisfied when Franklin D. Roosevelt became President.
   (d) She sought to be faithful to traditional roles as a civil rights activist.

31. Q: What can be inferred about Eleanor Roosevelt from the passage?
   (a) She was the most revered person in the area of politics.
   (b) She couldn't distinguish herself from other female politicians.
   (c) Her life was quite different from that of other First Ladies.
   (d) She was reluctant to meet reporters due to personal traits.

R

The idea of product placement in mass media such as television programs and movies originated due to movie producers' and directors' efforts to promote the reality of movies by featuring real brands and products. However, much to the surprise of marketing professionals, the placement of products in movies was followed by increase in sales. After recognizing the efficiency of product placement, a profusion of companies began to engage in a wide range of product placement activities. Compared with other marketing strategies, each product can be displayed or used in a specific context and environment.

Marketing professionals have verified the synergy effect created by integrated marketing communication by placing products. As evidenced by their research, a combination of visual effects and verbal references to products is the most effective advertising method, albeit one of the most expensive. Product placement in mass media develops familiarity and a sense of being associated with the brand of each product displayed. Furthermore, the lifespan of brand placements is considerably longer than other advertising strategies.

32. Q: What is the main topic of the passage?

(a) An innovative way to promote reality in movies and TV programs
(b) Research on a variety of advertisements to create synergies
(c) An effective method of advertisement through product placement
(d) The pros and cons of product placement in the field of marketing

33. Q: Which of the following is correct about product placement according to the passage?

(a) It deteriorates reality in each movie and television program.
(b) It targets a wide range of customers in just one placing.
(c) It facilitates customers' familiarity with brands and products.
(d) It shortens the lifespan of each product in customers' memory.

Questions 34-35

Serious Unemployment Rate

by Chris Williams

The paradoxical title of Franco Montiel's article *More Opportunities for the Old Population* seems to well describe the increasing concern in the United States of having a lost generation. Joblessness among youths has gradually increased since companies in distress release junior employees first and refuse to pay statutory redundancy payments on the basis of seniority. Even when they employ new workers, they are looking for experienced workers, so younger people are placed at the back of the queue and don't have the opportunity to augment their own careers.

The average youth unemployment rate in the United States is 21%, approximately double that of adult workers. Admittedly, the youth unemployment rate is not the best indicator to estimate young people's labor market, as many of them are enrolled in the education system. However, while hundreds of thousands of unemployed young people visit job fairs organized in many cities, many of them don't get recruited. Rather, the high unemployment rate precipitates the economic recession, devastating the labor market and eventually accelerating the flexibility of the country's labor market.

34. Q: What is the main purpose of the article?
   (a) To criticize an article explaining loss of opportunities in the job market
   (b) To address the seriousness of young people's unemployment rate
   (c) To endorse the flexible labor market found in the United States
   (d) To advertise job fairs for young job seekers in many cities

35. Q: Which statement would the writer most likely agree with?
   (a) Experienced workers are usually working in adverse condition.
   (b) Young employees can build more careers in a flexible labor market.
   (c) The unemployment rate is a good indicator showing economic situations.
   (d) Organizing job fairs is not conducive to entry-level applicants.

ACTUAL TEST

4

Reading
Comprehension

Part I **Questions 1—10**

Read the passage and choose the option that best completes the passage.

---

1. A worker's satisfaction with his job can partly depend on _____. Those in the job market are primarily looking for jobs with strong companies that fit their talents and pay them well. So, salary and working conditions certainly influence satisfaction most. But when employees are underpaid or overworked, the feeling that they're doing something beneficial to society can make it easier to accept a small paycheck or long hours. But unfortunately, it's often only employees in the health care, social services, and education fields who feel they are helping others.

(a) the quality of his health care benefits

(b) how much money he makes working

(c) how well he gets along with coworkers

(d) whether he finds the work valuable

2. The discovery of a vast, complex structure on the British island of Orkney _____. It covers several miles of land and was constructed more than 5,000 years ago, before the Egyptian pyramids or Stonehenge. Based on artifacts at the site, it's clear that distinctive forms of building and material design, such as pot making, originated in Orkney and spread to other parts of the British islands. Those studying the site closely say it was the seat of new ideas at the time.

(a) explains how Britain gained its power as a nation

(b) provides new insights into an influential civilization

(c) reveals new theories on the origin of British religion

(d) shows early advancements in scientific and cultural theories

3. In democratic nations, courts often debate _____. For example, if someone falsely yells, "Fire!" in a crowded movie theater, is this a form of free speech? This action could cause harm to the audience as they try to exit the building in a panic. Similarly, should citizens in a free country be allowed to make hateful comments in public about groups they unfairly dislike? There might not be an immediate risk of danger, but the government might reasonably fear that this form of speech could potentially lead to violence.

(a) which groups in society should be allowed to speak
(b) the proper level of punishment for violent acts
(c) the line between individual liberty and public safety
(d) the effects of citizens sharing opinions honestly

4. A historic watercraft built in 2010 changed the way we _____. It's called Plastiki. It was designed by David de Rothschild, who later sailed it 8,000 miles across the Pacific Ocean. Plastiki's inner structure is made from recyclable plastics and holds together thousands of plastic bottles that keep the boat afloat. De Rothschild also invented a glue made from cashews and sugar, whereas most marine glues use toxic chemicals. Rather than using gas or electricity, Plastiki is equipped with solar panels.

(a) travel long distances over the water
(b) recycle the plastics we use every day
(c) understand the cause of ocean pollution
(d) think about environmental engineering

5. Driverless cars will be introduced into the market in the next few years, but their popularity is hard to predict. Electronic sensors and GPS navigation have been around for years, and luxury automobiles already offer camera views for parking. Attaching all these with the car's steering is the next step for a vehicle that drives itself. But cars that can park themselves have been slow to catch on. Consumers have expressed doubt about their necessity. Perhaps driverless vehicles will also _____.

(a) offer more advantages for inexperienced drivers
(b) face a similar response with drivers' turning away
(c) have the same technology that has been highly praised
(d) gain loyalty from both existing and potential consumers

6. Did you know that adults in America eat twice as much sugar today as they did 40 years ago? We've always known too many sweets aren't healthy. But a new study says sugar may be toxic. Using mice as test subjects, scientists discovered that increased sugar in the diet can cause early death. When mice were given 25 percent more sugar, they were less likely to protect their territory or produce baby mice. These were signs the animals had lost _____.

(a) the extra weight they had gained
(b) the ability to care for themselves
(c) tolerance for other food sources
(d) thinking skills for problem solving

7. At the age of three, children begin to more actively engage with their peers at school or on the playground. By watching others who are slightly more advanced, they find the courage and inspiration to try something new. At the same time, their budding egos make them possessive and sensitive to the actions of others, which often causes crying and hurts feelings. It's a challenging time of growth when toddlers must learn to

_____.

(a) communicate more efficiently with their classmates
(b) channel their confidence and regulate their moods
(c) test their limits and practice skills that are new to them
(d) contribute to the family in more noticeable ways

8.

Movie Review

The film *Elysium* is set more than 100 years in the future. Earth has become a wasteland, where the poor struggle to survive. The planet's wealthy citizens have moved to a luxurious space station called Elysium, where they live comfortably and enjoy the best health care technology. The story unfolds as the suffering people on Earth try to force their way into the world of the wealthy so they can live better lives. Yet the rich use their money to prevent them from entering. The result is a film that _____.

(a) explores how humans respond to class differences
(b) creates high drama with advanced special effects
(c) offers a general description of life in the future
(d) details the real experiences of modern societies

9. Early in his career, the American writer Truman Capote was known for his portraits of high society in New York City. _____, Capote wanted to tackle weightier subjects. He traveled to a small town in Kansas to write his next book, *In Cold Blood*, a novel based on the true story of an innocent family's brutal murder, as well as the men who committed the crime. The novel, a groundbreaking blend of fiction and truth, sold out immediately, and it remains a modern classic.

(a) For all that
(b) Afterwards
(c) Thus
(d) Indeed

10.

Book Review

Marla Johnson's new fantasy novel imagines what would happen if vampires established their own communities within large cities. In her story, humans force blood-thirsty vampires to live in separate neighborhoods where they won't cause harm. _____, the vampires establish successful businesses and use their money to throw extravagant parties that are broadcast on TV. The humans look on, growing jealous of the vampires' way of life. The result is a fascinating and smart description of the complex relationships between different groups of people.

(a) Besides
(b) Otherwise
(c) Likewise
(d) Nevertheless

Part II **Questions 11—12**

Read the passage and identify the option that does NOT belong.

R

11. Recent reports about the extent of secret surveillance have again fueled the debate on privacy versus security. (a) The 9/11 attacks provided the motivation for broad presidential powers to fight terrorism using nearly any means necessary. (b) These could include military actions, unmanned air strikes, and intelligence gathering. (c) WikiLeaks started in 2006 to expose to the public documents and videos that reveal classifiable information. (d) A computer analyst claimed that the National Security Agency, which he worked for, spies on ordinary citizens to an unlawful extent.

12. Citron tea is a popular herbal tea in Korea drunk as a remedy for the common cold. (a) It is traditionally prepared by marinating pieces of the yuja in honey. (b) This gets rid of the sour and bitter taste of the fruit and helps preserve it for the winter months. (c) A spoon of the yuja marmalade dissolves more easily in hot water than in cold. (d) It's considered a reliable natural treatment for an illness most people experience each year.

Part III Questions 13—25

Read the passage, question, and options. Then, based on the given information, choose the option that best answers each question.

13.

≡ **THE SOUTHVILLE TIMES**   🔍

Science > Technology

Scientists are now able to control cockroaches using remote devices. By connecting a tiny device into the roaches' antennae, humans can direct the bugs' movements using a computer. These "roach robots" could even save lives. For example, a tiny microphone or cameras can be added to an insect's computer backpack. Then the tiny creatures can be sent into the rubble of damaged buildings after an earthquake. The audio and visual devices could detect cries for help from those trapped after a disaster.

Q: What is the news report mainly about?

(a) Training insects to do human jobs

(b) New robots that behave like cockroaches

(c) Tiny technology to eliminate pests

(d) Computerized bugs to the rescue

14. The basic structure is simple — each number is the result of adding the two previous numbers, starting with 0 and 1. A similar idea had already existed in ancient India when counting all the possible combinations of two items. But the world knows this technique today in its medieval form created by Leonardo Fibonacci. This series of numbers is truly greater than the sum of its parts. Its attraction is that it also closely describes patterns found in the branches of a tree or the shape of seashells.

Q: What is the main topic of the passage?

(a) The cultural significance of a mathematical formula

(b) How an idea can spread from country to country

(c) A sequence of numbers which can characterize nature

(d) Applying an old method to current problems

15. If you are seriously searching for a local job, know that finding a job is easy when you know where to search. One popular place to search is a job center. Job centers provide numerous vacancies for different kinds of work. Local and national newspapers also provide advertisements on current job vacancies. Also, every industry has its own magazines or journals and many employers go to these publications for employing professionals. The most cost-effective way to find local jobs is through the Internet. Getting the job you want may be a challenge but locating the right channels for a job search will increase the possibility of landing a job.

Q: What is the passage mainly about?

(a) Hiring the right employees
(b) Effective methods to get hired
(c) The challenges of job hunting
(d) Different ways to post a job

16. According to Dr. Ian Joint, carbon dioxide increases in the atmosphere are turning the world's oceans into weak acids that are affecting marine life and oxygen levels. Further, the effect on marine life may be significant enough to amount to the loss of a major food source for humankind. Millions of types of bacteria, responsible for keeping the planet fertile and assist in reducing the amount of toxins in the oceans, are at risk of dying due to the imbalance being created by the acidification of the oceans. In terms of oxygen, microbial plant matter in the oceans creates almost half of the oxygen globally. Putting microbes at risk puts humankind at risk.

Q: What is the main topic of the passage?

(a) Oxygen levels in marine ecologies
(b) Oceanic bacteria harmful to animal life
(c) Acidic oceans killing marine microbes
(d) Acidification slowed by greenhouse gases

17. One in six people who snore suffer from the severe condition of Obstructive Sleep Apnea (OSA). This is caused when the muscles in the tongue and back of the throat relax to the point of blocking airways, making it difficult to breathe. A person can be awakened by this sometimes hundreds of times a night, making it impossible for the person to get a good night's sleep. The effects of this disorder on the person's health can be quite serious, resulting in constantly feeling tired, gaining weight, raised blood pressure, and even heart failure or stroke. Sufferers need to treat their snoring through surgeries or use of sleeping devices that prevent their snoring.

Q: Which of the following is correct about Obstructive Sleep Apnea?

(a) People with this disorder are awoken at night and cannot fall asleep again.
(b) This condition affects the functioning of the heart.
(c) Almost all people who snore suffer serious health disorders.
(d) The throat muscles of a person with sleep apnea tighten up.

18. A U.S. Immigration Society report found that 45.8% of the total labor force for agriculture and fishing was comprised of immigrants. That represents approximately 5,725,000 of the 12.5 million workers in that sector. This is higher than the 16% of the total labor force of 128 million workers in the U.S. who are immigrants. Near the other end of the spectrum, about 5.8% of all lawyers and legal professionals in the U.S. are immigrants.

Q: Which of the following is correct according to the passage?

(a) A large percentage of immigrants are lawyers.
(b) Immigrant workers represent 16% of all U.S. workers.
(c) There are roughly 12 million immigrant workers in the U.S.
(d) Almost half of all immigrants work in agriculture or fishing.

19. Rocket science is usually associated with advanced scientists. But a look at ancient history shows that basic rocket fuel, or gunpowder, may have been developed accidentally. The first devices that fit the definition of a rocket were invented in China. Based on a small collection of documents, historians believe Chinese chemists discovered gunpowder for their fireworks while trying to create a medicine that would make people live forever. While testing combinations of different substances, the Chinese eventually uncovered an idea that could make an object launch into the air.

Q: Which of the following is correct about rocket science?

(a) It was a medical treatment in ancient China.
(b) Its history is not completely documented.
(c) It was quickly evolved to make weapons.
(d) It was the product of a planned experiment.

20. What's known as Dutch coffee was actually discovered by chance. In the 17th Century, Dutch merchants would sail from Indonesia, bringing exotic goods back home. One of these ships carrying coffee was soaked in cold water during high seas. The remaining coffee had a unique but pleasant taste. In today's cafés, the cold brewing of Dutch coffee takes several hours and brings out a different taste from the ground beans than when using boiling water. Less of the acid and caffeine are extracted from the beans, making it smoother to drink.

Q: Which of the following is correct about Dutch coffee?

(a) It is richer but milder in taste than coffee brewed with hot water.
(b) The Dutch intended to invent an alternative way of brewing coffee.
(c) Its time-consuming manufacturing procedure makes it expensive.
(d) It is usually made from coffee beans that were grown in Indonesia.

21. The broad definition of cancer covers any kind of uncontrolled cell growth that forms dangerous tumors in the body. The cause of most outbreaks of cancer is difficult to find because several factors can be involved. It's thought that the vast majority of cases are due to lifestyle factors with only a small percentage due to genetics. The fact that immigrants to a country often develop the diseases common to their new surroundings indicates the importance of lifestyle in influencing disease.

Q: Which of the following is correct according to the passage?

(a) Immigrants' health is affected by their new environment.
(b) Most cancers' origins can be identified by studying patients.
(c) Genetics may have a greater influence than doctors believed.
(d) Air and water pollution are to blame for most deadly tumors.

22. The Encounters Festival in South Africa is the largest film festival in the continent dedicated entirely to documentaries. Since it started in 1999, it has helped draw attention to the genre, promoted new productions, and brought international movies to Africa. The festival also makes a directed effort to encourage new filmmakers. First-time directors can propose projects to a team of experienced experts; the best projects win money for production. Since it started, the festival has supported nearly 1,500 new documentaries.

Q: Which of the following is correct about the festival?

(a) It introduces a variety of different types of movies.
(b) It celebrates filmmakers at all levels of their career.
(c) It has had little impact on the world of documentaries.
(d) It tours globally to bring cinema to other countries.

23.

> To All Our Staff:
>
> The development team announces a new logo and brand image for the company. They've worked hard to transform our image to meet a changing business environment. They are distributing a new Standards Guide covering all media, including webpages, company documents, stationery, and business cards. Download the latest template from our website and the instructions will walk you through the switching process. An up-to-date presentation of our logo will go a long way to distinguish our brand.

Q: What can be inferred about the company according to the announcement?

(a) It wants people to see both the new and old logos.
(b) The company is trying to adapt to the market.
(c) The new logo will mostly alter its online presence.
(d) Workers can make suggestions about the new logo.

24. Australia Day is an annual celebration commemorating the arrival of British settlers on the island of Australia in 1788. It was first celebrated in the early 1800s. Later, in the 1900s, Australian aborigines, who had lived on the island for centuries, founded their own holiday in protest. They called it Day of Mourning and marched through the streets, objecting to years of cruel treatment by the British, including the takeover of land and the removal of aboriginal children from their family homes into English schools. The aborigines demanded equal rights and claimed that British "progress" had come with a price.

Q: What can be inferred from the passage?

(a) The two opposing sides were able to finally make peace.
(b) A colonial tradition was replaced with a positive protest.
(c) Hosting two celebrations enriched the cultural experience.
(d) Actions taken to establish the country weren't entirely just.

25.

Plan your next exotic trip with Gift of Travel!

We'll give you ample time to relax and sightsee, but you'll join local groups working to address environmental issues.

· You can visit Myanmar's beaches and assist with a project that prevents erosion on the country's coastline.

· Or you can travel to Brazil and enjoy its cuisine and beautiful scenery while helping restore the nation's rainforests.

· Journey to South Africa, view its historical monuments and participate in rhino repopulation efforts.

Q: What can be inferred about the travel plans from the passage?

(a) They are greatly helping local people in Brazil.

(b) They were designed for environmental causes.

(c) They have significantly affected the rhino population in Africa.

(d) They are very popular among many travelers.

Part IV **Questions 26—35**

Read the passage, questions, and options. Then, based on the given information, choose the option that best answers each question.

R

Questions 26-27

Glaxokline Probiotics+ Vitamin D

As a dietary supplement, Glaxokline Probiotics+ Vitamin D functions as "good" bacteria in your gastrointestinal tract, guaranteeing general health and wellness inside your body. Keeping a healthy balance of bacteria in your gut makes your digestive health optimum.

As all of you know well, the popularity of vitamin D has surged due to a myriad of health benefits such as improvement in digestive and immune systems, influencing bone health as well as your emotional wellness.

Glaxokline Probiotics+ Vitamin D features lactobacillus acidophilus, one of the most frequently researched bacteria as to digestive health. This formula contains more than 60 micrograms of vitamin D for additional immune support, providing nutritional benefits in a convenient capsule.

Though refrigeration is not required, you should refrigerate to ensure maximum potency once opening it. Natural color variations might occur from batch to batch. Take one capsule per day with water, but consult your physician before using it if you are pregnant or trying to conceive.

26. Q: What benefit is NOT mentioned in the advertisement?
   (a) Digestive health
   (b) Blood circulation
   (c) Bone health
   (d) Immune system

27. Q: Which of the following is correct about Glaxokline Probiotics+ Vitamin D according to the advertisement?
   (a) It is an effective treatment for gastrointestinal disorders.
   (b) It features bacteria frequently studied by researchers.
   (c) It should be refrigerated to prevent discoloration.
   (c) It is beneficial in improving pregnant women's health.

R

To whom it may concern,

On April 15th of this year, I was treated in your emergency room because of my painful leg. I waited for more than one hour while in extreme pain before being X-rayed and examined by Dr. Steve Lohan. After the examination, I was told that no serious problem was found in my leg and was just prescribed some pain killers.

However, since the excruciating pain lasted for two more days, I went to the University Hospital of Alabama, where an X-ray was taken that showed my leg was fractured. Because of my unnecessary suffering, I'd like the doctor reprimanded for this misdiagnosis and negligence. Enclosed are copies of the X-ray and documents from the second opinion as well as copies of the prescription and receipt I received in your hospital. Although I fully understand the crowdedness of the emergency room, I expected a professional accurate diagnosis. Please let me know what, if any, measure I should take in this case.

Sincerely,

Ellie Hudson

28. Q: What is the main purpose of the letter?

(a) To petition for reimbursement for the medical cost the writer paid

(b) To require the hospital to reexamine the writer's fractured leg

(c) To ask about the action the writer can take about the misdiagnosis

(d) To complain about the crowdedness in the emergency room

29. Q: Which of the following is correct according to the passage?

(a) Not until after the passage of an hour was Ellie examined by a doctor.

(b) The X-ray found some problems in Ellie's leg in the emergency room.

(c) Ellie sought a second opinion at Alabama State Hospital.

(d) Ellie doesn't have any prescription or receipt from Alabama State Hospital.

Questions 30-31

\<Editorial\> Voter Registration: Effects and Controversy

Many political pundits have asserted that voter registration requirements discourage many people, especially the destitute, from exercising the right to vote, triggering a lower voter turnout. Voter enrollment is the requirement with which a person should register on an electoral roll before he or she is permitted to vote. The regulation is applied at most federal, state and local elections. Many states set their own deadline dates for voter registration, ranging from 2 to 4 weeks before an election.

However, many reformers in some counties where registration is each individual's accountability have proposed easy process to register in order to maximize voter turnout. They insist that such an innovative enrollment system be automatic or that application be made on the Election Day. Thereby, voters can have voting rights automatically if the government agency forwards the information to the electoral agency to update the voter registration information.

30. Q: Which of the following is correct according to the passage?
- (a) The current registration system facilitates the voting process.
- (b) Voter registration regulation is not applied on local elections.
- (c) Some counties attribute the responsibility of registration to individuals.
- (d) The government agency has been reluctant to reveal voters' information.

31. Q: What can be inferred from the passage?
- (a) An automatic registration process can increase voter turnout.
- (b) Most states set the same deadline dates before elections.
- (c) The voter registration requirements are discriminatory based on wealth.
- (d) Many voters would choose not to register to keep their information confidential.

R

Saki monkeys are among several New World monkeys living in northern and central South America. They are relatively smaller monkeys with black, grey or reddish-brown furry skin and long, bushy tails. Though their head is covered with fur, their faces are naked. With strong hind legs allowing them to make jumps and a long tail weighing up to 2 kilograms, their bodies are adapted to life in trees. Living in the trees of the rainforests, they occasionally go onto the land.

Saki monkeys live a communal life as a family group consisting of parents and their offspring. Moving from a tree to another one, they are territorial animals, defending their habitat against other families. They also communicate with other monkeys in their family through shrill cries or bird-like twitter as a means of connection among family members and a loud roar as a warning against other animals. Being omnivores, they eat a variety of food, including fruits, insects and small vertebrates.

32. Q: What is the main topic of the passage?
   (a) The appearance and life of Saki monkeys
   (b) The difference among Saki monkey species
   (c) The physical attributes of Saki monkeys
   (d) The cohabitation of a unique monkey species

33. Q: Which of the following is correct about Saki monkeys in the passage?
   (a) Most members of their species live throughout South America.
   (b) Their tail is not strong enough to support their body on trees.
   (c) They live harmoniously with other families on their habitat.
   (d) They use distinct sounds according to some purposes.

Electric Cars: Not the Answer to Air Pollution

Officials have recently been forced to make plans to produce less air pollution, only to generate woefully inadequate results. Electric motors have long been known to provide a clean and safe alternative to the environment. Most people believe that driving an electric vehicle could reduce harmful air pollution from exhaust emissions. Renewable energy used to recharge the electric vehicle has been considered to reduce the greenhouse gas emission even further. These reduced harmful exhaust emissions seem to be good news for our health. Better air quality is expected to lead to fewer health problems and less cost from air pollution.

Much to the surprise of officials, however, new research has shown that the so-called clean and cost-effective measure to cut pollution is actually urging dirty cars to enter the urban center. According to some experts, while electric vehicles emit no exhaust fumes, they produce large amounts of tiny pollution particles from brake and tires. Therefore, one of the safe and efficient movements around the cities can only be achieved by using a cleaner and more expanded mass transit system. Consistently clean, cheap and reliable vehicles could be the ultimate alternative to air pollution.

---

34. Q: What is the main purpose of the article?
(a) To show the compromising effects of traditional automobiles
(b) To abate harmful greenhouse gas emissions around cities
(c) To point out the unsettled problem of alternative vehicles
(d) To prevent drivers from using electric vehicles on roads

35. Q: Which statement would the writer most likely agree with?
(a) Recharging electric cars doesn't require a great amount of energy.
(b) Electric automobiles have received undeserved positive ratings.
(c) Air pollution is the most serious problem caused by vehicles.
(d) The government has nothing to do to reduce air pollution.

ACTUAL TEST

5

TEPS

Reading
Comprehension

DIRECTIONS

This section tests your ability to comprehend reading passages. You will have 40 minutes to complete 35 questions. Be sure to follow the directions given by the proctor.

Part I   Questions 1—10

Read the passage and choose the option that best completes the passage.

R

1. The river Ganges is an important symbol in the ancient Veda traditions of India. The goddess Ganga is said to travel the heavens as well as earth and the underground world of the dead. As a result, the holy river named after her is a place for the faithful to purify the body and soul and even journey to the afterlife. With so many using the river for bathing and cremation, the unfortunate consequence has been high levels of pollution. Yet millions of people continue to visit the river as a spiritual place, thereby _____.

   (a) reviving a practice that has been ignored
   (b) spreading a major religious belief system
   (c) contributing to environmental problems
   (d) sparking interest in a famous landmark

2. When a government steps in to build infrastructure, it is setting in motion a fiscal policy that _____. These efforts can help boost activity during a slump, or accomplish projects too large and complicated for a single company to handle. Either way, the infrastructure is viewed as necessary, so public funds are mobilized by the government. Not only is the infrastructure itself useful to society but the workers employed to complete the job also benefit from the work.

   (a) seeks to strengthen the economy on several fronts
   (b) allows companies to share the profits they bring in
   (c) provides needed natural resources in the right places
   (d) takes workers away from their jobs into new projects

3. Getting away from the physical buttons of the earliest models, touchscreens have taken over on mobile devices. The first on-screen keyboards required that physical pressure be applied to the screen. As such, many phones offered a stylus, shaped like a pen, which could be used to touch and type on the screen. Today's cell phone keyboards do away with any pressure signal and rely solely on the tiny electric signals that radiate from the human body. With this form of design taking over the market, the latest phones _____.

(a) represent buttons on the screen with visual icons
(b) use a smaller stylus to navigate the gadget's menu
(c) use touch and voice recognition for their operations
(d) simplify the user's interaction with the digital device

4. In ancient times, it was common to _____. Thinkers in classical times would compare human features to a corresponding animal. Included in all this was the comparison of face shapes and body types. These were used to make predictions about human behavior. Though it fell out of favor in the Middle Ages, a revival of sorts came about in the wake of Darwinism. This modern version, in a certain sense, was more aggressive than ancient theories. Racial differences, eugenics, and criminal behavior were instead the primary focus.

(a) assign psychological attributes to physical appearance
(b) identify the differences in the appearances of men and animals
(c) define humans as the single rational creature ever made by God
(d) consider each racial group's connections to different ancestors

5. The world knows the devastation caused by the bombing of Hiroshima, but many people don't understand that survivors faced painful social challenges, not just physical difficulties. People affected by the bomb were called "hibakusha," meaning "explosion-affected people." Though "hibakusha" received benefits from the Japanese government, their neighbors would not hire them for jobs out of fear that radiation sickness could spread. For the same reason, they were rarely able to marry or have children. So, after living through one of the world's worst events, _____.

(a) the government ignored and forgot about them
(b) "hibakusha" overcame painful memories
(c) America offered to permit immigration
(d) they were rejected by their own people

6. Very little of a child's learning is focused on how to determine one's values and make decisions accordingly. Schools emphasize only academic areas, like math and science, but avoid lessons that help young people learn early on what matters to them and how they ought to treat others. As a result, many adults make decisions that may not reflect their true values because they have little practice in such situations. But if schools can broaden their approach to teaching, _____.

(a) children will have more complete educations
(b) teachers will be more satisfied with their classes
(c) our youth can make more learning tools
(d) instruction in difficult subjects will be easier

7.

> ### Business News
>
> For big city dwellers who mainly rely on bikes and buses, a new business helps
> _____. It's called Zipcar, and it places cars in parking spots
> around the city. Those who need to drive on special occasions can reserve the cars
> online or by phone in advance or at the last minute. You have to subscribe to the
> service and pay a yearly fee, but you're given an access card that unlocks the car
> during your reserved time.

(a) people test cars they want to buy
(b) those without reliable transportation
(c) promote new types of automobiles
(d) cities reduce increasing traffic online

8. Urban areas are traditionally where the people of a country congregate and interact. Even within them, some areas are spatially designated for this purpose. In ancient Greece, almost every city had a meeting place where citizens not only bought and traded goods, but also exchanged ideas about politics, science, and philosophy. These gathering spots called "agora" were usually the focal points of the towns and were visited by people _____. Community leaders, scientists, government administrators, merchants, philosophers, nobles, and even outlaws and slaves gathered at the agorae to discuss and develop some of history's greatest ideas such as the concept of democracy. It was at these Greek agorae where men such as Socrates, Plato, Aristotle, Hippocrates, and Pythagoras shared their ideas.

(a) from only the highest social class
(b) dissatisfied with the government
(c) from a wide array of professions
(d) who strictly wanted to trade goods

9.

Health News

Many people believe MSG, an ingredient often used in foods to enhance flavor, is highly dangerous, more so than alcohol or smoking. American foods, _____, use MSG in numerous canned and packaged foods, like crackers and salad dressings. Many people aren't aware they're eating large amounts of it, nor do they realize its downside. MSG excites cells in the body to the point that they become damaged. It mostly affects the brain and nervous system, and can cause learning disabilities or Parkinson's disease.

(a) despite this
(b) in contrast
(c) on top of that
(d) in particular

10. Many people rely on chicken soup and orange juice when they feel a cold coming on. But other foods, those containing phytochemicals, can truly help fight off illness. These compounds occur naturally in plants like carrots and bell peppers. They're not considered essential nutrients. Rather, they contain strong biological properties that can boost the immune system, slow bacterial and viral attacks, and increase cell repair. Eating phytochemical sources only when you feel sick won't suddenly cure you. _____, it's important to include them regularly in your diet.

(a) Indeed
(b) After all
(c) Instead
(d) In other words

Part II   **Questions 11—12**

Read the passage and identify the option that does NOT belong.

11. For a megabug — a particularly contagious virus — to spread across the planet in a year, certain conditions would need to be met. (a) First, it should be a strain of influenza that is prevalent especially in cold weather. (b) Unfortunately, there is no vaccine to kill an influenza virus although there has been a persistent research. (c) Because it affects the respiratory tract, sneezing and coughing make it easy to infect anyone within a three-foot radius. (d) Lastly, the virus must originate in a major city with plenty of airport traffic to ensure that it jumps continents.

12. The bones in our body are as alive as our skin or any other part of us. (a) Our bones have blood vessels and grow larger as our bodies grow taller and bigger. (b) Bones have nerves that respond to injury, most of which are well protected and are touched only in the case of a severe injury. (c) The hardest bone in the body is the thigh bone, which is stronger than concrete. (d) As people grow older, their bones contain more mineral material, which causes them to become more brittle and more susceptible to breaking.

Part III **Questions 13—25**

Read the passage, question, and options. Then, based on the given information, choose the option that best answers each question.

R

13. In the early part of the 19th century, monarchy was being restored in Spain, and Russia was expanding into Alaska and along the America's western coast. U.S. foreign policy then announced that the spheres of Europe and America were to be politically separate from that point on. In what was later known as the Monroe Doctrine, Washington declared that the newly created nations of the American continents were to remain free of any further interference by European colonial powers.

Q: What is the main topic of the passage?

(a) European threats to America
(b) How the U.S. won the west
(c) Independence for the Americas
(d) James Monroe as fifth president

14.

Movie Reivew

Behind the box office success of Disney's animated film *Frozen* lie some surprising story elements which may in fact help to explain its popularity. What looks like a conventional fairy tale plot at first turns out to contain themes running counter to stereotypes. While it is usually the villains in children's stories who are shunned by society and live alone in solitude, Princess Elsa is here a sympathetic heroine who finds empowerment in her isolation. Her upbringing, which stressed denying her natural instincts, ended in her exiling herself from society, a sort of failure of parenting.

Q: What is the main point of the passage?

(a) Plot inconsistencies enliven an otherwise tired story.
(b) An old-fashioned fairy tale makes a villain sympathetic.
(c) Breaking with convention adds to a story's appeal.
(d) Exile in isolation is the downfall of a story's character.

15. Punk is defined as a loud, fast paced, and aggressive type of rock music that was common in the 70's and 80's. Punk rock surfaced in the mid 70's when the US, UK and Australia saw the arrival of quick, edgy, straightforward songs that shocked the music business. Punk advanced from the genre of garage rock and stripped songs of its complexities to produce a quick, sharp edge that contrasted drastically with the glam-rock and roll and disco of the era. Punk showed up with such a fierce intensity, but its popularity was inevitably short-lived as the anarchic and angry rage of punk became diluted and lost its flavor. Punk bands did the right things to make some cash but only for a short period.

Q: What is the main topic of the passage?

(a) The reasons behind punk
(b) The rise and fall of punk
(c) The history of punk fashion
(d) The origin of punk music

16. Addiction is one of the greatest problems that our modern society is facing. To help the addicts around you, it is necessary to know what types of addictions there are and how they come about. There are two types of addictions: substance addictions (e.g., alcoholism, drug abuse, and smoking); and process addictions (e.g., gaming, gambling, computer, shopping, and eating). So how do we become addicted? In certain areas of the brain when dopamine is released, it gives one the feeling of pleasure or satisfaction. These feelings of satisfaction become desired and the person will grow a desire for the satisfaction. To satisfy that desire, the person will repeat behaviors that cause the release of dopamine and this repetition becomes addiction.

Q: What is the purpose of the passage?

(a) To inform about ways to prevent addiction
(b) To explain how a person becomes addicted
(c) To educate about the symptoms of addiction
(d) To teach how to help addicts around you

17. In English, you may hear someone say a person is the "spitting image" of someone else, meaning they strongly resemble one another, usually with relatives. While it might seem strange to use "spit" in connection with one's appearance, it has been part of the language for hundreds of years. For example, "It's as if he were spit from his father's mouth." The idea is that two people look so alike that one must have been created from the body of the other. According to the rules of reproduction, the idiom carries a lot of truth.

Q: Which of the following is correct about the idiom according to the passage?

(a) At present, it has lost its original form.
(b) It describes how personalities are shared by relatives.
(c) It shows similarities in people with major differences.
(d) It points out those people who look almost identical.

18. The rates of graduation will now become the biggest factor in the annual school rankings from U.S. News & World Report. Another category that counts the number of freshmen entering a school each year will have less importance. This new method reflects the latest trends and attitudes that look more at the practical results of higher education. The top schools remain at the top, but some colleges are seeing large jumps. The Education Department is also adjusting its own rating system to focus on helping disadvantaged students.

Q: Which of the following is correct about college rankings according to the passage?

(a) The government is requesting magazines change their focus.
(b) Rates of freshman who are disadvantaged are now rising.
(c) Perspectives and values about education are shifting.
(d) The best positions have changed under the new system.

19.

Society > Education

Today, college students take out one large loan to be paid after they graduate. But in a tough economy, there are few high-paying jobs, and graduates spend decades struggling to get out of debt. A new plan would lessen the burden. It would pay students' tuition up front. After graduation, borrowers would give up a set percentage of their income each year, regardless of how much money they make. It sounds similar to the current system, but it would spare students earning lower wages from years of financial difficulty.

Q: Which of the following is correct about the proposed plan?

(a) It would force universities to lower tuition rates.
(b) It rewards those who perform best academically.
(c) It considers a borrower's earnings after graduation.
(d) It encourages colleges to spend less and save more.

20. It's commonly believed that life formed out of unique chemical combinations that existed on earth billions of years ago. But geochemist Steven Benner believes the current theory about life on earth is actually wrong, at least partly. Benner says that a certain key ingredient was missing on our planet. He thinks this essential mineral was delivered from Mars by a meteorite. It's called molybdenum, and without it most organic matter turns to tar, a sticky mixture of carbons. As it happens, billions of years ago Mars was rich with molybdenum.

Q: Which of the following is correct about Steven Benner according to the passage?

(a) He studies and records the mineral composition of meteorites.
(b) He believes earth would be empty of life if it weren't for Mars.
(c) He searches for signs of life on other planets in the solar system.
(d) He thinks organic matter originated on our planet.

21. People generally agree that young minds are extremely adaptable to their surroundings. These days, this includes a technologically rich world, and public concern is growing as children spend long hours staring at computers and cell phones. This trend was labeled "digital dementia" for the way it affects children's attention spans, memory, and emotional state. While this condition isn't permanent, as it is with elderly dementia, the effects can persist as young people continue to spend years focused on their devices.

Q: Which of the following is correct about digital dementia according to the passage?

(a) It is very similar to dementia in older people.

(b) It poses a minor danger to teens' learning abilities.

(c) It is extremely adaptable to the users of digital media.

(d) If allowed to go on a long time, its effects can endure forever.

22. Pathos — the appeal to emotion — is one of three key components in Aristotle's theory on persuasive argument. Ethos and logos — ethics and logic — are the others. Aristotle believed a listener's emotional response to an idea or theory was crucial in changing a person's judgment, though he said all three techniques should be used together for the best effect. Philosophers in later years turned away from pathos as a form of rhetoric and emphasized logic almost exclusively. They believed pathos was an unfair approach when trying to change people's minds.

Q: Which of the following is correct about pathos according to the passage?

(a) It was emphasized less in more modern contexts.

(b) It relies on logic to persuade others to action.

(c) It is used as a reason to justify an idea.

(d) It contradicts the other two components.

23.

Notice to New Students!

Next year, according to the Education Department, all 9th-grade students must meet new academic standards.

- All students must take six hours of fine arts instead of four.
  Students who want to graduate with honors must pass Calculus I and Calculus II.
- Requirements for physical education now allow students to attend a gym or exercise class outside school.
- All students must perform six more hours of certified volunteer work, for a total of 30.

Please speak with your counselor to plan accordingly and ensure you have everything you need to graduate.

Q: What can be inferred from the passage?

(a) Students can graduate if they attend Calculus I and Calculus II.
(b) The hours of fine art classes students need to take has decreased.
(c) Students are not allowed to take any classes provided outside school.
(d) Some requirements student have to meet have been enhanced.

24. Online shopping malls function much like physical malls. Through a single Web site, consumers can shop at a variety of different stores, purchasing home improvement products, clothes, books, and accessories. The sites aim to attract shoppers by making the online buying experience more convenient. Some companies are beginning to incorporate customer reviews with the online mall concept. That is, the malls can determine the top ranked winter jackets, for example, even if they come from different stores, and help consumers more easily find the product that best suits them.

Q: What can be inferred about online shopping malls according to the passage?

(a) They are ordering only the products customers demand.
(b) Their business model has changed that of physical malls.
(c) Their success is putting physical malls out of business.
(d) They are combining services to enhance shopping.

25. The rise of the Phoenician city-states near present-day Lebanon came along after the invasions of sea-going people around 1200 B.C. This attack from the north, though not well documented, greatly weakened the Egyptian and Hittite empires. Into this power vacuum, the Phoenicians built their trading empire at the eastern end of the Mediterranean. The people of Phoenicia quickly distinguished themselves through their ability to organize urban centers and build reliable ships. The start of their decline came when they fell under Persian rule by Cyrus the Great in 539 B.C.

Q: What can be inferred about Phoenician from the passage?

(a) They moved around and never lived in one location for long.

(b) They escaped by ship when the ocean invaders came to attack.

(c) Their religious beliefs were unlike those of their neighbors.

(d) They were effective in building cities and commerce.

Part IV Questions 26—35

Read the passage, questions, and options. Then, based on the given information, choose the option that best answers each question.

R

Questions 26-27

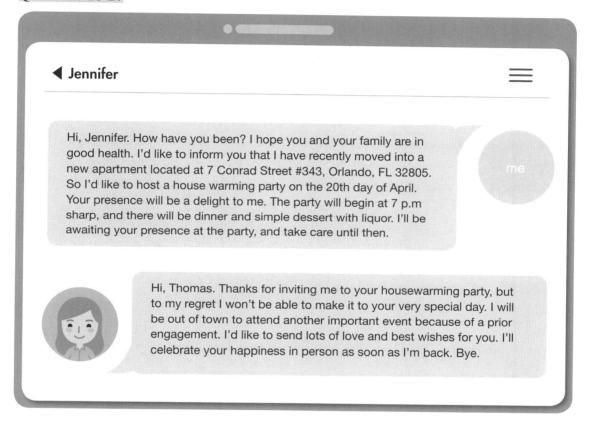

26. Q: What will be served at the housewarming party?

(a) Noodles

(b) Alcoholic drinks

(c) Fruit juice

(d) Soda

27. Q: Which of the following is correct according to the messages?

(a) Thomas will move into a new apartment next week.

(b) Thomas will invite all of his friends to his housewarming party.

(c) Jennifer is going to attend Thomas's housewarming party.

(d) Jennifer will meet Thomas after she returns from her prior arrangement.

R

Medical Records Request

From: Paul Smith (Patient No.: 289423)

To: Customer Service Representative at Houston City Hospital

Number of Copies: 2

This is a letter to request copies of my medical records your hospital has. I understand that patients are entitled to have copies of their medical records according to the Health Care and Insurance Policy Act.

I was treated and hospitalized at your hospital from March 23rd to April 2nd. I'd like copies of all of my medical records, including blood test results, imaging studies, operative reports, notes from doctors, consultations with specialists, and any other record in my medical file.

I understand you charge a reasonable fee for copying and sending the records to my address, which you have at your hospital. I hope to receive the above-mentioned records within 30 days after you receive this request form, or a letter stating the reason for any delay.

I can be reached at 222-555-4652 or paulsmith@gmail.com if you have any questions.

---

28. Q: What is the main purpose of the form?

(a) To ask a hospital to correct the errors in a patient's medical records

(b) To call for notes from a doctor for a second opinion

(c) To request a hospital to post a patient's medical records

(d) To complain about the excessive fee charged by a hospital

29. Q: Which of the following is correct according to the form?

(a) Patients can ask for copies of their medical records only in special cases.

(b) Paul was treated at the hospital for ten days as an outpatient.

(c) Paul got the blood test conducted to treat his illness.

(d) The medical records are usually sent to customers by e-mail.

Math Genius: Emmy Noether

Considered a genius in mathematics, the Jewish woman Emmy Noether continually suffered gender discrimination in academic circles since contemporary women weren't allowed to pursue higher education in the late 1800s and early 1900s. She is described in the *Encyclopedia Britannica* as the most creative mathematician of modern times. Even Albert Einstein publicly recognized her as the most significant mathematical genius.

After receiving her Ph. D. in math, she initially worked as a university lecturer without a title and sometimes under a male pseudonym. She went on to publish more than 40 academic papers while working alongside notable physicists and mathematicians.

In 1933, the Nazi Party overtook Germany and banned all Jewish professors from teaching in schools. Because of the persecution, Noether immigrated to the United States, where she was promptly embraced as a scholar and studied mathematical and physical theories. But in the middle of the 1930s, she died abruptly due to complications from surgery to remove an ovarian cyst.

30. Q: Which of the following is correct about Emmy Noether?
(a) She was not treated equally in the academic world.
(b) She has been estimated to be the most creative scientist in history.
(c) The lectures offered under her name were very popular among students.
(d) She moved to the United States despite the Nazis' attempts to retain her.

31. Q: What can be inferred about Emmy Noether from the passage?
(a) She could pursue higher education in a favorable environment.
(b) She was able to publish over 40 papers, supported by the Nazi Party.
(c) She was discriminated against because of her gender and race.
(d) She still encountered gender discrimination in her new country.

R

AMERICAN JOURNAL OF CRIMINOLOGY

| Home | Articles | About Us | Submit Paper | Subscribe | Most Cited | Browse |

With more than 1.6 million people behind bars, the United States has the second highest incarceration rate in the world. An increasing number of people are held in prisons operated by for-profit private companies. Proponents say these private prisons can be a solution to saving government expenditures. The private prisons currently house about 10 percent of all the inmates in the U.S. according to the government statistics. What's more, hundreds of thousands of undocumented illegal immigrants are often detained in privately run facilities each year.

Yet recent academic research suggests that whereas privately run facilities might be less expensive, they often infringe on inmates' human rights and raise moral and ethical questions. Some criminologists are concerned that private prisons are often more dangerous and less effective at rehabilitating inmates than facilities run by the federal and state governments. Therefore, some opponent representatives proposed a bill to stop companies from being funded from governments and taking advantage of legal loopholes. They also require private prisons to maintain the same level of transparency as that of government-run prisons.

32. Q: What is the main topic of the passage?

(a) A solution suggested to save government expenditures

(b) The status and controversies of privately run prisons

(c) The seriousness of the violation of inmates' rights

(d) Several legal loopholes in privately run facilities

33. Q: Why do some criminologists oppose the privately run prisons?

(a) A large amount of tax money is paid to maintain private prisons.

(b) Prisons run by governments can house much fewer prisoners.

(c) The transparency in running private prisons is often considered dubious.

(d) Private prisons are found to fail to rehabilitate inmates.

Native to the mountains of New Zealand's South Island, kea parrots suffer from predation by mammals and impact caused by human activities. Cats are known to be one of the primary predators, especially when cat populations make invasions on the kea habitat. Opossums also prey on kea parrots and disturb their nests though their threats are not as severe as those of stoats. Their nests are particularly vulnerable since they are just holes in the ground, which are easy to locate and break into.

Studies have shown that kea parrots in areas where they are fed are at risk from accidents by man-made objects such as buildings and cars. Buildings made with lead nails are posing a threat to kea parrots since lead has a sweet taste to them, resulting in lead poisoning. They also have a tendency to damage motor cars for their wiper blades and windshield rubbers. They are also compromising properties around campsites and parking lots, causing conflicts between kea parrots and humans. Therefore, albeit illegal, humans are shooting and killing kea parrots.

34. Q: What is the main point of the passage?
   (a) The vulnerable underground nests of kea parrots
   (b) Several factors threatening kea parrot populations
   (c) Harmful artificial objects attracting kea parrots
   (d) Causes to induce conflicts between humans and kea parrots

35. Q: What can be inferred about kea parrots from the passage?
   (a) Their habitat is meticulously and safely disguised like holes in the ground.
   (b) Opossums are the most dangerous predator to them as invaders.
   (c) They are often in danger because of their particular tastes in some material.
   (d) Most human beings are seeking to protect their populations.

SINCE 1999
ALL PASS

○ 1999년 정기시험 최초 시행
○ 2018년 뉴텝스 시행 (총점 600점 변경)
○ 국내 대학 수시, 편입, 졸업인증 활용
○ 전문대학원 입시 반영
○ 공무원 선발 및 국가자격시험 대체
○ 공공기관, 기업 채용 및 인사고과 활용

텝스로 올패스!

고교부터 대학(원), 취업, 승진을 잇는
" 대한민국 대표 영어시험 TEPS "

[자격명] TEPS 영어능력검정, [자격종류] 공인민간자격, [등록번호] 2008-0167, [공인번호] 교육부 제 2018-2호

 02.886.3330   www.teps.or.kr   www.facebook.com/teps4u   @teps

기본부터 실전까지, 가장 빠르게 점수를 올리는 뉴텝스 독해

NEW TEPS 독해

실력편 실전 400+

정일상·넥서스TEPS연구소 지음

Reading

부가 제공 자료 www.nexusbook.com

모바일 단어장
VOCA TEST
정답 자동 채점

모바일 단어장

모바일 VOCA TEST

정답 자동 채점

+

어휘 리스트 & 테스트

ACTUAL TEST 5회분 수록

정답 및 해설

NEXUS Edu

NEW
TEPS

실력편
실전 400+ 독해

Reading

정답 및 해설

NEXUS Edu

I 올바른 독해를 위한 문법

Unit 01 to부정사와 동명사

EXERCISE 1
p 31

1 <u>To fly over ten hours to this corner of Indonesia's North Sulawesi province</u> will not be a waste of time once you see the panoramic view of the Sulawesie Sea. (주어)

인도네시아의 북 술라웨시 주의 이 외딴 곳까지 열 시간 이상 비행해서 오는 일은 술라웨시 바다 전경을 보면 시간 낭비가 아닐 것이다.

2 If it is a breathtaking picture of the sea that you want, the trick is <u>to find the perfect time and place.</u> (보어)

만약 숨이 막힐 듯한 바다 사진을 원한다면 그 비법은 완벽한 시간과 장소를 찾는 것이다.

3 The mayor plans <u>to attract more tourists this year</u> to cover the losses coming from the city's falling real estate prices. (목적어)

시장은 시의 하락하는 부동산 가격에서 오는 손실을 약화시키기 위하여 올해에 더 많은 관광객을 유치할 계획이다.

4 <u>To lend a helping hand to the needy</u> is not only rewarding but also comforting. (주어)

어려운 사람들에게 도움의 손길을 주는 것은 보람이 있을 뿐만 아니라 위안도 된다.

5 The job of the 15-member team is <u>to feed, clean, and care for the orphaned animals.</u> (보어)

15명으로 구성된 팀의 임무는 어미를 잃은 동물들을 먹이고, 씻기고, 돌봐 주는 것이다.

6 For the first time in its 43-year-old history, the New Orleans Saints managed <u>to reach the Super Bowl.</u> (목적어)

43년 역사상 처음으로 뉴올리언스 세인트가 슈퍼볼에 가까스로 참여하게 되었다.

7 The proposed plan by the committee is <u>to expand its niche in the lucrative market</u>. (보어)

의회가 제안한 계획은 이익성이 높은 시장에서 틈새를 넓히는 것이다.

8 According to Doctor Holmes, <u>to understand that book, which abounds with mysteries and ironies,</u> will not be easy for his first-time readers. (주어)

홈즈 박사에 의하면 미스터리와 아이러니로 가득한 그 책을 이해하는 것은 박사의 책을 처음 읽는 독자에게는 쉽지 않을 것이다.

9 As an administrator who swore <u>to serve the country,</u> the new secretary failed <u>to resist getting involved in corruption.</u> (목적어)

나라를 위해 일하겠다고 맹세한 행정관으로서 신임 장관은 부패의 유혹을 뿌리치지 못했다.

10 To appease frantic investors, the new chief executive needs <u>to articulate a clear and unified vision for the company.</u> (목적어)

극도로 흥분한 투자가들을 달래기 위하여 신임 최고경영자는 회사를 위한 명확하고 통일된 비전을 분명하게 설명해야 한다.

EXERCISE 2
p 32

1 Mr. Zhou, the zoo keeper, reports that the favorite activities of these furry creatures in this scorching season are <u>slumbering in the shade and going for a dip in the water.</u> (보어)

동물원 관리인인 자우 씨는 이 무더운 계절에 털이 많은 동물들이 가장 즐겨 하는 것은 그늘에서 자고 물속에 몸을 담그는 것이라고 한다.

2 <u>Escaping from the economic crisis gripping the entire continent</u> will be on the top of the agenda at the summit meeting. (주어)

대륙 전체를 움켜쥐고 있는 경제 위기에서 탈출하는 것이 정상 회담에서 최우선 협의 사항이 될 것이다.

3 With another round of heavy rainfall anticipated, the immediate concern is <u>housing the possible flood victims in school auditoriums and sports stadiums.</u> (보어)

또 한 번의 폭우가 닥칠 것으로 예상되는 상황에서 당면한 우려는 발생 가능한 홍수 피해자들을 학교 강당과 체육관에 수용하는 것이다.

4 For a team who was widely expected to win the cup, <u>getting eliminated in the preliminary round</u> was more than a rude awakening. (주어)

많은 사람들이 우승하리라 예상했던 팀에게 예선 탈락은 갑작스럽고 불쾌한 일 이상이었다.

5 The town residents favored <u>relocating the landfill to the outskirts of the town</u> in hopes of raising their real estate values. (목적어)

마을 거주자들은 부동산 가격 상승의 희망을 품고 쓰레기 매립지를 마을 변두리로 옮기는 것을 지지했다.

6 Educators in this country must realize that the toughest part of the problem is <u>weighing the merits and demerits of rewarding teachers for their performance.</u> (보어)

이 나라의 교육자들은 문제점의 가장 어려운 부분이 선생님들을 성과에 따라서 보상을 해주는 것에 대한 장점과 단점을 저울질하는 것임을 깨달아야 한다.

7 Whenever the government proposes a new measure, the leftist critics love <u>slamming it as unconstitutional and evocative of nationalist sentiments</u>. (목적어)

정부가 새로운 조치를 제안할 때마다 좌파 비평가들은 그것이 헌법 위반이고 민족주의적 감성을 불러일으킨다며 공격하기를 즐긴다.

8 The president learned the hard way that <u>pursuing domestic political objectives</u> is more bureaucratic than achieving foreign policy goals. (that절의 주어)

대통령은 국내의 정치 목적을 달성하는 일은 해외 외교 정책 목표를 달성하는 것보다 더 관료적이라는 것을 비싼 대가를 치르고서야 알게 되었다.

9 In order to preserve the essence of the original work, the artist suggested <u>recreating fabric and upholstery based on the original designs</u>. (목적어)

원작의 본질을 유지하기 위해서 예술가는 원작 디자인을 바탕으로 구조와 커버를 다시 만들자고 제안했다.

10 The government has begun <u>sending the refugees back to their war-stricken homeland,</u> drawing criticism from the neighboring countries. (목적어)

정부는 난민을 전쟁 중인 모국으로 돌려보내기 시작하면서 주변 국가로부터 비판을 샀다.

EXERCISE 3   p 33

과학자들로 구성된 팀의 12년간의 연구에 따르면 뇌의 지적인 활동이 치매를 늦추거나 심지어 예방을 하는 것으로 발견되었으나, 거기에는 대가가 있다. 수년 동안 의사들은 카드놀이를 하고 책을 읽고 다른 뇌 운동을 하면서 치매를 예방하는 방법인 뇌에 지적인 자극을 주는 것을 권했다. 그러나 새로운 발견에 의하면 치매가 시작되면 지적으로 활동적인 사람들이 그렇지 않은 사람보다 지적인 감퇴가 더 빨라지는 것으로 조사되었다. 사실 1,157명의 65세 이상의 남녀를 대상으로 한 연구에서 치매 증상이 시작되었을 때 지적으로 활동적인 연구 대상자들에게 52% 더 빨리 진행되는 것으로 나타났다.

Q: 글의 주요 내용은?
(a) 치매의 증상과 예방 대책
(b) 운동의 위험성을 보여 주는 연구
(c) 지능 운동과 치매의 관계
(d) 치매에 대항하기 위한 정신 운동 방법

discover 발견하다 **intellectual** 지적인 **delay** 미루다, 연기하다 **dementia** 치매 **at a price** 상당한 비용을 들여 **recommend** 추천하다 **stimulate** 자극하다 **engage in** ~에 관여[참여]하다 **set in** 시작하다 **conduct** (특정 활동을) 하다 **symptom** 증상 **progress** 진행되다

EXERCISE 1   p 35

1 Before granting the lease to the developers, the residents are asking just <u>how many homes can be powered by the proposed number of wind turbines</u>. (목적어)

임대차 계약을 개발자들에게 승인하기 전에 주민들은 제안된 풍력 발전용 터빈의 숫자가 얼마나 많은 가정에 전기를 공급할 수 있는지 물어보고 있다.

2 <u>How anyone can find seclusion from the hustle and bustle from this urban life</u> is still a mystery to many city dwellers. (주어)

복작거리는 도시 생활에서 어떻게 은둔을 찾을 수 있는지는 아직도 많은 도시인에게 미스터리다.

3 Your next question will be <u>if we can make use of its geographic features in the same way as our ancestors did centuries ago</u>. (보어)

다음 질문은 수세기 전에 우리 조상들이 했던 것과 똑같은 방식으로 우리가 그 지리적 특징을 활용할 수 있느냐이다.

4 I could not concentrate on my work for the rest of the day because <u>what I had for breakfast</u> gave me heartburn. (주어)

아침에 먹은 것 때문에 속이 쓰려서 하루 종일 일에 집중할 수 없었다.

5 The association estimates <u>that about two out of five women suffered from anorexia or bulimia in their teens</u>. (목적어)

협회는 여성 다섯 중 둘은 10대에 거식증이나 폭식증을 겪은 것으로 추정하고 있다.

6 As there is no visible end to the current deadlock between the local residents and the developers, <u>when the construction will be completed</u> is beyond anyone's knowledge. (주어)

지역 주민들과 개발자들 사이의 현 교착 상태가 끝날 것 같지 않아 보이기 때문에 공사가 언제 완공될지는 아무도 모른다.

7 Perhaps the biggest mistake committed by the lawyer was <u>that he entrusted his colleague with sensitive information about the plaintiff</u>. (보어)

변호사가 저지른 가장 큰 실수는 아마도 동료에게 고소인에 대한 극히 신중을 요하는 정보를 맡겼다는 것이다.

8 Some people are wondering <u>why the decision made by the president is a magnet for anti-government demonstrations</u>. (목적어)

어떤 사람들은 대통령이 내린 결정이 왜 반정부 시위를 자석처럼 끌어들이는지 궁금해 한다.

9 Although the Federal Reserve Board is expected to nudge down long-term interest rates soon, <u>when exactly it will do so</u> is anybody's guess. (주어)

연방 준비 제도 이사회가 장기 금리를 곧 내릴 것이라고 기대되지만 정확히 언제 할 것인지는 아무도 모른다.

10 The city's educational leaders are deciding <u>how much penalty would be sufficient under the "3 Strikes, you're Out" system</u>. (목적어)

시 교육 지도자들은 '삼진 아웃 제도'에 얼마나 많은 벌칙이 충분한지 결정 중이다.

EXERCISE 2   p 41

인구 과잉이 환경오염과 기근을 낳는다는 것에 경제학자와 인구 통계학자 거의 다 동의한다. 그러나 국가 인구 조사국의 코헨 박사는 인구 증가가 빈곤, 기아, 환경 파괴와 같은 문제와 관계가 매우 표면상이라는 점에 주목한다. 코헨 박사에 의하면 사람들은 이러한 문제의 원인이 되는 정치적인 요소들을 무시한다고 한다. 예를 들어, 부유한 나라가 개발도상국에게 농업 지원금을 주면 개발 도상국의 굶주림을 더욱 악화시키며 농업 수입이 줄어든다. 더 나아가 교육 지원금과 더 발전된 농업 기술, 의료 지원 부족은 인구 증가가 아닌 정치적 부패와 남용으로 발생하지 인구 증가로 일어나지 않는다.

Q: 다음 중 지문에 따르면 옳은 것은?
(a) 인구 과잉은 사회 문제와 환경 문제의 가장 위협적인 원인이다.
(b) 정치 부패는 사회 문제와 환경 문제의 가장 심각한 원인이다.
(c) 인구 증가와 사회 문제의 관계는 반대이다.
(d) 인구 과잉이 아니라 정치 남용이 낳는 문제가 있다.

overpopulation 인구 과잉   **conducive** 공헌하는   **destruction** 파괴
famine 기근   **economist** 경제학자   **demographer** 인구 통계학자
poverty 빈곤   **starvation** 기아   **degradation** 오염, 붕괴   **factor** 요소
subsidy 보조금   **aggravate** 악화시키다   **bring about** 일으키다
corruption 부패   **abuse** 남용

Unit 03 연결어

EXERCISE 1   p 39

1 당국은 해안 마을에 미리 허리케인에 조기 경보를 발령하지 못했다. **결국** 200명 이상이 홍수로 집을 잃었다.

(a) 대조적으로
(b) 구체적으로
(c) 대신
(d) 결국

2 보건 당국은 가축에게 예방 접종을 하기 위해 24시간 일을 하고 있다. **게다가** 야생 조류의 이동이 자세히 관찰되었지만 조류 독감의 발발이 아직 보고되지 않았다.

(a) 구체적으로
(b) 게다가
(c) 의심할 여지없이
(d) 따라서

3 칠레 농산물은 한국 식탁에 오를 수 있었다. **마찬가지로** 한국 제품은 칠레에서 판로를 찾았다.

(a) 마찬가지로
(b) 이것이 사실일지라도
(c) 이런 이유로
(d) 대조적으로

4 질병의 증상은 걸리고 나서 수년 후에도 감지하기 힘들다. **사실** 오직 27%만이 치료가 가장 가능한 초기 단계에서 발견된다.

(a) 마찬가지로 중요하게
(b) 게다가
(c) 사실
(d) 그러나

5 지방 선거가 다가오면서 행정부는 농민을 달래려는 의지를 보였다. **예를 들어,** 농림부 장관이 쌀 시장을 개방하기 위해 공격적인 시도로 농민을 분노하게 만들어서 해임되었다.

(a) 마찬가지로 중요하게
(b) 이런 이유로
(c) 그러므로
(d) 예를 들어

6 많은 성공한 비즈니스 거물은 경쟁자보다 더 일찍 하루를 시작하는 것으로 알려져 있다. **그러나** 나같이 일찍 일어날 수 없는 올빼미도 있다.

(a) 유사하게
(b) 그러나
(c) 따라서
(d) 그 후에

7 7개의 다른 나라에서 온 십 대들은 가뭄으로 피해를 입은 마을에 우물을 짓는 하나의 목표를 달성하기 위해 차이를 극복하는 것을 배웠다. **즉,** 서로 다른 사람들은 처음에는 함께 어울리지 않지만, 동일한 목표가 있으면 결국에는 협동을 한다.

(a) 설명하자면
(b) 사실
(c) 반면
(d) 즉

8 OPEC 회원국들은 지난주 생산량을 늘리자는 합의에 이르렀다. **그에 따라서** 원유 가격이 하락하여 제조업자의 부담이 줄어들었다.

(a) 그러면
(b) 정말
(c) 분명히
(d) 그에 따라

9 소매 산업은 가장 좋은 철에 그다지 좋은 실적을 내지 못 했다. **대조적으로** 금융 산업은 이익 감소에도 불구하고 활발한 4사분기를 지냈다.

(a) 게다가
(b) 대조적으로
(c) 동시에
(d) 즉

10 전쟁으로 황폐화된 지역에 더 이상 개입하는 것에 반대하는 대중의 감정이 그 어느 때보다 높다. **그럼에도 불구하고** 대통령은 이라크에 부대를 추가 파병하는 것을 허락했다.

(a) 사실
(b) 또한
(c) 그럼에도 불구하고
(d) 의심할 여지없이

EXERCISE 2
p 34

무엇이 사람들이 행동하는 방식을 형성할까? 유전자일까 아니면 어린 시절의 환경일까? 어떤 사람들은 그들이 성인이 되어 형성하는 라이프스타일에 대한 선택일지도 모른다고 생각한다. **그러나** 태어였을 때 인생이 만들어진다고 생각해 본 적이 있는가? 엄마의 자궁에서 보내는 9달이 인생에서 가장 많은 영향을 미치는 기간이라는 흥미로운 주장이 있다. 뇌가 연결되고 심장, 간과 같은 주요 장기가 형성되는 시기이다. 신체적인 형성과 더불어 태아의 시기의 성장은 지능, 성격, 심지어 분별에 영향을 미칠지도 모른다. 새로운 발견은 주제에 대한 폭발적인 연구로 이어질 것으로 기대된다. 태아 단계에 대한 심도 있는 연구로 과학자들은 인간성이 어디에서 오고 언제 발달하기 시작하는지 더욱 정확히 알 수 있을 것으로 기대한다.

(a) 그러므로
(b) 사실
(c) 특히
(d) 그러나

turn out 모습을 드러내다 **gene** 유전자 **childhood** 어린 시절 **fetus** 태아 **provocative** 도발적인 **assert** 주장하다 **womb** 자궁 **critical** 대단히 중요한 **vital** 필수적인 **organ** 장기[기관] **liver** 간 **influence** 영향을 주다 **temperament** 기질 **sanity** 온전한 정신, 분별 **explosion** 폭발적인 증가 **optimistic** 낙관적인 **accurate** 정확

EXERCISE 1
p 44

1 The movie, <u>which premiered last week in New York</u>, features new faces with no track record in the film industry. (movie)

지난주 뉴욕에서 개봉한 그 영화에는 영화계에서 이력이 없는 신인 배우들이 출연한다.

2 The new controversial ad provides a few tips for guys <u>who need to get out of hot water</u> thereby helping them cheat on their wives. (guys)

논란이 많은 새 광고는 곤란에 빠진 남자들을 위한 팁을 제공하면서 아내 몰래 바람을 피도록 도와주고 있다.

3 The young artist made some changes to the Prime Minister's image from a picture taken in 1965 <u>when the nation won its independence</u>. (1965)

젊은 예술가는 나라가 독립한 1965년에 찍힌 사진에서 총리의 사진을 변형시켰다.

4 A recent series of bullying-related suicides is the reason <u>why American moms are up in arms and determined to fight the problem</u>. (reason)

최근 왕따로 인한 일련의 자살 사건이 미국의 어머니들이 격분하여 그 문제와 싸우기로 결심한 이유다.

5 Mr. Harris, <u>who was admired among atheists as their role model</u>, has been losing his followers after claiming that he believes in a spiritual being. (Mr. Harris)

무신론자 사이에서 우상으로 존경받는 해리스 씨는 영혼의 존재를 믿는다고 주장한 후 지지자들을 잃고 있다.

6 An economist and former executive at the World Bank, Mr. Hymer believes that the destitute country <u>where there seemed to be no end to famine</u> will finally find a ray of hope. (country)

세계은행에서 경제학자이며 전 임원이었던 하이머 씨는 굶주림이 끝이 없어 보였던 그 빈곤한 나라가 드디어 희망 한 줄기를 볼 것이라고 믿는다.

7 The ironic fact is that highly visible business people and celebrities <u>that are recognized for lending a hand to the world's poor</u> are not actively involved in the issue of domestic poverty. (business people and celebrities)

모순적인 사실은 세계의 가난한 사람들을 돕는 것으로 알려진 크게 존경받는 사업가들과 유명 인사들이 자국의 빈곤에 대해서는 활발히 개입하지 않는다는 것이다.

8 With the New York Fashion Week finally over, the design house headed by Jesse Miller, <u>whom the critics praised as a rising star in the industry</u>, is busy filling orders from buyers. (Jesse Miller)

뉴욕 패션 위크가 끝나면서 디자인 업계에서 뜨는 별이라고 비평가들의 찬사를 보낸 제시 밀러가 이끄는 디자인 회사는 구매자들로부터 들어온 많은 주문을 처리하느라 바쁘다.

9 More working moms are finding it nearly impossible to juggle work and house chores while trying to nurture their children right in a society <u>where the term "housewife" has become anachronistic.</u> (society)

'전업주부'라는 말이 시대착오적인 표현이 된 사회에서 더 많은 일하는 엄마들은 아이들을 제대로 양육하면서 일과 집안일을 잘 처리하는 것이 거의 불가능하다고 느끼고 있다.

10 Wage disparities <u>which discourage many female graduates from entering the corporate world</u> will not be eradicated without a change in people's attitude. (wage disparities)

많은 여성 졸업생이 기업 세계에 들어가는 것을 낙담시키는 임금 격차는 사람들의 태도가 변하지 않는 한 근절되지 않을 것이다.

EXERCISE 2
p 45

19세기 전반에 걸쳐 영국은 1815년부터 1870년까지 유럽 대륙이 여러 차례 겪어야 했던 일종의 사회 반란을 가까스로 피할 수 있었다. 많은 영국 역사학자는 영국이 이렇게 할 수 있었던 이유를 영국 의회가 일찍이 민주주의를 채택했기 때문이라고 한다. 이런 주장은 어느 정도 사실이지만 의문의 여지도 있다. 예를 들어 1832년 더 많은 남자에게 투표권을 주는 영국 선거법 개정은 역사적인 법안이었지만 여전히 남성 인구의 20%만 투표를 할 수 있었다. 1867년에 통과된 선거법 개정안은 더 많은 투표권을 주었지만, 그 권리는 일반적인 배경을 가지고 보통 교육을 받았으며 나라 안팎의 정치에 일반적인 견해를 가진 소수에게만 주어졌다. 영국은 다른 어느 유럽 나라보다 더 빨리 개정을 실행시켰지만 진행에는 시간이 걸렸다.

Q: 글의 주요 내용은?
(a) 의회 민주화에 실패한 영국
(b) 체제 민주화에 성공한 영국
(c) 유럽을 민주화하기 위한 영국의 점진적인 접근법
(d) 개정을 위한 영국의 초기 시도, 그러나 충분히 빠르지 못했던 시도

manage 용케 해내다 **uprising** 반란 **on and off** 때때로, 불규칙하게 **give credit for** ~에 관한 공적을 인정하다 **adopt** 채택하다 **parliament** 의회 국회 **claim** 주장 **doubt** 의심, 의문 **legislation** 법률, 제정법 **expand** 확장시키다 **reform bill** 개정안 **perspective** 견해, 관점 **domestic** 국내의

EXERCISE 1
p 48

1 <u>Hailed as an extraordinary engineering achievement</u>, the tunnel was completed by over 26,000 workers who had to battle dust and danger for 12 years. (the tunnel)

엄청난 공학 기술의 업적으로 찬사를 받으며 그 터널은 12년 동안 먼지와 위험과 싸워야 했던 26,000 노동자들에 의해 완공되었다.

2 <u>Creating a super-fast rail-link under the sea</u>, the two countries hope to boost trade and travel while cutting down cost and congestion. (the two countries)

바다 밑에 초고속 고속철도를 만들면서 그 두 나라는 비용과 교통 혼잡을 줄이면서 무역과 관광을 증가시키기를 기대한다.

3 <u>Published last week in the *Parenthood*</u>, the article introduces a study that suggests women's brains may actually grow bigger with motherhood. (the article)

지난주에 〈Parenthood〉라는 잡지에 실리면서 그 기사는 처음 엄마가 되면서 여성의 뇌가 실제로 점차 더 커질 수 있다는 연구를 소개했다.

4 <u>Found to have violated the law</u>, the insurance companies will be penalized for collaborating to fix the price. (the insurance companies)

위법한 것이 발견되어 그 보험 회사들은 가격을 고정하기로 담합한 것으로 처벌을 받을 것이다.

5 <u>Being extremely cautious not to spoil the trial</u>, the official spoke on condition of anonymity because the investigation was just getting under way. (the official)

그 재판을 망치지 않기 위해 매우 조심해야 하므로 그 공인은 조사가 얼마 전 시작되었기 때문에 익명으로 말했다.

6 <u>Possessing all the classic elements of successful internet start-ups</u>, the new socializing website was never expected to sink. (the new socializing site)

성공한 인터넷 신규 업체의 전형적인 모든 요소들을 갖추고 있었기 때문에 그 새로운 사교 사이트는 절대로 실패할 것이라고 보지 않았다.

7 <u>Encouraged by rising incomes and red-hot growth attributing to exploding numbers of visitors</u>, China has launched construction of new airports throughout the country. (China)

방문객 수의 폭발적인 증가 덕분으로 소득 증대와 고도성장에 고무된 중국은 전국에 새로운 공항들을 짓기 위한 건설을 시작했다.

8 <u>Concerned about the stricter rules and harsher fines for dirty plays</u>, the players are bemoaning that the new regulations will spoil the fun of the game. (the players)

반칙에 대한 더 엄격한 규정과 더 가혹한 벌금에 대해서 걱정을 하며 선수들은 새로운 규정이 게임을 재미없게 만들 것이라고 탄식하고 있다.

9 Deprived of their helmets, football players would be less likely to use their heads as weapons, according to some experts. (football players)

헬멧을 못쓰게 한다면 미식축구 선수들은 머리를 무기로 사용할 가능성이 적을 것이라고 전문가들은 말한다.

10 Sitting through the entire movie for three hours, I realized that I had almost no memory of its content. (I)

세 시간 동안 그 영화 전체를 다 보고 난 후, 나는 그 내용에 대한 기억이 거의 없다는 것을 깨달았다.

EXERCISE 2 P 49

우주여행이 더 길고 잦아지면서 우주 비행사들의 건강에 대한 우려가 새로이 제기되었다. 마케트 대학의 연구에 의하면, 우주에서 6개월 이상 보낸 우주 비행사는 80세 노인처럼 약해질 수 있다. 연구에 의하면 우주에 더 오래 있을수록 우주비행사의 근육이 위축되어 힘을 잃는 것으로 나타났다. 이런 현상은 일시적이라고 주장하면서도 연구 담당자 로버트 피츠는 고려해야 할 심각한 위험이 있음을 인정했다. 만약 우주 비행선이 비상 착륙을 하고 우주 비행사들이 오도가도 못하면 어떨까? 지구에 잠시 머문 후에 당장 긴급 수리를 위해서 우주로 돌아가야 한다면 어떻게 할까? 이것은 우주 비행사들을 우주에서도 신체적으로 젊고 강하게 만들기 위해 답해야 하는 단지 몇 안 되는 질문들이다.

Q: 다음 중 옳은 것은?
(a) 우주 비행사들은 비행이 잦을 때만 운동을 해야 한다.
(b) 우주 비행사들의 충분한 휴식을 위해 비행을 덜 해야 한다.
(c) 우주 비행사들은 우주에서 반년 이상 머물지 말아야 한다.
(d) 우주의 조건으로 우주에서 인간의 근육은 더 빨리 약해진다.

frequent 빈번한　**regarding** ~에 관하여　**astronaut** 우주 비행사　**reveal** 드러내다　**atrophy** (신체 부위의) 위축　**prolong** 연장시키다　**temporary** 일시적인　**threat** 위험, 위협　**strand** 좌초시키다, 오도가도 못하게 하다　**immediately** 즉시, 바로

Ⅱ 유형별 독해 전략

Unit 01 앞 빈칸 채우기 p.53

1 (a)	**2** (d)	**3** (b)	**4** (c)	**5** (b)
6 (d)	**7** (a)	**8** (d)	**9** (c)	**10** (b)

1

식량 공급에 대한 늘어나는 요구를 충족시키기 위해 농부들은 비료와 유전자를 조작한 식량 종자에 의지해 왔다. 하지만 이러한 관행은 소비자의 건강을 심각하게 위협하는 결과를 초래했기 때문에, 많은 소비자들이 **무기농 원두보다 건강에 유익한 유기농 원두를 선호하기 시작했다.** 유기농 원두는 합성 비료로 재배한 원두보다 맛있고, 커피를 끓였을 때 맛이 더 풍부하다는 장점이 있다. 또 다른 장점은 무기농 원두가 살충제와 화학 비료로 재배되는 반면 유기농 원두는 환경에 이롭다는 점이다. 농부들이 커피 재배를 위해서 유기농을 선택한다면, 환경에 도움이 되고 인간과 동물의 건강에 대한 위험도 감소시킬 수 있다. 또 다른 장점을 들자면, 농부들이 반드시 정부의 엄격한 인증 절차를 거쳐야 하기 때문에 커피 애호가들은 유기농 원두의 품질을 확신할 수 있다는 것이다. 따라서 다음에 상점 진열대에서 원두를 고를 때는 유기농 제품을 구입하고 싶어질 것이다.

(a) 무기농 원두보다 건강에 유익한 유기농 원두를 선호한다
(b) 건강을 개선하고 환경을 보호하기 위해 아침에 마시는 커피량을 줄인다
(c) 유기농 원두 대신 무기농 원두를 재배하는 농민들에게서 커피를 구입한다
(d) 예전보다 커피의 품질과 영양가에 대해서 신경을 더 쓴다

살충제와 화학 비료로 키운 무기농 원두보다 유기농으로 재배한 원두가 맛이 풍부하고 건강에 유리하며 환경에 이롭다는 것이 지문의 요지이다. 유기농 원두의 장점을 주로 나열하고 있으므로 정답은 (a)이다.

resort to 의지하다　**fertilizer** 비료　**genetically engineer** 유전자를 조작하다　**practice** 관행　**prefer A to B** B보다 A를 선호하다　**flavor** 맛　**pesticide** 살충제

2

유럽의 세력 균형은 단일 민족 국가의 세력 증대를 지리적 또는 정치적인 경쟁국의 세력 증대와 짝을 맞춤으로써 국제 질서와 평화를 유지하기 위한 목적으로 도출된 체계였다. **이러한 세력 균형에 대한 가장 좋은 예 중 하나가** '유럽의 병자'로 알려진 오토만 제국과 유럽의 관계이다. 세력의 정점에 있을 때 오토만 제국은 중동, 북아프리카 일부, 보스니아-헤르체코비나를 포함한 북부 지역을 지배했다. 오토만 제국은 지배력 약화에도 불구하고 발칸 반도를 통제했기 때문에, 대부분의 유럽 국가들은 어느 한 유럽 국가가 발칸 반도에 대해 영향력을 행사하는 것을 방지하기 위해 오토만 제국이 **스스로** 지탱할 수 있도록 도움을 주었다. 오토만 제국의 수도인 콘스탄티노플이 존속하도록 도움으로써 유럽의 세력 균형이 유지될 수 있었다. 그러나 결국 유럽 세력 균형의 기반을 흔들었던 것이 바로 불안한 발칸 반도였다.

(a) 이러한 국제 체제에서 발견되는 결점의 한 예
(b) 학자들이 이 이론을 통해서 설명하지 못하는 것
(c) 세력 균형에 대해 주목할만한 모순점
(d) 이러한 세력 균형에 대한 가장 좋은 예 중 하나

빈칸 앞에 나오는 한 국가의 세력 증대를 경쟁국과 짝을 맞추어 세력의 균형을 유지했다는 내용이 나오고, 지문 뒷부분에는 대부분의 유럽 국가들이 어느 한 국가에 의한 득세를 막기 위해서 쇠약해진 오토만 제국이 존속할 수 있도록 도왔다는 내용으로 이어지므로 정답은 (d)이다.

international order 국제 질서 **one nation-state** 단일 민족
dominate 지배하다 **Middle East** 중동 **sustain** 지탱하다 **exert**
행사하다 **capital** 수도 **volatile** 불안한 **peninsula** 반도

3

Freelancing.com은 우리나라에서 **기업이 프리랜서를 고용하기 위한 가장 큰 시장입니다.** 당사는 만족해하는 수천 명의 고객을 보유하고 있습니다. 270개 지역에 있는 110만 명이 넘는 고용주와 프리랜서를 연결해 줍니다. 기업은 당사 웹 사이트에서 프로그래밍, 자료 입력, 영업, 회계와 같은 분야에서 일할 프리랜서를 고용할 수 있습니다. 당사는 보안 대금 결제 시스템을 통해서 고용주를 위한 안전한 환경을 조성하였습니다. 당사는 수천 명의 프리랜서 작가, 프로그래머, 디자이너, 마케팅 담당자 등을 확보하고 있습니다. 가장 훌륭한 웹 디자인, 전문적인 프로그래밍, 맞춤 집필 또는 예산에 맞는 마케팅 서비스를 받기가 그 어느 때보다도 쉽습니다. 오늘 무료로 아웃소싱 서비스를 이용해 보세요! 귀하의 다음 프로젝트나 업무를 위해 당사의 홈페이지를 즐겨찾기에 추가하는 것도 잊지 마세요.

(a) 프리랜서 일자리를 찾는 구직자를 위한 가장 인기 있는 웹 사이트
(b) 기업이 프리랜서를 고용하기 위한 가장 큰 시장
(c) 온라인 보안 결제 프로그램의 가장 안전한 제공자
(d) 대기업을 위한 최고의 지원자를 찾아주는 최대 사이트

Freelancing.com이 전 세계적으로 270개 국가와 지역의 110만 명이 넘는 고용주와 프리랜서를 연결해 주고 있다는 내용이다. (a)는 구직자들을 위한 사이트라는 것이고, (c)는 결제 시스템을 설명하는 것이며, (d)는 대기업 지원자를 찾기 위한 사이트라는 것으로 내용과 무관하다. 따라서 정답은 (b)이다.

employer 고용주 **freelancer** 프리랜서 **software writing** 소프트웨어
제작 **accounting** 회계 **affordable** 감당할 수 있는 **bookmark** 즐겨
찾기에 추가하다 **outsource** 외부에서 조달하다

4

학교는 아이들이 시험을 치르기 위한 준비를 갖춰 주는 장소이므로 아이들이 **교실 밖의 경험을 통해서** 교실에서 배우는 모든 수업 내용을 늘릴 수 있는 다양한 방법을 찾아내는 것은 부모들에게 달려 있다. 연극과 음악에서 과학과 운동에 이르기까지 아이들을 다양한 관심을 가진 다재다능한 사람을 만들고자 하는 목적으로, 부모들은 학교 활동량을 보충하는 방법을 배울 수 있다. 예를 들면, 예술 회관이나 강습소에서 가르치는 연극 강좌들이 많이 있고, 학교 음악 교사가 추천하는 자격 있는 개인 교사가 제공하는 음악 교습도 있다. 물론, 모든 아이들이 연극이나 음악에 관심이 있는 것은 아니다. 어떤 아이들은 과학 분야를 좀 더 심도 있게 탐구하기를 원할지도 모른다. 만약 자녀가 생물학이나 물리학에 강한 흥미를 보이면, 지역의 과학 클럽이나 보이 스카우트 또는 걸 스카우트와 같

은 사교 클럽에 가입할 수 있는 기회를 찾아보아라. 자녀 교육에 예술이나 과학을 추가하는 것은 아이들에게 다양한 경험을 제공하고 흥미와 창의력을 개발하는 데 도움을 줄 것이다.

(a) 일일 교사로 참여함으로써
(b) 학부모 회의를 통해
(c) 교실 밖 경험을 통해
(d) 자녀의 숙제를 도와줌으로써

교실 수업 내용을 보완하기 위한 방법을 부모들이 어떻게 찾아야 할 것인가에 관한 내용이다. 아이들이 접할 수 있는 연극, 음악, 과학, 운동, 과학 클럽이나 사교 클럽 활동은 모두 교실 밖에서 이루어진다. 따라서 정답은 (c)이다.

gear up 준비를 갖추다 **add to** 늘리다 **well-rounded** 다재다능한
heightened 증가된

5

손목시계는 이제 한물간 것 같다. 왜냐하면 한 연구 결과가 더욱 많은 사람들이 약속이나 회의 시간에 맞추기 위해서 **더 새로운 기술에 의존하기 시작했다고** 밝혔기 때문이다. 맥클랜의 소비자 성향 분석가들에 의한 연구는 일곱 명중 한 명은 이동 전화와 컴퓨터가 기존의 시계를 더 이상 쓸모가 없는 것으로 만들었다고 말했다고 밝혔다. 또한 이 연구에 의하면, 86%는 더 이상 정확한 시간을 알기 위해 손목시계에 의존하지는 않지만 여전히 손목시계를 소유하고 있다고 한다. 분석가들에 의하면 이동 전화를 휴대하면서 성장한 25세 미만의 사람들은 구세대에 비해 절반 정도가 시계를 소유할 것이라고 한다. 맥클랜의 수석 패션 분석가인 티모시 샌더는 '많은 소비자들이 기술과 함께 성장했고, 시간을 이동 전화기로 확인한다는 생각을 시계로 확인한다는 생각과 연관 짓는 것 같다'고 말했다. 이동 전화가 크게 유행하고 있고 모든 연령에서 사용이 증가하고 있어 아마도 장기적으로 일반 손목시계에 대한 수요에 위협이 될 수 있다.

(a) 손목시계가 패션 품목이라고 생각하기 시작한다
(b) 더 새로운 기술에 의존하기 시작한다
(c) 탁상용 컴퓨터와 노트북 컴퓨터를 사용한다
(d) 손목시계가 불편하다는 것을 알게 된다

최신 기술과 함께 성장한 많은 사람들이 이동 전화나 컴퓨터로 시간을 확인하고, 이동 전화의 소유 및 사용 증가로 장기적으로 손목시계에 대한 수요가 감소할 것이라는 것이 지문의 요지이다. 사람들은 시간을 맞추기 위해서 이동 전화와 컴퓨터에 의존하는데 이는 신기술의 산물이므로 정답은 (b)이다.

wristwatch 손목시계 **obsolete** 쓸모가 없는 **generation** 세대
pose (위험성을) 지니다 **in the long-term** 장기적으로

6

보험 정책상 자동차 보험 회사가 여성보다 남성에게 보험료를 매기는 데 있어서 차별을 한다고 불평하는 남성들을 위해서 **더 비싼 보험료에 대해 간단히 설명을** 하겠습니다. 남성보다 여성이 치명적인 자동차 사고에 덜 연관됩니다. 게다가 차 사고를 낸 적이 없는 여성 수가 남성 수보다 많습니다. 지나치게 포괄적인 일반화는 불공평한 것처럼 보이겠지만 사실은 거짓을 말하지 않습니다. 통계적으로 남성들이 더 많은 사고를 낸다는 것은 보험 회사가 그들에게 더 많은 돈을 지불해야 한다는 것을 의미합니다. 물론 보험 회사가 매기는 보험료는 운전 경력에 상당히 좌우됩니다. 그럼에도 불구하고 남성의 자동차 보험료는 남성들이 더욱 조심해서 운전하지 않는 한 내려가지 않을 것입니다.

(a) 보험료는 줄이는 데 도움이 되는 방법
(b) 높은 비용에 대해서 불평을 하는 이유
(c) 보험료를 올리는 효과적인 방법
(d) 더 비싼 보험료에 대한 간단한 설명

여성보다 남성에게 더 높게 매기는 보험료에 대해서 불평하는 남성들에게 그 이유를 설명하고 있다. 남성이 더 많은 자동차 사고를 내기 때문에 사고 수가 줄지 않는 한 보험료는 내리지 않을 것이라고 한다. 따라서 정답은 (d)이다.

discriminatory 차별적인 **premium** 보험료 **sweeping** 전면적인 **generalization** 일반화 **dictate** ~을 좌우하다 **statistical** 통계적인

7

천문학자들은 허블 망원경을 이용해서 <u>우주가 아마도 영원히 팽창할 것이라는 것을</u> 알아낼 수 있었다. 그렇다면 어떻게 그것을 알 수 있을까? 그들이 망원경을 통해 찾아낸 것은 아벨 1689라고 이름 붙여진 거대한 은하 성단인데 이 성단은 별빛의 방향을 변경시킨다. 은하 성단은 주변의 빛을 휘어지게 함으로써 멀리 있는 물체가 보이도록 하는 확대경과 같은 역할을 한다. 빛이 어떻게 이 우주의 렌즈 주변에서 휠 수 있는가에는 세 가지 요소에 달려 있다. 그것은 물체의 거리와 은하 성단의 질량, 부근에 있는 암흑에너지의 분포이다. 그리고 끊임없는 팽창으로 예상되는 우주의 운명을 밝혀내는 것이 암흑 에너지의 존재이다. 과학자들은 암흑에너지는 우주의 팽창을 촉진하는 신비한 힘으로 우주를 차갑고 생명력 없는 불모지로 만든다고 한다. 암흑에너지는 전혀 볼 수 없지만, 우리는 아벨 1689와 같은 간접적인 증거를 통해서 그곳에 암흑에너지가 있다는 것을 알고 있다.

(a) 우주는 아마도 영원히 팽창할 것이다
(b) 우주는 암흑에너지 없이도 팽창할 것이다
(c) 미래에 우주가 사라질 것이다
(d) 암흑에너지는 우주에 항상 존재할 것이다

천문학자들이 허블 망원경을 이용해서 무엇을 알아냈는가에 대한 내용이다. 은하 성단 부근에 존재하는 암흑에너지가 우주의 팽창을 촉진해서 결국 우주가 황폐해 질 것이라는 내용이 있으므로 (b)와 (d)는 제외되고, (c)는 지문에 없는 내용이다. 따라서 정답은 (a)이다.

astronomer 천문학자 **galactic** 은하계의 **distort** 뒤틀다 **magnifying glass** 확대경 **cosmic cluster** 은하 성단 **in the vicinity** ~의 부근에 **incessant** 끊임없는 **expedite** 촉진시키다

8

이렇게 급변하는 사회에서 만성 피로는 현대인들이 당면하고 있는 공공의 적이다. 이 질병과 싸우는 데 도움이 되려면 반드시 옳은 식단을 선택해야 한다. 그러면 옳은 식단이란 무엇인가? 바로 **알칼리성 식단이다.** 인간의 신체는 약 75%가 물로 구성되어 있고 우리의 식단은 산성이 높거나 알칼리성이 높을 수 있다. 산성 식품은 물에 분해되지만 몸에 축적될 수 있는 '산성 잔여물'을 남김으로써 신체 기능을 저하시킨다. 하지만 알칼리성 식품은 물에 쉽게 용해되고 혈류에 신속하게 흡수되므로 신체가 최적의 기능을 발휘할 수 있도록 돕는다. 불행히도 서구 사회의 평균적인 식단은 골다공증과 심장 마비와 같은 여러 가지 건강 문제를 야기하는 높은 수준의 산을 생성한다. 산과 알칼리의 최적 균형을 유지하기 위해서는 식단의 알칼리 수준을 높이라고 권장할 만하다.

(a) 산이 풍부한 식단
(b) 서구 식단
(c) 균형 잡힌 식단
(d) 알칼리 식단

산성 식품은 신체의 기능을 저하시키고 여러 가지 질병을 유발시키는 반면, 알칼리 식품은 신체가 최적의 기능을 발휘할 수 있도록 돕는다는 내용이 있으므로 정답은 (d)이다. (c)의 균형 잡힌 식단도 옳은 식단이나 지문의 요지와 무관한 내용이므로 정답에서 제외된다.

fast-paced 급변하는 **chronic** 만성의 **fatigue** 피로 **acidic** 산성의 **residue** 잔여물 **accumulate** 축적 **dissolve** 용해하다 **absorb** 흡수하다 **osteoporosis** 골다공증 **optimum** 최적의 **alkaline** 알칼리성의 **recommendable** 권장할 만한

9

지도자란 따를 모범이자 귀 기울일 조언자이다. 그렇다면 사람들이 따르는 지도자의 자질은 무엇인가? 훌륭한 지도자는 자신이 속한 조직의 성공 요구를 충족시키기 위해서 **다음 특성을 지녀야 한다.** 우선, 지도자는 사람들이 자신에게 기대하는 바에 있어서 유능해야 한다. 유능함은 업무를 훌륭히 해내어 사람들이 따르도록 만드는 것이다. 또 다른 지도력의 면모는 의사소통이다. 능력 있는 지도자는 자신의 의견을 효율적으로 전달해서 부하들을 잘 이해하도록 하는 것뿐만이 아니다. 훌륭한 지도자는 또한 강한 목적의식을 가져야 한다. 어떤 지도자는 냉정하고 거리가 있는 것 같아 보일 수 있지만, 그의 목적이 정직하고 진실하다면 사람들이 여전히 따를 것이다. 세상에는 좋은 사람들이 많이 있지만, 위에서 언급한 자질이 있는 사람이 능력 있는 지도자가 되기에 적합하다.

(a) 부하들을 현명하게 훈련시켜야 한다
(b) 장애물을 신중하게 피해야 한다
(c) 다음의 특성을 지녀야 한다
(d) 인간적으로 많은 신뢰를 받아야 한다

훌륭한 지도자의 자질을 묻고 있는 지문이다. 빈칸 뒤에는 지도자는 유능함, 의사소통 능력, 강한 목적의식, 진실성을 갖추어야 한다는 내용이 나오므로 정답은 (c)이다.

quality 자질 **entice** 유인하다 **organization** 조직 **competent** 유능한 **subordinate** 부하 **transmit** 전달하다 **attribute** 자질

10

철인 경기 참가를 준비하면서 **전반적인 목적의식을 잃게** 만드는 경기 전 초조함이 있으면 안 되니 몇 가지를 명심해야 한다. 마지막 주는 무엇보다도 왜 이 운동을 좋아하는지 스스로 상기하는 시간이다. 철인 3종 경기가 제공하는 극기, 즉 육체적 훈련과 전 세계 멋진 장소를 방문할 수 있는 기회, 참가 선수들과 쌓는 우정 때문에 철인 3종 경기에 끌렸을지도 모른다. 그 다음, 목표를 정하라. 경기를 완주하는 것은 항상 중요하다. 그러고 나서 자신의 개인 기록을 갱신하는 것과 같은 두 번째 목표를 정하라. 또한, 경기를 할 때까지 훈련에서의 일관성과 집중은 필수다. 철인 경기는 장애물을 극복하는 것이 전부인 경기이며, 투지를 가진다면 해법을 찾아 결승선까지 도달할 것이다.

(a) 경기를 시작하기도 전에 부상을 입는다
(b) 전반적인 목적의식을 잃는다
(c) 철인 경기를 성공적으로 마치는 데 더할 나위 없이 적합하다
(d) 경기에서 경쟁하겠다는 동기를 솟구치게 만든다

경기 전 초조함 때문에 목적의식을 잃는 문제를 방지하기 위해 경기 전 명심해야 하는 몇 가지를 알려주고 있다. 경기에 앞서 철인 경기를 좋아하는 이유와 목표를 세우라고 조언하고 있는 것으로 보아 (b)가 답이다.

keep in mind ~을 명심하다   **jitter** 초조   **triathlon** 철인 3종 경기   **discipline** 극기   **beat one's own personal record** 개인 기록을 갱신하다   **consistency** 일관성   **determination** 투지

02 중간 빈칸 채우기   p.59

1 (d)	**2** (d)	**3** (a)	**4** (b)	**5** (a)
6 (c)	**7** (b)	**8** (c)	**9** (a)	**10** (c)

1

어떻게 이민자들을 외국 생활에 순응시킬지에 대해 '용광로'와 '모자이크'라 불리는 대조적인 두 이데올로기가 부상했다. 미국은 용광로를 고수하는 **반면** 캐나다는 모자이크 접근 방식을 따른다고 한다. 용광로 이데올로기에 따르면 언어를 포함한 민족 특유의 관습과 풍습을 버림으로써 이민자들은 사회 주류에 융화하기를 시도해야 한다. 이와 대조적으로, 모자이크 이데올로기는 이민자들이 민족적 정체성을 사회에서 다른 민족과 통합하면서 유지하도록 장려한다.

(a) 그렇기는 해도
(b) 비록 ~일지라도
(c) 사실상
(d) 반면

이민에 대한 미국의 접근 방식과 캐나다의 접근 방식을 대조하여 설명하고 있다. 두 가지를 비교 대조할 때 쓰는 접속사인 whereas가 빈칸에 적절하므로 정답은 (d)이다.

acclimate 순응시키다   **emerge** 부상하다   **melting pot** 용광로   **adhere to** ~을 고수하다   **relinquish** 포기하다   **distinctive** 독특한   **ethnic** 민족의   **blend into** ~와 뒤섞이다   **mainstream** 주류   **integrate** 통합시키다

2

튼튼한 600D 나일론으로 제조된, 보통 고가의 제품에서 볼 수 있는 내구성이 더해진 새로운 컨퍼런스용 가방 세트는 굉장한 기능성이 특징입니다. 주요 수납공간의 밸크로 잠금**뿐만 아니라** 튼튼한 손잡이와 추가 지퍼 주머니가 있는 이 가방은 여러 가지 용도로 사용될 수 있기 때문에 확실히 긍정적인 측면에서 귀하의 브랜드를 나타내 줍니다. 오늘 이런 종류의 선물을 제공하는 최고 회사 대열에 합류하세요!

(a) ~없이
(b) ~에 관하여
(c) ~에 대하여
(d) ~뿐만 아니라

컨퍼런스용 가방은 회의 자료나 기업 안내 책자 등을 담아 회의 참가자들에게 나눠 주는 가방을 말한다. 새로운 컨퍼런스 가방의 특징과 관련 정보를 계속 나열하고 있으므로 빈칸에는 (d)가 가장 적절하다.

manufacture 제조하다   **rugged** 튼튼한, 질긴   **durability** 내구성   **feature** ~을 특징으로 하다   **tremendous** 굉장한   **functionality** 기능성   **compartment** 수납공간   **sturdy** 튼튼한, 견고한   **rank** 대열   **top notch** 최고의

3

시장에서 신선하고 잘 익은 배를 고르는 데 어려움을 겪은 적이 있었나요? 만약 그런 경험이 있다면, 배를 사러 갈 때 유용한 조언에 주의를 기울이고 싶을 것입니다. 우선 배는 쉽게 멍이 드는 과일이고, 나무에서 완전히 익기 전에 수확해야 합니다. 따라서 찍힌 자국, 상처 또는 멍 등이 없는 배를 구입해야 한다는 것을 항상 기억할 필요가 있습니다. 또한 색이 너무 짙지 않고, 꽤 단단한 배를 구하도록 하십시오. **이제 집에서 배를 익히고 싶다면**, 배를 사과나 오렌지와 같은 과일과 함께 통기 구멍을 몇 개 낸 상자에 담아서 보관해야 합니다. 다른 과일에서 나오는 에틸렌 가스는 숙성 과정을 도울 것입니다. 상자를 며칠간 실온에 둘 수 있습니다. 배가 먹기 좋은지의 여부는 꼭지 부위 근처에 매끄러움과 부드러움으로 알 수 있습니다. 이러한 점만 유념한다면, 가정에서 신선한 배를 즐길 수 있을 것입니다.

(a) 이제 집에서 배를 익히고 싶다면
(b) 비록 배가 이미 익었더라도
(c) 수확된 배는 빨리 숙성되기 때문에
(d) 과일의 변색을 방지하기 위해

빈칸 뒤에는 완전히 익지 않은 배를 다른 과일과 함께 상자에 보관하라는 숙성 방법이 소개되고 있으며, 이러한 점만 유념하면 가정에서 신선한 배를 즐길 수 있다는 마지막 문장의 내용으로 보아 정답은 (a)이다.

bruise 멍들다   **ventilation hole** 통기 구멍   **ethylene** 에틸렌   **room temperature** 실온

4

지금까지 발견된 행성이 많은 태양계 중 하나에서 글리저 581g라고 명명된 새로운 행성이 천문학자들에 의해서 발견되었다. 우선 새로 발견된 행성은 우리 지구보다 3배 또는 4배 질량이 무거운데, 이는 생물체가 살 수 있는 단단한 표면이 있을 가능성을 시사한다. **더욱 중요한 사실은** 이 행성이 환경이 알맞은 구역 한가운데에 위치해 있다는 것인데, 이는 물이 얼거나 끓어서 사라지지 않고 액체 형태로 남을 수 있을 정도로 항성에서 적당히 떨어진 거리에서 궤도를 돌고 있다는 것을 의미한다. 우리가 아는 한 그것은 생물체를 존속시키는 데 필요한 최소 조건이다. 수세기 동안 과학자들은 지구와 같은 또 다른 행성의 존재 가능성을 상상해 왔고 그 어느 때보다 가능성에 가까워지고 있었다. 분명히 과학자들은 마침내 가능성이 큰 행성을 찾은 것이다.

(a) 대조되는 점은
(b) 더욱 중요한 사실은
(c) 기이한 현상은
(d) 이에 대한 설명은

빈칸 앞에는 새로 발견된 행성이 생물체가 살 수 있을 조건을 갖추었을 정도라고 하며 빈칸 뒤에는 관련 내용이 이어지고 있으므로 문맥상 내용을 더 강조하는 연결 어구가 적합하다. 따라서 정답은 (b)이다.

populous 개체수가 많은 solar system 태양계 designate 명명하다 orbit 궤도를 돌다 hospitable 환경이 알맞은 boil away 끓어서 사라지다 the minimum 최소 조건

5

1형이든 2형이든 당뇨병 진단을 받았다면, 혈당을 낮추는 방법을 찾는 것의 중요성을 반드시 알아야 한다. 약물 치료는 혈중 당 수치를 효과적으로 낮추는 데 도움이 된다. 그러나 최선의 방법은 자연적인 방법을 통하는 것이고 이 방법은 사용하기 쉽다. 혈당 수치에 큰 영향을 미치는 가장 중요한 요인은 사람들의 먹거리이다. 섭취하는 음식에는 풍부한 섬유질, 소량의 포화 지방, 더 적은 양의 당이 함유되어야 한다. 식사 간격 및 섭취량도 당 수치에 영향을 미친다. **구체적으로 말하자면** 하루에 많은 양을 세 번 먹는 것보다 소량을 5~6회 먹는 것이 낫다. 하루에 소량씩 먹는 것은 소화액을 조절하는 데 도움이 되며, 이는 혈당을 낮추는 좋은 방법이다. 운동 역시 혈당을 낮추는 좋은 방법인데 이것은 지방을 연소하고 인슐린에 대한 몸의 민감도를 증가시킨다. 이것은 몸이 당 수치를 낮추는 데 필요한 인슐린 덜 필요하다는 의미이다. 당뇨병과의 싸움은 긴 싸움이며, 당뇨병 환자들은 최선의 방법을 이해함으로써 건강하게 오래 살 수 있다.

(a) 구체적으로 말하자면
(b) 대조적으로
(c) 게다가
(d) 이런 사실에 비추어 보아

빈칸 앞에서는 당뇨병 치료에 있어서 먹거리, 식사 간격 및 섭취량의 중요성에 대해서 설명하고 있다. 빈칸 뒤에서는 혈당 감소를 위한 식사 방법을 좀 더 자세하게 설명하고 있으므로 정답은 (a)이다.

diagnose 진단하다 diabetes 당뇨병 blood sugar 혈당 ingest 섭취하다 digestive system 소화기 계통 intake 섭취하다 medication 약물 치료 digestive juice 소화액

6

제1차 세계 대전의 종전과 더불어 경제적 정치적 보수주의에 대한 미국인들의 욕구가 1920년 워렌 G. 하딩의 대통령 선출에 반영되었다. 하딩이 임기를 시작한 후, 의회는 관세법을 통과시켰는데 이는 수입에 대한 평균 관세를 거의 40% 인상시킬 것이다. 외교 정책에 관한 한, 하딩은 강경한 고립주의 입장을 고수했고 해외에 대한 미국의 영향력을 줄이고자 했다. **예를 들어**, 그는 1922년에 태평양에 있어서 미국과 영국, 일본의 해군 함선을 제한하는 5개 강대국 해군 조약을 감독했다. 같은 해 미국은 태평양에서의 현상 유지를 보장하기 위해서 4개 강대국 조약에 서명했다. 하딩의 대내외 정책은 이전의 행정부가 수립해 놓은 진보적인 법안의 잔재를 완전히 없애는 데 많은 역할을 했다.

(a) 그러나
(b) 또한
(c) 예를 들어
(d) 틀림없이

빈칸 앞은 외교 정책에 관한 한 하딩이 고립주의 입장을 고수해서 미국의 대외 영향력을 줄이고자 했다는 내용이고, 빈칸 뒤에는 이러한 정책의 일환으로 미국이 다른 국가들과 체결한 조약들이 열거되어 있다. 따라서 정답은 (c)이다.

conservatism 보수주의 reflect 반영하다 tariff 관세 foreign policy 외교 정책 stance 입장 oversee 감독하다 naval 해군의 status quo 현상 유지 administration 행정부

7

전 직원 여러분께
1월 9일부터 올더스는 연차 휴가에 관한 당사의 방침 수정을 실시하게 됨을 알려 드립니다. 매년 각 부서의 직원 1명에게 뛰어난 업무 성과에 대한 포상으로 연차 보너스 휴가가 주어집니다. 해당 직원들은 1월 9일에 연차 휴가 5일을 추가로 받게 됩니다. 총 연차 휴가 일수에 대한 제한 **에도 불구하고** 보너스 휴가는 사용할 때까지 유용합니다. 당사는 12월 15일 오전 10시에 회의를 열어서 금년도 업무 평가 결과를 논의하고, 보너스를 받을 자격이 있는 최종 직원 명단을 발표할 것입니다. 질문이나 의견이 있으시면 회의 전에 제게 알려 주시기 바랍니다.
제럴드 에반스 상무

(a) 게다가
(b) 그럼에도 불구하고
(c) 결과적으로
(d) 제외하고

부서별로 우수한 성과를 낸 직원 1명에게 추가로 5일의 연차 보너스 휴가를 준다는 회사의 변경된 방침을 알리는 내용이다. 빈칸 뒤의 총 연차 휴가 일수 제한에 관한 내용과 보너스 휴가는 사용할 때까지 유용하다는 내용의 관계를 파악해 보면 정답은 (b)이다.

implement 실행[실시]하다 amendment 수정 with regard to ~에 관해서 annual leave 연차 휴가 performance 성과 eligible 자격이 있는 evaluation 평가 comment 의견

8

루나 르코네상스 오비터 카메라의 고해상도 영상이 달 표면에 걸쳐서 가해지는 지질적 압력에 의해 유발되는 일련의 단층선을 드러냈다. 열편 모양의 절벽으로도 알려진 14개의 단층선이 영상에 포착되었다. 호주 행성 과학 연구소의 전문가에 따르면, 단층선의 구조가 달이 축소와 연관된 지질적 압력을 받고 있다는 것이 분명하게 입증되고 있다. 달의 열편 모양의 절벽은 도장칠을 한 풍선이 칠이 마른 후 점차 바람이 빠지는 형태로 이해될 수 있다. **바람이 빠지면** 마른 칠에 금이 가고 풍선은 쪼글쪼글해진다. 이것이 단층선 절벽에 나타나고 있는 것이다. 달의 축소 현상은 40억년 이전에 달이 용융된 상태로 생겨난 이후로 서서히 식어가는 것으로 볼 수 있다.

(a) 풍선이 터질 때
(b) 칠이 완전히 마르기 전에
(c) 바람이 빠지면
(d) 풍선이 작아지면서

달에 있는 열편 모양의 절벽과 페인트칠을 한 풍선이 바람이 빠지면서 발생하는 균열을 비교하고 있는 내용이다. 따라서 정답은 (c)이다. 풍선이 작아지면서 칠이 마르는 것이 아니라 칠이 마른 후 바람이 빠지는 것이기 때문에 (d)는 답이 될 수 없다.

high resolution 고해상도 reveal 드러내다 fault line 단층선 induce 유발하다 exert 가하다 capture 포착하다 lobate scarp 열편 모양의 절벽 deflate 공기가 빠지다 phenomenon 현상

9

어떤 사람들은 수년간 불안과 공황 발작으로 고통 받고 있는데, 첫 번째 증상은 아마도 불쑥 경고가 거의 없거나 전혀 없는 상태에서 와서 자신에게 무슨 일이 일어났는지 의아할 것이다. 이러한 장애와 싸우려면 불안 발작의 원인을 밝혀내고 불안 발작을 야기하는 증상을 이해해야 한다. 한 가지 확실한 원인은 아마 모든 원인의 어미 격인 스트레스이다. **사실** 약간의 스트레스는 도움이 되지만, 장래성이 없는 직업이나 가까운 사람의 죽음과 같은 심각한 스트레스 요인은 공황 발작을 촉발시킬 수 있다. 스테로이드제나 항우울제와 같은 일부 약물이 이러한 발작을 초래한다고 알려져 있으므로 이러한 약물을 복용하기 전에 의사와 상의해야 한다. 불안 발작의 몇 가지 공통적인 증상으로는 심박과 호흡 횟수의 급격한 상승, 동공 확장, 헐떡거림, 몸의 떨림 등이 있다. 다른 원인과 증상이 있지만, 가장 중요한 것은 발작이 일어나기까지의 순간과 일어나고 있는 동안 무슨 일이 일어나고 있는지를 인지하는 것이다.

(a) 사실
(b) 앞으로
(c) ~이긴 하지만
(d) 비록 ~이기는 하나

빈칸 앞의 문장에서 불안과 공황 발작의 원인 중 하나가 스트레스이며 스트레스 강도에 따른 영향을 소개하고 있으므로 (a)가 가장 자연스럽다.

attack 발작 **blue** 우울증 **symptom** 증상 **stressor** 스트레스 요인 **trigger** 촉발시키다 **dead-end** 장래성이 없는 **antidepressants** 항우울제 **respiratory** 호흡의 **dilation** 팽창 **pupil** 눈동자

10

사회주의자이자 민족주의자인 호치민은 제2차 세계 대전 당시 베트민 혹은 베트남 독립 연맹을 창설할 수 있는 기회를 잡았다. 전쟁 중 독일이 프랑스를 침공했을 때 일본은 1940년에서 1945년까지 베트남을 점령했다. 이때가 호치민이 일본의 침략을 모든 베트남 사회에 호소력을 가지는 새로운 민족주의 군사력을 증강할 기회로 사용했던 시기이다. **그 결과**, 호치민은 1941년 베트민을 세웠다. 당시 미국은 제2차 세계 대전에서 일본과 전쟁을 했기 때문에 호치민은 새로운 일본 억압자들을 몰아낼 수 있도록 베트민이 비밀리에 무기를 갖추게 해 달라고 미국 지도자들을 설득할 수 있었다. 이때가 호치민이 휘하의 장군 보응우옌잡에게 게릴라 전술을 채택해서 성공적으로 일본군과 대항해 싸울 수 있도록 조언을 했던 시기이다. 전쟁 내내 베트민은 통킹과 안남에서 성공적으로 세력 기반을 확장했고 베트남 국민들로부터 엄청난 인기를 얻었다.

(a) 그럼에도 불구하고
(b) 놀랍게도
(c) 그 결과
(d) 예를 들면

빈칸 앞에 있는 문장에는 호치민이 일본의 침략을 베트남 사회에 호소력을 가지는 새로운 민족주의 군사력을 증강할 기회로 이용했던 시기에 대한 언급이 있고, 빈칸 뒤의 문장에 호치민이 1941년에 베트민을 세웠다는 내용이 있으므로 두 문장의 관계는 원인과 결과이다. 따라서 정답은 (c)이다.

socialist 사회주의자 **grab** 손에 쥐다 **occupy** 점령하다 **appeal** 호소하다 **convince** 설득하다 **drive out** 몰아내다 **guerilla tactic** 게릴라 전술 **power base** 세력 기반

| 1 (c) | 2 (a) | 3 (b) | 4 (a) | 5 (d) |
| 6 (b) | 7 (c) | 8 (d) | 9 (a) | 10 (b) |

1

경제 불황에도 불구하고 사탕 산업의 매출과 인기는 상승하고 있다. 경제는 제과 산업에 불리하게 작용했을지 모르나, 사실 이윤 증가를 가져왔다. 2017년 초콜릿 매출은 800억 달러를 약간 밑돌았다. 모든 종류의 초콜릿 매출이 2016년에서 2017년 사이에 증가했고, 앞으로도 다시 증가할 것으로 기대된다. 2016년 비초콜릿 사탕 산업의 매출은 450억 달러인 반면, 2017년에는 490억 달러에 육박했다. 이런 상승 추세는 앞으로 몇 년간은 계속될 것이라 예상된다. 의심할 여지없이 제과 산업은 앞으로 수년간 성공적일 것으로 기대할 수 있다. 사탕 도매업과 사탕 상점은 **신규 업체들의 시장 진입에도 불구하고** 여전히 강세를 보일 것이다.

(a) 신규 업체들이 시장에 진입하기 때문에
(b) 신규 업체들이 시장에 진입한 후
(c) 신규 업체들의 시장 진입에도 불구하고
(d) 신규 업체들이 시장에 있는 한

지문은 불경기에도 불구하고 사탕 산업과 제과업이 성장하고 있다는 내용이다. 신규 업체들이 시장에 진입하면 기존 업체의 매출이 감소하는 것이 보통이지만 사탕 도매업과 사탕 상점이 계속 강세를 보일 것으로 전망하고 있다. 따라서 정답은 (c)이다.

confectionery 과자류 **recession** 불경기 **popularity** 인기 **without a doubt** 확실히 **despite** ~에도 불구하고

2

제1차 세계 대전을 촉발한 바로 그 사건은 우연한 일의 결과였다. 1914년 6월 28일, 오스트리아의 대공 프란츠 페르디난드와 부인이 공식적인 방문으로 보스니아 헤르체코비나의 도시인 사라예보에 가고 있었다. 오스트리아-헝가리 제국으로부터 독립하고자 싸우고 있던 세르비아 과격 단체는 방문 기간 동안 대공의 암살을 계획했다. 그가 사라예보에 도착했을 때, 과격 단체가 대공의 차에 폭탄을 던졌지만, 폭탄이 차를 맞고 튕겨 나가 계획은 무산되었다. 그날 늦게, 대공은 앞서 있던 공격에서 부상을 입은 장교를 방문하기 위해 병원으로 가는 동안 그날 아침 암살 시도에 참가했던 19살의 보스니아계 세르비아인 가브릴로 프린치프가 마침 그곳에 있게 되었다. 기회를 잡은 프린치프는 차로 다가가 바로 대공 대공과 부인에게 총을 쐈다. 아마도 역사상 가장 비극적인 사건 중 하나가 **약간의 운만 있었다면 피할 수 있었던** 것을 보는 일은 매우 흥미로운 동시에 불행한 일이다.

(a) 약간의 운만 있었다면 피할 수 있었던
(b) 치밀한 계획을 통해 일어났던
(c) 인간의 탐욕 때문에 발생할 수밖에 없었던
(d) 자유를 향한 오도된 투쟁에 의해 유발되었던

제1차 세계 대전을 촉발시킨 원인에 관한 지문으로 계획된 사건이 아닌 우연에 의한 사건으로 비극이 발생했고, 전쟁도 일어났다는 내용이다. 따라서 정답은 (a)이다.

incident 사건   spark 촉발시키다   chance happening 우연한 사건
archduke 대공[왕자]   militant 과격 단체   assassinate 암살하다
officer 장교   point-blank 매우 가까운 거리에서

3

감사의 표현은 전 세계적으로 성공한 사람들의 두드러진 특징이다. 그렇
다면 이것이 그렇게 중요한 이유는 무엇인가? 크고 작은 인생사에 고마
워하는 사람들은 삶에 대해 잘못된 것보다는 무엇이 옳은가에 초점을 맞
춘다. 결국 사람은 자신들이 종일 생각한 대로 된다. 다시 말해 사람들이
정신적으로 자주 생각하는 대상은 그들의 삶에서 끌어들이는 것들이다.
따라서 감사의 이유가 된 대상에 의식적으로 집중하는 법을 배우면, 그것
을 많이 얻게 된다. 게다가 감사하는 사람은 다른 사람들의 어려움을 이
해하고 웃으며 도와준다. 그래서 그들의 축복이 이웃의 축복이 되는 것이
다. 에이브러햄 링컨은 "자신의 짐을 함께 덜지 않으면서 다른 사람의 짐
을 덜어주는 것은 가능하지 않다."라고 말했다. 성공적이고 기뻐하는 사람
은 **축복을 헤아리는 데 매우 능숙하므로** 더 많은 축복을 삶에 끌어들인다.

(a) 인생에서 대단한 일의 진가를 알지 못하는
(b) 축복을 헤아리는 데 매우 능숙한
(c) 자기 자신에게만 감사하는
(d) 인생에 있어서 가지고 있는 것을 염두에 두지 않는

살면서 크고 작은 일에 감사하는 사람들은 긍정적인 자세로 남을 이해하고
도우면서 성공한다는 것이 지문의 요지이다. 따라서 성공적이고 기뻐하는 사
람들이 더 많은 축복을 자신들의 삶에 끌어들이므로 정답은 (b)이다.

characteristic 특징   focus on 집중하다   dwell on 숙고하다
blessing 축복   burden 짐, 부담   lift 들어내다   conjointly 공동으로

4

생물의 다양성을 연구하는 연구원들의 새로운 논문은 조류가 우리에게
에너지를 공급하는 미래의 가능성을 탐구한다. 전문가들에 의하면 조류
에는 연료로 채취할 수 있는 커다란 잠재력이 있다. 일반적으로 조류는
박테리아나 효모보다 낮은 밀집도로 자라지만, 성장률은 박테리아나 효
모보다 훨씬 우수하다. 이러한 특징이 이 생물의 기름 생산 능력을 향상
시킨다. 더욱이 기름을 얻기 위한 일반적인 씨앗 작물보다 최소한 10배
이상의 기름을 조류에서 수확할 수 있다. 게다가 이산화탄소와 폐수와 같
은 환경 폐기물을 먹으며 자랄 수 있다. 조류를 이용한 연료 생산 공정이
개발되면, **조류는 가장 널리 사용되는 친환경 에너지원이 될 것이다.**

(a) 조류는 가장 널리 사용되는 친환경 에너지 원천이 될 것이다.
(b) 세계 대부분 지역에서 기름이 고갈될 것이다.
(c) 세계는 조류가 만들어 내는 오염 물질과 싸워야 할 것이다.
(d) 비산유국에서 조류에 대한 수요가 급증할 것이다.

지문의 요지는 조류가 연료로써 커다란 잠재력을 가지고 있고 친환경적이
라는 것이다. 빈칸 앞에서 조류가 폐수와 같은 환경 폐기물을 이용해서 성
장할 수 있다고 하므로 정답은 (a)이다.

biodiversity 생물 다양성   algae 조류   potential 잠재력   yeast
효모   enhance 개선하다   waste 폐기물   eco-friendly 친환경적인
energy source 에너지원

5

여성의 심장병 징후를 아는 것은 특히 심장 질환을 앓고 있는 부인을 둔
남편이라면 더욱 중요하다. 문제는 여성에게 나타나는 심장병의 징후가
남성에게 나타나는 것과 다르다는 것이다. 남녀 모두에게서 가장 흔히 나
타나는 심장 마비의 증상은 흉부 내 가벼운 통증이다. 하지만 이 증상이
특히 여성에게 있어서 심각한 심장 상태를 항상 나타내는 것은 아니다.
가슴 통증 외에, 여성에게 심장 마비가 일어나기 전에 흔히 겪는 증상에
는 현기증, 호흡 곤란, 구토 또는 메스꺼움, 피로, 발한 또는 어깨, 목, 배
또는 허리 윗부분을 포함한 신체 부분 통증이 있다. 하지만 여성에 있어
서 이러한 심장 마비 징후는 찌르는 듯한 가슴 통증보다 더 억제된다. 이
것은 여성의 대동맥뿐만 아니라 작은 동맥이 막혀 있기 때문일 수도 있
다. 이러한 심장병의 징후를 알면 심장 마비나 뇌졸중과 같이 심각한 심
장 질환이 **일어나는 것을 방지할 수** 있다.

(a) 치료하고 고치다
(b) 증상을 피한다
(c) 결과를 알아채다
(d) 발생을 방지하다

여성의 심장 마비의 사전 징후를 알아야 한다는 내용이다. 심장병의 징후를
알면 심장 마비나 뇌졸중과 같이 심각한 심장 질환 예방에 도움이 된다는
것을 예상할 수 있다. 따라서 정답은 (d)이다.

discomfort 가벼운 통증   dizziness 현기증   vomiting 구토   nausea
메스꺼움   fatigue 피로   abdomen 배   restrain 억제하다   stab 찌르다
artery 동맥   incidence (사건의) 발생   restrained 막힌   stabbing 찌르
는 듯한   blockage 장애물, 폐색

6

1947년 국무부 분석가 조지 F. 케넌은 마침내 소비에트 연방의 공산주
의 확산을 막는 미국의 봉쇄 정책의 근간이 되었던 화합하는 외교 정책의
개요를 제시하는 데 도움을 주었다. 케넌에 따르면, 소비에트 연방은 이
웃 국가를 정복하거나, 정치적인 격동을 겪는 나라에서 공산주의 혁명을
몰래 도움으로써 전 세계 구석구석에 공산주의를 확산시키기 위한 기회
를 잡으려 했다는 것이다. 공산주의의 세계 지배를 방지하기 위해서 미국
은 봉쇄 전략을 채택할 수 있었다. 케넌에 따르면, 영토의 현상 유지를 위
해 미국은 해외에서 공산주의 공격을 좌절시켜야 했다는 것이다. 케넌의
아이디어는 빠르게 인기를 얻었고 1990년대 초반에 냉전이 끝날 때까지
공산주의를 저지하는 전략으로 사용되었다.

(a) 전 세계에 민주주의를 교육하다
(b) 공산주의를 저지하다
(c) 공산주의 혁명론자들을 전향시키다
(d) 정치적으로 불안정한 나라들을 봉쇄하다

지문은 냉전 시대에 소련의 공산주의 확장을 막기 위해서 미국이 채택했던
케넌의 정책에 관한 것이다. 미국이 무슨 목적으로 냉전이 끝날 때까지 케넌
의 생각을 전략으로 이용했는가를 묻는 문제이므로 정답은 (b)이다.

sketch 개요를 제시하다   cohesive 화합하는   containment 봉쇄
ward off 막다   conquer 정복하다   turbulent 격동의   domination
지배   communism 공산주의   aggression 공격   catch on 인기를 얻다
convert 전향시키다

7

〈사회적 유동성에 있어 고등 교육의 역할〉이라는 논문에서 저자들은 대부분의 미국인이 강한 동기와 충분한 능력을 가진 사람은 누구나 성공적으로 미국 대학교에 간다는 생각을 믿는데 이는 연구가 시사하는 바와 완전히 다르다고 한다. 고등 교육에의 접근과 성공 측면에서 소득 관련 격차는 커지고 있다. 자격이 있는 젊은이 집단은 입학 허가를 받고 등록할 수 있는 수를 훨씬 능가하는데, 이는 대학이 <u>학생 집단의 질을 떨어뜨리지</u> 않으면서 등록을 늘리는 것이 가능할 것이라는 것을 의미한다.

(a) 그들의 긍정적인 행동 기록에 흠집 내기
(b) 보호 집단을 목표로 하기
(c) 학생 집단의 질을 떨어뜨리기
(d) 약화된 유형 만들기

마지막 문장을 보면 충분한 자격을 가진 젊은이가 대학교에 입학할 수 있는 수보다 훨씬 많으므로 대학에서는 더 많은 학생을 입학시켜도 등록한 학생들의 질이 떨어지지 않을 것이라고 유추할 수 있다. 따라서 정답은 (c)이다.

social mobility 사회적 유동성[이동성]   **state** 말하다   **notion** 생각
sufficient 충분한   **convey** 시사하다   **balloon** 커지다   **pool** 집단
blemish 흠집을 내다   **affirmative** 긍정의   **dilute** 약화시키다

8

속독은 본문의 일부만을 읽고 본문 전체를 읽고 이해하는 능력이다. 속독자가 되기 원하는 사람에게 먼저 다음과 같은 전략을 연습할 것을 일반적으로 권장하고 있다. 우선 독자는 단어에 있는 몇 개의 문자만으로 단어를 인지할 수 있는 방법을 배운다. 예를 들어, control은 cntrl, expert는 exprt, reader는 rdr 등이 될 수 있다. 또 다른 방법은 문장을 연결하는 단어들을 무시하는 것이다. 예를 들자면, but, the, which 같은 단어는 문맥이나 이해력에 영향을 주지 않고도 무시할 수 있다. 모든 종류의 독서에 있어서 독해력은 중요하며 속독 또한 예외가 아니다. 따라서 읽는 속도가 빨라질수록 속독자가 더 많은 정보를 보유하는 것이 매우 중요하다. 위에서 언급한 전략들은 <u>완전 초보 독자가</u> 속독과 독해력에 대한 전문 기술을 <u>획득하기 위한 첫걸음을 내딛는 데</u> 도움이 될 것이다.

(a) 초보 독자를 가르치는 데에 도움을 준다
(b) 중요성을 이해하는 것을 돕는다
(c) 아마추어 독자가 배우는 것을 방해한다
(d) 완전 초보 독자가 획득하기 위한 첫걸음을 내딛기 시작한다

속독과 독해력을 위한 전략을 소개하고 있다. (a)와 (c)의 내용처럼 속독에 대한 전문 기술 자체를 초보 독자에게 가르치거나, 아마추어 독자가 이를 배우는 것을 방해하거나 또는 (b)의 내용처럼 속독의 중요성에 대한 이해를 돕기 위한 것과는 거리가 멀다. 지문은 속독하는 방법을 설명하는 내용이므로 정답은 (d)이다.

speed reading 속독   **context** 문맥   **crucial** 결정적인   **retain** 보유하다
aforementioned 앞서 말한   **expertise** 전문 지식   **novice** 초보자
brand-new 완전 초보의

9

가로등 시스템은 도시 조명의 필수 부분 중 하나이다. 중국의 여러 대도시에서는 전통적인 가로등이 LED조명으로 교체될 예정이라고 하는데, 그 이유는 LED조명이 전통적인 가로등에 비해서 많은 장점이 있기 때문이다. 우선, LED조명은 수명이 매우 길다. 금속 할로겐 램프의 수명이

6,000에서 12,000시간인 점에 비해서 LED조명의 수명은 25,000 시간에 이른다. 둘째, LED조명은 구조가 강한 외부 충격으로부터 내부 부품을 보호할 수 있도록 설계되어 있기 때문에 내구성이 있다. 셋째, LED조명은 매우 효율적이고 환경 공해를 유발시키지 않는다. LED조명은 '차가운 조명'이라고 불리는데, 이는 전통적인 전등과 같은 밝기에서 거의 발열을 하지 않는다는 것을 의미한다. 마지막이지만 역시 중요한 것인 LED의 전력 소비량은 상당히 낮다. LED조명은 전통적인 광원보다 전력을 80%이상 절약한다. 전통적인 에너지원이 고갈되고 공해에 대한 규제가 가해지고 있는 상황에서 <u>낮은 전력 소비와 무해한 특성 때문에</u> LED조명에 대한 수요가 증가하고 있다.

(a) 낮은 전력 소비와 무해한 특성 때문에
(b) 구입 가능성과 내구성 때문에
(c) 환경친화적 특성에도 불구하고
(d) 전 세계적으로 오르는 에너지 가격으로

기존의 조명과 비교하여 LED조명의 장점을 열거하면서 에너지 절약과 친환경적인 면을 언급하고 있다. 이와 관련해서 기존의 에너지원이 고갈되고 공해에 대한 규제가 가해지고 있는 상황에서 어떤 점 때문에 LED조명에 대한 수요가 증가하고 있는지를 묻는 문제이므로 정답은 (a)이다.

lifetime 수명   **halide lamp** 할로겐 등   **durable** 내구성이 있는
component 부품   **power consumption** 전력 소비   **deplete**
대폭 감소시키다   **restriction** 규제

10

생후 4개월에서 6개월의 아기들은 배 같이 영양이 풍부한 과일을 섭취해야 한다. 아기에게 유동식보다는 고형식을 더 많이 먹이기 시작할 때가 되면 배와 같은 과일을 먹이는 것이 탁월한 선택이 될 수 있다. 의사와 보육 전문가들은 이런 저알레르기 식품(부작용이나 알레르기를 유발하지 않는 과일)을 권장하고 있다. 배를 선택해야 하는 또 다른 이유는 아기에게 먹이기 전에 과일을 쉽게 조리하거나 찔 수 있기 때문이다. 또한 배는 조리된 형태나 신선한 상태에서 좋은 퓌레를 만들 수 있다. 생후 8개월이 지난 아기라면 찐 과일을 먹이는 것을 권한다. 이는 유아가 배에 들어 있는 당분과 섬유질을 분해하는 데 도움을 줄 것이다. 또한 이 과일은 비타민 A와 비타민 C가 풍부하고 칼륨, 마그네슘, 칼슘과 같은 무기질의 보고이다. 일반적으로 배는 아기들을 위한 <u>건강에 좋고 영양이 풍부한 훌륭한 고형식</u>이 될 수 있다.

(a) 채소와 우유를 대신할 수 있는 영양가 높은 대체 식품
(b) 건강에 좋고 영양이 풍부한 좋은 고형식
(c) 단백질을 공급하는 좋은 보조 음식
(d) 쉽게 삼키고 소화될 수 있는 음식

유동식에서 고형식으로 넘어가는 단계에 있는 아기들을 위해서 배의 장점을 설명하면서 권장하는 내용이다. 이 시기의 아기에게 배가 어떤 음식이 될 수 있는지 이해하면 (b)가 정답임을 알 수 있다.

feed 먹이다   **solid food** 고형식   **hypo allergic** 저알레르기성의
negative effect 부작용   **child care specialist** 보육 전문가
steam 찌다   **puree** 퓌레 (과일이나 삶은 채소를 으깨어 물을 조금 넣고 걸쭉하게 만든 음식)   **potassium** 칼륨   **magnesium** 마그네슘
calcium 칼슘

04 불필요한 문장 고르기 p.71

1 (c)	2 (d)	3 (c)	4 (a)	5 (b)
6 (c)	7 (d)	8 (d)	9 (a)	10 (c)

1

생활 방식 위험이라는 범주로 분류되는 스트레스는 사실 많은 신체적 및 정신적 질병의 근원이다. (a) 스트레스의 신체적 징후 중 하나는 두통의 형태로 오기도 한다. (b) 또는 아마도 당신은 그저 정신과 몸이 최적의 수준에서 업무수행을 하고 있지 않다고 느끼고 있을 수도 있다. (c) 스트레스가 다른 것들뿐만 아니라 이러한 증상의 원인일 수 있지만 누구와 의논을 한다든지 활력을 되찾기 위해 어떤 운동을 하는 것과 같은 스트레스를 해소하기 위한 간단한 방법들이 많이 있다. (d) 스트레스는 그것으로부터 고통 받는 개인을 약화시킬 뿐만 아니라 종종 가족과 가까운 친구들에게도 전염된다.

글의 주 내용은 스트레스가 일으키는 문제를 알리는 것이다. (a), (b), (d)는 이러한 맥락에 비추어 볼 때 일관적이지만, (c)는 스트레스를 관리하는 방법에 대해서 언급하고 있으므로 정답은 (c)이다.

manifestation 징후 **optimal** 최적의 **vent** (감정을) 터뜨리다 **wear down** 약화시키다 **rub off** 옮다, 전염되다

2

시간 생물학자들은 인간의 체내 생체 시계와 우리 건강에 있어 빛과 잠의 영향을 연구한다. (a) 그들은 밤 시간 동안 인공적인 빛에 노출되는 것은 사람들이 더욱 암에 취약하게 만들 수 있음을 알아냈다. (b) 동시에, 사람들이 야외에서 많은 시간을 보내지 않아, 건강한 바이오리듬을 조절하는 데 도움이 되는 햇빛이 몸에서 빠져나가고 있다. (c) 이런 문제들은 사람들이 밤낮으로 하루 종일 일하고 놀 수 있게 하고, 게다가 수면 패턴을 방해하는 새로운 기술들로 인해 악화되고 있다. (d) 유사한 혁신으로 시간 생물학자들은 현대적 생활 방식과 그것들이 삶의 질에 미치는 영향을 연구하고 평가할 수 있다.

빛과 잠이 건강에 미치는 영향을 연구하는 시간 생물학자들이 제시하는 여러 외부 현상으로 인해 나타날 수 있는 문제점들이 나열된 내용으로 볼 때, 문맥상 글의 흐름에 어울리지 않는 문장은 (d)이다.

chronobiologist 시간 생물학자 **internal** 체내의 **body clock** 생체 시계 **exposure** 노출 **artificial** 인공의 **susceptible to** ~에 취약한, 걸리기 쉬운 **regulate** 조절하다 **biorhythms** 바이오리듬, 생체 리듬 **be compounded by** ~로 인해 악화되다, 더 심각해지다 **interrupt** 방해하다 **innovation** 개혁, 혁신 **assess** 평가하다

3

제2차 세계 대전에서의 핵폭탄의 사용은 오랫동안 전 세계적으로 토론과 논쟁의 대상이 되어왔다. (a) 비평가들은 일본이 이미 1945년 여름에 항복할 준비가 되어 있었고 핵폭탄이 수십만의 무고한 민간인들을 비인도적으로 죽였다고 주장한다. (b) 반면, 폭탄 투하를 지지하는 사람들은 이오지마와 오키나와 침략은 일본 군대가 항복할 의사가 없었고 어마어마한 사상자들을 방지하며 핵폭탄이 전쟁을 끝냈음을 보여준다고 말한다. (c) 첫 번째 폭탄은 히로시마에 떨어졌고, 두 번째는 나가사키에 떨어졌다.

(d) 폭탄 투하에 대한 유일한 다른 선택은 미국과 일본의 양쪽의 엄청난 사상자를 낼 수도 있었던 일본의 지상 침략이었다.

제2차 세계 대전에서 원자 폭탄 투하가 세계적으로 논란의 대상이 되어왔다는 것이다. (a)는 원폭에 대해서 비난하는 내용이고, (b)는 원폭에 대해서 지지하는 내용이며, (d)는 원폭에 대한 대안과 관련된 내용으로 모두 논쟁에 대한 내용이다. (c)는 단지 원폭 장소에 대한 사실적 내용이므로 정답이 된다.

inhumanely 비인도적으로 **civilian** 민간인 **unwilling** 꺼리는 **surrender** 항복하다 **casualty** 사상자

4

미국의 도시 인구는 빠른 산업화와 도시화로 인해 1920년대에 폭발적으로 증가하였다. (a) 농촌 지역과 교외 지역은 이민자들이 도시의 일자리와 서비스를 제공받지 않았기 때문에 이민자들에게 인기 있는 목적지는 아니었다. (b) 첫째, 당시 10년간 수백만 명의 사람들이 시골의 농경 지역에서 무리지어 도시로 몰려들었는데, 특히 아프리카계 미국인 흑인들이 제1차 세계 대전 이후 흑인 이동기에 남부에서 북부 도시로 달아났다. (c) 이민자들, 특히 동유럽인 또한 다양한 종류의 직업과 자국민에게 접근하기 위해서 도시로 밀려들었다. (d) 이러한 변화의 결과로 미국 도시 거주자들의 수는 미국 역사상 최초로 농촌 지역에 살고 있는 인구의 수를 초과하게 되었다.

1920년대 빠른 산업화와 도시화로 인한 미국 도시 인구의 폭발적인 증가에 관한 내용이다. (b)와 (c)는 도시 인구 유입에 관한 사실 내용이고 (d)는 도시 인구 유입에 의한 농촌과 도시 인구의 역전에 관한 내용으로 일관성이 있다. (a)는 도시 인구 유입과 관련이 있는 내용이 아니라, 단지 미국에 온 이민자들이 농촌 지역과 교외 지역을 선호하지 않았다는 내용이다. 따라서 정답은 (a)이다.

population 인구 **explode** 폭발하다 **industrialization** 산업화 **urbanization** 도시화 **suburb** 교외 **immigrant** 이민자 **flock** 무리지어 모여들다 **African-American** 흑인 **migration** 이동 **dweller** 거주자

5

티셔츠는 착용도 편안하고 자신의 취향에 꼭 맞는 티셔츠도 주문할 수 있는 등 여러 가지 이유로 좋습니다. (a) 티셔츠의 또 다른 장점은 원하는 방식대로 만들기가 매우 쉽다는 것 입니다. (b) 주문 제작한 티셔츠를 세탁할 때는 잘못 세탁하면 디자인이 바랠 수도 있기 때문에 반드시 주의해야 합니다. (c) 다른 사람에게 돈을 주고 셔츠를 디자인해서 만들어 달라고 하거나 자신이 쉽게 직접 디자인을 할 수 있습니다. (d) 가능성은 끝이 없고 티셔츠에 세상에 말하고 싶은 모든 상상을 표현할 수 있습니다.

티셔츠의 장점을 소개하는 내용이다. (a), (c) 그리고 (d)는 모두 티셔츠의 장점을 기술하는 반면, (b)는 세탁 시 주의해야 할 점을 말하고 있다. 따라서 정답은 (b)이다.

customize 주문 제작하다 **distinguish** 돋보이게 하다 **design** 디자인하다, 설계하다 **come up with** 고안하다 **imagination** 상상

6

부엌의 수도꼭지에서 물이 뚝뚝 흘러서 이 사실을 4월 12일 일요일에 제가 건물 관리인에게 말씀드렸고, 그가 그 주에 수리하겠다고 했습니다. (a) 그로부터 거의 세 달이 지났는데 아직도 수리가 되지 않았습니다. (b) 큰 문제는 아니지만 낭비되는 수도 요금은 제가 내야 하는 비용입니다. (c) 새로운 수건걸이도 설치해 주시면 고맙겠습니다. (d) 또한 계속해서

물 떨어지는 소리에 짜증이 나기 시작하니 이 문제를 건물 관리인에게
말씀해 주시면 감사하겠습니다.

부엌의 수도에서 새는 물에 대해 조치를 취해달라고 부탁하는 내용이다.
(a), (b), (d)는 모두 문제가 된 수도꼭지와 관련된 내용인 반면 (c)는 수도꼭
지 고장과는 관련이 없는 내용이다. 따라서 (c)가 정답이다.

water tap 수도꼭지 **leak** 새다 **drip** 똑똑 떨어지다 **grateful** 고마워하는
install 설치하다 **towel rack** 수건걸이 **constant** 계속되는 **drip** 물이
똑똑 흐르다 **irritate** 짜증나게 하다

7

개발 교육은 학생들은 다른 방식으로 배우고 교사들은 이러한 차이점에
세심할 필요가 있다는 것을 이해한다. (a) 조기 유아기 발달 프로그램과
고등학생을 위해 고안된 개발 프로그램이 있다. (b) 조기 유아기 프로그
램은 생후 3개월쯤 시작해서 아이가 유치원에 갈 준비가 될 때까지 계속
된다. (c) 고등학생을 위한 프로그램은 중학교 이후에 시작되며 14세에서
18세 사이의 좀 더 성숙한 학생들을 대상으로 고안되었다. (d) 조기 유아
기 개발 프로그램을 받고 있는 학생은 고등학교에서 더 잘하고 대학으로
진학할 가능성이 크다.

개발 교육에 관한 내용으로 (d)는 조기 유아기 프로그램의 장점에 대한 내
용으로 문맥에서 다소 벗어나 있으므로 정답이다.

sensitive 세심한 **go through** 받고 있다, 거치다 **no matter when**
언제 ~ 해도 **prospects** 전망

8

성형 치과 산업은 치아 표백과 치아 미백이라는 두 가지 주요 시술을 발
전시켰다. (a) 치아 미백은 수년간 축적된 먼지와 때를 제거해서 치아의
본래 색을 되돌려 주는 과정이다. (b) 반면에 치아 표백은 타고난 색깔을
넘어 밝고 새하얗고 광택이 나는 치아가 되도록 시술된다. (c) 즉, 치아 미
백 시술은 노란 치아를 이전의 상태로 되돌리는 것이 목적이고 표백은 하
얀 미소를 만들기 위한 목적으로 행해진다. (d) 치아 표백과 미백은 유명
인사들 사이에서 똑같이 인기 있는 방법인데, 그 이유는 치아가 더 하얗
게 되기 때문이다.

전체 주제는 치아 표백과 치아 미백의 몇 가지 차이점에 대한 내용이다. (a),
(b), (c)는 두 시술의 차이점에 관한 내용인데 반해 (d)는 두 시술이 모두 유
명 인사들에게 인기가 많다는 동떨어진 내용이다.

cosmetic dental industry 성형치과 산업 **evolve** 발전시키다
procedure 시술 **teeth whitening** 치아 미백 **accumulate** 축적하다
teeth bleaching 치아 표백 **beyond** ~을 지나서 **white smile** 환한
미소 **celebrity** 유명 인사

9

엄청난 수의 발암성 합성 화합물의 개발로 인해서 더 많은 사람들이 암에
걸리고 있다. (a) 발암 물질은 방향제와 세제에서 낮은 농도로 검출된다.
(b) 이러한 화합물은 식품 업계에서 조미료, 색소, 그리고 방부제로 사용
된다. (c) 식품 산업에서 사용되는 합성 화학 물질은 특히 간암과 신장암
을 많이 유발하는 것으로 의심을 받고 있다. (d) 이는 간장은 음식의 대사
가 이뤄지는 부위이고 신장은 이러한 화합물을 몸에서 내보내는 곳이기
때문에 그렇다.

발암성 물질을 포함하는 합성 화합물에 관한 내용이다. (b), (c), (d)는 모두
발암 물질이 포함된 화합물이 식품 산업에서 사용됨으로써 발병하는 암과
관련이 있는 내용인 반면, (a)는 발암 물질이 방향제와 세제에서 검출된다는
사실적 내용일 뿐이다. 따라서 정답은 (a)이다.

synthetic 합성의 **compound** 화합물 **carcinogenic** 발암성의
contract cancer 암에 걸리다 **air freshener** 방향제 **detergent** 세제
flavor compound 조미료 **pigment** 색소 **preservative** 방부제
be suspected of ~으로 의심되는 **liver** 간 **kidney** 신장
metabolism 신진대사

10

미국의 포효하는 20년대는 문화적 개화뿐만 아니라 더 많은 여성의 권리
와 자유를 보여줬다. (a) 1920년의 19조 수정 조항은 미국 여성에게 투
표권을 주었다. (b) 마찬가지로 중요하게 많은 수의 여성들이 노동인구가
됨에 따라 재정적인 독립을 획득했다. (c) 대부분의 회사에 있는 보이지
않는 승진 제한 때문에 그들이 승진하는 것은 불가능했다. (d) 여성의 권
리와 독립이 번성함에 따라 단발머리, 짧은 치마와 진보적인 태도를 가진
신여성현상에서 보여지듯이 그들의 사회적 자유도 그러했다.

요지는 여성의 자유와 권리 증진에 관한 것이다. (a)는 미국 여성들에
게 대한 투표권의 부여 (b)는 여성의 재정적 독립, (d)는 여성의 사회
적 자유에 관한 내용으로 모두 여성의 사회적 지위의 향상에 관한 것
인 반면, (c)는 직장에 있어서 여성 차별에 관한 내용이다. 따라서 정답은
(c)이다.

roar 포효하다 **amendment** 수정 **acquire** 획득하다 **glass
ceiling** 유리 천장(눈에 보이지 않는 장벽) **flapper** 1920년대의 신여성
phenomenon 현상 **bobbed** 단발의 **liberal** 자유민주적인

Unit 05	주제 찾기	p.76

1 (a) **2** (a) **3** (c) **4** (b) **5** (c)
6 (b) **7** (d) **8** (a) **9** (b) **10** (b)

1

현재 우리는 지구 온난화를 겪고 있고, 지구 온난화의 유해한 영향에 맞
서기 위해 시급히 에너지를 절약할 필요가 있다. 놀라운 것은 돈을 절약
하면서 에너지 절약 방법을 찾을 수 있다는 것이다. 텔레비전과 DVD 플
레이어 등과 같은 전기 제품을 사용하지 않을 때 플러그를 뽑는 것으로
가정에서 시작할 수 있다. 이런 종류의 가정용 전기 제품들은 켜있지 않
아도 전원에 연결만 되어 있으면 에너지를 소비한다. 건조기를 사용하는
대신 세탁물을 넣어서 자연 건조시키는 것과 같은 작은 행동을 바꾸는 것
으로 에너지가 절약되고, 가까운 장소는 차를 가져가는 대신 걸어가거나
자전거를 타고 가는 것도 또 다른 에너지 절약 습관이다. 우리가 참여해
서 에너지 절약을 위해서 옳은 일을 하기만 해도 에너지 절약은 우리의
손이 미치는 곳에 있다는 것을 반드시 알아야 한다.

Q: 지문은 주로 무엇에 관한 것인가?
(a) 에너지를 아껴 쓰는 것은 돈을 절약하는 것뿐만 아니라 환경도 아끼는 것이다.
(b) 에너지 절약 실패가 지구 온난화의 주된 이유이다.
(c) 에너지 정책으로 인해서 심각한 환경적인 결과가 초래되었다.
(d) 전기 제품은 에너지를 덜 낭비하도록 설계되어야 한다.

지구 온난화를 막고 비용 절약을 위해서 주변에서 쉽게 할 수 있는 에너지 절약 방법을 소개하고 있다. 지문에는 (b), (c), (d)와 같은 내용이 없다. 따라서 정답은 (a)이다.

go through 겪다 **global warming** 지구 온난화 **conserve** 보존하다 **unplug** 플러그를 뽑다 **electrical device** 가정용 전기 제품 **turn off** (스위치를) 끄다 **within one's reach** 손이 미치는 곳에

2

범죄의 공범은 범죄를 저지르는 데 있어 간접적으로 개입을 했다. 직접적으로 개입을 했던 법적인 처벌에 직면한다. 예를 들어, 강도질을 위해 알고도 무기를 제공한 사람은 공범으로 지목된다. 범행에 있어서 공범을 정의하는 데 도움을 주기 위해서, 법률은 다음과 같이 정의를 규정하고 있다. 공범은 반드시 범죄에 있어 주범의 범행 의도를 알고 있어야 한다. 공범은 반드시 직접 또는 간접적으로 범행에 자발적으로 가담해야 한다. 범행 현장에는 없었지만 범행 계획을 도운 사람 또한 공범이다. 요약하면, 의식하고 있으면서 어떤 식으로든 범행을 도운 사람은 주범처럼 유죄가 될 수 있다.

Q: 다음 중 지문의 목적을 가장 잘 설명한 것은?
(a) 범죄에서 무엇이 공범을 정의하는가를 설명하기 위해
(b) 공범과 범죄자 간의 차이점을 명확히 하기 위해
(c) 공범이 왜 유죄가 되어야 하는지 설명하기 위해
(d) 공범이 왜 유죄가 되어서는 안 되는지 보여 주기 위해

범행에 적극적으로 가담하지 않았더라도 범행을 도왔다면 공범으로서 유죄 판결을 받을 수 있다는 것과 법률에 규정된 공범에 대한 정의를 자세히 인용하고 있는 내용이다. 따라서 정답은 (a)이다.

accomplice 공범 **legal** 법적인 **participate** 가담하다 **knowingly** 알고서, 고의로 **robbery** 강도(질) **intent** 의도 **willing** 자발적인 **awareness** 의식 **principal criminal** 주범

3

데이비슨 씨께

귀하의 회계사 보조 지원서를 잘 받았습니다. 귀하의 이력서에서 경력 부분이 가장 인상적이었습니다. 이곳에서 일할 가능성에 대해 논의하기 위해 개인적으로 만났으면 합니다. 저는 이번 달 2일에서 4일까지 가능합니다. 제 비서 애나 드와이트에게 555-1473으로 연락하시면 그녀가 약속 시간을 잡도록 도와줄 겁니다. 질문은 그녀에게 직접 하시면 됩니다. 그러면 만나 뵙기를 기대하겠습니다. 좋은 하루 보내세요.

대니얼 애빌라

Q: 다음 중 편지의 목적은?
(a) 장래의 고용주와 면접 일정을 잡기 위해
(b) 대리를 찾기 위해 구직자와 회의 일정을 잡기 위해
(c) 입사 지원자와 면접 약속을 잡기 위해
(d) 지원자가 이력서 쓰는 것을 도와주기 위한 약속을 정하기 위해

담당자가 입사 지원서를 제출한 지원자에게 구체적인 면접 약속을 자신의 비서와 정하라는 내용의 편지이다. 비서와 약속을 잡는 것이기 때문에 (a)는 답이 아니고, (b)는 수신인이 이미 회계사 보조로 지원했기 때문에 제외되며, (d)는 지문에 없는 내용이다. 따라서 정답은 (c)이다.

application 지원서 **contact** 연락하다 **arrange** 정하다, 조정하다

4

남성형 대머리를 성공적으로 치료하는 새로운 줄기세포 치료법을 이용할 수 있게 되었기 때문에 탈모는 마침내 과거의 일이 될 수 있다. 잘 알려져 있지 않은 한 영국 회사가 세계적으로 1억 명이 훨씬 넘는 탈모 환자 시장에 이러한 치료법을 성공적으로 내놓았다. 지난 몇 년 동안 최첨단 실험실에서 연구하면서 이 회사는 마침내 줄기세포 기술을 이용하여 성공적으로 환자의 두피에서 머리카락이 다시 자라나게 할 수 있게 되었다. 이 회사는 자가 조직 접근법, 즉 환자의 몸에서 채취한 줄기세포를 머리카락을 재생하는 데 이용하는 방법을 완벽하게 만들고 있는 중이다. 이 혁신적인 치료법으로 많은 남성들이 아침에 일어나서 하루하루 머리카락이 서서히 빠지는 것을 보는 데 익숙했던 것과는 반대로 머리카락이 하루하루 다시 자라는 것을 볼 수 있게 될 것이다.

Q: 지문의 주제로 가장 알맞은 것은?
(a) 대머리를 위한 다양한 치료 방법
(b) 머리카락을 회복하기 위해 줄기 세포 이용
(c) 대머리를 위한 자연적인 치료
(d) 줄기 세포를 이용한 조직 재생

탈모 치료를 위해 이용되는 줄기세포 치료에 관한 내용이다. (a) 지문에는 대머리 치료를 위한 한 가지 치료 방법, 즉 줄기세포 치료법만 소개되고 있고, (c) 자연적인 치료에 대한 언급은 없으며, (d) 머리카락도 조직에 포함되나 지문은 줄기세포를 이용한 머리카락 재생에 대해서만 기술하고 있으므로 모두 정답에서 제외된다. 따라서 정답은 (b)이다.

lose one's hair 탈모가 일어나다 **stem cell** 줄기세포 **baldness** 대머리 **sufferer** 환자 **perfect** 완벽하게 하다 **autologous** 자가 조직의 **regenerate** 재생하다 **shed** 탈모하다

5

귀하는 자신이 하는 일에 최고인 것을 알고 있습니다. 귀하는 누구에게나 가정이나 사무실 청소를 귀하의 회사에 맡기도록 권고하려 할 것입니다. 귀하의 마술 같은 손길로 모든 것들이 마침내 아주 말끔해집니다. 그렇다면 귀하가 같은 일을 하고 청소 업체 광고를 최고에게 맡기면 안 되나요? 귀하가 실제로 얼마나 잘하는지 아무도 모른다면 최고가 되는 것이 무슨 소용이겠습니까? HousekeepingandCleaners.com은 귀하가 어디서든 찾을 수 있는 가장 양질의 청소 광고를 해드립니다. 요즘 같이 뒤숭숭한 경기에 개인이나 가족들이 청소하는 데 들이는 시간이 그 어느 때보다도 적습니다. 또한 그들은 인터넷을 통해 손가락만으로 전 세계를 만나는 데 익숙해졌습니다. 청소 업체 광고는 적절한 사람들이 볼 때만 효과가 있습니다. HousekeepingandCleaners.com에서는 매번 양질의 청소 광고를 귀하에게 제공하고 귀사의 고객들이 볼 수 있는 완벽한 곳에 배치하여 이를 실현시켜 드립니다.

Q: 지문의 목적을 가장 잘 나타내는 것은?
(a) 사무실 청소하는 법을 알려주는 웹사이트를 소개하기 위해
(b) 좋은 청소 업체를 찾는 고객들을 위한 웹사이트를 소개하기 위해
(c) 청소 업체들이 고객들을 찾는 데 도움을 주는 웹사이트를 광고하기 위해
(d) 전문 청소 업체를 광고하기 위해

지문은 HousekeepingandCleaners.com이란 회사가 청소 업체들을 대상으로 인터넷에서 효율적인 광고를 해 주겠다고 자사를 소개하는 내용이다. 따라서 정답은 (c)이다.

turn … over to ~에게 …을 맡기다   touch 손길   spic and span 아주 깔끔한   fingertip 손가락 끝

6

클리런 씨께

귀사에서 보내신 장비의 첫 번째 선적분이 예상 도착일보다 빨리 도착했습니다. 신속한 선적에 감사드리고자 합니다. 모든 부품에 만족합니다. 따라서 당사는 다시 한 번 결정했습니다. 총액이 70만 달러인 추가 상품에 대한 구매 주문서 3422번을 첨부합니다. 귀사에서 지속적으로 당사에 동질의 서비스와 상품을 공급해 주시기를 바랍니다. 귀사에서 이미 당사의 조달 지침을 가지고 있기 때문에 이번 주문에서는 첨부하지 않겠습니다. 이전처럼 신용장을 개설할 예정입니다. 제게 선적일을 알려 주십시오. 배려에 감사합니다.

로버트 윌리엄스

Q: 편지의 목적을 가장 잘 나타낸 것은?
(a) 조기 선적에 불평하기 위해
(b) 추가 구매 주문을 하기 위해
(c) 이전에 했던 주문을 취소하기 위해
(d) 주문 물품의 도착에 대해 문의하기 위해

지문은 업무 서신으로 고객이 선적분의 품질에 만족해서 구매량을 늘려서 추가 주문하는 내용이다. 따라서 정답은 (b)이다.

shipment 선적(물)   equipment 장비   estimated 예상된   prompt 신속한   attach 첨부하다   procurement 조달   guideline 지침   letter of credit 신용장   shipping date 선적일

7

세계가 계속해서 발전함에 따라 많은 과학자들이 무공해인 대체 친환경 에너지를 개발하는 방법을 찾고 있다. 전기의 많은 친환경 에너지원 중 하나는 태양 에너지다. 태양 에너지는 수백만 년 동안 지속적으로 에너지를 공급해 줄 태양에서 생산된다. 또 다른 친환경 에너지원은 생물량으로 더 잘 알려진 식물 발전이다. 이 에너지원은 생물, 생분해 산물 또는 쓰레기에서 나오는 생물질을 이용한다. 풍력도 산들바람이 많이 부는 곳에서 실질적이고 효과적으로 운용되는 친환경 에너지원의 또 다른 좋은 예이다. 풍력 발전에서는 발전기를 켜기 위해서 풍차, 풍력 터빈, 풍력 펌프를 이용한다. 이러한 에너지원을 활용하기 위해서 기반 시설을 짓는 것은 많은 비용이 들지만, 친환경 에너지원을 활용해서 지구 보호에 종사하는 많은 사람들이 있다.

Q: 지문은 주로 무엇에 관한 것인가?
(a) 풍력과 태양 에너지 사용의 혜택
(b) 시급한 새로운 에너지원 개발의 필요성
(c) 태양 에너지 이용의 필요성
(d) 다양한 친환경 에너지원에 대한 탐구

지문은 과학자들이 다양한 무공해 대체 친환경 에너지를 개발하는 방법을 찾고 있다는 것을 언급하고, 몇 가지 친환경 에너지원을 소개하고 있다. (a)는 풍력과 태양 에너지만을 소개하고 있고, (b)의 그린 에너지원 개발의 시급성에 대한 언급이 없으며, (c) 또한 (a)와 마찬가지 이유로 정답에서 제외된다. 따라서 정답은 (d)이다.

alternative 대체의   pollution-free 무공해의   solar 태양의   biomass 생물량   biological material 생물질   biodegradable 생분해성의   breezy 산들바람이 부는   wind mill 풍차   generator 발전기   engage in ~에 종사하다   harness 이용하다

8

탈수증이 무엇이고 신체에 어떤 영향을 미치는지를 이해하는 것은 신체에 끼치는 피해를 방지하고 건강한 신진대사를 촉진하는 데 도움이 된다. 탈수증은 체내 수분 부족이나 과다 손실을 의미한다. 탈수증의 심각한 영향으로 장기가 손상되며 최악의 경우 죽음을 초래한다. 대부분 사람들의 인체는 전체 몸무게의 70%가 물로 이루어져 있다. 따라서 체내에서 신진대사가 적절하게 이루어지도록 2리터 이상의 물을 마시도록 권장하고 있다. 적당량의 수분 소모는 몸을 튼튼하고 건강하게 하는 데 도움이 된다. 반면에 물이 부족하면 몸에 급격한 변화가 일어난다. 예를 들어 인체는 호흡, 소변, 대변 및 땀을 통해서 독소를 배출하기 위해서 물이 필요하다. 그렇기 때문에 세포의 원기 회복 촉진과 장수를 위해서 충분한 물을 마시도록 권장하고 있다.

Q: 지문의 주제로 가장 알맞은 것은?
(a) 충분한 수분으로 건강 유지하기
(b) 물이 어떻게 몸을 정화하는가
(c) 식수를 평가하는 방법
(d) 물을 대체할 수 있는 식품

탈수증이 인체에 미치는 피해와 함께 충분한 물의 섭취가 인체에 주는 이점을 설명하는 내용이다. (b), (c), (d) 모두 지문에 있는 내용이지만 단편적인 내용이므로 정답에서 제외되며, 원기 회복 장수를 위해서 충분한 물을 마시도록 권장하는 것이 마지막 문장이 지문의 요점이다. 따라서 정답은 (a)이다.

dehydration 탈수증   metabolism 신진대사   organ 장기   encourage 권장하다   consumption 소모   drastic 급격한   flush out 배출하다   toxin 독소   urination 소변   rejuvenation 원기회복   longevity 장수

9

오프쇼링(업무위탁)의 의미는 10년 이상 익숙해져 왔지만, 이제 또 다른 용어 '인쇼링'의 사용이 두드러지게 증가하고 있다. 사전은 인쇼링을 외국 회사가 생산 활동의 일부를 국내 경제로 옮겨올 때 오프쇼링과 반대되는 용어라고 정의한다. 국가들이 인쇼링의 장점을 인식하기 시작하면서 각국 정부는 인쇼링에 더욱 우호적인 사업 환경을 조성하고 있다. 회사는 인쇼링을 통해 사업을 더욱 통제를 할 수 있다. 또한 인쇼링은 회사가 비용 효율적인 영업 이득을 최대화할 수 있는 자율권을 부여한다. 게다가 회사는 문화적 차이와 시차를 최소화할 수 있다. 하지만 가장 좋은 점은 회사는 국내 인재들을 개발할 수 있다는 것이다. 국내 인쇼링은 현지 노동과 자원, 기술을 이용하고 사업 가치를 높이며 국가의 경제적, 사회적 이득을 보장한다.

Q: 지문의 주제로 가장 알맞은 것은?

(a) 오프쇼어링과 인쇼어링의 장점

(b) 인쇼어링의 장점 이해하기

(c) 전 세계에서 인쇼링하는 법

(d) 왜 인쇼링이 세계적으로 퇴조하는 추세인가

사용이 두드러지게 증가하고 있는 용어인 인쇼링의 장점이 지문 전체에 걸쳐서 기술되고 있다. 지문에는 인쇼링과 오프쇼어링의 우열을 가리는 내용이 없어 (a)는 정답이 될 수 없고, 지문에는 단지 인쇼링에 대한 정의와 그 장점만이 기술되어 있고 방법은 기술되어 있지 않기 때문에 (c)도 답이 아니다. (d)는 지문과 반대되는 내용이다. 따라서 정답은 (b)이다.

familiar to ~에게 익숙한 **prominence** 두드러짐 **firm** 회사 **domestic economy** 국내 경제 **empower** 자율권을 부여하다 **time-zone differences** 시차 **talent** 인재 **wane** 약해지다

10

케네디 대통령의 기릴 만한 많은 업적 중에는 많은 사람들이 그에 대해 실패라고 기억하는 한 사건이 있다. 바로 '피그스 만' 사건이다. 쿠바의 공산주의 지도자인 피델 카스트로를 타도하기 위한 시도로 케네디는 1961년 쿠바를 침입하기 위해 CIA가 망명한 친민주주의 쿠바인들을 훈련하고 무장하게 했다. 미국 정부는 훈련 받은 망명군이 미국 공군의 도움으로 카스트로 세력을 격파하고 민중 봉기의 도화선이 되기를 기대했다. 쿠데타 시도 직전에 케네디는 지상 부대에 공군을 지원하지 않기로 결정했다. 공군의 도움 없는 피그스 만 급습은 실패로 돌아갔다. 카스트로의 군대는 쿠데타였을 뻔한 사건을 좌절시키고 미국에 대한 승리를 선언했다. 이 침공은 완전한 재앙이었고 케네디는 대실패에 대한 모든 책임을 받아들였다.

Q: 지문은 무엇에 관한 것인가?

(a) 카스트로와의 불화를 매듭짓고자 했던 케네디의 실패

(b) 케네디의 카스트로 축출 실패

(c) 케네디 행정부가 저지른 다른 실수들

(d) 카스트로를 전복시키려는 미국의 성공적인 노력

케네디 대통령이 쿠바의 지도자인 피델 카스트로를 실각시키기 위해 미국이 지원했던 쿠바 침공에 관한 내용이다. (a) 지문에 언급된 내용은 카스트로와 불화를 매듭짓는 내용이 아니다. (c) 케네디 행정부가 저지른 다른 실수는 언급되지 않았다. (d) 미국의 이러한 노력은 실패로 돌아갔다. 쿠바 침공의 실패는 카스트로의 권력을 제거하려는 시도의 실패를 의미한다. 따라서 정답은 (b)이다.

achievement 업적 **overthrow** 타도하다 **communist** 공산주의의 **authorize** 권한을 위임하다 **exile** 망명하다, 망명자 **defeat** 물리치다 **spark** 도화선이 되다 **popular uprising** 민중 봉기 **storm** 급습하다 **cover** 엄호하다 **utter** 전적인, 완전한 **fiasco** 대실패

1 (d)	**2** (a)	**3** (d)	**4** (b)	**5** (d)
6 (a)	**7** (b)	**8** (d)	**9** (c)	**10** (d)

1

부모들이 하이킹을 하기 위해서 자녀를 산에 데려갈 때, 집에서 몇 가지 준비를 꼭 해야 한다. 우선, 부모는 보호자와 어린이의 이름, 전화번호가 적혀 있는 연락 카드를 준비해서 아이의 주머니나 배낭에 넣어 두어야 한다. 다음으로, 아이들이 가볍고 통기성이 좋으며 편안한 옷을 입도록 해서 열사병으로부터 보호해야 한다. 또한 아이들이 자외선을 차단하는 챙이 있는 모자를 쓰도록 하는 것도 권장 사항이다. 좋은 자외선 차단 크림을 발라줄 때는 쉽게 햇볕에 노출되는 얼굴, 손, 다리에 특히 신경을 써야 한다. 부모는 또한 고열량 음식과 비상 약품 상자를 준비해야 한다. 이와 같은 간단한 조치를 따른다면 숲 속에서 아이들이 위험에 맞닥뜨린다 하더라도 안전하게 보호할 수 있다.

Q: 지문에 따르면 다음 중 옳은 것은?

(a) 아이들은 얼굴에만 자외선 차단 크림을 바르면 된다.

(b) 부모는 자기 주머니나 배낭에 명함을 넣어 두어야 한다.

(c) 부모는 햇볕으로부터 보호하기 위해 선글라스를 써야 한다.

(d) 하이킹을 할 때 아이들은 열량이 높은 음식을 먹을 필요가 있다.

자녀와 함께 산으로 하이킹을 갈 때 자녀의 안전을 위해서 부모가 미리 준비해야 할 몇 가지를 설명하고 있다. (a) 아이들의 얼굴뿐만 아니라 손, 발에 모두 자외선 차단 크림을 발라야 하고, (b) 아이들의 주머니나 배낭에 명함이 아닌 연락 카드를 넣어 두어야 하며, (c) 부모가 아니라 아이들을 햇볕으로부터 보호하기 위해 챙이 있는 모자를 쓰도록 해야 한다. 따라서 정답은 (d)이다.

guardian 보호자 **breathable** 통기성의 **heat stroke** 열사병 **visor** 자외선을 차단하는 챙이 있는 모자 **first aid kit** 비상 약품 상자

2

체인, 엔진 또는 컨베이어 벨트에 끼어 쌓여서 기능 장애를 일으키는 아주 작은 조각들을 어떻게 제거하십니까? 자, 정답은 에어 나이프입니다. 에어 나이프는 체인과 벨트에서 액체나 고형 부스러기를 불어서 제거하기 위해서 사용되는 공구입니다. 에어 나이프는 보통 기계 부품의 제작, 유지 보수 및 세척에 사용됩니다. 이 나이프는 때때로 유선형 흐름으로 알려진 고강도의 균일한 공기 흐름으로 이루어집니다. 압축 공기로 인한 충격 범위는 물리적 접촉 없이 표면을 세척할 수 있도록 미풍 수준에서 마하 0.6까지입니다. 에어 나이프는 표면을 건조시키거나, 냉각시키는 데에도 사용할 수 있습니다. 에어 나이프는 어떤 표면 위든 원치 않는 물질이나 이물질을 제거하는 가장 효율적인 방법입니다.

Q: 에어 나이프에 관해 다음 중 옳은 것은?

(a) 건조와 세척을 위해 고속의 바람을 분사한다.

(b) 플라스틱을 자를 만큼 강력하다.

(c) 제조업뿐만 아니라 가정에서도 사용될 수 있다.

(d) 기계 부품 제작에 사용되는 휴대가 매우 간편한 도구이다.

광고문으로 에어 나이프가 최고 마하 0.6의 압축공기를 불어서 건조, 세척 및 부품의 제작과 유지 보수에 사용되고 있다는 내용이다. (b)는 지문에 없는 내용이고, (c) 에어 나이프는 가정용이라는 내용이 없으며, (d) 에어 나이프가 휴대용이라는 내용도 없다. 따라서 정답은 (a)이다.

particle 아주 작은 조각   wedge 끼다   debris 부스러기
manufacture 제작하다   maintain 유지하다   intensity 강도
streamline 유선형   compressed air 압축 공기   Mach 마하, 음속
foreign substance 이물질   velocity 속도

3

포스터 씨께
지난주에 주문하신 가구 세트가 낮은 수요로 더 이상 제조되지 않아 유감스럽게 생각합니다. 그 스타일은 중단됐지만 고객님의 필요에 응해 뭔가 다른 것을 찾으시도록 새로운 최신 카탈로그를 첨부했습니다. 카탈로그 7쪽에 있는 품목은 고객님이 주문품에서 찾으신 몇몇 특징을 제공할 것입니다. 어떤 품목이든지 관심 있으시다면 저희에게 알려 주세요.

조이스 와일더스
Q: 편지에 따르면 옳은 것은?
(a) 낡은 가구를 교체할 새 가구가 배달될 것이다.
(b) 처음에 주문됐던 가구가 모두 품절이다.
(c) 배달되기로 예정됐던 가구는 늦게 도착할 것이다.
(d) 사전에 요청한 가구는 생산이 중단되었다.

편지의 목적은 고객이 주문한 가구가 더 이상 생산되지 않아서 다른 가구를 제안하는 것이므로 정답은 (d)이다. (a)는 다른 가구를 제안만 하지 아직 다른 가구를 산 것이 아니기 때문에 오답이다.

regret 유감스럽게 생각하다   manufacture 제조[생산]하다
discontinue 중단하다   enclose 동봉하다   feature 특징
arrange ~의 예정을 세우다

4

언어 능력은 아이들이 어릴 때 이해하고 의사소통을 하는 것을 배우는 방법이다. 하지만 아이들이 나이가 들면서 언어 학습은 더 어려워진다. 사실 대부분의 언어 능력은 뇌가 아직 발달하고 있는 생후 3년 내에 학습된다. 어떤 사람들은 언어 능력은 아이가 태아일 때부터 발달하기 시작해서 엄마의 목소리와 말투를 인식할 수 있다고 믿는다. 언어 능력은 간단한 옹알이와 흉내내기로 시작된다. 생후 9개월까지 아기는 보통 간단한 단어나 명령을 이해할 수 있고 심지어 단어 몇 개를 말할 수도 있다. 아이는 나이를 먹으면서 단어를 조합해서 간단한 문장을 만들기 시작한다. 5살이 되면 아이의 언어 능력은 성인의 능력과 비슷해진다. 이것이 많은 부모가 유아기 때부터 활발한 상호 작용을 통해 아이들과 의사소통 연습을 하는 이유이다.

Q: 지문에 따르면 다음 중 옳은 것은?
(a) 아기는 생후 3년이 되면 처음으로 단어를 이해하기 시작한다.
(b) 첫 3년이 언어 학습에 가장 중요하다.
(c) 언어 발달은 성인 후반기가 되어야만 멈춘다.
(d) 언어 학습은 아이가 태어난 이후에 시작된다.

아이의 언어 능력 발달에 관한 내용이다. 지문에 의하면 (a) 생후 3년이 아니라 9개월까지 단어를 이해할 수 있고, (c) 5살이 되면 언어 능력이 성인과 비슷해지며, (d) 언어 학습은 태아일 때부터 발달하기 시작된다. 대부분의 언어 능력이 뇌가 아직도 발달하고 있는 생후 3년 내에 학습된다는 내용에 미루어 정답은 (b)이다.

fetus 태아   speech pattern 말투   babbling 옹알이   mimicry 흉내내기   interaction 상호 작용   infancy 유아기

5

일상적인 운전을 위한 내비게이션 시스템을 제공해 주는 용도 외에도 GPS에는 다른 몇 가지 용도가 있다. 지구 전체를 훑는 인공위성 네트워크인 GPS는 지상에서 발견되는 길뿐만 아니라, 땅에 대한 정보를 추적할 수 있다. 다시 말하자면 GPS는 토양의 구조를 실제로 분석할 수 있다. 이는 농부들이 농경지를 최선으로 관리하는 방법을 정하는 데 도움이 된다. 도움이 필요한 사람들을 추적할 때에도 사용할 수도 있다. 알츠하이머 환자는 GPS 기기를 가지고 다니며 길을 잃었을 때에 다른 사람들이 환자의 위치를 찾을 수 있다. 이는 오늘날 GPS의 용도의 일부일 뿐이며 향후 다른 용도를 분명히 찾을 것이다.

Q: 지문에 따르면 다음 중 옳은 것은?
(a) GPS는 지구의 위치를 나타낸다.
(b) GPS는 잃어버린 소지품을 찾는 데 유용한 기기다.
(c) GPS는 환자들이 훌륭한 의사를 찾는 데 도움을 준다.
(d) GPS는 농부들이 좋은 농지를 찾는 데 쓰인다.

GPS의 다양한 용도에 대한 내용이다. (a) GPS는 지구 자체가 아니라 지구상의 위치를 나타낸다. (b) 잃어버린 소지품을 찾을 때 GPS를 이용한다는 것은 알 수 없다. (c) GPS가 정보 검색용이라는 내용은 없다. 지문 중반부에는 GPS가 농부들이 적합한 농지를 찾는 데 도움이 된다는 내용이 있다. 따라서 정답은 (d)이다.

application 용도   track 추적하다   analyze 분석하다   composition 구조   soil 지면   keep track of ~의 진로를 쫓다

6

르네상스 시대 여성의 삶은 대부분 제약과 예속을 특징으로 한다. 여성은 어린 시절 내내 부모에 의해 통제 받은 뒤, 아마도 자신이 선택하지 않았을 것이고 둘 중 하나가 죽을 때까지 자신을 통제했을 남편의 손으로 바로 넘어갔다. 어떤 이유에서든 결혼하지 않은 여성은 남자 친척의 집에 살거나 여성에게 유일하게 허용되었던 직업인 수녀가 될 수 있는 수녀원에 살면서 생각과 행동의 독립이 허용되지 않았다. 여성은 흔히 예술과 과학에 참여하는 것이 좌절되었고, 따라서 그 시대에는 여성의 온전한 문학적, 예술적 잠재력을 결코 알지 못했다. 그 시대는 여성이 유명해지거나 자신을 표현하는 것을 허용하지 않았다.

Q: 다음 중 르네상스 시대에 여성에게 허용되었던 것은?
(a) 여성 종교 단체의 일원이 되는 것
(b) 연극을 위한 대본을 쓰는 것
(c) 과학 실험을 하는 것
(d) 초상화와 풍경화를 그리는 것

르네상스 시대의 여성은 수녀 외에는 직업을 가질 수 없었고 예술이나 과학에 참여하는 것이 좌절되었으며 미혼녀들은 친척의 집이나 수녀원에 살았다는 내용이 있다. 따라서 정답은 (a)이다.

limitation 제약 subjugation 예속 relative 친척 convent 수녀원
literary 문학적인

7

덴트 씨께

11월 1일 일요일 자 〈시카고 타임즈〉에 광고된 것과 같이, 현재 스피드웨이 트래블에 자리가 있는 대리직에 지원하기 위해 이 지원서를 보내니 접수해 주십시오. 제 이력서를 동봉하니 검토와 숙고 부탁합니다. 저의 이력에는 견실한 사무 경력과 학력뿐만 아니라 사무 자동화에 있어서 폭넓은 실무 경력이 반영되어 있습니다. 저의 경력으로는 월례 보고와 행정 관리가 있습니다. 저는 제 능력으로 스피드웨이 트래블에 즉각적이고 가치 있는 기여를 할 수 있다고 확신합니다. 시간 내주셔서 감사합니다. 가까운 시일 내에 귀하가 편리한 시간에 면접 일정을 정하기 위한 연락을 기다리고 있겠습니다.

헬렌 뎀시

Q: 편지에 따르면 다음 중 옳은 것은?
(a) 지원서를 쓴 사람은 예비 고용주이다.
(b) 지원서를 쓴 사람은 신문에서 일자리에 대해 읽었다.
(c) 지원서를 쓴 사람은 이력서를 별도로 보낼 예정이다.
(d) 지원서를 쓴 사람은 최근에 대학을 졸업한 사람이다.

지문에는 지원자가 대리를 구한다는 광고를 시카고 타임즈에서 보고, 지원서에 자신의 실무 경력이 반영된 이력서를 동봉해서 제출했다는 내용이 있다. 따라서 (a)와 (c)는 정답이 될 수 없고, 지원자의 경력으로 보아 (d)도 정답에서 제외된다. 따라서 정답은 (b)이다.

extensive 넓은 범위에 걸친 administrative 행정의 currently
현재에 letter of application 지원서 position 직위 resume 이력서
practical experience 실무 경력 office automation 사무 자동화
contribution 기여

8

1811년까지 나폴레옹은 유럽에 지배적인 통제력을 행사했다. 하지만 나폴레옹의 제국은 강해 보였어도 점점 나약함으로 가득하게 되었다. 프랑스의 지배는 독일과 스페인 현지의 민족주의를 고취시켰고, 더 확고해진 그의 적들은 프랑스 군대가 약할 때 공격하기 위한 호기를 기다리고 있었다. 폴란드를 지배하고자 했던 러시아의 알렉산더 1세는 나폴레옹이 독립한 폴란드를 인정하고 바르샤바의 대공국이라고 칭하면서 황제를 모욕한 이후 나폴레옹을 불쾌하게 생각했다. 게다가 추방당한 프로이센의 슈타인 남작은 이제 알렉산더의 궁전에 있으면서 과거 동맹이었던 나폴레옹을 공격하라고 그에게 속삭였다. 이렇게 불리한 상황과 사태의 전환으로 나폴레옹 제국의 궁극적인 몰락의 길이 열렸다.

Q: 지문에 따르면 다음 중 옳은 것은?
(a) 나폴레옹은 폴란드의 독립을 인정하지 않았다.
(b) 러시아는 나폴레옹의 가장 큰 적이었다.
(c) 독일과 스페인은 프로이센의 적이었다.
(d) 러시아는 폴란드의 독립을 원하지 않았다.

(b) 러시아가 나폴레옹을 불쾌하게 생각했지만 나폴레옹의 가장 큰 적이었다는 내용은 없고, (c) 또한 없는 내용이다. 나폴레옹이 독립된 폴란드를 인정한 이후 러시아의 알렉산더 1세가 나폴레옹을 불쾌하게 생각했다는 내용으로 보아 러시아가 폴란드의 독립을 승인하지 않았다는 것을 알 수 있다. 따라서 (a)도 제외되고 정답은 (d)이다.

be riddled with ~으로 채워지다 nationalism 민족주의
established 확고한 czar 황제 acknowledge 인정하다 court 궁전
ally 동맹

9

귀하의 방이 집안에서 언제나 에어컨 냉방이 가장 안 되는 방인가요? 그렇다면 분리형 에어컨이 귀하의 노여움과 방을 식혀줄 수 있습니다. 분리형 에어컨은 서로 떨어져 있는 두 개의 주요 부품으로 구성된 에어컨으로 하나는 건물 내부에 다른 하나는 외부에 둡니다. 분리형 에어컨 시스템의 두 주요 부품은 서로 다른 기능을 가집니다. 실외에 놓는 압축기라고 부르는 장비가 공기를 식히고 물방울을 처리합니다. 이렇게 함으로써 실내의 공조 과정에서 발생한 물의 배수 방법을 찾아야 하는 수고를 덜게 됩니다. 송풍기라고 부르는 내부 장비는 공기를 집안 구석구석에 분배하는 역할을 맡습니다. 에어컨을 고를 때는, 모든 가족의 요구 사항을 가장 효율적으로 처리할 수 있는 능력을 가진 장비를 선택해야 한다는 것을 명심하십시오.

Q: 지문에 따르면 다음 중 옳은 것은?
(a) 실내에서 사용되는 에어컨 장비를 압축기라고 부른다.
(b) 송풍기는 실내에서 생기는 물방울을 처리한다.
(c) 분리형 에어컨의 두 장치는 다른 기능을 가진다.
(d) 분리형 에어컨은 일반 에어컨보다 비싸다.

분리형 에어컨은 서로 다른 기능을 가진 2개의 부품으로 구성되는데, 하나는 실내에 놓는 송풍기이고, 실외에 놓는 압축기는 공기를 식히고 물방울을 처리하는 기능을 한다는 내용으로 보아, (a)와 (b)는 어긋나며 (c)가 정답이다. (d)는 지문에 없는 내용이다.

temper 노여움 split 분리된 component 부품 compressor
압축기 condensation 응결수 drain 배수하다 distribute 분배하다
household 가정

10

터너 씨께

페어웨이 아트 센터는 다음 시즌의 티켓이 다음 주에 할인에 들어가게 됨을 알려드리게 되어 기쁩니다. 시즌 티켓 소지자인 귀하를 소중히 여기며 저희 공연을 계속해서 성원해 주시길 바랍니다. 하지만 비용과 임대료의 상승으로 다음 시즌의 요금이 인상될 것임을 알려드리게 되어 유감스럽습니다. 티켓 가격은 현재의 265달러에서 292달러로 인상될 것입니다. 1회 공연 가격도 인상될 것입니다. 이런 불가피한 요금의 상승에도 불구하고 예술을 기념하는 흥미로운 한 해를 보내도록 저희와 함께 해주시길 진심으로 바랍니다.

특히 저희 페어웨이 심포니 오케스트라는 24번째 해를 함께 기념하여 객석의 4분의 1을 시즌 티켓 고객께서 채워주시길 기대합니다. 귀하와 같은 충실한 후원자가 없이는 호평을 받는 저희 오케스트라의 운명은 불확실해집니다. 다가오는 시즌 저희 행사에 다시 와 주시기를 고대합니다.

테레사 핸리

Q: 이 지문에 따르면 다음 중 옳은 것은?
(a) 티켓 가격은 청중의 부족으로 인상되었다.
(b) 1회 관람권 가격은 동일할 것이다.
(c) 페어웨이 심포니는 25년 전에 설립되었다.
(d) 청중의 약 4분의 1이 정기 구매권 소지자이다.

교향악단이 연주회를 하는 페어웨이 아트 센터의 임대료 인상으로 인해서 정기 입장권 가격과 함께 1회 관람권 가격도 인상이 될 것이라는 내용이 있으므로 (a)와 (b)는 정답에서 제외되며, 내년에 25주년이라는 내용으로 보아 교향악단이 24년 전에 설립된 것을 알 수 있다. 교향악단이 매 행사마다 좌석의 4분의 1(25%)을 채우는 정기 입장권 소지자에게 의지해 왔다는 내용이 있으므로 정답은 (d)이다.

patronage 성원 **observe** 기념하다 **loyal** 충성스러운 **patron** 고객
acclaimed 호평을 받고 있는 **function** 행사

Unit **07** 추론하기   p.88

| **1** (d) | **2** (d) | **3** (c) | **4** (a) | **5** (c) |
| **6** (d) | **7** (b) | **8** (b) | **9** (a) | **10** (c) |

1

약초는 면역 체계를 강화시키는 데 매우 중요한 역할을 할 수 있다. 그중 하나인 자운영속은 주로 중국에서 사용되는 인기 있는 약초로 폐를 상당히 강화시키는 것으로 알려졌다. 영지는 꽤 유익한 다른 약초이다. 영지는 활력을 주며 피를 정화하는 데 사용된다. 이 약초는 몸에 있는 백혈구 수치를 높이며 박테리아와 바이러스의 성장을 억제한다. 시중에 건강에 좋고 침입에 대한 신체의 자연 방어 시스템을 강화하는 전체적이고 자연적인 방법을 제공하는 약초가 많이 나와 있다.

Q: 약초에 대해 유추할 수 있는 것은?
(a) 영지는 감기를 예방하기로 인기 있는 약초이다.
(b) 자운영속은 많은 의학적 용도가 있다.
(c) 약초는 향기가 안 좋은 것으로 알려져 있다.
(d) 자운영속은 숨 쉬는 데 어려움이 있는 사람들에게 권장된다

면역력을 높여주는 약초를 소개한다. 자운영속은 특히 폐를 강화시키기 때문에 숨 쉬기 어려운 사람들에게 도움이 된다고 추측할 수 있다. 따라서 정답은 (d)이다. (b)는 자운영속이 많은 효능을 가지고 있는지는 알 수 없으므로 오답이다.

medicinal herb 약초 **immune system** 면역 체계 **astragalus**
자운영속 **considerably** 상당히 **ganoderma** 영지 **purify** 정화하다
white blood cell 백혈구 **holistic** 전체론의 **application** 특정 용도

2

세계가 직면한 공중 보건 문제 중 쉽게 간과되는 것이 FNB-3으로 알려진 박테리아이다. 이 유형의 박테리아는 대부분의 항생 물질의 공격을 억제하고 견뎌내 항생제에 저항성을 가진 박테리아가 되는 것으로 알려져 있다. 이 박테리아는 돌연변이를 통해 유전적 구성을 바꿈으로써 쉽게 항생제에 저항성이 생길 수 있다. 그런 다음 이 돌연변이 좋은 버저 현재 시장에서 구입할 수 있는 항생제에 저항성이 있는 또 다른 새로운 군집을 만들어 낸다. 현재 감염에서 우리 스스로를 보호할 수 있는 최선의 방법은 규칙적으로 손을 씻고 위생 상태를 유지하는 것이다.

Q: FNB-3에 관해 유추할 수 있는 것은?
(a) 항생제에 취약하다.
(b) 항상 그 형태를 유지한다.
(c) 공기를 통해 감염된다.
(d) 확실한 예방 백신이 없다.

FNB-3과 같은 박테리아가 항생제 공격을 제압하고, 자체의 유전적 구조를 변화시켜서 항생제에 쉽게 적응한다는 것과, 위생을 유지하는 것이 이 박테리아에 의한 감염을 피할 수 있는 최선의 방법이라는 내용으로 보아 (a)와 (b)는 정답에서 제외되고 정답은 (d)가 된다. (c)는 지문에 없는 내용이다.

public health 공중 보건 **overlook** 간과하다 **antibiotic** 항생 물질
mutation 돌연변이 **hygiene** 위생

3

오늘날 인적 자원 개발자들은 성공적인 직원이 활용하는 듯한 소위 소프트 기술에 대해 점점 더 많이 이야기하고 있다. 직원들의 소프트 기술을 강화하기 위해서 조직은 소프트 기술이 무엇인지 알아야 한다. 소프트 기술은 자질, 성격적 특성 그리고 모든 사람이 어느 정도는 갖고 있는 사회적 기술이다. 직장에서의 성공은 원활한 의사소통, 정보 공유, 의사 결정 능력, 유연성, 진실성, 좋은 유머 감각에 관한 직원의 기량에 크게 의존한다. 인생에 대한 긍정적인 관점과 친근함 또한 다른 팀 구성원들과 좋은 관계를 형성하기 위해 필요한 소프트 기술이다. 직원들이 소프트 기술을 향상시키는 최선의 방법은 세미나, 연수회, 회사 행사 등 함께 모여 그들의 식견을 나눌 수 있는 곳에 참석하는 것이다.

Q: 다음 중 필자가 가장 동의할 것 같은 의견은 무엇인가?
(a) 일류 대학교를 졸업하는 것이 소프트 스킬이다.
(b) 훌륭한 수학 실력은 소프트 스킬이다.
(c) 다른 사람의 이야기를 경청하는 것은 소프트 스킬이다.
(d) 훌륭한 컴퓨터 실력은 소프트 스킬이다.

소프트 스킬이 무엇이고 얼마나 중요한지 기술하는 내용이다. 자질, 성격, 사교 기술, 의사소통 기술, 유머 감각, 긍정적인 인생관, 호의 등을 소프트 스킬에 포함시키는 것으로 보아, 소프트 스킬은 학력이나 특정 분야에 있어서 전문 기술이 아니라 좋은 인간관계를 유지하는 능력을 의미한다. 따라서 다른 사람의 이야기를 경청하는 것도 좋은 인간관계를 유지하는 데 도움이 되므로 정답은 (c)이다.

soft skills 대인 기술 **capitalize on** ~을 활용하다 **fortify** 강화하다
trait 특성 **flexibility** 유연성 **integrity** 진실함 **rapport** 관계
enhance 향상시키다 **insight** 식견

4

맥애비티 씨께
이 서신은 당사가 9월 5일에 귀사에 주문해서 귀사가 당사에게 9월 20일에 보낸 선적분에 관한 것입니다. 주문 내용을 상기시켜드리자면, 당사가 주문한 것은 보쉬 이어폰 250,000개와 뎅크 스피커 60,000개였습니다. 그런데 당사의 창고에서 검사해 보니 이어폰 선적 물량이 50,000개 초과된 것으로 밝혀졌습니다. 당사로 보내주신 스피커 브랜드 또한 저희가 요청한 것이 아니었습니다.
당사는 이것을 귀사의 단순한 실수라고 생각합니다. 따라서 잘못된 선적분을 반송합니다. 또한 귀사에서 참고할 수 있도록 당사의 정확한 주문 내용을 보여주는 판매 송장 원본 1부를 동봉합니다. 늦어도 9월 25일까지 정확한 주문량을 받을 수 있도록 해 주시면 감사하겠습니다.

신속한 조치를 부탁드립니다.

샌디 록하트

Q: 이 편지에서 유추할 수 있는 것은?
(a) 이어폰과 스피커 둘 다 반송될 것이다.
(b) 이 편지는 9월 20일 전에 보내졌다.
(c) 뎅크 스피커 60,000개가 배달되었다.
(d) 이어폰 200,000개만 도착했다.

주문한 물건이 잘못 납품되었다고 알리는 사업상의 서신이다. 상대 회사는 9월 20일 선적했다고 했으므로 이 서신은 선적일 이후 보내진 것이다. 이어폰이 50,000개 초과 납품되었고 주문하지 않은 브랜드의 스피커가 왔다고 했으므로 이어폰은 총 300,000만대가 납품되었고 뎅크 스피커는 하나도 납품되지 않았다. 잘못된 선적분을 반송한다는 내용으로 보아 이 회사는 초과된 이어폰과 스피커 전량을 반송할 것으로 보인다. 따라서 정답은 (a)이다.

shipment 선적 examination 검사 warehouse 창고 oversight 실수
return 반송하다 enclose 동봉하다 invoice 송장 at the latest 늦어도

5

어떤 역사가들은 세계 2차 대전에서 독일의 폴란드 침략을 단순한 군사적 전술로 들지만, 많은 역사가들은 그것을 폴란드 인구를 멸살하기 위한 사악한 시도로 본다. 예를 들어, 수도인 바르샤바로 바로 향하기 보다는 독일군은 군사적이거나 정치적이지도 않은 목표물을 파괴하며 지방을 휩쓸고 다녔다. 그들은 그저 폴란드 군대를 물리치는 것뿐만 아니라 폴란드 국민의 저항도 탄압하기 위해 애썼다. 유태인과 비유태인 민간인 모두 항복 또는 저항에 상관없이 박해를 받았다. 도시 전체가 완전히 파괴되고 모든 생존자들이 무자비하게 색출되었다. 이런 전시 잔혹 행위는 그 뒤에 일어난 일에 비하면 작은 것일 수 있지만 히틀러의 폴란드 침략은 독일 전쟁광의 능력과 의도를 섬뜩하게 보여주는 것이었다.

Q: 다음 중 필자가 가장 동의할 것 같은 의견은 무엇인가?
(a) 독일이 폴란드를 침공한 유일한 목적은 정부를 타도하는 것이었다.
(b) 폴란드 침공은 독일이 저지른 최악의 잔혹 행위였다.
(c) 민간인은 전쟁에서 적법한 군사적 목표가 아니다.
(d) 히틀러가 전쟁에서 승리하기 위해서는 폴란드 국민을 전멸시킬 필요가 있었다.

독일군이 폴란드 정부를 파괴하고 국민을 말살하려고 했으므로 (a)는 정답에서 제외되며, 저지른 잔혹 행위들이 다가올 일 때문에 작아 보였다는 내용으로 미루어 그 후 더 큰 잔혹 행위가 저질러졌음을 알 수 있으므로 (b)도 정답에서 제외된다. 히틀러가 전쟁의 승리를 폴란드 국민을 전멸시킬 필요가 있었다는 내용이 지문에 없으므로 (d)도 정답에서 제외된다. 지문 중 '군사적이지도 않고 정치적이지 않은 목표'는 민간인임을 의미한다. 여기에서 민간인은 적법한 군사적 목표가 아님을 알 수 있다.

cite 인용하다 tactic 전략 sinister 사악한 wipe out 완전히 파괴하다
civilian 민간인 persecute 박해하다 raze 완전히 파괴하다 atrocity
전시의 잔혹 행위 gruesome 섬뜩한

6

150년간의 영광스러운 역사에서 알파는 기술 혁신 선도자의 역할을 해 왔습니다. 끈기와 개척 정신으로, 당사의 손목시계는 혹독한 날씨에 도전하기 위해서 광활한 우주부터 심해에 이르기까지 여러 지역을 여행했습니다. 알파는 또한 스포츠 시간 측정 분야에서도 선도자입니다. 누구도 따라잡을 수 없는 기술 분야의 전문 지식으로 인해서 알려진 알파는 시간

측정 서비스를 필요로 하는 수많은 국제 행사를 위한 공식 업체입니다. 국제 수영 경기의 시간 측정 시스템 전광판은 알파의 자랑스러운 상품이고, 알파는 북유럽 겨울 스포츠 경기를 위한 시간 측정 서비스를 제공합니다. 알파는 고품질 상품과 개척 정신의 브랜드입니다. 1849년에 창립된 이래로 알파는 업계의 영광스러운 역사를 창조하는 데 헌신해 오고 있습니다.

Q: 지문에서 유추할 수 있는 것은?
(a) 알파는 150개가 넘는 국가에 국제 지사가 있다.
(b) 알파는 1849년 이래로 올림픽의 주요 후원업체였다.
(c) 알파는 최근 겨울 스포츠 기구를 제조하기 시작했다.
(d) 알파는 극한의 환경에서도 정상적으로 작동하는 제품을 개발하려고 노력한다.

두 번째 문장에서 알파의 제품이 극한의 기후를 견딜 수 있도록 우주나 바다로도 제품을 보낸다고 했으므로 정답은 (d)이다.

innovation 혁신 perseverance 끈기 pioneering spirit 개척 정신
wristwear 손목시계 elements 악천후 foundation 설립 dedicate
to ~에 헌신하다

7

국가들의 결정을 이해하고 예측하기 위해 많은 정치인들이 국제 관계 이론이라는 렌즈를 통해서 바라본다. 국제 관계 이론의 매우 인기 있는 유파는 자유주의이다. 자유주의는 세상이 가혹하고 위험한 곳이지만 군사력을 사용해서 얻은 결과는 흔히 혜택을 능가한다고 주장한다. 그러므로 국제 협력은 모든 나라의 관심사이다. 또한 군사력이 유일한 힘의 형식이 아니다. 경제력과 사회적인 힘도 매우 중요하다. 경제력의 행사가 군사력의 행사보다 더 효과적인 것으로 입증되었다. 게다가 국제 규정과 기구는 협력, 신뢰, 번영을 조성하는 것을 도울 수 있다. 빠른 세계화와 통신 기술의 향상으로 자유주의는 국가의 행동을 이해하는 데 있어서 많은 지지를 얻고 있다.

Q: 지문에 따르면 자유주의에 관해 유추할 수 있는 것은?
(a) 전쟁은 국제적 갈등을 해결하는 방법이다.
(b) 국가는 가능한 한 많은 관계를 형성해야 한다.
(c) 세계에는 우호적인 국가들이 많이 있다.
(d) 세계 평화는 돈으로 살 수 있다.

자유주의에 대해서 기술하는 내용이다. 자유주의는 군사력 보다 경제력을 더 효과적인 것으로 보고 있으므로 (a)는 제외되며, (c)의 내용은 지문에서 유추할 수는 있지만 자유주의와 관계가 없는 내용이다. 경제력의 행사가 돈으로 세계 평화를 사는 것을 의미하는 것이 아니므로 (d)도 제외된다. 국제 협력이 모든 나라의 관심사이고, 국제 규정과 국제기구가 협력, 신뢰, 번영을 조성하는 것을 도울 수 있다는 내용으로 미루어 (b)가 가장 적절하므로 정답이다.

predict 예측하다 school 유파, 학파 liberalism 자유주의
consequence 결과 outweigh 능가하다 cooperation 협력
matter 중요하다 prosperity 번영

8

컴퓨터 시스템은 우리에게 엄청난 효용과 편의를 제공할 뿐만 아니라 심신을 꽤 쇠약하게 만들 수 있는 사이버 공격의 가능성도 열어 놓는다. 이러한 위협의 희생물이 되지 않기 위해서는 명심해야 하는 몇 가지 사항이 있다. 인터넷에서 찾아보고 선호하는 검색 엔진을 이용하여 우선 실질적

인 위협에 익숙해져야 한다. 데이터 손실을 피하기 위해 할 수 있는 또 다른 일은 컴퓨터에 저장되어 있는 중요한 파일의 백업 파일을 만들어 두는 것이다. 이 파일을 USB 플래시 드라이버나 외장 하드 디스크와 같은 휴대용 저장 장치에 저장할 수 있다. 또는, 온라인 저장 사이트를 이용해서 중요한 파일의 백업 파일을 만들 수도 있다. 또한 바이러스로부터 시스템을 보호하는 데 도움이 되는 신뢰할 만한 바이러스 방어 소프트웨어를 설치하기를 권장한다. 데이터를 보호하는 것은 결국 외부 위협에 대해서 얼마나 준비하고 경계를 하고 있는지에 달려 있다.

Q: 지문에서 유추할 수 있는 것은?
(a) 휴대용 저장 장치는 데이터를 외부적으로 저장할 수 있는 유일한 공간이다.
(b) 인터넷에는 컴퓨터 바이러스에 대한 많은 정보가 있다.
(c) 바이러스 방어 소프트웨어가 효력이 있으려면 반드시 지속적인 업데이트가 되어야 한다.
(d) 내장 하드 디스크에 데이터를 저장하는 것은 백업 파일을 만드는 방법이다.

컴퓨터에 대한 공격으로부터 데이터를 보호하기 위한 방법을 알려 주는 내용이다. '데이터의 손실에 대비해서 백업 파일을 만드는 방법으로 USB 플래시 드라이버나 외장 하드 디스크와 같은 휴대용 저장 장치 또는 온라인 저장 사이트를 이용해야 한다'는 내용이 있다. 따라서 (a)와 (d)는 정답에서 제외된다. (c)는 맞는 말이지만 지문에는 없는 내용이다. 지문 중에 '인터넷에서 찾아보고 선호하는 검색 엔진을 이용하여 우선 실질적인 위협에 익숙해져야 한다'는 내용으로 보아 인터넷에 데이터를 보호하기 위한 정보가 있다는 것을 알 수 있다. 따라서 정답은 (b)이다.

debilitate 쇠약하게 하다　**portable** 휴대할 수 있는　**storage** 저장
install 설치하다　**dependable** 신뢰할 만한　**ultimately** 궁극적으로

9

외부인이 한 무리의 십 대들을 본다면 임의적으로 만들어진 그룹이라고 생각할지 모른다. 그러나 이는 마치 재갈매기 무리를 보고는 새가 많다고 묘사하는 것처럼 잘못된 해석이다. 사실 갈매기의 집단은 지도자와 이를 따르는 무리가 있는 매우 조직화된 사회로서 십 대 그룹과 같다. 그룹에 속한 모든 사람들은 누가 리더인지 알고 있다. 아마 매우 주의 깊은 관찰자는 서 있거나 걷는 모습에서 드러나는 특유의 자신감을 보고 그 그룹의 리더를 알아차릴 수 있을지도 모른다.

Q: 글로부터 유추할 수 있는 내용은?
(a) 십 대 무리는 갈매기 무리처럼 매우 조직화되어 있다.
(b) 십 대들은 갈매기처럼 임의적으로 무리를 짓는다.
(c) 갈매기 무리가 십 대보다 더 조직화되어 있다.
(d) 십 대 무리를 보면 사람들은 쉽게 리더를 알아볼 수 있다.

저자는 십 대 그룹이 상당히 조직화된 그룹임을 보여 주고자 재갈매기 예를 들고 있으므로 정답은 (a)이다. (b)와 (d)는 본문의 내용과 다르며, (c)는 본문의 내용만으로는 확인할 수 없는 내용이다.

herring gull 재갈매기　**gullery** 갈매기의 집단 서식처　**observer** 관찰자
spot 찾아내다

10

근무 또는 공부를 하는 장소에 상관없이 간단한 글쓰기는 길러야 하는 필수적인 능력입니다. 작문 능력을 향상시키기 위해서 따르기 쉬운 이 지시 내용을 숙고해 볼 수도 있습니다. 첫째, 정확한 글의 분량을 확인하십

시오. 교수나 상사가 특정의 글의 분량을 요구한다면 반드시 그에 따라야 합니다. 그리고 좋은 작문의 3S를 준수하십시오. 다시 말해, 간결하고 간단하고 구체적으로 쓰십시오. 이것은 주제에 대해서 풍부한 자료를 제공하는, 짧고 이해가 가능하면서도 빈틈이 없는 분석을 쓰라는 것을 의미합니다. 셋째, 충분히 조사를 하십시오. 글의 정보는 균형 잡힌 다양한 출처에서 나와야 합니다. 이러한 원칙을 이용한 꾸준한 연습을 통해서 직업이나 학업에 도움이 되도록 작문 실력을 상당히 향상시킬 수 있습니다.

Q: 작문 실력에 관해 유추할 수 있는 것은?
(a) 할당된 분량보다 더 많이 쓰면 좋은 점수를 받을 수 있다.
(b) 모든 독자는 장문의 글을 이해한다.
(c) 간결한 동시에 빈틈없는 글을 쓰는 것이 가능하다.
(d) 대학을 졸업한 후에는 훌륭한 작문 실력은 필요가 없다.

이 지문의 내용은 글을 쓰는 데 도움이 되는 방법들을 소개하는 것이다. 글 분량에 대한 요구를 받았다면 반드시 따라야 한다는 내용이 있으므로 (a)는 제외되고, (b)는 지문에 없는 내용이며, 좋은 작문 실력이 직업이나 학업에 도움이 된다는 내용이 있으므로 (d)도 제외된다. 짧고 이해가 가능하고 빈틈없는 글을 쓰라는 내용이 있으므로 정답은 (c)이다.

irrespective of ~에 관계없이　**indispensable** 필수적인
ascertain 확인하다　**succinctness** 간결성　**specificity** 구체적임
comprehensible 이해가 가능한　**adequate** 충분한　**derive** 비롯되다
source 출처　**proficiency** 실력

Unit 08 1지문 2문항　　　　　　　　p.95

1 (a)	2 (b)	3 (b)	4 (d)	5 (d)
6 (a)	7 (b)	8 (c)	9 (b)	10 (c)

1

이스턴 포스트
천식 흡입기 리콜
다이엘 호프만

수십 종의 천식 흡입기들이 환자들의 생명에 위협을 가할 수도 있는 잠재적인 결함 때문에 최근에 리콜이 되었다. 약 8,000가지 종류의 흡입기들이 미국에서만 해도 시장에서 천식 환자들에 의해 이용되고 있다. 그것들 중에서, 200여 종 이상의 흡입기들이 부정적인 영향을 받고 있으며, 반환될 필요가 있다고 보고되고 있다. 리콜은 공공의료기구조사국 (PHPRA)의 관리들이 천식 환자들에게 천식 증상에 대한 응급 치료에 이용되는 흡입기들을 반환하라고 촉구한 이후에 진행되고 있다. 왜냐하면 그것들이 요구되는 복용량을 제공하지 못한 것으로 밝혀졌기 때문이다.

PHPRA의 조사부의 제품분석과의 매니저인 제시카 맥레인은 천식 흡입기를 이용하고 있는 환자들이 그들의 흡입기가 리콜 대상인지를 확인해야 한다고 말했다. 그녀는 환자들과 그들의 가족들이 그들의 치료 장치들이 안전하고 효과적인지를 확인해야 한다고 말했다. 그녀는 인터뷰에서 잘못된 흡입기들을 가지고 있는 사람들이 위험에 처할 수도 있다고 말했다. 그들은 기침, 무호흡증, 헐떡거림, 혹은 가슴 통증과 같은 악화시키는

천식 증상을 경험할 수도 있다. 천식 흡입기를 이용하고 있는 사람들은 흡입기 바닥에 있는 일련번호를 확인해야 한다. 만약 그것들이 리콜 목록에 있다면, 그들은 의학적 조언을 받아야 하며, 교환을 위해 약국에 반품해야 한다.

Q1: 글쓴이가 하고자 하는 것은?
(a) 건강에 해를 끼치는 결함이 있는 천식 흡입기들의 리콜을 보도하기
(b) 공공의료기구조사국의 역할에 대해 환자들에게 알려주기
(c) 천식 증상을 완화하기 위해 안전하고 효과적인 치료 기구를 홍보하기
(d) 제약회사들의 근무태만에 대해 불평하기

Q2: 글쓴이가 동의할 것 같은 것은?
(a) 시장에 출시된 대부분의 천식 흡입기들은 환자들의 요청에 따라 환불될 수 있다.
(b) 환자들 스스로 그들의 흡입기들이 리콜될 것인지를 확인해야 한다.
(c) 단지 적은 양의 복용량이 천식 증상을 치료하는 데 효과적일 수 있다.
(d) 리콜 목록은 공공의료기구조사국의 웹사이트에 게시되어야 한다.

Q1. 천식 흡입기들의 문제점에 대해 지적하는 글이며, "Dozens of kinds of asthma inhalers have recently been recalled due to potential defects"라는 문장을 통해, 결함이 있는 천식 흡입기들의 리콜을 보도하고 있으므로, "리콜을 보도하기 위한" 글이라는 것을 알 수 있으므로, 정답은 (a)이다.

Q2. 천식 흡입기들의 결함 확인과 리콜의 경우, "Those who are using asthma inhalers should check the serial number on the bottom of their inhaler"라는 문장을 통해, 고객들이 직접 일련번호를 확인해서 흡입기가 리콜 대상인지 확인해야 한다는 것을 알 수 있으므로, 정답은 (b)이다.

recall 리콜하다, 회수하다 asthma 천식 inhaler 흡입기 potential 잠재적인 defect 결함, 결점 pose a threat 위협하다 adversely 역으로, 거꾸로 emergency 응급, 긴급 assessment 평가 be subject to ~을 따르다 faulty 결함이 있는 aggravate 악화시키다 wheeze 헐떡거리다 pharmacist 약사 detrimental 해로운 ameliorate 개선하다 negligence 근무태만 at the request of ~의 요구에 따라

2

동료 연구원 여러분께,

조직위원회를 대신하여, 20번째 국제토목공학회가 5월 16일부터 20일까지 개최될 것이라는 점을 알리게 되어 기쁘게 생각합니다. 우리의 명망 있는 오랜 전통이 있는 국제회의는 연구자들이 그 분야에서 최신 연구 결과물들에 대해 배울 수 있는 이상적인 학계의 플랫폼으로서 중요한 역할을 해왔습니다. 저희는 토목공학의 모든 분야에서 새로운 연구 결과물들을 제시하고 공유하는 데 기여하기 위해 노력해 왔습니다.

우리 학회는 그들의 경험과 최신 연구 결과물들을 교환하기 위해 주요 학자들과 연구자들을 하나로 모으는 데 기여해 왔습니다. 우리 학회는 전 세계적으로 과학자들, 공학자들, 그리고 전문가들 사이에서 최고의 학제간 포럼을 경험할 수 있는 기회를 전문가들에게 계속해서 제공해 왔습니다.

학회가 진행되는 동안, 몇 개의 세부 토론회들이 몇몇 배정된 회의실에서 개최될 예정입니다. 그 프로그램들은 토목공학의 연구, 생산, 그리고 이용에서의 다양한 현재의 진보에 초점을 맞출 것입니다. 학회와 세부적인 토론회의 목적은 전 세계의 명망 있는 학자들에게 포럼을 제공하는 것이며, 최신 지식의 상호 교환을 촉진시키기 위한 것입니다. 만약 관심이 있다면, 늦어도 4월 10일까지 참여할 것인지를 알려주시기 바랍니다.

진심을 다하여,
앨리스 맥도웰 교수
인디애나 주립 기술 대학교
토목공학과

Q1: 맥도웰 교수는 왜 편지를 보냈는가?
(a) 명망 있는 학회의 업적에 대해 연구자들에게 알리기 위해
(b) 특정 분야의 연구자들에게 국제학회에 참석해 줄 것을 요청하기 위해
(c) 토목공학 학자들 사이에서 최신 연구 결과물을 공유하기 위해
(d) 전통적인 국제학회를 조직하기 위한 혁신적인 생각들을 요구하기 위해

Q2: 편지에 따르면 옳은 것은?
(a) 그 학회는 토목공학에 대한 국내 문제들을 다룰 것이다.
(b) 조직위원회는 조사 보고서들을 미리 기고하도록 요구하고 있다.
(c) 다른 학술계의 연구자들은 그 학회에 참석할 수 없다.
(d) 그 학회에 참석한 사람들은 그들 분야에서 최신 정보를 얻을 수 있다.

Q1. 20번째로 개최되는 국제토목공학회(the 20th International Conference on Civil Engineering)에 대해 알리는 편지글이며, "If you are interested, please let me know if you will attend by April 10 at the latest."라는 문장을 통해 참가의사를 알려달라고 했으므로, 학회에 초청하는 글이라는 것을 알 수 있으므로 정답은 (b)이다.

Q2. 국제토목공학회에서 다양한 주제를 다루지만, 특히 "promote the interactive exchange of state-of-the-art knowledge"라는 내용을 통해 토목공학과 관련하여 최신 지식 및 정보를 얻을 수 있다는 것을 알 수 있으므로, 정답은 (d)이다.

colleague 동료 on behalf of ~을 위하여, 대신하여 prestigious 유명한, 신망있는 seek to ~하기 위해 노력하다 conference 회의, 학회 consistently 지속적으로 premier 최고의 interdisciplinary 학제간의 practitioner 개업자, 실행자 subdivision 부분, 구획 state-of-the-art 최신의, 최근의 accomplishment 업적, 실적, 실행 innovative 혁신적인 conventional 전통적인

3

세계에서 최신 전기 개인 운송 수단의 주요 공급업체들 중의 하나인 세그웨이는 두 개의 새로운 전기 스쿠터인 세그스쿠터 1과 세그스쿠터 2를 출시하여 개인 운송 수단 제품군을 확장할 것이라고 발표하게 되어 기쁘게 생각합니다. 각각의 세그스쿠터를 타는 동안, 고객들은 라이딩을 하면서 스마트폰 앱을 이용할 수 있으며, 다른 편리한 장치들을 이용할 수 있습니다. 디자인부터 생산까지 전체 과정에 참여했던 개발자들은 우리의 전기 세그스쿠터들이 뛰어날 것이라고 확신하고 있습니다.

세그스쿠터 1
세그스쿠터 1은 한번 충전하여 약 15마일(24 km)의 거리를 최대 시속 6마일(10 km/h)로 달릴 수 있습니다. 그것은 또한 자가 균형 장치, LED 디지털 디스플레이, 그리고 잠김 방지 브레이크 시스템을 장착하고 있습니다.

세그스쿠터 2
세그스쿠터 2 모델은 한번 충전으로 최대 15마일(24 km)까지 최대 시속 12마일(20 km/h)에 도달할 수 있습니다. 세그스쿠터 1에서 발견되는 모든 특징들 이외에도, 그것은 편안한 라이드를 보장하기 위해 후방 충격 흡수 기능을 가지고 있습니다.

용이성

모든 제품은 현재 미국 전역의 주요 소매업체에서 구매하실 수 있습니다.

여러 해 동안, 세그웨이는 상업용의, 전기로 운용되는, 자가 균형이 가능한 개인 운송 수단에서 세계적인 리더라고 알려져 왔습니다. 우리는 일상적으로 그리고 여가활동으로 타는 라이더들을 돕기 위해 제품에 우리의 지적 재산권을 적용하고 있습니다. 더 많은 정보를 원하신다면, www.segscooter.com을 방문해 주세요.

Q1: 배터리가 완충이 되면, 고객들은 얼마나 멀리까지 세그스쿠터들을 운행할 수 있는가?

(a) 6마일

(b) 10마일

(c) 12마일

(d) 15마일

Q2: 광고에서 추론할 수 있는 것은?

(a) 세그스쿠터 2는 세그스쿠터 1보다 기능이 더 많다.

(b) 잠김 방지 브레이크 시스템은 시장에 출시된 대부분의 스쿠터들에 널리 이용되어 왔다.

(c) 두 개의 새로운 세그스쿠터들은 충격 흡수 장치들이 장착되어 있다.

(d) 세그웨이는 전국에 고객들이 연락을 취할 수 있는 지역 대리점들을 가지고 있다.

Q1. 세그스쿠터 출시를 홍보하는 글이며, "15 miles (24 km) out of a single charge"라는 내용을 통해, 한번 충전하면 15마일을 달릴 수 있으므로, 정답은 (d)이다.

Q2. 세그스쿠터 2는 세그스쿠터 1의 기능 전부를 가지고 있고 후방 충격 흡수 기능도 가지고 있다고 했으므로 정답은 (a)이다.

transportation 운송 수단 release 출시하다 leverage ~을 다양하게 이용하다 convenient 편리한 feature 특징, 특성 confident 확신하는 approximately 대략, 약 anti-lock braking system 잠김 방지 브레이크 시스템 absorption 흡수 availability 용이성, (입수) 가능성 retailer 소매업자 intellectual property 지적재산권 distributor 배급업자, 유통업자

4

조나단 스위프트: 걸리버 여행기

많은 문학비평가들은 아일랜드 작가 조나단 스위프트가 인간혐오적인 시각을 통해 인간의 본성을 묘사했으며, 영국 사회의 변화와 상황을 풍자했다고 주장한다. 그의 대표적 소설 〈걸리버 여행기〉는 영국인 레뮤엘 걸리버의 여정과 독특한 경험을 다룬다. 이 작품은 18세기 영국의 정치적 사회적 문제뿐만 아니라 인간 본성에 대한 풍자적 논평 때문에 수많은 논쟁을 유발해왔다. 걸리버는 인간의 이기심에 대해 이야기하며, 인간의 허영심을 보여주는 수많은 예들에 대해 이야기한다.

실제로, 〈걸리버 여행기〉에서 스위프트는 분명하게 인간성의 절망에 대한 걸리버의 관점을 공유하는 것 같다. 특히, 걸리버의 네 번째 여행은 야후들에 대한 명백한 공격 때문에 인간의 본성에 대한 공격으로 이해될 소지가 있다. 그러나 그 소설을 세심하게 읽어 보면, 스위프트는 걸리버와 야후들에 대해서만 풍자적인 것 같다. 그는 대규모로 인간성을 표적으로 삼지 않지만, 분명히 인간성이 결함이 있다고 생각한다. 한 에세이에서, 그는 인간에 대한 유사한 분노를 표현하지만, 그러한 분노 속에서 그는 여전히 인간들이 그들의 결함을 수정함으로써 그들의 본성을 개선할 수 있다는 희망을 표현한다. 인간에서 내재된 모든 결함에도 불구하고, 그는 실제로 인간에 대해 신경 썼으며, 그들의 개선을 기원했다.

Q1: 본문의 주요한 논점은 무엇인가?

(a) 조나단 스위프트의 풍자적이고 인간혐오적인 글쓰기 양식을 비판하기 위해

(b) 조나단 스위프트가 인간혐오주의자라는 오해를 반박하기 위해

(c) 영국에서 인간의 이기심의 불가피한 면들을 강조하기 위해

(d) 독자들에게 〈걸리버 여행기〉에 등장하는 등장인물들의 결함에 대해 알리기 위해

Q2: 조나단 스위프트에 대해 옳은 것은?

(a) 그는 영국 사회의 정치적 변화와 상황에 대해 호의적이었다.

(b) 그는 〈걸리버 여행기〉에서 인간의 본성에 대해 스스로 충분히 밝히지 않았다.

(c) 그는 야후를 인간과 비슷한 본성을 가진 것으로 여겼다.

(d) 그는 자신들의 결함을 개선하기 위해 노력하지 않는 점 때문에 인간에게 분노했다.

Q1. 조나단 스위프트의 소설 〈걸리버 여행기〉의 내용을 통해, 스위프트가 인간혐오주의자라는 세간의 평가가 있다는 점을 지적하고 있으나, "a careful reading on the novel suggests that Swift is just satirical toward Gulliver and the Yahoos"라는 문장을 통해, 실제 스위프트는 인간혐오주의자가 아니었다는 것을 밝히고 있으므로, 정답은 (b)이다.

Q2. 걸리버의 네 번째 여행에서 조나단 스위프트는 야후와 인간의 모습을 대비시키고 있으며, "Gulliver's fourth travel is ostensibly understood as an attack on the human nature due to the vivid attack on the Yahoos"라는 문장을 통해 개선되지 않은 인간의 본성이 야후와 유사하다고 판단하고 있으므로, 정답은 (c)이다.

literary 문학의 misanthropic 인간혐오의 parody 희화화하다, 풍자하다 representative 대표적인 peculiar 특별한, 독특한 a myriad of 수많은 controversy 논란, 논쟁 satirical 풍자적인 a profusion of 수많은 vanity 자만심, 허영심, 무가치 perspective 관점 ostensibly 표면적으로 vivid 선명한, 강렬한 indignation 분노, 화 rectify 개정하다, 수정하다 inherent 타고난, 선천적인 refute 반박하다 misconception 오해 highlight 강조하다 inevitable 불가피한 in favor of 호의적인 sufficiently 충분히 conceive 이해하다, 고안하다 be indignant with ~에 분노하다

5

www.usatoday.com/opinion/nuclearplants

일리노이주를 위한 핵발전소 추가

기사 전문 읽기 ▼

의견

알렉스 라우리 | 8월 10일

핵에너지를 평화롭게 이용하는 것은 핵무기의 확장에 대해 우려했던 아이젠하워 대통령의 통치 시기였던 1954년 미국에서 시작되었다. 미국 정부는 핵무기를 개발하는 것을 포기한 약속의 대가로 다른 나라들에게 평화로운 핵 기술에 대한 접근을 허용했다. 결과적으로, 몇몇 국가들에 의한 핵폭탄 실험에도 불구하고, 극소수의 국가들만이 최근에 핵무기를 개발해왔다. 안전은 특히 핵발전소에서 평화로운 핵에너지 이용을 위한 필수적인 요구사항이었다.

핵에너지는 수많은 장점을 가지고 있지만, 그것은 항상 심각한 위험을 줄 가능성이 있다. 일본에서 후쿠시마 핵발전소가 2011년에 붕괴되었을 때, 세계는 이러한 에너지가 얼마나 위험할 수 있는지 알게 되면서 충격에 빠

졌다. 일본과 같은 매우 발전된 국가들도 예상치 못한 사고가 일어났을 때 그 상황을 통제할 수 없었다. 게다가, 폐기물을 저장하는 문제는 환경에 매우 해로우며, 폐기물을 처리하는 것은 가장 심각한 문제들 중의 하나이다. 따라서 몇몇 국가들은 새로운 핵발전소를 건설하는 것을 금지하기로 결정했으며, 곧 모든 기존의 핵발전소를 정지시키기로 결정했다.

Q1: 본문의 주제는 무엇인가?
(a) 평화로운 핵 기술은 많은 현재의 문제를 해결해 줄 것 같다.
(b) 많은 장점에도 불구하고, 핵에너지는 해결해야 할 것이 많다.
(c) 대부분의 선진국들은 핵발전소를 통제하에 유지한다.
(d) 몇몇 국가들은 이미 핵폐기물을 저장하는 문제를 해결했다.

Q2: 본문에 따르면 옳은 것은?
(a) 미국 정부는 한때 핵무기의 확장을 환영했다.
(b) 미국 정부의 노력 덕분에, 모든 국가들은 핵기술을 폐기했다.
(c) 대부분의 사람들은 후쿠시마에서의 붕괴 이전에 핵에너지의 위험성을 인지하지 못했다.
(d) 핵발전소를 제거하려는 노력이 이루어졌으나, 효과는 미미하거나 아예 없었다.

Q1. 핵에너지의 이용과 한계에 대해 지적하는 글이며, "Though nuclear power has a great number of advantages, it always has the possibility of posing serious threats"라는 문장을 통해, 핵에너지의 위협을 해결하는 것이 중요한 문제이므로, 정답은 (b)이다.

Q2. 핵에너지의 위험성을 지적하면서, 일본의 후쿠시마 핵발전소의 사고에 대해 언급하고 있으며, "When the Fukushima nuclear power plant in Japan began to melt down in 2011, the world was shocked to know how dangerous this sort of power could be"라는 문장에서 세계가 깜짝 놀란 이유는 위험성을 예상하지 못했기 때문임을 알 수 있으므로, 정답은 (c)이다.

nuclear 핵의 **reign** 지배, 통치 **expansion** 확장, 확대 **in return for** ~에 대한 대가로 **pledge** 약속, 서약 **forgo** 포기하다 **pose a threat** 위협하다 **melt down** 붕괴하다 **detrimental** 해로운 **dispose of** 버리다, 폐기하다 **prohibit** 금지하다 **merit** 장점 **hail** 환영하다 **forsake** 포기하다 **eliminate** 제거하다, 없애다

Ⅲ 주제별 독해 훈련

Unit 01 과학

p.102

| 1 (b) | 2 (a) | 3 (c) | 4 (a) |
| 5 (d) | 6 (c) | 7 (b) | 8 (c) |

1

오존은 성층권과 대류권이라는 <u>2개의 지구 대기권 층에</u> 존재한다. 70년대 후반 이후로 남극 대륙 위에 있는 성층권의 오존은 감소하고 있다. 이 오존 구멍은 대략 북아메리카의 크기이고 전 세계에 퍼져나가는 감염과 유사하다. 오존 감소로 인해 대두되는 문제는 피부암, 눈의 손상, 지구 온난화, 작물 피해 등 많은 문제를 발생시키는 자외선에 대한 노출이다. 대류권의 오존은 사실 '나쁜 오존'이고 스모그와 인구 과밀 지역에서 발견된다.

(a) ~을 형성하는 우라늄과 더불어
(b) 2개의 지구 대기권 층에
(c) 빛을 제공하기 위한 목적으로
(d) 태양을 공전하는 대부분의 행성을 위해

지구 대기권의 오존층에 대해 설명하고 있다. 첫 문장에서 stratosphere는 지구 대기권의 성층권이고, troposphere는 대류권을 의미하는데 오존이 그 두 개의 대기권 중에 존재하므로 (b)가 정답이다.

stratosphere 성층권 **troposphere** 대류권 **Antarctica** 남극 대륙 **deplete** 감소하다 **analogous to** ~와 유사한 **ultraviolet radiation** 자외 복사선 **highly populated** 인구 밀도가 높은

2

오존층이 대기 중에 중요한 역할을 하는 것을 알게된 건 그리 오래 전은 아닙니다. 하지만 오존층의 위험한 파괴를 되돌려 놓는 것은 전 세계 국가들의 생활 방식과 정치적 변화를 요구하는 일입니다. 오존층 파괴 물질은 오존 분자를 없애는 합성 화학 물질이며 이 화학 물질 제조업자들의 수를 줄이면 오존의 파괴를 되돌려 놓는 데 보탬이 될 것입니다. ODS가 생산되지 않으면, 자연적인 오존 생성이 약 50년간 오존에 입혔던 과거의 훼손을 되돌릴 것으로 기대됩니다. <u>이를 고려하여</u>, 오존을 고갈시키는 화학 물질의 사용을 멈추기 위한 전 세계적으로 노력을 하고 있습니다. 불행히도 이 기회는 영원히 계속될 수 없습니다. 왜냐하면 어느 시점에서는 훼손이 너무 극심해서 태양 자외선의 영향이 너무 많은 피해를 야기해 우리는 영구적인 환경 문제를 경험하게 될지도 모르기 때문입니다.

(a) 이를 고려하여
(b) 그럼에도 불구하고
(c) 이전에
(d) 예를 들어

빈칸 전에 오는 문장을 보면 오존을 파괴하는 물질을 줄이면 오존층을 보존할 수 있다고 이야기하고 있다. 그리고 빈칸 뒤에 오는 내용은 전 세계적으로 오존을 파괴하는 화학품의 사용을 금지하는 노력을 하고 있다고 언급하고 있다. 따라서 빈칸 전 내용과 빈칸 뒤 내용의 관계는 원인과 결과이기 때문에 정답은 (a)가 된다.

crucial 중대한 **atmosphere** 대기 **reverse** 뒤바꾸다 **deplete** 고갈시키다 **substance** 물질 **synthetic** 합성한 **extinguish** 없애다 **molecule** 분자 **permanent** 영구적인

3

새로운 타입의 젤이 갑작스런 충격이나 심지어 총상과 같은 물리적 외상으로 인한 뇌 손상을 되돌려 놓을 기회를 제공할 것으로 보인다. 이 획기적인 발명품은 액체의 형태로 부상 자리에 주입되어 그곳의 줄기세포의 성장을 자극한다. 과학자들은 이미 기증자의 뇌세포를 가지고 상처에 위치시켜 손상된 조직을 복구하는 실험을 했다. 그러나 이것은 뇌 부상을 치료하는 데 다만 부분적으로 효과적임을 증명했다. 기증자의 세포는 염증과 흉터 때문에 상처를 복구하지 않는지도 모른다. 그러나 새로운 젤은 기증자 세포가 자랄 수 있는 더 나은 환경을 만들어 좀 더 많은 성공을 유도할 수 있다. 쥐를 이용한 연구에서 젤의 사용은 뇌부상 자리에 혈액 공급을 다시 확고히 하도록 도왔다. 더 나은 발전과 함께 새로운 젤은 머리의 신체적 손상을 치료하는 데 더 안전하고 확실한 방법의 문을 열도록 도울 수 있다.

(a) 뇌에서의 줄기세포 연구를 진행시키는 데
(b) 성공적인 장기 이식을 하는 데
(c) 머리의 신체적 손상을 치료하는 데
(d) 정신병자가 회복되도록 돕는 데

지문의 핵심 내용은 뇌의 외상을 치료하는 데 도움이 되는 새로운 젤을 소개하는 것이다. 그렇다면 마지막 문장에서 새로운 젤은 머리에 입은 물리적인 부상을 치료하는 확실하고 안전한 방법을 제공한다는 내용이 와야 자연스러우므로 정답은 (c)이다.

trauma 외상 **impact** 충격 **breakthrough** 획기적 발전 **stimulate** 자극하다 **inflammation** 염증 **scar** 흉터

4

많은 국가에서 뎅기열과 말라리아가 발생하여, 세계는 다시 모기로 인한 위험에 주목하고 있다. 대부분의 사람들은 모기의 박멸을 큰 소리로 외치지만 이는 현실적인 해결책이 아닐 수 있다. 따라서 일부 과학자들은 모기의 유전자를 변경하는 방안을 고민하고 있다. 그러나 우리는 모기의 유전자 변형을 허용하기 전에 우선 이 질문에 답을 해야 한다. 만약 모기가 유전적으로 변형되어 오래 살지 못하거나 제대로 날지 못하면, 생태계에서 모기의 역할을 맡기 위해 무슨 일이 발생할 것인가? 돌연변이와 다른 종으로 바뀔 가능성이 있는가? 모기가 퍼뜨리는 질병과 모기를 더 잘 통제하는 것과 관련된 인간의 고통 감소량은 엄청난 반면, 우리는 이러한 변화가 야기할 결과에 대한 철저한 요령이 필요하다.

Q: 지문의 주제는 무엇인가?
(a) 모기를 전멸시키는 것에 대한 우려
(b) 모기를 몰살시키는 확실한 방법
(c) 모기로부터 보호하는 법
(d) 위험하고 반갑지 않은 손님

이 지문의 핵심 내용은 모기들을 모두 없애는 것이 다른 문제를 야기할 수 있다는 것이며 이는 두 번째 문장에서 알 수 있다. 그렇다면 가장 어울리는 주제는 모기를 없애는 것이 나쁜 아이디어가 될 수 있다는 답인 (a)가 맞다.

outbreak 발병 **eradication** 근절, 박멸 **genocide** 학살 **genetics** 유전적 특징 **modification** 변경 **alter** 변경하다, 바꾸다 **niche** 생태적 지위 **ecosystem** 생태계 **mutation** 돌연변이 **downstream effect** 앞선 사건이 야기한 결과 **exterminate** 근절하다

5

옥스퍼드 대학의 과학자들은 뇌를 통과하는 전기에 의한 새롭고 흥미로운 부작용을 발견했다. 연구자들은 몇 분 동안 약한 전류를 이용해 치료를 받은 대상을 시험했고 수학적 기술에 있어서 그들의 능력이 실제로 고조되었음을 발견했다. 전기적 자극이 수적 인지 기능이 일어난다고 여겨지는 두정엽에 보내졌기에 이 결과를 완전히 예상치 못했던 것은 아니었다. 그러나 오히려 놀라운 발견은 인지할 수 있는 수학능력의 향상이 치료 6개월 후에도 관찰되었다는 것이다. 옥스퍼드팀은 이런 종류의 정신적 향상 서비스를 대중에게 제공한다는 생각을 품고 있다. 그런 서비스가 인기를 끌게 되든 어떻든, 심각한 수학적 장애를 가진 우리를 도와 줄 잠재력이 있는 듯하다.

Q: 이 지문은 주로 무엇에 관한 것인가?
(a) 수학을 연습하는 것은 뇌의 능력을 키워 준다.
(b) 전류는 기억력을 향상시켜 줄 수 있다.
(c) 대부분의 사람들은 TDCS가 필요하다
(d) 전류는 수학 능력을 향상시켜 준다.

지문의 핵심 내용은 첫 문장에 나오는 뇌에 전류를 흐르게 하면 수학 능력을 개선시킬 수 있다는 것이다. 따라서 정답은 (d)가 적합하며 (a)는 수학을 연습하면 뇌가 좋아진다는 뜻이라서 오답이다.

heighten 고조되다 **stimulation** 자극 **parietal lobe** 두정엽 **cognitive** 인식의 **perceivable** 인지할 수 있는 **entertain** 즐겁게 해주다 **catch on** 인기를 끌다 **handicap** 장애

6

과학자들과 공학자들은 과학 연구를 위한 최신 세대 수중 잠수정을 생각해 냈다. 이 새로운 급의 자율 수중 차량(AUV)은 프로펠러 운송수단의 단거리 기동성을 가진 수중 글라이더의 장거리 능력을 특징으로 한다. 개발자에 의해 테티스라고 명명된 원형은 굉장한 속력으로 수백 마일을 여행하거나 수 주 동안 해류를 따라 단순히 미끄러지듯이 움직일 수 있다. 그리고 탑재된 과학 도구의 고급 무기를 가진 테티스는 광범위한 연구를 위해 더 많은 해양을 개발할 것을 약속한다. 현재 원형은 약 십만 달러로 글라이더와 같은 가격이지만 최신 첨단 기술 장비들이 탑재되어 있다.

Q: 지문에 따르면 다음 중 일치하는 것은?
(a) 테티스는 장거리 여행을 할 수 있지만 과학 기구가 부족하다.
(b) 테티스는 많은 과학 기구를 갖추고 있지만 장거리를 달리지 못한다.
(c) 테티스는 장거리 여행이 가능하며 많은 과학 기구를 갖추고 있다.
(d) 테티스는 장거리 여행도 못하며 과학 기구도 별로 갖추지 않고 있다.

잠수정 테티스에 관한 내용으로 많은 과학 장비를 가지고도 장거리 여행을 할 수 있다는 장점이 있다. 따라서 정답은 (c)가 된다.

come up with ~을 생산하다 **submersible** 물속에서 쓸 수 있는 **autonomous** 자치의 **maneuverability** 기동력 **prototype** 원형 **velocity** 속력 **arsenal** 무기

7

핀란드의 한 남자가 시각 장애를 위한 혁신적인 새로운 치료법의 중심 대상이다. 새로운 실험적인 칩은 시신경에 양분을 제공하기 위해 기계적인 카메라와 합성 수정체를 이용하는 대신 눈의 수정체를 이용한다. 이 장치를 착용한 핀란드 남자는 글자, 회색 색조, 그리고 심지어 시계 판과 같은 일부 일상 사물도 알아볼 수 있었다. 다른 환자들과의 차후 임상 실험은 이 장치를 한 사람들은 사물을 알아보고 방 주변에서 방향을 찾을 정도로 충분히 잘 볼 수 있음을 확인시켜 줬다. 이런 장치들은 언젠가 노화에 따른 시력 감퇴를 포함한 다른 형태의 망막의 시력 장애를 가진 환자들을 도울 수 있을 것이다.

Q: 지문에서 유추할 수 있는 것은?
(a) 특별한 칩을 사용하는 맹인은 꽃 색깔을 구분할 수 있다.
(b) 특별한 칩을 사용하는 맹인은 앞에 있는 탁자를 볼 수 있다.
(c) 특별한 칩은 안경에 설치되어 눈 위에 쓰는 것이다.
(d) 특별한 칩을 사용하는 맹인은 보기 위해서 빛이 필요 없다.

지문의 주제는 시력을 잃은 사람들을 보게끔 도와주는 특별한 칩인데 칩을 이식하면 사물을 인식할 수 있다고 했으므로 유추할 수 있는 내용은 (b)이다.

lens 수정체 **optic nerve** 시신경 **make out** 알아보다 **subsequent** 그다음의 **clinical trial** 임상 실험 **navigate** 길을 찾다 **retinal** 망막의 **macular degeneration** (노화에 따른) 시력 감퇴

8

분자 생물학자들로 구성된 팀이 만들어 낸 신약의 한 종류는 세포를 그대로 살리면서 세포 안에 있는 바이러스를 없앨 수 있다. (a) 세포를 죽이면서 바이러스를 죽일 순 있지만 지나치게 하면 몸에 너무 해롭다. (b) 그러나 이 팀이 개발한 신약은 세포의 면역을 강화시키며 바이러스가 세포 안에 들어온 후에도 세포를 죽일 수 있는 능력을 준다. (c) 이 신약의 개발은 두 개의 큰 제약 회사의 자금으로 가능했다. (d) 세포의 면역력을 돕는 것은 세포가 바이러스를 죽이고 나서도 온전하게 해준다.

이 지문의 핵심 내용은 세포를 죽이지 않고 세포를 침입한 바이러스를 죽이는 신약을 소개하는 것이다. 그리고 그다음 문장에는 그 원리를 설명하는데 (c)는 제약 회사들의 지원을 통해서 이 약을 만들 수 있었다는 이야기이므로 글의 흐름과 맞지 않다.

immunology 면역학 **cell** 세포 **eliminate** 제거하다 **pharmaceutical** 제약의 **viral** 바이러스에 의한

Unit
02 건강
p.106

1 (b)	**2** (a)	**3** (d)	**4** (c)
5 (a)	**6** (a)	**7** (b)	**8** (b)

1

초콜릿을 사랑하는 분들에게 희소식이 있다. 퇴폐적이지만 맛있는 간식이 __건강에 도움이 될 수 있다고__ 발견되었다. 심장 협회의 정기 간행물은

8년 동안 40세에서 82세 사이의 스웨덴 여성 34,000명을 대상으로 한 연구 결과를 실었다. 연구는 20에서 30그램의 다크초콜릿을 일주일에 한두 번 먹으면 심장 질환의 위험을 30% 줄인다고 주장한다. 한 달에 한 번에서 세 번을 먹으면 위험이 26%로 떨어졌다. 연구는 영양사들이 초콜릿을 너무 많이 먹으면 건강을 해칠 수 있다는 경고를 반박한다. 그러나 초콜릿바 포장지를 하나 더 뜯기 전에 두 가지 요점들을 기억하라. 첫 번째, 혜택을 보려면 다크초콜릿만 적당히 먹어야 한다. 두 번째는 과일이나 채소와 같은 대체 음식으로도 동일한 혜택을 즐길 수 있다는 것이다.

(a) 너무 자주 먹어서는 안 된다
(b) 건강에 도움이 될 수도 있다
(c) 심장 마비의 위험을 증가시킬 수 있다
(d) 당뇨병을 앓고 있는 사람들에게 도움이 될 수 있다

세 번째 문장부터 내용을 살펴보면 초콜릿이 심장 질환의 발병을 낮출 수 있다는 실험 결과를 보여준다. 그리고 마지막 부분에서는 초콜릿의 혜택을 즐기기 위해서 해야 하는 두 점을 강조한다. 따라서 빈칸에는 초콜릿이 건강에 좋을 수 있는 내용의 (b)가 들어가야 자연스럽다.

decadent 타락한 **delectable** 아주 맛있는 **consume** 소비하다 **confute** 반박하다 **rip** 뜯다 **diabetes** 당뇨병

2

남자가 여자보다 심장 마비와 당뇨병과 같은 비만과 관련된 질환에 더 걸리기 쉽다는 점은 잘 알려진 사실이다. 흥미롭게도 병가와 식료품 구입비, 병원 치료비, 심지어 기름 비용(자동차가 더 무거우면 기름도 더 많이 먹는다)과 같은 여러 가지 요소를 고려하면 남자보다 여자들에게 비만은 거의 50% 더 많은 비용을 들게 한다. __이 계산에 따르면__ 여자들은 매년 4,500달러가 들고 남자는 2,500달러가 든다. 비만으로 인한 조기 사망 비용을 고려했을 때 이 비용은 여자에게는 8,300달러, 남자에게는 6,500달러로 올라간다. 주목해야 할 점은 비용의 차이에 병원비는 별로 영향을 미치지 않는다는 점이다. 그것보다는 임금에 미치는 영향이 더욱 컸다. 비만 여성은 일반 여성보다 임금이 낮은 반면 남성은 체중과 관련 없이 비슷한 임금을 받았다.

(a) 이 계산에 따르면
(b) 결과와 반대로
(c) 증명된 대로
(d) 그 결과로

빈칸 전에서는 남자보다 여자에게 비만이 더 많은 비용을 낳는다고 하며 빈칸 다음에는 구체적으로 얼마나 더 많은 비용을 낳는지 보여 준다. 그렇다면 정답은 (a)가 가장 적절하다. 그 이유는 전 문장에서 공식에 넣는 다양한 요소들을 제시한 다음 그 결과를 보여주기 때문이다.

susceptible (~의) 영향을 받기 쉬운 **obesity** 비만 **diverse** 다양한 **variable** 변수 **guzzle** 꿀꺽꿀꺽 마시다 **premature** 너무 이른

3

공중 보건 정기 간행물에 실린 최근 보고서는 운전보다는 자전거를 타거나 걷는 것과 같은 '능동적인 이동'이 개인의 의지보다는 도시의 물리적인 환경에 더 좌우된다고 주장한다. 미국 15개의 도시에서 인구와 주변 지역, 기본 시설을 조사한 후 연구원들은 대중교통과 거리 연결성과 주택 밀집과 토지의 다양한 사용 용도가 걷거나 자전거를 타기에 좋은 지역을 만들고 사람들이 운전하는 것을 덜 선호하게 만드는 데 커다란 요인이되는 데이터에 주목했다. 이러한 요인이 사람들이 운전하는 것을 덜 선호

하게 만들었다. 그러나 이러한 영향을 극대화하기 위해서는 시는 자동차 **주행 속도의 감소와** 더 비싼 주차비와 같은 자동차에 대한 제한을 실행해야 한다.

(a) 무단 횡단에 대한 더 높은 벌금
(b) 공용 주차장에 더욱 쉬운 이용
(c) 더 많은 신호등의 설치
(d) 주행 속도 감소

이 지문은 도시의 물리적인 환경이 사람들을 얼마나 능동적으로 이동하게 하는지 좌우한다는 내용이다. 마지막 문장은 물리적인 환경이 미치는 영향을 극대화하기 위해서 추가로 할 수 있는 것들을 이야기 한다. 그렇다면 자동차 사용을 자제시키는 조치를 골라야겠다. 따라서 정답은 (d)가 된다.

engagement 참여 **will** 의지 **transit** 교통체계 **connectivity** 접속 가능성 **density** 밀도 **compile** 엮다 **conducive to** ~을 조장하다 **optimize** 최고로[가장 능률적으로] 활용하다

4

습득된 행동과 물려받은 행동의 차이를 연구하기 위해서 일란성 쌍둥이는 훌륭한 연구 대상이다. 쌍둥이의 일치하는 유전자 덕분에 과학자들은 제품을 고르는 선호도는 습득된 행동인지 물려받은 행동인지 연구할 수 있었다. 컨슈머 리서치가 발간한 저널에서 일란성 쌍둥이의 제품 선호도를 다른 형제와 유전적으로 비슷한 이란성 쌍둥이들의 선호도와 비교했다. 그 연구는 일란성 쌍둥이들이 초콜릿, 자동차, 영화, 음악과 같은 다양한 제품에서 동일한 취향을 보이는 경향이 있는 것으로 나타났다. 물론 일란성 쌍둥이는 비슷하게 생각하고 행동할 것이라는 사회적인 기대를 받음으로 비슷한 선호도를 보일 것이라고 기대할 수 있다. 그래도 그 결과는 시장 경영자들이 왜 특정한 소비자는 특정 제품에 푹 빠지고 다른 소비자는 그러지 않는지 이해하는 데 도움이 될 것이다.

Q: 지문은 주로 무엇에 관한 것인가?
(a) 일란성 쌍둥이의 다른 쇼핑 습관
(b) 일란성 쌍둥이와 이란성 쌍둥이
(c) 취향에 대한 유전적 영향에 대한 연구
(d) 제품 선호도와 마케팅

지문의 핵심 내용은 일란성 쌍둥이를 상대로 한 연구가 제품 선호도는 습득한 행동이 아닌 타고난 행동이라고 한다. 그래서 가장 적합한 주제는 (c)이다.

inherit 상속하다 **identical twins** 일란성 쌍둥이 **innate** 타고난 **fraternal twins** 이란성 쌍둥이 **exhibit** (감정·관심 등을) 나타내다

5

생강 있으세요? 병든 임산부와 항암 치료를 받는 환자들, 약한 위를 달래기 위해서 뿌리를 사용하는 여행자들에게 유명한 민간요법으로 생강이 진통제 역할을 한다는 것이 발견되었다. 조지아 대학교의 과학자들은 익히거나 익히지 않은 생강 2그램 또는 플라시보를 2주 동안 매일 섭취한 건강한 성인 74명을 연구했다. 실험 대상자들은 팔꿈치 주변에 염증이나 근육통을 일으키는 운동에 참여했다. 연구의 목적은 근육통을 치료하는 데 생강의 효력을 보기 위함이었다. 연구 결과는 플라시보를 복용한 그룹보다 익히지 않은 생강을 먹은 그룹에서 운동을 하고 24시간 후 근육통이 23% 완화된 것으로 나타났다. 비슷하게 익힌 생강을 먹은 그룹은 플라시보를 먹은 그룹보다 근육통이 21% 더 줄었다.

Q: 지문은 주로 어떤 내용인가?
(a) 통증을 없애는 생강의 효력
(b) 집에서 사용하는 약으로써 생강의 다양한 용도
(c) 운동 효과를 더욱 높이기 위한 생강의 혜택
(d) 생강 과다 섭취의 부작용

지문의 핵심 내용은 생강이 진통제로 사용될 수 있다는 것이다. 따라서 정답은 (a)이다. (b)는 진통제뿐만이 아닌 다른 치료제로도 사용된다는 것을 의미하기에 너무 광범위하다.

remedy 치료 **ailing** 병든 **pregnant** 임신한 **chemotherapy** 화학 요법 **root** 뿌리 **soothe** 달래다 **analgesic** 진통제 **placebo** 플라시보, 위약

6

최근 몇 년 동안 하와이 사람들이 백인이나 흑인보다 더 일찍 죽는다는 근거 없는 이야기가 있었다. 그러나 연구에 근거를 둔 새로운 증거는 이 이야기가 사실이라는 것을 확인시켜 준다. 연구원들은 미국 백인보다 하와이 사람들이 더 일찍 사망할 위험이 컸으며 65세 이상인 사람들은 흑인 미국인보다 더 일찍 사망할 가능성이 있다는 것을 발견했다. 이러한 추측은 당뇨병과 비만, 마약 문제와 영아의 높은 사망률로 이어지는 태교의 부족 같은 다양한 요인을 포함한다. 연구는 미국인들이 최근 누리는 장수를 하와이 사람들이 즐길 수 있도록 특정 그룹을 위한 건강 및 행동 프로그램을 시작하도록 도와줄 것이다.

Q: 지문에 따르면 옳은 것은?
(a) 하와이 사람들은 대개 백인, 흑인 미국인보다 일찍 죽는다.
(b) 65세 이상의 흑인 미국인은 하와이 사람들보다 더 일찍 죽는다.
(c) 하와이 사람들이 일찍 사망하는 원인은 식단 때문이다.
(d) 하와이 사람들이 다른 미국인들과 비슷한 건강 통계를 가지고 있는지는 밝혀지지 않았다.

지문의 핵심 내용은 하와이 사람들이 백인이나 흑인보다 더 일찍 사망한다는 것이며 그 이유를 소개하고 있다. 하지만 하와이 사람들과 다른 아시아 사람들과는 비교를 하지 않는다. 따라서 정답은 (a)이다.

ungrounded 근거 없는 **evidence** 증거 **premature** 너무 이른 **speculation** 추측 **longevity** 장수

7

겨울은 사람들과 바이러스가 가까워져 아이들이 쉽게 감기에 걸리게 하는 계절이다. 보통 아이들은 며칠 후 감기를 털어 버리지만 감기와 싸우는 과정이 비만으로 이어질 수 있다는 나쁜 소식이 있다. 일반 감기와 비만의 새로운 관계는 8세부터 17세 아이들 120명을 연구한 후 발견되었다. 일반 감기에 대한 항체의 흔적이 있는 아이들은 항체의 흔적이 없는 아이들보다 비만일 확률이 3배 정도 된다. 실제로 항체를 가진 아이들은 없는 아이들보다 35파운드 정도 더 나갔다. 연구는 감기 바이러스가 세포의 발달 과정 속도를 올리면서 미성숙한 지방 세포를 더 빨리 자라게 하며 수를 늘린다고 설명했다. 연구는 식전 손을 씻는 것과 기침을 할 때 입을 막는 것처럼 예방 조치의 중요성도 지적한다.

Q: 필자가 동의할 것 같은 의견은?
(a) 아이들은 감기에 걸리면 체중이 줄어든다.
(b) 아이 안에 있는 일반 감기에 대한 항체가 자랄수록 아이는 비만이 될 확률이 크다.
(c) 비만인 아이들은 감기에 더 잘 걸린다.
(d) 아이가 체중을 줄이면 아이 안에 있는 항체 수도 줄어든다.

지문의 핵심 내용은 감기가 비만을 일으킨다는 것이다. 그리고 감기에 대한 항체를 많이 가진 아이들이 다른 아이들보다 더 비만일 가능성이 크다고 하기에 항체가 몸에 많을수록 비만일 가능성도 커진다고 추측할 수 있다. 따라서 정답은 (b)가 된다.

render 어떤 상태가 되게 만들다 **vulnerable** ~에 취약한 **shake off** 문제나 병 따위를 없애다 **sniffle** 훌쩍거림 **battle** 싸우다 **antibody** 항체 **rev up** 속도를 올리다

8

급성 치료 환자에게 매일 비타민 C를 복용시킨 후 의사들은 비타민 C가 사람들의 기분을 향상시키고 성생활까지도 활발하게 만든다는 예전 주장을 뒷받침해주는 새로운 증거를 갖게 되었다. (a) 비타민 C의 결핍은 급성 치료 환자들에게 일반적으로 발견되는 특징이고, 실험은 80명의 환자들로 구성된 대조군이 규칙적으로 비타민 C를 섭취하고 나서 기분이 좋아지는 것을 보여 줬다. (b) 결론은 충분한 양의 비타민이 하루를 평소보다 더 즐겁게 시작할 수 있게 해준다는 것을 보여 주었다. (c) 대조적으로, 같은 환자들이 정상적인 양의 비타민 D를 섭취를 했을 때에는 기분이 달라지지 않았다. (d) 결과는 비타민 C와 D의 결핍과 정신적인 이상의 관계를 설명해 주는 데 도움이 될 것이라는 점이다.

지문의 핵심 내용은 비타민 C가 사람들의 기분을 향상시킨다는 것인데 (b)를 보면 지문 중간에 결론을 이야기한다. 그리고 그 다음 문장은 지문에서 소개한 연구의 결과를 이야기하고 있으며 마지막 문장에서 지문의 결론을 또 소개한다. 따라서 어색한 문장은 (b)가 된다.

acute care 급성 환자 치료의 **dose** 복용량 **sufficient** 충분한 **bottom line** 요점 **deficiency** 결핍

Unit 03 역사

p.110

| 1 (c) | 2 (b) | 3 (b) | 4 (a) |
| 5 (d) | 6 (d) | 7 (c) | 8 (a) |

1

태평양 전쟁으로 유명한 전쟁 영웅인 맥아더 장군은 한국 전쟁 동안 **트루먼 대통령과의 대립** 때문에 그의 지휘권을 포기해야 했다. 중국이 공산주의 북한을 돕기 위해 전쟁에 참여했을 때 장군은 중국에 핵폭탄을 사용하도록 트루먼 대통령을 압박했다. 이것이 그가 한국 전쟁에서 이기도록 할 뿐만 아니라 베이징 공산주의자 정부의 붕괴를 강요할 것이라고 그는 판단했다. 그러나 트루먼과 그의 군사 고문들은 미국이 당시 유럽과 아시아에서 소련 연방과의 냉전으로 바쁜 와중에 중국과의 싸움을 해나갈 수 있다고 믿지 않았다. 지도부의 의견을 우회하여 맥아더는 자신의 주장을 미국 대중에게 호소하며 그 과정에서 대통령을 비난했다. 이것이 불복종과 마찬가지라 느낀 트루먼은 한국 전쟁이 진행 중이었음에도 1951년 그를 해임했다.

(a) 국가에 대한 배신
(b) 대통령에 출마하려는 바람
(c) 트루먼 대통령과의 대립
(d) 중국 병력을 막지 못한 실패

맥아더 장군과 트루먼 대통령의 갈등으로 맥아더 장군이 지휘권을 박탈당했다는 내용으로, 특히 마지막 두 문장을 보면 맥아더 장군이 트루먼 대통령과 군 관계자들의 주장을 무시하고 트루먼 대통령을 공개적으로 비방한 후 지휘권을 잃었다고 한다. 따라서 정답은 (c)가 된다.

celebrated 유명한 **relinquish** 포기하다 **bypass** 우회하다 **tantamount to** ~와 마찬가지의 **insubordination** 불복종 **disloyalty** 불충 **presidency** 대통령 직 **clash** 충돌, 대립

2

북대서양 조약 기구(NATO)는 오늘날까지도 활발하게 유지되고 있는 냉전 시대의 잔재이다. 동유럽에서 공산주의가 빠르게 확산됨에 따라, 미국의 트루먼 대통령은 NATO 동맹을 이용해 소련의 침투로부터 서유럽을 보호하고자 했다. 1949년 다국적 협약에 서명하면서 미국, 캐나다와 함께 유럽의 주요 국가들인 이탈리아와 노르웨이, 프랑스, 영국이 상호 방위 조약으로 동맹을 맺었다. NATO 헌장에 의하면 회원국 중 어느 한 나라에 대한 공격은 회원국 전체에 대한 공격으로 간주되었다. 1952년에 그리스와 터키, 뒤이어 1955년에 서독도 가입했다. 나토의 가장 위대한 족적은 미국이 서유럽을 보호하기 위해 서약한 것과 1차 세계 대전 후에 그랬던 것처럼 미국의 고립주의에 대해 또 다시 세계에서 들려오는 보수적인 목소리를 막았다는 것이었다.

(a) NATO 헌장과 반대로
(b) NATO 헌장에 의하면
(c) 헌장이 쓰여지기 전에
(d) 헌장이 만들어졌지만

빈칸 전에서는 NATO의 출범을 소개하고 있으며 그다음 문장은 NATO회원국들의 의무를 설명하고 있다. 그렇다면 의무는 NATO 헌장에 나오는 내용이라고 유추할 수 있으므로 정답은 (b)이다.

remnant 잔재 **alliance** 동맹 **secure** 안전하게 지키다 **infiltration** 침입, 침투 **multi-national** 다국적의 **agreement** 협정 **mutual defense treaty** 상호 방위 조약 **pledge** 맹세, 서약 **conservative** 보수적인 **isolate** 고립시키다

3

비록 미국인이 자동차를 발명하지는 않았지만, 그들이 확실히 자동차 생산과 사용을 확산시켰고 이 업적 대부분의 공적은 헨리 포드와 그의 조립 라인 방식에게 돌아갔다. 포드 덕분에 자동차는 사치품에서 현대인의 생활에 있어 필수품으로 완전히 변화되었다. 1920년대 중반까지 많은 노동자 계층 가족들은 250불을 약간 넘는 비용으로 새 T형 포드 자동차를 구입할 수 있었다. 자동차에 대한 수요 증가는 결국 다른 많은 산업으로 확산되었다. 예를 들어, 석유에 대한 수요는 호황을 누렸고, 석유 시추자들은 사실상 하룻밤 사이에 텍사스와 서남부지역에 새로운 유정을 세웠다. 새롭고 매끄러운 도로가 미국 전역에 건설되면서 군데군데 주유소가 들어섰다. **고속도로의 확장에 힘입어** 1930년까지 미국인 3명 중 1명꼴로 자동차를 몰았다.

(a) 유가 하락이 발단이 되어
(b) 미국 고속도로의 확산 때문에
(c) T형 자동차의 성공이 도화선이 되어
(d) 헨리 포드의 조립 라인에도 불구하고

자동차의 수요 증가는 여러 다른 산업에 영향을 미쳤는데 석유 수요가 늘고 고속도로 건설이 증가했기 때문에 마지막 문장과 같은 결과가 나타날 수 있다. 따라서 정답은 (b)가 된다.

feat 공적 assembly line 조립 라인 practically 사실상
prospector 탐사자 innovativeness 획기적인 면 service station 주유소

4

비록 많은 비평가들이 프랭클린 D. 루스벨트 대통령의 뉴딜 정책이 미국인의 일상생활에 미국 정치를 너무 많이 연관시켰다고 안타까워하지만, 뉴딜 정책은 사실 수백만의 미국인들이 대공황에서 헤어나올 수 있도록 도움을 주었다. 전임자인 허버트 후버와 달리 루스벨트 대통령은 의회의 보수주의자들과 대법원이 허락하는 한 많은 사람을 직접적으로 도우려고 애썼다. 그의 뉴딜 정책 법안은 새로운 일자리를 창출하고, 노숙자를 위한 집과 쉼터를 건설했으며 굶주린 자들에게 음식을 나누어 주었다. 또한 뉴딜 정책의 방침은 농산물 가격을 인상시켰고, 은행이 다시 견고한 기반을 갖도록 했으며, 국가의 기반 시설을 크게 향상시켰다. 증가하는 재정 적자와 국가 부채에도 불구하고 뉴딜 정책은 미국인이 역사상 최악의 경제적 대실패에서 헤쳐 나오는 데 큰 도움을 주었다.

Q: 지문의 주제로 가장 알맞은 것은?
(a) 미국인이 불황에서 살아남도록 한 뉴딜 정책
(b) 뉴딜 정책이 어떻게 미국 정치를 변화시켰는가
(c) 뉴딜 정책의 혜택에 대한 논란
(d) 뉴딜 정책, 불황의 치료약이 아닌 독약

지문의 핵심 내용은 루스벨트 대통령의 뉴딜 정책이 대공황에서 헤어 나올 수 있게 해줬다는 것이다. 따라서 (a)가 가장 적합한 주제이다. (b)는 뉴딜 정책이 미국 정치를 바꿨다고 하기 때문에 정치에만 한정되어 있다. 그리고 (c)처럼 뉴딜 정책의 논쟁을 이야기하는 것도 아니다.

lament 애통하다 predecessor 전임자 commodity 상품 deficit 적자 national debt 국가 부채 debacle 대실패

5

1970년대와 1980년대에 다국적 기업들은 할리우드의 예술적인 실험기를 끝내고 대중을 매료시키는 화려한 영화의 대량 생산의 길을 열며 많은 미국 영화사를 사들여 합병했다. 다국적 기업들 덕분에 영화 산업은 블록버스터 시리즈의 개발과 대규모 마케팅 캠페인, 어린이들을 겨냥한 콘텐츠를 통해 재정적인 성공과 세계적 지배를 되찾았다. 기업 투자자들 또한 관객을 영화관으로 끌어들이기 위해 극적인 특수 효과에 더욱 중점을 두었다. 심지어 독립 영화 제작자들도 시나리오가 많은 관객을 끌어들일 수 있는 잠재성을 보여주기만 한다면 자금을 조달받을 수 있었다. 이러한 과도기의 최종 생산물은 대다수의 영화팬의 관심을 끄는 다양한 장르의 영화 제작이었다.

Q: 지문은 주로 무엇에 관한 것인가?
(a) 어떻게 다국적 기업이 영화의 예술적 가치를 훼손했는가
(b) 어떻게 독립 영화 제작자들이 할리우드에서 성공할 수 있었는가
(c) 어떻게 할리우드 영화가 외국 시장에서 성공할 수 있었는가
(d) 어떻게 다국적 기업이 할리우드 영화가 유명해지는 데 도움이 되었는가

다국적 기업이 영화사를 합병해 화려한 영화의 대량 생산의 길을 열어줬다고 하므로 정답은 (d)가 된다. (a)는 틀린 사실은 아니지만 지문의 핵심 내용은 아니다. 그리고 (b)처럼 독립 영화를 만드는 사람들의 이야기도 아니다.

merge 합병하다 spectacular 장관을 이루는 dominance 지배
emphasis 강조 special effect 특수 효과 draw into 끌어 들이다
lure 유혹하다

6

제2차 세계 대전 종전 이후, 국제 체제는 두어 번 이동했다. 전쟁 이후, 미국과 소비에트 연방 이렇게 두 열강만 남았다. 비록 다른 중요 국가들도 존재하기는 했지만, 거의 모든 국가들은 두 초강대국과의 관계상 정황에서 이해되었다. 이 국제 체제는 두 열강을 중심으로 이루어졌기 때문에 양극화 체제로 불린다. 냉전의 종식과 그로부터 수십 년 뒤 소비에트 연방의 붕괴 이후, 세계 유형은 다시 변화를 겪었다. 단 하나만의 초강대국이 남아 몇몇 학자들은 이 새로운 세계 체제를 단극화 체제라고 명명했다. 그러나 다른 학자들은 몇몇의 유럽 및 아시아 국가들의 경제력이 증가하는 점을 들어 이 새로운 국제 체제를 다극화 체제라고 명명하였다. 어느 정도까지는 두 용어 모두 정확하지만, 곧 세계는 급속히 성장하는 세력인 중국으로 인해 또 다른 국제 체제의 변동을 목격하게 될 것이다.

Q: 지문에 따르면 다음 중 옳은 것은?
(a) 냉전 이후 세계는 양극화 체제가 되었다.
(b) 지정학적으로 단극 체제는 내재적으로 불안정하다.
(c) 전쟁은 세계 사회가 마치 다극화처럼 행동할 때 나타난다.
(d) 현 세계는 단극화이거나 다극화이다.

제2차 세계 대전 이후 세계의 권력 체제가 어떻게 바뀌었는지에 대한 내용으로 냉전 시대 때는 양극화 체제였지만 소련의 붕괴 이후 세계는 단극화이거나 다극화 체제에 있다고 지문 끝 부분에서 설명하고 있으므로 정답은 (d)가 맞다.

shift 바꾸다 context 정황 맥락 superpower 강대국 bipolar 양극 geopolitics 지정학 label 딱지를 붙이다 unipolar 단극
extent 정도 inherently 내재적으로 unstable 불안정한

7

1800년대 중반 유럽의 혁명 시대는 전성기를 맞이했다. 평등과 자유에 대한 이상에 자극 받은 유럽인들은 낡은 정권을 타파하고 새로운 자유의 시대를 열기 위해 봉기했다. 직접 영향을 받은 입장에서는 혁명의 바람은 가혹했을지도 모른다. 하지만 유럽 대륙의 총체적인 상황을 주시하던 역사가들은 다가오는 폭풍의 몇몇 징후를 제시할 수 있다. 1846년에 널리 확산된 기근은 유럽 역사상 마지막이었을 엄청난 식량 위기로, 그로 인해 식량 가격이 급등해 사람들은 뭔가를 사먹을 수 없었다. 가격 상승만큼 임금은 인상되지 않아, 사람들은 갈수록 적은 물품을 구입했고 이윤 폭도 떨어졌다. 부정적 악순환이 뒤따랐고 대량 실업을 야기하며 경제가 침체되었다. 이것이 반란과 혁명의 배경이었다. 일련의 사건들이 시발점이 되어 혁명적 열기가 눈에 띄게 무르익으면서 그 무엇도 혁명을 막을 수 없었다.

Q: 다음 중 필자가 가장 동의할 만한 의견은 무엇인가?

(a) 사람들이 혁명의 징후를 알아차렸다면, 이를 막을 수 있었다.

(b) 사람들은 혁명의 조짐을 알아차리지 못했을 것이다.

(c) 임금이 인상되었더라면 수익률이 상승했을 것이다.

(d) 식품 가격이 높았기 때문에 수익률이 엄청났다.

19세기 중반 유럽에서 일어난 혁명에 이미 여러 경고 징후가 있었다는 내용으로 그 중 하나는 식량이 모자르고 가격이 급등했지만 임금은 낮았다. 그래서 소비가 줄었고 이익도 줄어서 산업도 무너지기 시작했다. 따라서 임금이 증가했다면 이익 마진도 증가했을 것이기 때문에 정답은 (c)이다.

heyday 전성기 **spurred by** ~에 자극 받은 **rise up** 봉기하다 **old regime** 구체제 **bring about** 야기하다 **harsh** 거센, 가혹한 **overall** 전체의, 종합적인 **continent** 대륙 **famine** 기근 **skyrocket** 급등하다 **wage** 임금 **profit margin** 이윤 폭 **spiral** (물가·임금 등의) 연쇄적 변동, 악순환 **ensue** 뒤따르다 **shrink** 위축[침체]되다 **revolt** 반란 **ignite** 불을 붙이다 **fervor** 열정 **ripen** 무르익다

8

국제 관계 면에서 크림 전쟁은 유럽 대륙에서 러시아의 군사 정복의 끝을 나타낸다. (a) 러시아 경제는 전쟁의 장기적 개입으로 매우 피해를 입었다. (b) 나폴레옹을 타파한 후 유럽의 질서를 유지해 주겠다고 약속한 것은 러시아였지만, 전쟁 이후 그 권력은 사실상 제거되었고, 따라서 권력은 다른 유럽 국가들로 이동했다. (c) 국가적인 규모로 크림 전쟁은 1917년 러시아 혁명으로 가는 길의 시작을 나타낸다. (d) 크림 전쟁 이후 줄곧 많은 러시아인들, 특히 해외에서 복무했던 장병들은 유럽의 더욱 커져 가는 민주화 운동에 고무되었다.

이 글은 처음 부분에서 국제 관계적 측면에서 봤을 때 러시아에게 크림 전쟁이 갖는 의미로 시작하며 어떻게 구체적으로 영향을 미쳤는지 설명하고 있으나 (a)는 러시아가 전쟁 개입으로 타격을 많이 입었다는 사실만 나오므로 문맥상 어색하다.

element 요소 **personnel** 직원들 **inspire** 고무하다 **beget** 결과를 부르다 **mark** 나타내다

Unit 04 교육   p.114

1 (c)	2 (a)	3 (c)	4 (b)
5 (d)	6 (d)	7 (d)	8 (d)

1

경험 많은 교육가들에 의해 입증된 만큼, 리포트 작성뿐만 아니라 사고력을 향상시키기 위해 **대학 작문은** 모든 대학생들이 충분히 조율해볼 만한 방법이다. 연구원들은 논문과 에세이를 쓰는 행위가 장기적으로 대학생들의 주제 파악 능력 및 분석 능력을 향상시킬 수 있다고 말한다. 논문을 쓰는 학생들은 내용을 보다 깊은 수준에서 깨우치고 문제들을 다양한 각도에서 볼 수 있다. 250개 대학 캠퍼스에서 진행된 교육 위원회의 설문 조사에서 조차도 글쓰기가 학생들과 교수들간에 보다 활발한 상호 작용

과 참여를 가능하게 한다는 것을 보여 주었다. 대학 강의실에서 제시하는 글쓰기 과제는 명백히 매우 교육적인 것으로 학습 과정 전체에 큰 도움이 된다.

(a) 서면 연구하기

(b) 대학에서 작문 가르치기

(c) 대학 수준의 글쓰기

(d) 글쓰기 설문 조사하기

논문과 에세이를 쓰면 대학생들의 주제 파악 능력과 분석 능력이 향상되고, 대학에서 글쓰기 과제를 내주는 것이 매우 교육적이며 학습 과정 전체에 도움을 줄 수 있다고 주장하는 내용으로 볼 때, 빈칸에 들어갈 가장 적절한 말은 (c)이다.

attested 입증된 **tune** 조율하다 **collegiate** 대학생 **grasp** 파악, 이해 **facilitate** 가능하게 하다 **interaction** 상호 작용 **engagement** 참여 **conduct** 시행하다

2

대학에 다니며 일하는 것은 단단한 마음가짐이 없는 학생들이 할 만한 것이 아니다. 파트타임 일이라고 해도 대학생들의 바쁜 스케줄을 방해한다. 일을 지속할 경우 정신적, 육체적 부담으로 학과 공부와 더불어, 캠퍼스에서 친구들과 어울리는 것과 같은 대학 생활의 모든 경험은 줄어들게 된다. 보통 학생들에게 주어지는 일상적인 제약 사항 중에 출석해야 하는 수업이 있다. **게다가** 공부와 일은 학생의 남은 시간과 에너지를 거의 모두 소진시킨다. 몇몇 대학생들은 시련을 통해 적어도 대학에 있는 동안에는 일보다 학업에 집중해야 한다는 것을 깨닫기도 한다.

(a) 게다가

(b) 반면

(c) 그렇지 않으면

(d) 따라서

학생이 아르바이트를 하며 공부하는 것이 힘들다고 언급하며 아르바이트가 학생에게 미치는 부작용에 대해 나열하며 이야기하고 있다. 빈칸은 나열하는 문장 사이에 있으므로 추가적인 내용이기 때문에 (a)가 정답이다.

faint of heart 용기 없는 **intrude** 방해하다 **socialize** 사람들과 어울리다 **diminish** 줄어들다 **mental** 정신적인 **demand** 요구, 부담 **constraint** 제약 **trial** 시련

3

대부분의 학생들은 대학을 선정하는 일이 자신의 미래에 얼마나 중요한지 알고 있다. 그리고 어느 학교가 최고인지 아마 나름 의견이 있을 것이다. 그러니 당신은 어떻게 맞는 학교를 선택하겠는가? 첫 단계는 자기 나름의 우선순위를 정하는 것이다. 당신에게 어떤 것이 중요한가? 어떤 것을 공부하고 싶은지 스스로에게 물어보라. 무엇을 잘 하는가? 일단 공부하고 싶은 것의 범위를 좁히면, 그 전공을 제공하는 학교를 겨냥하라. 당신에게 중요한 것들의 목록을 작성하고 스스로에게 더 많은 질문을 하라. 학교까지 통학하고 싶은가, 아니면 교내에 살고 싶은가? 큰 학교나 작은 학교 어느 쪽을 선호하는가? 고려해야 할 다른 사항은 학생의 총체적인 경험을 포함한다. 교수들은 높이 평가받고 있는가? 근처에 기분 전환을 할 수 있는 기회가 있는가? 얼마나 많은 졸업생이 취업을 하는가? 대학을 선택하는 일은 중요하지만 흥미롭기도 하다. 그리고 대학 교육은 당신의 꿈을 이룰 수 있게 한다. 그러니 슬기롭게 빨리 <u>조사를 시작하라</u>.

(a) 목표를 정하라
(b) 전공을 선택하라
(c) 조사를 시작하라
(d) 공부를 시작하라

본인에게 맞는 대학을 고르기 위해서 따라야 하는 절차를 조언하며 마지막에는 대학 교육은 꿈을 이루기 위해 필요하다고 말하고 있고, 이런 질문 사항들에 대한 답을 찾기 위해서는 알아보고 조사해야 하므로 정답은 (c)이다.

priority 우선 순위 **narrow down** 좁히다 **zero in on** 목표를 겨냥하다
commute 통학[통근]하다

4

다민족 아이들의 많은 부모들이 처음으로 자녀를 학교에 보내려는 생각은 두려움과 걱정을 야기하기 때문에 적절한 학교를 선택하는 데 있어 매우 조심스러운 경향이 있다. 정보에 근거해서 현명하게 학교를 선택하려면 먼저 부모들이 학교가 얼마나 문화적 다양성에 민감한지에 대해 알아봐야 한다. 다민족 학생의 부모들은 학교에서 학생들에게 다문화주의를 가르치기 위해 역할 연기나 토론을 하는 탄탄한 교과 과정을 운영하는지를 판단해야 한다. 또한 교사와 관리자들이 다문화주의에 관련된 사안에 대한 부모들의 의견을 기꺼이 받아들이는지와 학생들의 다민족 정체성을 지지하는지를 알아야 한다. 부모들이 다민족 어린이들에게 친근한 분위기를 조성하기 위해 그들의 문화와 기념일, 역사를 나누기 위해 교실을 방문하는 것도 권장한다. 자녀를 어디에 보내고 있는지 앎으로써 다민족 어린이들의 부모는 자녀들을 잠재 능력을 최대로 발휘할 수 있는 안전한 안식처에 입학시킬 수 있다.

Q: 지문은 주로 무엇에 관한 것인가?
(a) 다문화 어린이를 이해하는 것
(b) 다문화성에 우호적인 학교를 찾는 것
(c) 다문화 어린이를 교육하는 것
(d) 학교에서 문화적 충돌을 극복하는 것

다문화가정의 부모가 자녀에게 좋은 학교를 고르기 위해 필요한 일을 설명하고 있으므로 가장 적합한 정답은 (b)가 된다.

multiracial 다민족의 **diversity** 다양성 **enroll** 입학시키다
haven 안식처

5

10대 청소년들에게 대학 면접은 초조할 수 있지만 모든 인터뷰가 다 같은 것은 아니다. 실제 면접은 학교마다 다르고 일반적으로 그 학교가 얼마나 까다로운가와 연관되어 있다. 인터뷰 방식이나 인터뷰를 진행하는 사람과 상관없이 기억해야 하는 기본 규칙이 있다. 첫째, 좋은 인상을 줄 수 있는 옷을 입어라. 모든 면접에 블레이저를 입거나 넥타이를 맬 필요는 없지만 운동복도 좋은 생각은 아니다. 학교와 복장에 대해 제대로 알아봐라. 둘째, 예절 재교육은 도움이 된다. 별다른 언급이 없다면 인터뷰하는 사람에게 'Mr.' 혹은 'Ms.'라는 호칭을 써라. 똑바로 앉고, 말하라고 할 때 말하라. 셋째, 휴대 전화기는 안 된다. 과학 기술에 기반을 둔 세상에서 휴대 전화기는 반드시 전원을 끄고 치워 놓아야 한다는 것을 명심해야 한다. 마지막이지만 중요한 것은 시간을 엄수하라는 것이다. 면접에서 자신의 최상의 모습을 보여주려면, 반드시 당신이 학교에 적합하고 학교도 당신에게 적합하도록 해야 한다.

Q: 지문은 주로 무엇에 관한 것인가?
(a) 면접관이 학생에게서 찾는 것
(b) 대학 면접에서 물어보는 질문의 유형
(c) 대학 면접에 갈 때 피해야 하는 것들
(d) 대학 면접에 대해 기억해야 할 중요한 조언

고등학생들이 대학교 면접을 볼 때 알아야 하는 팁을 얘기하고 있으므로 정답은 (d)가 된다. 지문에서는 해야 하는 것도 소개하기 때문에 (c)는 답이 안 된다.

nerve-wracking 안절부절 못하게 하는 **selective** 까다로운 **blazer** 블레이저, 콤비 상의 **refresher** 생각나게 하는 것 **display** 보이게 하다

6

대부분의 소아 정신과 의사는 어린이의 인격 발달이 음악에 지대한 영향을 받는다고 생각한다. 이 때문에 동요가 어린이들의 각자 다른 학습 스타일에 상관없이 배우는 데 도움을 줄 수 있는 이유이다. 어린이용 교육 음악의 전문적인 특성 중 하나는 주문 제작된 노래를 담은 CD는 어린이의 이름이 여러 번 나오도록 제작된다는 점이다. 또한 어린이 노래에 쓸 가사와 운을 고를 때 작가는 노래로부터 획득한 지식을 통해 세상을 탐험할 어린이들의 흥미에 염두에 둔다. 학습 형태로 운을 이용하는 것은 어린이 교육의 가장 중요한 과정 중 하나이다. 현대 과학의 관점에서 음악은 개인의 기억력뿐만 아니라 창의력까지 높여 준다. 따라서 다양한 유치원과 초등학교는 노래를 통해 학생들을 효과적으로 교육시키는 데 더욱 주목하고 있다.

Q: 어린이들이 학습하는 데 동요는 어떻게 도움을 주는가?
(a) 가사에서 어려운 단어를 반복함으로써
(b) 노래에서 이야기를 들려줌으로써
(c) 어린이들이 혼자 노래를 하도록 함으로써
(d) 창의성을 증진시켜 줌으로써

아동 심리학자들에 의하면 동요가 아이들에게 학습적으로 도움이 된다고 하고, 음악은 창의성과 기억력에 도움을 준다고 하므로 정답은 (d)다.

psychiatrist 정신과 의사 **immensely** 엄청나게 **primary school** 초등학교 **explore** 탐험하다 **lyrics** 가사

7

남녀 분리 교육을 지지하는 사람들은 여대가 다음과 같은 혜택과 더불어 젊은 여성들이 현실 세계를 준비할 수 있다고 생각한다. 우선, 그들은 남녀 공학에 다니는 또래보다 학업에 더 열중할 수 있다. 또한 높은 수준의 학업적 도움을 경험할 가능성이 더 크다. 그들은 수업 시간에 더욱 활발하고 협력적인 학습에 참여한다. 게다가 여대생들은 남녀 공학에 다니는 학생들보다 교실 내 수업과 교실 외 경험을 결합한 활동에 더욱 참여한다. 가장 중요한 것은 남녀 공학의 여성 졸업자들에 비해 졸업할 가능성이 더 크고, 박사 학위를 따고 의대에 진학할 확률이 두 배 이상 높다. 모든 대학들이 여성에게 다양한 기회를 제공하지만, 여대는 더 많은 기회를 제공한다.

Q: 작가가 가장 동의할 만한 의견은 무엇인가?
(a) 여대생들이 남자 대학생보다 학점이 더 좋다.
(b) 여대 졸업생이 남녀 공학을 나온 여성 졸업자보다 높은 봉급을 받는다.
(c) 여대의 교수들은 남녀 공학의 교수들보다 더 엄격하다.
(d) 여대의 수업은 아마 남녀 공학 대학교의 수업보다 더 어려울 것이다.

지문은 여자 대학의 장점을 소개하고 있는데 그 장점 중 하나는 높은 학구적인 도전을 받는 다는 것이며 이 내용은 세 번째 문장에서 나온다. 그렇다면 여자 대학의 수업이 다른 대학 수업보다 더 어려울 것이라고 유추할 수 있으므로 정답은 (d)가 된다.

collaborative 공동의   **coeducational** 남녀 공학의   **doctoral degree** 박사 학위

8

동기 부여는 내적인 것과 외적인 것, 두 가지의 광범위한 범주로 나타난다. (a) 내적 유형은 일에서의 흥미와 재미에서 비롯되며 내적으로 형성된다. (b) 연구에 따르면 이런 유형의 동기 부여는 고등 교육 학력과 상관관계가 있다. (c) 반면, 외적 유형의 동기 부여에는 돈이나 다른 종류의 보상, 게다가 힘이나 위협 같은 부정적인 요소 같은 것들이 포함된다. (d) 사람들이 내적으로 동기 부여될 때 그들은 고유의 가치, 흥미, 목표를 추구하는 경향이 높아진다.

지문의 핵심 내용은 두 가지의 동기 부여, 내적 동기와 외적 동기를 소개하는 것이다. (a)에서 내적 동기 부여의 특징을 언급한 후, (b)에서 이에 대한 부연 설명을 하고 있다. 그러므로 (c), (d)의 관계 역시 (c)에서 외적 동기 부여의 특징을 말하고 있으므로 (d)에서 부연 설명이 따르는 것이 자연스럽다. 하지만 (d)에서 다시 내적 동기에 대해 언급하고 있어 어색하다.

intrinsic 내적인, 본질적인   **extrinsic** 외적인   **originate from** ~에서 기인하다   **correlate** 상관관계가 있다   **advanced** 고등의   **attainment** 성취   **reliance** 의존, 의지   **associated with** ~와 관련 있는

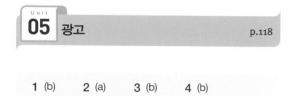

Unit 05 광고

p.118

| 1 (b) | 2 (a) | 3 (b) | 4 (b) |
| 5 (b) | 6 (c) | 7 (d) | 8 (b) |

1

플렉서릴은 근육을 이완시켜 주는 약입니다. 이 약은 염좌나 접질림 또는 다른 근육 부상으로 인한 **통증과 근경련을 감소시키기 위한** 안정과 물리 치료와 함께 사용됩니다. 플렉서릴은 사이클로벤자프린이라고도 불리는데, 근육 기능에는 아무런 영향을 미치지 않습니다. 플렉서릴은 경구 복용하는 정제로 보통 하루 2회에서 4회 복용합니다. 의사와 상의 없이 3주 이상 이 약을 복용해서는 안 됩니다. 처방지의 지시 사항을 따르고 이해되지 않는 부분은 의사나 약사에게 문의하십시오. 플렉서릴을 처방대로 복용하십시오. 플렉서릴을 근처 약국에 가지 않고 복용하시길 원하시면 온라인 약국을 이용하십시오.

(a) 관절 통증과 염증을 완화하기 위해
(b) 통증과 근경련을 감소시키기 위해
(c) 근력과 지구력을 키우기 위해
(d) 신체적 활동을 높이기 위해

플렉서릴이라는 근육 이완제의 효력을 소개하고 있는데 이 약은 근육을 이완시킨다고 첫 문장에 이야기하고 있기 때문에 빈칸에 들어가는 내용으로 근육통을 완화시킨다는 내용이 들어가야 자연스럽다. 따라서 정답은 (b)가 된다. (a)는 근육이 아니라 관절통을 이야기해서 틀리며 (c)는 근육 통증과는 관계없기 때문에 오답이다.

strain 좌상   **sprain** 삐다   **pharmacist** 약사   **prescribe** 처방하다   **alleviate** 완화하다   **spasm** 경련   **boost** 북돋우다

2

따뜻하고 질 좋은 양피 부츠를 찾고 있으시다면 아웃랜더 클래식 톨 부츠를 신어 보셔야 합니다. 우수한 마감으로 아웃랜더 부츠는 싸구려 유사품보다 4배에서 5배 더 오래 신을 수 있고, 착용자에게 더 높은 편안함을 제공해드릴 것을 약속드립니다. 아웃랜더 니트 부츠 구매를 가격 때문에 미루지 마십시오. **왜냐하면** 생각보다 저렴하게 구매하실 수 있기 때문입니다. 저희 일반 부츠 한 켤레 가격은 80불에서 120불 사이입니다. 이 가격으로 더 좋은 신축성뿐 아니라 무게도 덜 나가게 하는 이바 구두창으로 향상된 아웃랜더 부츠의 놀라운 편안함을 누리실 수 있습니다. 당신 옷장의 어떠한 의상과도 잘 어울리는 부츠를 찾으신다면 올 겨울 아웃랜더 클래식 부츠에 돈을 투자해 보시는 것을 생각해 볼 만합니다.

(a) 왜냐하면
(b) 비록
(c) ~전에
(d) ~일지라도

빈칸 뒤에 오는 내용은 아웃랜더 부츠를 기대 이상으로 저렴한 가격에 살 수 있다고 하고 빈칸 전 내용은 아웃랜더 부츠의 가격 때문에 구매를 망설이지 말라고 하니 빈칸 뒤 내용은 이유이고 전 내용은 결과이다. 그래서 정답은 (a)이다.

finish 마감   **put off** ~에 대한 흥미를 잃게 하다   **outsole** 구두창   **wardrobe** 옷

3

엘름허스트 퍼니처는 고급 가정용 가구에 있어 폭넓은 선택권을 제공합니다. 저희 제품들은 영국 전원풍인 것에서부터 동시대의 현대적인 것까지 그 스타일이 다양합니다. 저희는 가정의 각 방마다 특색 있는 제품들을 제공합니다. 저희 에스테이츠 가죽 소파는 친구와 가족들이 나눌 수 있는 안락한 경험을 선사합니다. 에스테이츠 침실용 탁자는 우아한 곡선이 살아 있고 미국 삼나무 베니어판을 이용한 단단한 원목으로 제작되어 독특한 느낌의 스타일을 제공합니다. 에스테이츠 식탁은 여러분의 주방에 어울릴 꿈의 제품입니다. 대리석 상판은 세련되고 고급스러운 외관을 돋보이게 합니다. 이것은 영국의 전통적인 자재와 마감재로 제작됩니다. 다음에 가정을 꾸밀 일이 있다면, **고급스럽고 우아한 가구를** 위해 엘름허스트 퍼니처를 방문해 보세요.

(a) 아름답고 편안한 아파트
(b) 고급스럽고 우아한 가구
(c) 최첨단의 가전제품
(d) 우아하고 전통적인 가정용 장식품

지문 앞부분에 나오는 핵심 내용은 엘름허스트 퍼니처에서 파는 다양한 종류의 가구를 광고하는 것이다. 그렇다면 뒤에 나오는 이야기도 가구에 대해 언급을 해야 한다. 그래서 정답은 (b)가 되고 나머지 답들은 가구에 대한 언급이 없다.

a wide range of 폭넓은   high-end 고급의   urban 도시의
contemporary 동시대의   gracious 우아한   curve 곡선   hardwood
원목   redwood 미국 삼나무   marble 대리석   top 상판
sophisticated 세련된   luxurious 고급스러운   material 자재
finishes 마감재   state-of-the-art 최신식의   gracious 우아한

4

회사 로고는 당신의 회사를 완전히 나타내기 때문에, 이미지를 진지하게 생각하는 회사라면 로고 이미지를 택하는 데 신중해야 합니다. 비록 수많은 서비스 제공 업체가 있지만, 모든 업체가 특별한 디자인을 제작하는 데 필요한 기술을 가지고 있다고 할 수는 없습니다. 일류 디자이너를 찾으신다면, 귀사의 로고 제작을 위해 아이브랜드를 생각해 보십시오. 저희 아이브랜드에는 솜씨 좋은 헌신적인 디자인 팀이 있습니다. 그리고 저희는 시간이 중요한 요소라는 것을 알고 있기 때문에 시간 엄수와 마감일을 정확하게 지킵니다. 저희 디자이너들의 작업 품질은 업계 최고이며 합당한 가격으로 서비스를 제공합니다. 저희 디자이너들은 귀사의 완벽한 이미지를 보여 줄 디자인을 만들기 위해 당신과 함께 일할 것입니다.

Q: 지문의 목적으로 적절한 것은?
(a) 브랜드 이름을 결정하기 위해서
(b) 잠재적 고객에게 사업체를 홍보하기 위해서
(c) 몇 개의 로고 디자인에 대한 의견을 구하기 위해서
(d) 디자인 회사의 일자리를 광고하기 위해서

로고의 중요성을 이야기하며 로고 디자인 회사를 잠재 고객인 다른 사업체에게 홍보하고 있으므로 정답은 (b)이다.

exceptional 특출한   top-notch 일류의 최고의   punctuality 시간 엄수

5

다음번 스키 여행을 계획하실 때, 스파이더 웨어 2를 가져가는 것을 기억하세요. 단열 처리가 되어 있는 스파이더 웨어 2는 추위, 비, 눈, 강풍, 우박을 포함한 모든 기상 상황에 적합한 재킷입니다. 다양한 디자인과 기능이 있어 어떠한 기상 변화에도 적응할 수 있게 해줍니다. 터맥스 양털 안감과 터매코어 단열 처리는 영하의 기온에서도 체온을 유지시켜 드립니다. 또한 저희 재킷 상품은 활동하기 쉽게 가볍고 항상 건조함을 유지할 수 있도록 재킷의 안쪽과 바깥쪽에 생길 수 있는 습기를 제어합니다. 다음번 고급 스키복으로 스파이더를 선택하세요.

Q: 광고의 주요한 목적은?
(a) 스키복의 열역학을 설명하기 위해
(b) 회사의 스키 재킷을 선전하기 위해
(c) 스키 탈 때의 패션에 대해 조언하기 위해
(d) 의류 기술에 대해 말하기 위해

스파이더 웨어 2라는 스키 재킷을 광고하는 글이다. 두 번째 문장 이후로 제품의 장점과 특징을 설명하고 있다. 따라서 가장 어울리는 제목은 (b)이다.

fleece 양털   insulation 단열   preserve 보존하다   moisture 습기
hail 우박   thermodynamics 열역학

6

며칠 안에 크리스마스 시즌이 다시 한 번 우리 모두에게 밝아 오고 재미와 즐거움을 누릴 수 있는 시간이 될 것입니다. 특히, 어린이들에게 크리스마스는 재미와 흥분, 즐거움, 산타로부터의 선물, 그리고 아마 가장 중요한 것인 친구들에게 자랑할 크리스마스 의상이 전부입니다. 코스튬포

미에서 자녀들을 위한 다양한 의상을 찾을 수 있습니다. 루돌프와 눈사람, 천사, 요정과 같은 다양한 고전적인 캐릭터뿐만 아니라 다양한 할리우드 영화에서 영감을 얻은 의상도 구비되어 있습니다. 인근의 오프라인 매장뿐 아니라 온라인으로도 수많은 다양한 크리스마스 복장을 제공하고 있습니다. 저희 의상은 당신의 자녀를 특별한 휴일에 특별하게 보이게 만들어 줄 것을 약속합니다. 저희 매장을 방문하시기 전에 www. costume4me.com에서 한번 살펴보시고 자녀를 위한 완벽한 의상을 찾으십시오.

Q: 지문에 따르면 다음 중 옳은 것은?
(a) 의상은 인터넷을 통해서만 주문 가능하다.
(b) 코스튬포미에서는 고전적인 캐릭터 의상만 판매한다.
(c) 코스튬포미에서는 영화 캐릭터 의상을 판매한다.
(d) 코스튬포미에서는 성인용 크리스마스 의상을 판매한다.

아이들을 위한 크리스마스 의상을 구입할 수 있는 코스튬포미라는 곳을 광고하는 있는데, 정통 의상뿐만 아니라 할리우드 영화에 나오는 인물의 의상도 구매할 수 있다. 따라서 옳은 것은 (c)이다. 인터넷에서만 살 수 있는 것이 아니라 매장 방문 구매가 가능하며 어린이용 의상을 주로 판매한다.

show off 자랑하다   check out 확인하다   costume 의상   pay a visit 방문하다

7

하루에 몇 번이나 집의 문을 여닫으십니까? 문을 여닫을 때, 집이 얼마나 도난 방지가 잘 되어 있는지 궁금한 적 있나요? 아름다운 해변과 경치를 가진 평화로운 지역에 거주하시는 것은 당신에게 잘못된 안전감을 줍니다. 사람들은 정직하고 나쁜 일은 일어나지 않을 것이라고 믿고싶지만, 때때로 나쁜 일은 일어나고, 안타깝게도 어딘가에는 다른 사람의 취약한 점을 찾아 착취하는 사람들이 있습니다. 그렇기 때문에 우수한 품질의 Lock & Key 가정용 보안 장치에 투자해야 합니다. Lock & Key 보안 장치를 설치함으로써 당신이 범죄의 피해자가 되지 않고 당신에게 안전을 드릴 것을 보장합니다. Lock & Key 보안 장치는 당신의 가정이 필요로 하는 약속, 이해, 헌신을 충족시켜 마음의 평화를 드리겠습니다.

Q: 광고에서 유추할 수 있는 것은?
(a) 해변과 아름다운 경치는 지역에서 범죄의 인식을 높인다.
(b) 독자들은 비교적 위험한 지역에 거주하는 것으로 보인다.
(c) Lock & Key는 타 브랜드와 근본적으로 다른 제품을 판매한다.
(d) 회사는 주거 침입에 대한 우려로부터 안심을 줄 것을 약속한다.

Lock & Key 보안 장치를 설치하면 범죄의 피해를 받지 않고 안전감을 준다 했으므로 정답은 (d)이다. 평화로운 지역에 거주하면 잘못된 안전감을 준다고 했으므로 (a)는 오답이고, (b)는 알 수 없는 내용이다.

burglarproof 도난 방지의   security 안전   vulnerability 취약성
victim 피해자   dedication 헌신   perception 인식

8

시 하우스 비치 리조트는 활기를 되찾거나 정신 없는 일상에서 벗어나고 싶은 사람들에게 완벽한, 루프 비치에 자리한 평온한 곳입니다. (a) 이곳은 태평양의 아름다운 해변에 있는 근처 크래비 국제공항에서 차로 30분 거리입니다. (b) 공항은 지역에 편의를 제공하기 위해 11년 전에 건설되었습니다. (c) 루프 비치는 아직도 자연적으로 훼손되지 않고 하이킹이나 항해 같은 실외 활동의 다양한 기회를 제공하는 새로운 개발 지역입니다. (d) 저희와 머무시는 동안, 차로 약 50분 거리에 있는 유명한 앱던 산도 방문하실 수 있습니다.

시 하우스 비치라는 리조트를 홍보하고 있다. 모든 문장에서 리조트에 대한 정보를 언급하고 있는데, (b)는 리조트 근처에 있는 공항에 대한 문장으로 글의 흐름에서 벗어난다. 따라서 (b)가 답이다.

rejuvenate 활기를 되찾게 하다 **hectic** 정신 없는 **unspoiled** 훼손되지 않은

06 편지글
p.122

| 1 (d) | 2 (a) | 3 (c) | 4 (d) |
| 5 (d) | 6 (c) | 7 (b) | 8 (a) |

1

존슨 씨께

저희가 귀하의 8월 15일자 편지를 받았음을 알려드립니다. 그 편지에서 귀하는 미지불된 대출 상환금의 기한을 3개월 연장해 달라고 요청했습니다. 화폐의 시간 가치 분석을 포함한 신중한 검토 후, 귀하의 지불 의무를 다하기를 요구할 수밖에 없는 상황에 놓였습니다. 귀하가 처한 어려움에 대해서는 유감스럽지만 9월 1일까지 저희에게 지불금을 보내 주시는 게 매우 중요합니다. 귀하의 어려움에 다른 해결책을 찾을 수 있기를 바랍니다.

질 테일러

미수금 회수부장

(a) 자금을 융통할 때가 왔다 생각해서 우리는
(b) 저희 지도부는 그 문제를 재정했고
(c) 저희는 귀하의 어려움을 이해하고 빚을 탕감하며
(d) 할 수밖에 없는 상황에 놓였습니다

편지를 쓴 사람인 질 테일러가 존슨 씨에게 대출금 상환 연장 요청을 거부하고, 9월 1일까지 미지불금을 모두 지불해달라고 요청하고 있다. 따라서 빈칸에는 그럴 수밖에 없는 입장을 설명하는 표현이 적절하므로 (d)가 정답이다.

acknowledge (수령했음을) 알리다 **outstanding** 미지불된 **mortgage** 대출 **payment** 지불금 **time value of money** 화폐의 시간 가치 **fulfill** 다하다 **obligation** 의무 **paramount** 가장 주요한 **furnish** 제공하다 **redefine** 재정립하다 **predicament** 곤경, 궁지

2

담당자님께

안녕하세요. 최근 인터넷을 하는 중에 www.buyright.com이라는 온라인 경매 사이트를 발견했고, 매우 좋은 인상을 받았습니다. 귀하는 귀찮은 절차 없이 구매자와 판매자를 연결하는 사이트를 구축했습니다. 제가 편지를 쓰는 목적은 간단합니다. 귀하의 사이트에 루미콘의 웹 사이트 링크를 걸고 싶습니다. 루미콘은 온라인 게임 선도 기업입니다. 귀하의 사이트를 탐색하는 사용자들이 루미콘에 대해 더 알고 싶어 하는 데 흥미를 가질 것이라고 생각합니다. 물론, 저희 사이트의 잘 보이는 곳에 www.buyright.com의 링크를 걸어 이에 보답할 것입니다. 이것이 우리 모두에게 가상현실의 장점을 취하도록 해 주고 혜택을 줄 것이라고 생각합

니다. 이 제안에 대해 논의하시려면 555-9484번으로 전화를 주시거나 contra@lumicon.com으로 이메일을 주십시오. 회신 기다리겠습니다.

헨리 애쉬포드

(a) 물론
(b) 그러나
(c) 사실
(d) 결과적으로

우선 이 편지를 쓴 사람은 루미콘을 대표해서 쓴 것이다. 그리고 편지의 목적은 buyright.com에 루미콘 링크를 걸기 위한 것이다. 그리고 빈 칸 뒤에 오는 내용을 보면 루미콘의 링크를 걸어주면 루미콘에도 바디라이트의 링크를 걸어 보답하겠다고 한다. 그리고 이것은 당연한 보답이 되기 때문에 정답은 (a)가 맞다. (b)는 상반되는 내용을 연결시키기 때문에 안 되고 (d)는 결과를 소개하는 표현이라서 적절하지 않다.

cruise 무엇을 찾아 천천히 가다 **navigate** 길을 찾다 **reciprocate** 비슷하게 화답하다 **prominent** 잘 보이는

3

관계자 분께

안녕하세요? 저희는 홍보 담당 매니저를 고용하려고 합니다만. 일반 경로로는 적합한 사람을 찾지 못했습니다. 혹시 최근 면접을 보았거나 저희 공석에 추천해 주실 분을 알고 계시는지 모르겠습니다. 연봉은 6만 5천 불이고 업무는 다양한 매체를 통해 회사 이미지를 제고하는 것입니다.

근면하고 이 분야에 경력이 있는 분을 아신다면 저에게 555-8934번으로 전화를 주시거나 후보자가 저에게 555-9898번으로 팩스를 보내도록 해주셔도 됩니다. 도와주셔서 매우 감사합니다.

(a) 비서에게 계속 업데이트하게 하다
(b) 고객이 연락하게 하다
(c) 후보자가 팩스로 이력서를 보내게 하다
(d) 부장님이 이 문제를 상의하게 하다

편지를 쓰는 사람은 직원을 고용하기를 원하며 편지를 받는 사람에게 좋은 후보를 소개해 달라고 하고 있으므로 마지막에는 좋은 후보가 있으면 연락을 주든지 아니면 이력서를 보내 달라고 하는데 이력서를 보내는 사람이 편지를 받는 사람이 아닌 이상 후보가 보내야지 논리적으로 맞다. 따라서 정답은 (c)가 된다.

locate 찾다 **appropriate** 적절한 **channel** 경로 **corporate** 기업의

4

관계자께

최근 귀사로부터 캐나다 캘로우 파인로 435번지에 위치한 건물을 구매했습니다. 공교롭게도 직업상의 이유로 근거지를 버밍햄으로 옮길 예정이라 이에 맞춰 청구서 주소를 변경해 주시기 바랍니다. 갑자기 이사하게 되어 제가 직접 변경하는 것이 불가능했기에 제가 없는 동안 이 편지를 가지고 있는 제 동료 커티스 잭슨에게 건물에 대한 청구서 주소를 여기 드리는 주소로 변경하는 것에 관한 모든 문제의 권한을 일임합니다.

존 스튜어트

Q: 다음 중 편지의 내용과 일치하는 것은?

(a) 앞으로는 동료 커티스 잭슨에게 발신자의 청구서가 발송될 것이다.

(b) 발신자는 결혼으로 이어질 수 있는 새로운 관계 때문에 다른 도시로 이사했다.

(c) 이 편지는 제3자에게 발신자가 부동산을 커티스 잭슨에게 매매했음을 알린다.

(d) 발신자가 없는 동안 커티스 잭슨이 발신자의 주소를 변경할 것이다.

편지의 발신자는 직업상의 이유로 갑자기 이사를 하게 되었고, 그래서 본인이 없는 동안 고지서 청구 주소 변경을 동료 커티스 잭슨에게 일임했으니 정답은 (d)이다.

property 부동산, 건물　**situated** 위치해 있는　**shift** 이동하다　**base** 근거지　**absence** 부재　**authorize** 권한을 부여하다　**colleague** 동료 **herein** 여기에

5

데이비스 씨께

저희 기록을 보니 귀하는 올해 1월부터 미불 매입금이 있습니다. 1월에 청구된 금액은 445불이었고 저희는 아직 이 금액을 받지 못했습니다. 청구서 한 부를 동봉합니다. 이 금액을 이미 지불하셨으면 이 안내문을 무시하십시오. 그렇지 않은 경우에는 3월 1일까지 전 금액을 저희에게 송부해 주십시오. 계약서에서 명시하는 바와 같이 30일 이후 미불 매입금에 대해서는 5%의 이자를 부과하기 시작합니다. 협조해 주셔서 미리 감사드립니다. 앞으로도 귀하와 비즈니스를 지속하기를 바랍니다.

메리 레이튼

Q: 이 편지의 주요한 목적은?

(a) 청구서상의 금액을 확인하기 위해

(b) 변경된 이율을 상기시키기 위해

(c) 초과 지불된 금액을 반납하기 위해

(d) 미지불 청구액을 수금하기 위해

첫 문장부터 미불된 금액이 있다고 하며 3월 1일까지 전 금액을 송부하라고 말하고 있다. 그래서 정답은 (d)가 된다. 다른 정답은 독촉을 하는 내용이 아니기 때문에 답이 안 된다.

outstanding balance 미불 매입금　**invoice** 송장　**cooperation** 협력 **disregard** 무시하다　**interest** 이자

6

애드리언 씨께

저희 팀에 오신 것을 환영합니다! 사일로 일렉트로닉스의 직원으로 귀하를 환영하게 되어 기쁩니다. 저희는 귀하가 저희 팀에 합류하게 되어 기쁘고, 회사에서 일하시는 것을 즐거워하시기를 바랍니다. 매월 첫 번째 월요일에 새로운 직원을 환영하는 특별한 직원 점심 모임을 마련합니다. 다음 주에 부디 참석하셔서 선임 직원들과 이달에 입사한 다른 신입 직원들도 만나 보십시오. 앨리스 피터스가 더 자세한 이메일을 보내드릴 것입니다. 교육 기간 중 궁금하신 사항이 있으시면 망설이지 마시고 저에게 연락 주십시오. 제 이메일 주소로 연락 주시거나 사무실 555-2222번으로 전화주세요.

비키 에반스

Q: 편지에 따르면 다음 중 옳은 것은?

(a) 애드리언은 화요일부터 회사 업무를 시작할 것이다.

(b) 월요일 점심은 신입 직원들만 참석할 것이다.

(c) 애드리언과 이 편지를 작성한 사람은 같은 팀에서 일할 것이다.

(d) 편지를 작성한 사람은 이미 애드리언을 만나 보았다.

신입 사원을 환영하면서 신입 사원 환영 행사에 초대하기 위한 편지인데 내용을 보아 편지를 쓴 사람과 애드리언은 같은 팀에서 일을 할 것이다. 첫 문장에 우리 팀에 온 것을 환영한다고 하고 있으므로 정답은 (c)가 된다. (d)는 편지를 쓴 사람과 애드리언이 만났는지를 알 수 없기 때문에 답이 안 된다.

staff 직원　**hold** 개최하다　**detail** 세부 사항　**hesitate** 주저하다 **contact** 연락하다

7

프레드에게

할아버지가 된 것에 대한 우리의 진심 어린 축하를 받아 주게나. 며느리가 예쁜 손녀를 낳았다는 소식을 매우 감격했어. 내가 자네를 알기에 새로운 가족을 얼마나 애지중지할지 상상이 가네. 아이들은 정말 빨리 자라기에 자네를 탓하는 것은 전혀 아닐세. 자네가 미처 깨닫기도 전에 손녀는 일어서고, 걸으며 자네를 할아버지라고 부를 거야. 그레이스와 나는 자네 손녀를 보고 싶어. 자네를 만나 꼬마 소녀에게 인사하기 언제가 적당한지 알려 줘.

피터와 그레이스

Q: 프레드에 대해 유추할 수 있는 것은?

(a) 아기의 외할아버지이다.

(b) 마음이 따뜻하고 친절한 것으로 알려져 있다.

(c) 아들에게 곧 딸이 생길 것이다.

(d) 피터는 프레드가 다정한 할아버지가 되지 않을 거라고 생각한다.

발신자인 피터가 수신자인 프레드를 잘 알고 있어서 가족을 얼마나 애지중지할지 상상이 간다고 하고 말하는 부분에서 프레드가 마음이 따뜻하고 친절하다는 사실을 유추할 수 있으므로 (b)가 정답이다.

heart-filled 진심 어린　**thrilled** 아주 흥분한, 신이 난　**dote** 애지중지하다 **blame** 비난하다, 탓하다　**suitable** 적당한　**maternal** 엄마의 **affectionate** 다정한

8

워터스 씨께

리지필드 약국에서 사직하려는 제 의사를 정식으로 통보 드리기 위해 편지를 드립니다. 저는 리지필드에서 2013년부터 업무를 시작하였습니다. 저의 마지막 근무일은 11일 14일입니다. 2주일이면 당신이 제 후임을 찾기에 충분하다고 생각합니다. 저는 당신이 뽑은 제 후임을 교육시키는 데 기꺼이 돕겠습니다. 지난해 동안 저를 고용해 주셔서 감사드립니다. 점원, 관리자 그리고 매장 총 담당자로서의 제 경력은 매우 도움이 되었고 제가 배운 여러 능력을 앞으로 필더스에서 잘 사용할 수 있으리라 확신합니다. 염려되는 사항이 있으시면 제 개인 이메일 주소로 연락 주십시오.

토마스 맨즈

Q: 편지에서 유추할 수 있는 것은?

(a) 토마스 맨즈는 장차 필더스에서 일할 것이다.

(b) 워터스 씨는 리지필드 약국의 사장이다.

(c) 새로운 후임은 토마스가 그만 두기 전에 교육 받는 것이 틀림없다.

(d) 맨즈 씨는 리지필드에서 약사로서 일했다.

첫 문장을 보면 알 수 있듯이 이 편지는 사직서다. 그렇다면 글을 쓴 사람이 자신이 배웠던 것들을 필더스에서 활용하겠다고 하므로 정답은 (a)가 된다. 워터스 씨가 약국의 사장인지, 후임의 교육에 적극적으로 돕겠다고 했지 교육 시기 등은 알 수 없다. 또한 리지필드 약국에서 했던 일은 약사는 아니었음을 알 수 있다.

resignation 사직   sufficient 충분한   replacement 대체(물)
supervisor 상사   floor manager 매장 관리자

Unit 07 기타
p.126

| 1 (d) | 2 (a) | 3 (b) | 4 (c) |
| 5 (d) | 6 (c) | 7 (b) | 8 (d) |

1

어쩌면 놀랍게도 게임 이론은 방송 전파 스펙트럼, 벌채권, 오염 감소 공제액 등을 망라한 정부 공공 자원 경매의 **표준화된 관행**이 되었다. 1940년대에 처음으로 포커 전략을 연구하기 위한 방법으로 숙고되었던 이 게임 이론은 해당 행동 수행에 따를 것 같은 보상과 더불어 상대방이 동일한 행동이나 대체 행동을 할 가능성과 그들의 잠재적 보상에 근거하여 플레이어의 행동을 결정한다. 기대되는 결과를 예측하고 계획을 세우기 위해 이 방법을 이용하는 것이 정부와 상업적 전략을 크게 발전시켜 왔다.

(a) 오래된 방법

(b) 계산된 속임수

(c) 비인간적으로 만드는 행위

(d) 표준화된 관행

포커 게임에서 쓰이는 게임 이론이 정부나 상업적인 전략을 세우는 데 이용되어 많은 전략적 향상을 가져왔다고 이야기하고 있으므로 빈칸에 적절한 표현은 (d)이다.

auction 경매   encompass 망라하다   airwave 방송 전파   timber 수목   credit (세금 등의) 공제액   contemplate 심사숙고하다
in concert with ~와 협력하여   obsolete 한물간   likelihood 가능성
deception 속임수   standardized 표준화된

2

요즘 새로운 이민자들을 위해 사용하기에 가장 적절한 교수법에 대해 상반되는 의견이 있다. 한 의견은 완전 몰입은 소용이 없고, 학습 향상을 위해 학생의 모국어가 활용되어야 한다고 주장한다. **이와 대조적으로** 몰입이 학생들이 그들이 필요로 하는 것을 소통하기 위해 필수 어휘와 문법을 배우게 하는 최고의 방법을 제공한다는 의견이 있다. 어쩌면 이 두 의견의 혼합이 가장 확실한 해결책을 제공할지도 모른다.

(a) 대조적으로

(b) 더욱이

(c) 게다가

(d) 일제히

이민자들에 대한 몰입 교육에 대해 상반된 두 의견을 빈칸 전후로 서술하고 있으므로 대조를 나타내는 접속어 (a)를 넣는 것이 적절하다.

conflicting 상충하는   appropriate 적절한   employ 이용하다
contend 주장하다   immersion 몰입   leverage ~에 영향을 미치다
postulate 상정하다   hybrid 혼합물   viable 확실한

3

〈양성적인 관리자〉라는 저서에서 앨리스 사전트는 유능한 관리자는 남성적이고 여성적인 장점 두 가지 면을 옹호한다고 가정했다. 이 가설을 연구하기 위해, 그녀는 다수의 관리자와 심층 인터뷰를 실시했다. 그러나 많은 이 중에서 한 사람이 눈에 띄었다. 이러한 개념에 대해 직설적으로 말하는 비평가인 버포드 맥클린은 회유적이고 동질화된 방식의 관리를 적용하는 것은 사람을 존재감 없고 무능하게 만든다고 말했다. 그는 계속해서 능력 있는 관리자는 **강하고 합리적인 방식을 활용하여** 유능하고 그들이 그 직책을 마땅히 맡을 만하다고 다른 사람들을 설득하는 끊임없이 힘겨운 투쟁을 한다고 말했다.

(a) 긍정적인 환경을 강조하며

(b) 강하고 합리적인 방법을 활용하여

(c) 침착하고 도움이 되는 처신을 표현하며

(d) 깊이와 도덕적 중심을 가지고

버포드 맥클린은 좋은 관리자는 회유적이고 특징 없는 동질화된 관리 방식을 써 보는 것에 대해 비판하고 있으므로 이런 방식과 상반된 내용을 담고 있는 (b)가 빈칸에 적절하다.

androgynous 양성적인   posit 가정[단정]하다   espouse 지지하다
hypothesis 가설   in-depth 심층의   multitude 다수   stand out 두드러지다, 눈에 띄다   outspoken 직설적인   conciliatory 회유하기 위한
homogenized 동질화된   render 만들다   apt 능한   uphill battle 매우 힘든 일, 힘겨운 투쟁   demeanor 행실, 처신   utilize 활용하다

4

건축학 학생들은 성공적으로 상업적 건물이나 주거 건물을 디자인하고 건설하기 위한 필수 도구를 얻고 이를 위한 기술을 발전시킨다. 그러나 이 분야에 뛰어들기 전에 학생들은 건축가라는 직업을 잘 이해해야 한다. 오늘날의 건축가란 혁신적이고 창의적으로 생각하는 사람들이다. 훌륭한 건축가가 되려면 고객의 요구를 이해하는 것은 필수이고, 인내심과 통찰력을 갖는 것이 도움이 된다. 건축가들은 모든 관계자들의 요구를 충족시킬 수 있는 건설 계획의 초안을 작성하기 위해 CEO, 조경사, 기술자와 함께 일한다. 예술과 모든 사물에서 발견되는 미학적 아름다움에 대한 사랑이 성공적인 건축가의 또 하나의 특징이다. 이 직업은 보통 불규칙적이고 긴 업무 시간을 지켜야 하므로 사랑해야 할 수 있는 일이다. 따라서 디자인에 대한 열정과 창작하고 싶은 욕구를 가진 창의적인 사람들은 이 수익성 좋은 직업에서 많은 것을 얻는다.

Q: 지문의 주제로 알맞은 것은?
(a) 건축학의 정의
(b) 훌륭한 건축 양식을 만들기
(c) 건축가의 일
(d) 역대 훌륭한 건축가들

건축학을 전공하고 싶어 하는 학생들이 건축이라는 직업에 대해서 알아야 하는 점을 소개하고 있기 때문에 주제는 (c)가 된다. 건축 학문에 관한 내용이 아니기 때문에 (a)는 맞지 않다.

architecture 건축학   **insight** 통찰력   **landscaper** 조경사   **irregular** 불규칙적인   **lucrative** 돈이 벌리는

5

나이가 지긋하고 혼자 살고 싶어 하는 친구나 가족이 있다면, 방문해서 안전을 위해 주거지를 살펴보고 싶을지도 모른다. 첫째, 화재 탐지기가 제대로 작동하는지 건전지는 완전히 충전되어 있는지 확인하기 위해 체크해야 한다. 또한 걸려 넘어지기 쉬운 울퉁불퉁한 곳이 있는지 확인하기 위해 러그와 카펫을 살펴보라. 전열 기구 주변에 수건과 같이 불에 잘 타는 물건이 없도록 확인하라. 집안의 특정 장소, 특히 욕실에 난간이나 잡을 수 있는 봉이 필요한지 판단하라. 마지막으로 주택에 불이 잘 켜지는지 확인하고 끊어진 전구는 교체하라. 우리 세계에서 어떠한 것도 100% 확신할 수 없다는 것을 기억하라. 특히, 연장자나 노인의 집에서의 사고 방지에 관해서라면 더욱 그렇다.

Q: 지문은 주로 무엇에 관한 것인가?
(a) 어르신들의 집을 개조하는 것
(b) 노인들에게 가정에서의 위험 요소에 대해 교육하는 것
(c) 어르신들을 화재 위험으로부터 보호하는 것
(d) 노인들을 위해 집을 안전하게 지키는 것

주변에 혼자 사는 노인이 있으면 그 집에 꼭 확인해야 하는 안전 사항을 소개하므로 정답은 (d)가 된다. 지문은 노인들을 위한 것이 아니라 혼자 사는 노인들과 가까운 사람들을 위한 글이므로 (b)는 오답이다.

detector 탐지기   **uneven** 고르지 못한   **flammable** 불에 잘 타는   **appliance** 가정용 기기   **dwell** 거주하다

6

11월은 전 세계 많은 지역에서 스키 시즌이 시작된다는 것을 알린다. 휴양지를 현명하게 선택한다면, 시즌이 시작할 때 바로 스키를 탈 수 있을 것이다. 프랑스의 발 토랑스는 11월 스키 휴가로 훌륭한 선택이다. 시즌의 성수기에 방문하는 것보다 훨씬 저렴하다. 또한 더 멀리 미국으로 가 타호 호 지역에서 스키를 타 볼 수도 있다. 이 지역은 캘리포니아 주와 네바다 주 경계의 시에라 네바다 산맥의 고지대에 위치해 있어 훌륭한 경치와 스키를 탈 수 있는 충분한 기회를 기대할 수 있다. 다시 유럽으로 돌아가서 만약 약간 색다른 곳을 시도해 보고 싶다면 핀란드를 고려하고 싶을지도 모른다. 레비는 눈이 보통 10월에 내리기 시작하기 때문에 최고의 선택이 된다. 스키 휴가를 떠나기 직전에 예약을 하더라도, 세상에서 가장 훌륭한 스키 경험을 일찍 누리기 위해 항상 선택지를 알고 있어야 한다.

Q: 지문에 따르면 다음 중 옳은 것은?
(a) 성수기에 발 토랑스에서 스키를 타는 것이 더 저렴하다.
(b) 타호 호는 핀란드에 위치해 있다.
(c) 핀란드에서는 10월에 스키를 타는 것이 가능하다.
(d) 타호 호 지역에서 스키 타기는 이르면 10월에 시작한다.

일찍 스키를 타고 싶어 하는 사람들에게 세계의 훌륭한 스키 휴양지를 소개하고 있다. 그중 핀란드에 있는 레비라는 휴양지의 장점은 10월부터 스키를 탈 수 있다는 것이다. 따라서 정답은 (c)이다.

get in action 참가하다   **height** 절정   **afield** 집에서 멀리 떨어져   **superb** 최고의   **last minute** 막판

7

인도는 극심한 인플레이션을 해결하기 위해 올해 6번째로 금리를 대폭 인상했다. 식품 가격의 막대한 인상은 인도가 끊임없이 극심한 인플레이션에 대처하면서 정부가 해결하기 가장 어려운 문제로 부상했다. 비록 전반적인 인플레이션은 약 8.5%로 하락했지만, 식품비 인플레이션은 15% 주위를 맴돌고 있다. 최우선시 되는 사안으로 인플레이션을 들며 중앙은행은 금리를 0.25% 인상했다. 정책 입안자들은 인상되는 금리가 경제 성장 탄력에 방해가 되지 않을 것이라고 말한다. 그러나 8.5% 정도의 성장으로 복귀하는 것은 중산층의 주머니에 부담이 되고 있다. 그럼에도 불구하고 이것은 성장하는 경제에 의해 소외된 국가의 수많은 빈곤층들이 높은 식량 가격에 대처하는 데 특히 어려움을 겪고 있기 때문에 필수적인 조치이다.

Q: 지문에서 유추할 수 있는 것은?
(a) 중산층은 극심한 인플레이션으로 가장 고통 받고 있다.
(b) 금리 인상은 상품과 서비스의 가격 인하를 가져온다.
(c) 식비 인플레이션은 항상 평균 인플레이션율보다 높다.
(d) 금리를 낮추는 것은 경제 성장 속도를 늦춘다.

이 지문의 핵심 내용은 인도의 물가 상승이 빈곤층에게 가지고 오는 부담을 알리기 위한 것이다. 그리고 물가를 안정시키기 위해서 정부가 내린 조치는 금리 인상이다. 그렇다면 금리가 인상할수록 물가가 내려간다고 추측을 할 수 있으므로 정답은 (b)가 된다.

hike 인상하다   **in a bid** ~하기 위해   **tackle** 씨름하다   **inflation** 물가 상승   **cope with** 대처하다   **hover around** ~주위를 맴돌다   **momentum** 탄력   **marginalize** 사회적으로 무시[과소평가]하다

8

환경친화적인 생활 방식은 실천해야 하는 것이 되어가고 있으므로, 이런 삶을 시작할 방법에 관한 몇 가지 팁을 제시하고자 한다. (a) 우선 식기 세척기와 세탁기 같은 가전제품들이 가득 채워졌을 때만 사용하도록 한다. (b) 또한, 뜨거운 물이 필요하지 않을 때는 찬물로 짧고 시원하게 샤워할 수 있다. (c) 샤워 시간을 1-2분 정도로 줄여 적은 양의 물이지만 쾌적한 온도로 샤워한다. (d) 이렇게 하면 건조한 날씨에도 피부를 촉촉하고 부드럽게 할 수 있고, 그 덕분에 환경을 보호하고 자원을 보존하는 것은 물론 건강도 유지하게 된다.

지문의 핵심 내용은 집에서 쉽게 환경친화적으로 살 수 있는 방법을 소개한다. (d)에서는 이런 방법들이 환경에 도움이 된다는 것보다 피부에 도움이 된다는 내용이 더 중심적으로 언급되기 때문에 글의 핵심 내용에 어긋난다. 따라서 정답은 (d)가 된다.

go about ~을 시작하다   **appliance** 가전제품   **capacity** 용량   **attempt** 시도하다   **conserve** 보존하다

Ⅳ NEW TEPS 실전 모의고사

ACTUAL TEST 1

p.134

Part I
1 (b)	**2** (c)	**3** (d)	**4** (a)	**5** (d)
6 (b)	**7** (d)	**8** (d)	**9** (d)	**10** (c)

Part II
11 (d)	**12** (c)

Part III
13 (b)	**14** (d)	**15** (a)	**16** (c)	**17** (b)
18 (a)	**19** (c)	**20** (b)	**21** (c)	**22** (a)
23 (d)	**24** (d)	**25** (c)		

Part IV
26 (a)	**27** (d)	**28** (b)	**29** (c)	**30** (d)
31 (c)	**32** (d)	**33** (c)	**34** (b)	**35** (d)

Part I

1

넷바이 경매 사이트를 통해 수익성 있는 홈 비즈니스 창업에 성공하려면, 다음과 같은 조언들을 유념해야만 한다. 우선, 제공해 판매하고자 하는 제품에 관한 내용을 가능한 상세히 명시한다. 키워드를 이용해 정확하게 기술한다. 또한, 판매하려는 제품을 잘 보여주는 이미지를 포함시켜 사람들이 판매하는 제품에 감을 느낄 수 있도록 한다. 더불어, 환불 정책도 아주 정확하게 명시하는 것이 중요하다. 마지막으로, 고객들이 여러분이 제공하는 서비스에 대한 평가 글을 쓸 수 있도록 한다. 이런 조언대로 경매 사이트를 만들면 **인터넷으로 돈을 버는** 목표를 달성할 수 있을 것이다.

(a) 가장 좋은 물건을 구입하는
(b) 인터넷으로 돈을 버는
(c) 가장 좋은 경매 사이트를 발견하는
(d) 가장 싼 물건을 파는

온라인 경매 사이트를 운영할 때 수익성을 높일 수 있는 팁을 소개하는 글이다. 따라서 결론 부분을 완성할 수 있는 내용은 (b)이다. (a)는 물건을 사기 위한 팁이며 (d)는 지문에 없는 내용이기 때문에 답이 될 수 없다.

profitable 수익성 있는 **take heed of** ~에 유념하다 **offering** 팔 물건 **promote** 판매를 촉진하다 **state** 기술하다 **refund policy** 환불 정책 **precisely** 명확하게

2

과학자들은 동물성 지방을 메탄올과 화합해 바이오디젤을 제조하는 새로운 기술을 개량했다. 이 화학 물질은 라드의 지방산 사슬 끝에 결합해 76갤런의 지방산 메틸 에스테르를 만들어내며 바이오디젤로 가공되어 대부분의 디젤 엔진에서 사용될 수 있다. 이 기술은 다른 지저분한 고체성 기름에도 응용될 수 있다. 많은 음식점이 튀기고 남은 기름을 생물 연료로 바꾸지만 많은 기름이 주방 배수관으로 내려가서 하수구에서 고체화된다. 새로운 과정은 지방 덩어리를 갤런당 2.50달러에 디젤로 바꿀 수 있다. 과학자들은 다음에 **지방 폐기물로** 만든 바이오디젤을 사용하는 버스의 연료를 채울 수 있는 시설을 설치하기를 기대하고 있다.

(a) 폐수에 존재하는
(b) 고체 기름으로 정제되는
(c) 지방 폐기물로 만든
(d) 메탄올이 더해진

폐 동물성 고체 지방을 연료로 만들어 디젤 엔진에 사용될 수 있다는 내용으로 결론 부분에서 적절한 내용은 이러한 지방폐기물로 만든 바이오디젤을 주입할 수 있는 시설 설치를 기대한다는 내용이 적절하므로 정답은 (c)가 된다. (b)는 바이오디젤이 고체 지방으로 만들어진다는 뜻이기 때문에 답이 될 수 없다.

bond to ~에 붙이다 **process** 화학적으로 (가공)처리하다 **solid** 고체 **convert into** ~으로 바꾸다 **biofuel** 생물 연료 **drain** 배수관 **solidify** 응고시키다 **sewer** 하수구 **refine** 정제하다

3

류머티즘성 관절염 치료법의 종류를 아는 것과 올바른 치료법을 고르는 일은 **환자들이 고통을 줄이는 데 도움이 될 수** 있다. 통증을 완화시킬 수 있는 한 가지 효과적인 방법은 침술이다. 이 과정에서 통증을 완화시키기 위해 몸의 특정 지점에 침을 놓는다. 또 하나의 자연 요법은 가게에서 구입 수 있는 모든 요구르트에 든 박테리아의 종류인 활생균을 먹는 것이다. 악마의 발톱이라고 불리는 허브도 치료에 있어서 효과적인 결과를 얻는 것으로 증명되었다. 올바른 형식의 치료법은 류머티즘성 관절염이 일으키는 통증을 더 잘 관리하게 해 줄 것이다.

(a) 관절염을 완전히 없앤다
(b) 환자들의 근육통을 완화시킨다
(c) 관절이 더 강해지도록 자극시킨다
(d) 환자들이 고통을 줄이는 데 도움이 된다

류머티즘성 관절염을 위한 치료법을 소개하며 침술, 활생균, 특정 허브를 예로 들어 올바른 치료법이 통증을 더 잘 관리할 수 있게 한다고 하였으므로 정답은 (d)이다. 통증을 완화시키는 치료이지 관절염을 완전히 없애는 것은 아니므로 (a)는 오답이며, (b)는 관절염이 아닌 근육통이라고 하였으므로 오답이다.

arthritis 관절염 **alleviate** 완화하다 **acupuncture** 침술 **insert** 꽂다 **consume** 먹다 **probiotics** 활생균 **once and for all** 완전히 **soothe** 완화시키다

4

왜 빅토리아 여왕 시대의 영국은 자유주의의 목소리와 노동자들을 제외한 귀족 계급이 통치했는데도 혁명적인 반란이 없었을까? 정답은 아마도 지배하는 엘리트들이 그 시대의 변화하는 요구와 의견에 따라 변하고 적응할 수 있었기 때문일 것이다. 자유당은 영국 중산층의 경제적, 정치적 소망을 대표했고 보수당은 사회의 보수적인 요소를 대표했다. 이것을 인정하지만, 사회의 다른 사람들은 투표에서 제외되었다. 하지만 많은 경우 두 당 모두 노동자들과 가난한 사람들의 요구에 반응을 보였다. 그 결과로 영국 통치 계급은 **자유민주적인 요구를** 더 빨리 **이해하고** 점진적인 변화로 이에 부응했다.

(a) 자유민주적인 요구를 이해하다
(b) 농부들을 억압하다
(c) 일반 시민들의 요구를 거부하다
(d) 중산층의 요구를 만족시키다

지문에서 영국이 혁명을 겪지 않은 이유를 엘리트들이 사회의 변화하는 요구와 의견을 잘 이해하고 대처했기 때문이라고 한다. 그렇다면 영국의 지도층은 자유민주적인 요구를 이해했다고 하는 (a)가 가장 적합하다. (b)와 (c)는 지문의 내용과는 반대되고 (d)는 중산층의 필요를 만족시켰다고 했으므로 틀리다.

uprising 반란 **exclude** 제외하다 **adapt** 적응하다 **liberal** 자유주의자
bourgeoisie 중산층 **conservative** 보수주의자 **grant** 인정하다
party 정당 **gradual** 점차적인 **suppress** 억압하다 **peasant** 농부
commoner 서민

5

40인치 디지털 메뉴 보드는 몇 가지 이유로 시장에서 가장 인기 있는 디지털 포스터 크기 중 하나이다. 디지털 메뉴 보드의 주요 장점 중 하나는 지나가는 행인에게 틀림없이 영향을 미치기 때문에 모니터가 클수록 효과도 크며 수요를 이익으로 만든다는 것이다. 이 패널은 영화와 사진, 파워포인트 프레젠테이션과 완전한 디지털 광고 전체도 화면에 표시할 수 있다. 장치를 설치할 때 스탠드에 놓거나 창문이나 문에 걸 수도 있다. 다음에 회사에서 놀라운 광고를 전시하거나 인상적인 프레젠테이션을 하고 싶을 때 **다양한 성과를 올리기 위해 디지털 메뉴 보드를 설치하는 것을** 고려하는 것이 좋을 것이다.

(a) 디지털 메뉴 보드를 잠재 고객에게 판매하는 것
(b) 오래된 디지털 메뉴 보드 문제를 개선하는 것
(c) 고객을 끌기 위해 회사의 디지털 메뉴 보드를 광고하는 것
(d) 다양한 혜택을 누리기 위해 디지털 메뉴 보드를 설치하는 것

핵심 내용은 디지털 메뉴 보드를 소개하며 보드의 장점을 알리는 것이다. 따라서 회사가 멋진 광고나 프레젠테이션을 하고 싶을 때 이 메뉴 보드를 설치하라고 해야 맞다. 그러므로 정답은 (d)이다. (a)나 (c)는 메뉴 보드를 판매하거나 광고하라고 하기 때문에 오답이다.

create a stir 파란을 일으키다 **passer-by** 통행인 **display** 전시하다
unit 장치 **jaw-dropping** 크게 놀라운 **market** 팔다 **potential**
잠재하는 **reap** (성과·이익 등을) 올리다, 거두다

6

연예 뉴스

펑키한 새 미국 록 밴드인 원더스는 다음 달 유럽 투어를 시작할 것이다. 오래 기다린 그들의 두 번째 앨범 〈라이프 인 어 박스〉가 지난주 발매됐을 때 밴드는 유럽 앨범 차트에 4위로 데뷔했다. 원더스는 유럽에서 정상에 오른 데뷔 앨범인 〈다이아몬드〉로 단숨에 스타덤에 올랐다. 그들의 투어는 11월 26일 프랑스에서 시작해 크리스마스 콘서트를 위해 아일랜드와 영국에 도착하기 전에 벨기에와 독일, 이탈리아, 스웨덴에서 공연할 것이다. 티켓은 10월 20일에 판매가 시작될 것이다. 지금이 단 하나의 공연도 놓치지 않기 위해 **가장 좋은 자리를 구할 수 있는** 완벽한 시기이다.

(a) 그들의 최신 앨범을 예약해라
(b) 가장 좋은 자리를 구해라
(c) 그들의 미국 콘서트에서 자리를 예약해라
(d) 그들의 히트 앨범을 다운로드 받아라

원더스라는 그룹과 그들의 유럽 콘서트 일정을 소개하고 있다. 콘서트표 판매 개시일을 언급하고 있으므로 표를 구매하라는 내용인 (b)가 정답이다. (c)도 표를 구매하라고 하지만 유럽이 아닌 미국 콘서트이기 때문에 틀리다.

skyrocket (명성 등이) 급상승하다 **kick off** 시작하다

7

대학생들이 인턴사원으로 근무할 자리를 찾으려면, 먼저 이력서 작성에 관해 알아야 하는 것이 **어떤 순서로 무엇을 써야 하는가이다.** 이력서는 여러 부분으로 구성되는데, 먼저 목표 부분을 작성한다. 목표는 잠재적 고용주가 지원자의 정확한 의도를 파악할 수 있도록 한다. 그 다음은 학력인데 여기엔 학교 이름과 위치, 4.0 기준의 평점, 학생이 원하는 학위를 기록한다. 세 번째 부분은 지원자가 관련 경력을 기술하는 곳이다. 학생들이 이런 이력서 형식을 염두에 둔다면, 전문적으로 보이면서 자신들을 정확하게 나타낼 수 있는 이력서 작성법을 알게 될 것이다.

(a) 목표에 관해 심사숙고하는 것
(b) 적절한 도움을 찾을 곳
(c) 자신에 대해 연구하는 것
(d) 어떤 순서로 무엇을 써야 하는가

대학생에게 이력서 작성법을 알려주는 지문이다. 빈칸 뒤에서는 이력서 작성법을 3단계로 소개하고 있으므로 가장 적절한 정답은 (d)이다.

objective 목표 **intention** 의도 **coursework** 수업 활동 **work experience** 경력 **GPA** 평균 성적, 평점 **highlight** 강조하다 **relevant** 관련된 **represent** 나타내다

8

눈 아래 다크서클은 완벽히 숨길 수 없는 노화의 징후이다. 여기 다크서클을 없애기 위해 **다크서클이 어디서 생기는지** 알려 주는 정보가 있다. 다크서클은 종종 밀이나 밀가루에 알레르기 반응을 일으키는 글루텐 과민증이 있는 사람들에게서 흔히 나타난다. 충분한 수면을 취하지 않는 사람들에게도 종종 아래 눈두덩이 어두운 것을 볼 수 있다. 여러 피부 알레르기도 피부 변색을 가져오기 때문에 다크서클을 생기게 할 수 있다. 마지막으로 이것은 당신이 통제할 수 없는 것으로 유전이다. 원치 않는 눈가의 다크서클이 왜 생기는지를 알아내는 것은 그것을 치료하기 위해 무엇을 할 수 있는지 알아내는 데 도움이 될 것이다.

(a) 다크서클이 당신의 외모에 어떻게 영향을 미치는가
(b) 무엇이 다크서클을 위험하게 하는가
(c) 다크서클을 치료하는 법
(d) 다크서클이 어디서 생기는가

마지막 문장에 다크서클이 왜 생기는지 알면 치료를 하는 데 도움이 된다고 한다. 그렇다면 빈칸에는 다크서클을 없애기 위해서 다크서클의 원인을 알면 된다는 내용의 답이 들어가면 되므로 정답은 (d)이다.

tell-tale 숨길 수 없는 **intolerance** 과민증 **adequate** 충분한
discoloration 변색 **heredity** 유전

9

담당자께
8월에 자동차 보험과 관련하여 250달러짜리 수표를 보내셨습니다. 수표는 저의 결혼 전 성인 스미스로 발급되었습니다. 그러나 올해 6월 저는 결혼해 성을 존스로 바꾸었습니다. 유감스럽게도 이것은 은행에서 당신의 수표를 수리하지 않을 것을 의미합니다. 제 계좌는 현재 결혼 후의 성으로 되어 있습니다. 여기 수표를 돌려드리며 사라 존스라는 이름으로 재발급해 주시기를 부탁드립니다. 기록에 제 이름을 수정할 수 있도록 결혼 증명서 사본 한 통을 동봉합니다. 제 주소는 동일합니다. 도와주셔서 감사합니다.

사라 존스
(a) 반면에
(b) 다행히
(c) 의심의 여지없이
(d) 유감스럽게도

빈칸 전 내용을 보면 글을 쓴 여자는 결혼 후 성을 바꾸어서 은행이 결혼 전에 사용한 이름으로 발행된 수표를 받지 않을 것이라는 내용이다. 그렇다면 수표를 다시 발행해야 하는데 이는 예상하지 않았던 유감스러운 일이기 때문에 (d)가 적절한 답이다.

maiden name (여자의) 결혼하기 전 성 **surname** 성 **herewith**
여기 첨부하여 **enclose** 동봉하다 **certificate** 자격증 **amend** 수정하다
detail 정보

10

인생의 어떤 부분이든 관계없이 긍정적인 전망은 상황을 좋게 만들기 때문에 두어 가지 비결을 알려 주겠다. 문제를 문제로 보지 않고 도전으로 봐야 한다. '문제'라는 단어 자체가 정복하기 어렵다는 인상을 준다. 부정적인 생각을 더는 또 한 가지 방법은 자신이 처해 있는 상황을 긍정적으로 바꾸고 거기에 시간의 틀을 덧붙이는 것이다. 예를 들어 어떤 사람이나 상황을 견딜 수 없다고 말하는 대신 어떤 사람이나 상황을 특정 기간 동안 견딜 수 있다고 말할 수 있다. 그 시간이 지나갈 거고 불편한 일이 끝이 날 것이라는 것을 마음속으로 받아들인다. 이런 태도로 당신의 전반적인 화와 짜증이 가라앉을 것이다.
(a) 일반적으로
(b) 상세히 설명하자면
(c) 예를 들자면
(d) 그 후에

빈칸 전 내용은 살면서 부정적인 생각을 없애는 방법 하나를 소개하고 그 다음 문장에서 그 방법의 예를 보여주고 있기 때문에 정답은 (c)이다. 빈칸 뒤에 오는 문장이 전 문장 뒤에 일어나는 관계가 아니기 때문에 (d)는 오답이다.

outlook 견해, 시야 **unconquerable** 정복하기 어려운 **ease** 덜다
tolerate 견디다 **mentally** 마음속으로 **aggravation** 화남

Part II

11

불경기와 이민, 대출 산업의 붕괴는 잊어라. 미국 실업과 관련해서는 로봇이 원인이다. (a) 어떤 사람들은 이 나라에 제조업이 아직 안정되어 있다고 하지만 공장을 담당하는 것은 인간이 아니라 로봇이다. (b) 만약 자동화가 제조업과 의료업 및 다른 분야의 미래가 된다면 로봇이 교육을 덜 받은 미국인을 크게 앞지를 수 있다. (c) 덧붙여 말하자면 비서, 은행원, 그 밖의 사무원들은 매우 틀에 박힌 일을 해서 자동화에 쉽게 희생당할 수 있다. (d) 그러나 자동화는 제조비용을 낮추고 회사가 수백만 달러를 절약하게 해준다.

로봇 때문에 어떻게 미국인들이 일자리를 잃는지 설명하고 있는 지문이다. 로봇이 일자리에 미치는 부정적인 영향이 나와야 하는데 (d)는 로봇이 경제에 가져오는 장점을 이야기하기 때문에 흐름에 어긋난다.

mortgage 대출 **collapse** 붕괴 **blame** ~때문으로 보다 **man**
담당하다 **automation** 자동화 **leave in the dust** ~를 크게 앞지르다
routine 판에 박힌 **drive down** 인하하다

12

유럽 제국주의를 이야기할 때는 인정해야 하는 어두운 결과가 있다. (a) 제국주의는 유럽이 식민지 지도에 계획 없이 비논리적인 경계를 그었을 때 수천 개 작은 사회의 혼란을 일으켰다. (b) 산업 발달은 식민지의 본래 환경을 어지럽히고 전통 사회는 유럽인들로 인해 사라졌다. (c) 지금은 옛날로 돌아가고 과거에 잃어버렸던 풍습을 되찾기 위해 많은 노력을 하고 있다. (d) 노예 제도는 꽤 오래 전에 사라졌지만 아프리카와 아시아 남녀는 유럽 공장의 저렴한 노동력으로 간주되었다.

이 지문은 유럽 식민주의의 부정적인 결과를 이야기한다. 그리고 (a), (b), (d)는 그 부정적인 결과를 얘기하지만 (c)는 과거의 전통을 되살려야 한다는 얘기를 하므로 흐름상 어색한 문장은 (c)이다.

imperialism 제국주의 **haphazard** 계획성 없이 **disturb** 어지럽히다
pristine 본래의 **dissolve** 사라지다 **slavery** 노예 제도

Part III

13

세계 대부분의 나라들이 시민권에 '혈통주의' 이념을 채택하는데, 이는 자녀가 자동으로 부모의 국적을 갖는 것을 의미한다. 반대로 출생국의 시민권을 갖는 '출생지주의'는 대부분 인구가 부족한 서반구 국가들이 새로운 거주자가 절실히 필요하고, 동화 작용이 문화적 기준이나 때로는 법에 의해 강요되던 시기에 시작된 신세계 현상이다. 요즘 우리는 다문화 이념이 동화를 권장하지 않고 여행으로 국경을 넘는 것이 쉬워진 다른 세계에 살고 있다.

Q: 글의 요점은 무엇인가?
(a) 이민자들이 자녀의 시민권 국가를 결정하도록 허용되어야 한다.
(b) 출생국의 시민권 획득은 구식 관행이다.
(c) 불법 이민이 유행하고 있다.
(d) 시민권은 그 나라의 문화적 기준에 기꺼이 동화되려는 사람들에게 주어져야 한다.

출생국에 따라 시민권이 주어지는 것은 인구가 부족한 서반구 국가들이 새로운 인구가 절실히 필요하고 그 나라에 동화 흡수되기를 강요하던 시기로 거슬러 올라간다. 그런데 우리는 지금 다문화가 장려되고 여행으로 국경 이동이 쉬워진 시대에 살고 있으므로 출생국에 따라 시민권을 주는 것은 현 시대에 어울리지 않는다고 할 수 있기 때문에 정답은 (b)이다.

jus sanguinis 혈통주의 **citizenship** 시민권 **conversely** 반대로, 역으로 **jus soli** 출생지주의 **date** 연대를 추정하다 **assimilation** 동화, 흡수 **enforce** 강요하다 **norm** 기준 **epidemic** 급속한 확산

14

과일과 채소의 즙을 짜는 일은 무척 수고러운 데도 최근에 보편화되었다. 그러나 주스로 만드는 것에 대한 장점은 확실히 노력한 가치를 한다는 것이다. 많은 과일과 채소는 심장 질환과 일부 암과 같은 어려움으로부터 몸을 보호해 주는 훌륭한 비타민과 무기물을 제공한다. 몸이 제대로 기능하기 위한 효소도 많은 과일과 채소에 들어 있다. 게다가 당근 주스 한 컵에 있는 영양소의 양과 동일한 양을 얻기 위해서는 주스와 동등한 양의 당근을 씹고 먹는 시간을 들여야 할 것이다. 매일 아침 주스를 마시는 습관이 포함된 생활 방식으로 바꾸면 많은 멋진 이점을 얻을 것이다.

Q: 주로 무엇에 관한 글인가?
(a) 가정에 가장 좋은 과즙기를 구입하는 법
(b) 주스가 단단한 과일보다 더 좋은 이유
(c) 과일과 채소를 주스로 만드는 법
(d) 과일과 채소를 주스로 만들면 좋은 이유

이 지문은 과일과 채소를 즙으로 만들어서 먹으면 좋은 점을 이야기한다. 그래서 맞는 정답은 (d)이다. (a)와 (b)는 핵심 내용에 어긋나므로 오답이다.

juice ~의 즙을 짜다 **mineral** 무기물 **guard** 보호하다 **enzyme** 효소 **acquire** 얻다 **equivalent** 동등한 **transform** 바꾸다 **reap** 얻다

15

미국예술디자인학교

거대한 분야인 멀티미디어는 가상의 마법을 만들어내기 위해 이미지와 애니메이션, 그래픽, 오디오, 비디오를 합칩니다. 멀티미디어의 한 흥미진진한 분야는 애니메이션입니다. 애니메이션 전문가가 되기 위해서는 최고의 기관에서 교육을 받아야 하며 미국예술디자인학교(ACAD)는 이 분야에서 최고가 되는 데 도와드릴 수 있습니다. 만약 기본 스케치 기술과 애니메이션에 대한 열정을 가지고 있다면 이 분야에서 커리어를 시작할 수 있습니다. 애니메이션 학위를 받기 위한 최소 교육 조건은 110학점입니다. 저희 협회에서 분야에서 가장 뛰어난 실력을 가진 전문가들로부터 최고의 교육을 반드시 받으실 겁니다.

Q: 글에서 광고하는 것은?
(a) 애니메이션 학교
(b) 멀티미디어 기관
(c) 애니메이션 수업
(d) 애니메이션 직업

ACAD라는 애니메이션 학교를 광고하는 것인데, 이는 두 번째 문장에서 ACAD가 애니메이션 전문가가 되기 위해 도와준다는 것에서 알 수 있다. 따라서 정답은 (a)이다.

enormous 거대한 **merge** 합치다 **virtual** 가상의 **degree** 학위 **qualification** 조건 **credit hour** (이수의) 단위 시간 **qualified** 자격이 있는

16

대학 입학시험 몇 주 전은 부모와 학생 모두에게 스트레스를 주는 기간이 될 수 있다. 그러나 스트레스를 풀기 위해서 부모가 할 수 있는 것들이 있다. 부모는 스스로에게 지나친 스트레스를 주면 안 된다. 그들은 학습적으로 아이들을 지원하기 위해 최선을 다했다는 것을 기억해야 한다. 게다가 시험 성과를 아이들의 유일한 미래 직업 전망의 잣대로 보는 것은 잘못된 것이다. 더 중요한 것은 부모는 자신을 위해 가치 있는 시간을 보내야 한다. 왜냐하면 부모의 스트레스 수준은 아이들의 스트레스 수준에도 영향을 미치기 때문이다. 자신이 하고 싶은 대로 하면서 부모는 중요한 시험 날을 기다리는 아이들에게 알맞은 집안 환경을 만들어 줄 수 있다.

Q: 글의 주제로 적절한 것은?
(a) 중요한 시험 전 부모가 꼭 해야 할 것들을 알려주기
(b) 학생들이 좋은 성적을 얻을 수 있도록 조치를 취하기
(c) 아이들의 시험 전에 부모의 스트레스를 풀게 도와주기
(d) 부모가 아이들의 시험 스트레스를 줄이게 도와주기

지문의 주제는 중요한 시험을 앞둔 아이를 가진 부모가 어떻게 본인의 스트레스를 풀 수 있는지 가르쳐 주는 것이다. 따라서 정답은 (c)이다. (b)는 학생들이 높은 점수를 받을 수 있는 조치에 대해서 말하지만 이 지문은 학생들이 아닌 부모들이 스트레스를 푸는 방법을 소개하기 때문에 오답이다.

vent 발산하다 **quality time** 가장 재미있고 가치 있는 시간 **congenial** 알맞은 **notify** 알리다 **prior to** ~에 앞서 **take steps** 조치를 취하다 **let out** 풀어 주다

17

자동차 랩핑은 매우 효과적인 광고 방식이다. 처음에는 버스에 사용되면서 유명해졌지만 현재는 시각 효과 때문에 소형차와 승합차에 자주 사용된다. 다른 형태의 광고보다 눈길을 끌 뿐만 아니라 비교적 저렴하다. 또한 여러 부류의 사람들이 당신의 광고를 보기 때문에 당신은 회사에 폭넓은 대중 인식을 가져온다. 마지막으로 3D 자동차 광고는 쉽게 제거하고 바꿀 수 있다. 이 혁신적이고 매우 시각적인 자동차 광고 형태는 기업 홍보에 잘 사용되며 광고가 갖는 긍정적인 효과는 당신의 사업을 확장시킬 것이다.

Q: 글에 따르면 옳은 것은?
(a) 광고를 위해 자동차를 사용하는 것은 효과적이지만 비싸다.
(b) 자동차 전체에 광고하는 것은 메시지를 크고 명확하게 전달한다.
(c) 자동차 랩핑은 승합차와 버스에만 가능하다.
(d) 광고지를 자동차를 덮어 싸면 자동차에 영구적으로 접착된다.

자동차를 광고물로 포장해서 홍보하는 방법을 소개하고 있는데 이 광고의 장점은 누구나 볼 수 있다는 점이다. 따라서 정답은 (b)이다. (a)는 이 광고는 값비싸다고 하기 때문에 오답이고, (c)는 밴과 버스뿐만이 아니라 일반 승용차도 사용이 되기 때문에 답이 안 된다.

form 방식 **visual** 시각의 **relatively** 상대적으로 **eye-catching** 눈길을 끄는 **broad** 폭이 넓은 **expand** 확장하다

18

각양각색의 국제 관계 이론은 세계 국가가 서로 어떻게 상호 작용하는지에 대해 서로 다른 개념을 나타낸다. 한 가지 주요 이론은 현실주의로 국가는 오로지 다른 국가보다 더 많은 권력을 쌓기 위해 애쓴다고 진술한다. 이런 맥락에서 현실주의는 세계를 적대적이고 경쟁적인 곳이라고 주장한다. 더구나 국가의 주요 관심사는 자기 보존이다. 그러므로 국가는 권력을 추구하고 자신을 항상 보호해야 한다. 도덕적인 행동은 매우 위험하다. 국가가 자신을 보호할 수 있는 능력을 약화시킬 수 있기 때문이다. 정치인들은 국가들이 존재하는 한 현실주의를 준수했다. 특히 냉전 시대에 학자들과 정책 입안자들은 현실주의의 교의를 널리 사용했다.

Q: 현실주의에 관해 옳은 것은?
(a) 국가가 비윤리적인 것은 정당하다.
(b) 살아남기 위해서는 기습 공격이 가장 좋은 방어이다.
(c) 국가들 간의 협력이 반드시 이뤄져야 한다.
(d) 자급은 나라의 부수적인 이해관계이다.

현실주의라는 국제 관계 이론의 특징 중 하나는 한 나라가 도덕적인 행동을 하는 것은 그 나라의 방어를 약화시키기 때문에 위험하다고 한다. 따라서 정답은 (a)이다. 현실주의 국가가 살아남기 위해서는 권력을 쌓아야 하나 다른 나라에게 선제공격을 할 필요가 있다는 이야기는 없기 때문에 (b)는 틀리며, 나라는 스스로 살아남는 것이 최우선 목표이기 때문에 (d)도 답이 안 된다.

realism 현실주의 **self-preservation** 자기 보존 **undermine** 약화시키다 **practice** 준수하다 **as long as** ~하는 한은 **policy maker** 정책 입안자 **tenet** 교의 **unethical** 비윤리적인 **collaboration** 협력

19

1800년대 말에 두 가지 새로운 혁신 사상인 진화론과 마르크시즘이 대두되었다. 그의 저서 〈종의 기원〉에서, 찰스 다윈은 성공적인 개체는 변화하는 환경에 적응하면서 살아남는 반면, 변화하지 못한 개체는 죽게 되는 도태 과정을 통해 영속된다고 주장했다. 1848년에 칼 마르크스는 그의 〈공산당 선언〉에서 계급 구분을 기반으로 한 사회는 그 계급 구분이 결국 억압된 계급, 즉 프롤레타리아 계급의 불만과 혁명을 야기하기 때문에 그 사회 실패의 열쇠를 쥐고 있다고 주장했다.

Q: 글에 따르면 옳은 것은?
(a) 다윈은 마르크스의 자본주의에 대한 비판을 지지했다.
(b) 마르크스는 자본주의 사회가 결속을 향유한다고 믿었다.
(c) 다윈은 변화는 살아남기 위해서 필수적이라고 주장했다.
(d) 마르크스는 최하층 계급이 억압적이라고 주장했다.

19세기에 변형을 일으킨 새로운 생각 두 가지를 소개하고 있다. 하나는 다윈의 진화론이고 다른 하나는 마르크스가 〈공산당 선언〉에서 주장한 생각이다. 진화론에서 다윈은 살아남기 위해 변화를 해야 하며 이 내용은 지문에서 두 번째 문장에 변화하지 않으면 도태된다는 말에 나온다. 따라서 (c)가 답이고 (d)는 최하층 계급이 억압하는 것이 아니라 억압받기 때문에 틀렸다.

evolutionism 진화론 **perpetuate** 영속시키다 **selection** 도태, 선별 **adapt** 적응하다 **undoing** 실패 **dissatisfaction** 불만 **suppressed** 억압된 **proletariat class** 무산 노동자 계급

20

석면은 화재 단열부터 지붕 잇기까지 거의 모든 곳에 사용되었기 때문에 우리 주변 모든 곳에 있다. 안타깝게도 이 물질은 큰 산업 장해물이다. 무엇이 한때 이렇게 유용했던 원료를 치명적으로 만들었을까? 석면의 심각한 문제는 이 섬유가 폐를 관통하면 그곳에 박혀 계속해서 해를 끼친다는 것이다. 증상으로는 심한 천식과 폐의 벽이 두꺼워지는 현상과 심지어 폐암이 포함된다. 정상적으로 증상은 석면에 노출되고 10년에서 40년 이상 지나고 나서 나타난다. 이와 비슷하게 석면의 노출로부터 안전한 한도는 없다. 이 소리 없는 살인자와 싸우기 위해 사람들은 재료의 치명적인 특성을 알아야 하며 사용을 금지해야 한다.

Q: 다음 중 석면에 대해 옳은 것은?
(a) 병의 증상이 즉시 나타나게 한다.
(b) 몸에 들어오면 나가지 않는다.
(c) 소화 기관은 석면에 취약하다.
(d) 석면은 쉽게 접하기 힘들다.

석면의 위험성을 소개하고 있는 글로 석면이 치명적인 이유 중 하나는 폐에 들어가면 다시 나오지 않기 때문이라고 했으므로 정답은 (b)이다. (a)는 증상이 곧바로 나타난다고 하는데 석면이 가지고 오는 질환의 증상은 오랜 시간 뒤 나타나기 때문에 정답이 될 수 없다. 호흡기를 공격하지 소화 기관을 공격하는 것이 아니기 때문에 (c)도 오답이다.

asbestos 석면 **insulation** 단열 **roofing** 지붕 잇기 **hazard** 위험 요소 **lethal** 치명적인 **penetrate** 관통하다 **lining** 내벽 **property** 특성

21

프랑스 음식이나 중국 음식 같은 세계 일류의 요리에 흔히 있는 일이지만, 태국 음식 또한 자국의 뿌리 외에 국제적인 면이 있다. 태국 본토의 향토 음식에 어느 정도의 다양성은 있겠지만 현지 태국 레스토랑 메뉴에 나타나는 미묘한 차이를 찾는 것은 매우 어려울 수 있다. 세계적인 기호에 더 잘 맞추기 위해 레스토랑은 가끔 맛에 전 세계적인 조화를 주려는 시도를 한다. 일부 극단적인 맛과 향신료 수준은 보통 낮춰진다. 다양한 사람들을 만족시키려는 이러한 노력의 성과는 이른바 음식의 표준화라고 불릴지도 모른다. 퓨전 레스토랑은 한 걸음 더 나아가 만인의 관심을 끌기 위해 서로 다른 요리를 융합한다.

Q: 글과 일치하는 것은?
(a) 해외의 태국 음식은 대개 정통이 아니다.
(b) 태국 음식의 양념을 조절할 수 있는 외국인은 거의 없다.
(c) 세계 요리는 다소 평범하고 일관된다.
(d) 음식은 그 나라 본토가 가장 맛이 좋다.

지문 첫 부분에 프랑스 음식이나 중국 음식에는 흔한 일이지만 태국 음식도 세계인의 입맛에 맞추려는 국제적인 면이 있다고 하였으므로 글과 일치하는 것은 (c)이다. 나머지 보기는 지문에 없는 내용이다.

as is the case with 흔히 있는 일이지만 **cuisine** 요리 **apart from** ~외에는 **proper** 본래의 **be hard pressed** ~하기 매우 어렵다 **subtle** 미묘한 **variation** 차이 **accommodate** 맞추다 **strike** ~의 인상을 주다 **cosmopolitan** 전 세계적인 **tone down** 좀 더 누그러뜨리다 **authentic** 진정한 **somewhat** 다소

22

심장병을 앓을 위험은 나쁜 콜레스테롤로 알려진 LDL (저밀도 지방 단백질) 콜레스테롤 수준이 높은 사람들에게 더 높다. LDL 콜레스테롤 수준을 낮추려면 다음 네 가지 조치를 따라야 한다. 첫째는 식단 조절이다. 포화 지방이 낮지만 식이 섬유와 비타민이 높은 식단을 권한다. 둘째는 비만은 높은 수준의 LDL 콜레스테롤과 관련 있기 때문에 이상적인 체중을 목표로 하는 것이 필수다. 셋째는 운동을 하면 LDL 콜레스테롤 수준을 낮출 수 있다. 넷째는 콜레스테롤 보조제를 먹으면 다른 영양소와 함께 건강에 좋은 콜레스테롤을 보충하는 데 도움이 된다. 생활 방식이 혈액 내 콜레스테롤 수준을 결정하는 데 중대한 역할을 한다는 것을 아는 것은 중요하다.

Q: 글과 일치하는 것은?
(a) 체중 감량은 LDL 콜레스테롤 수치를 낮출 수 있다.
(b) 간은 신체 내 대부분의 콜레스테롤을 생산한다.
(c) 포화 지방은 몸에 좋다.
(d) 식이 섬유가 높은 식단은 심장 문제를 일으킨다.

건강에 해로운 LDL 콜레스테롤을 줄이기 위한 방법들을 소개한다. 두 번째 방법을 보면 높은 LDL 콜레스테롤 수준이 비만과 연관되어 있다고 하므로 정답은 (a)이다.

density 밀도 **modify** 조절하다 **saturated fat** 포화 지방 **associate** 관련시키다 **must** 절대로 필요한 것 **supplement** 보충물 **make up for** 보충하다

23

니콜스 씨에게

임페리얼 문구점에서 고급 용지 케이스 15개를 주문해 주셔서 감사합니다. 고객님의 주문은 처리되어 목요일 아침에 배송되었으며 다음 평일 중 5일 안에 도착할 것입니다. 동봉된 총 800달러에 이르는 주문 청구서를 확인하시고 40달러 상당의 수표는 환불됩니다. 고객님이 선불을 하셨기 때문에 5% 할인해 드리며 주문액이 500달러를 초과했으므로 운송비도 지불해드립니다. 임페리얼 문구점은 고객 리스트에 귀하의 성함을 올리게 되어 기쁩니다. 고객님의 다음 주문을 고대합니다.
엘렌 해리스

Q: 편지로부터 유추할 수 있는 것은?
(a) 주문은 늦어도 월요일에는 도착할 것이다.
(b) 총 주문액이 500달러이면 운송비는 무료일 것이다.
(c) 니콜스 씨는 760달러에서 5% 할인 받을 것이다.
(d) 이 주문은 고객이 이 회사에 한 첫 주문이었다.

니콜스 씨의 주문을 확인하는 편지이다. 끝에서 두 번째 문장에서 니콜스 씨를 고객 리스트에 추가하겠다고 하기 때문에 첫 주문인 것으로 추측할 수 있다. 따라서 정답은 (d)가 된다. (b)는 운송비가 500달러를 초과해야 운송비가 무료이기 때문에 오답이고, 800달러에서 할인된 가격이 760달러이기 때문에 (c)도 틀렸다.

premium 고급의 **stationery** 문방구 **ship** 수송하다 **business day** 평일 **exceed** 초과하다

24

미국과 소련간의 '우주 경쟁'은 소련 과학자들이 처음으로 인간이 만든 위성인 스푸트니크 1을 1957년에 궤도로 성공적으로 발사했을 때 시작되었다. 인공위성 자체가 미국에게는 위험을 지니지 않았지만 미국인은 소련이 우주를 장악할 수 있어 핵탄두를 장비한 대륙간탄도미사일로 미국 영토를 공격할까 봐 염려했다. 이 사건은 1958년에 미국이 미국항공우주국(NASA)을 세우도록 촉구했다. 미국 의회는 그동안 방위 예산을 늘렸고 공립학교에 과학 수업 자금을 더 제공하기 위해 국방교육법을 1958년에 통과시켰다. 소련이 우주 경쟁에서 승리할 것이라는 두려움이 미국을 우주 탐사에 뒤떨어지지 않도록 박차를 가했다.

Q: 글에서 유추할 수 있는 것은?
(a) 스푸트니크의 발사 없이는 우주 탐사에 투자가 이뤄지지 않았을 것이다.
(b) 인공위성은 소련이 장거리 미사일을 시험하기 위해 발사했다.
(c) 소련은 대륙간탄도미사일을 발사할 기술이 없었다.
(d) 미국은 1957년 전에는 소련만큼 우주 탐험에 관심을 가지지 않았다.

소련이 스푸트니크를 발사하는 것이 어떻게 미국이 우주 개발에 더욱 신경을 쓰게 자극했는지 설명하므로 정답은 (d)이다. 미국은 소련의 대륙간탄도미사일 공격 여부를 염려했으므로 (c)는 옳지 않다.

launch 발사하다 **satellite** 위성 **orbit** 궤도 **nuclear-tipped** 핵탄두를 장비한 **intercontinental** 대륙 간의 **ballistic missile** 탄도 미사일 **urge** 촉구하다 **fund** 자금을 제공하다 **spur** ~에 박차를 가하다 **fire** 발사하다

25

뇌에 안 좋은 식습관

어떤 식습관은 두뇌 활동을 늦춘다는 것을 아시나요? 그렇다면 두뇌 활동을 촉진시키기 위해 어떻게 식습관을 바꿀 수 있을까요?

· 과식은 분명 금물입니다. 당신의 신체는 소화시키는 데 전념해야 해서 생각하기에 충분한 에너지가 남지 않을 것입니다.
· 설탕이 에너지를 공급한다고 생각할지 모르지만 오로지 짧고 강한 효과만 있기 때문에 두뇌가 필요로 하는 것은 아닙니다.
· 흰 밀가루는 너무 가공되어 뇌가 필요한 영양소를 얻을 수 없습니다.
· 카페인은 아침에 기운을 돋우는 데 좋을지 모르지만 지나치게 섭취하면 초조함과 신경과민을 느낄 것입니다.
· 과도한 양의 알코올은 건망증을 유발해 두뇌에 유익할 수 없습니다.

Q: 글에서 유추할 수 있는 것은?

(a) 시험 날 아침 식사를 많이 하면 점수를 잘 받을 것이다.

(b) 가공 음식은 여러 종류의 영양소를 가지고 있다.

(c) 두뇌는 안정되고 오래가는 에너지 공급이 필요하다.

(d) 커피에 설탕을 타면 두뇌에 좋다.

먹는 습관이 두뇌 활동에 영향을 미친다는 내용으로 식습관 중 설탕이 두뇌 활동을 자극시킨다고 착각을 하는데 실제로 설탕은 두뇌에 많은 에너지를 짧게 여러 번 주기 때문에 별로 도움이 안 된다. 그렇다면 두뇌에는 지속적으로 에너지 공급이 되어야 좋다고 볼 수 있기 때문에 정답은 (c)이다. (a)는 과식은 두뇌 활동에 좋지 않다고 했기 때문에 틀리고, 가공된 음식은 영양소가 별로 없기 때문에 (b)도 정답이 될 수 없다.

boost 촉진시키다 no-no 금물 suppose ~라고 생각하다 pick-me-up 기운을 돋우는 음료 uptight 초조해 하는 jittery 신경과민의

Part IV

26-27

"어머니들의 고통"

헨리 스티븐슨

우리 미국인들은 전쟁의 실상 혹은 불행, 특히 재앙과 같은 폭력, 회복할 수 없는 파괴 그리고 생존한 사람들에게 가하는 정신 외상적인 타격을 감추기 위해 노력하고 있는 사회에 살고 있다. 따라서 케이트 댄싱 팀(KDT)이 선보이는 "어머니들의 고통"이라는 공연은 폭력적인 갈등이 있는 몇몇 지역으로 성인이 된 아이들을 파병했던 미국 어머니들의 이야기를 다룰 것이다. 이 공연은 언론 매체의 주목을 받고 있다.

그것의 세계 최초의 공연은 그린우드 극장에서 6월 15일 금요일과 6월 16일 토요일에 진행될 예정이다. 감독은 평범한 여성들이 침략행위와 군사화의 시기에 살면서 다른 어려움들에 직면하고 있다고 언급했다. 그것은 모든 어머니들이 그들의 내면 이야기를, 그리고 그들의 아이들의 내면 이야기를 말할 수 있는 플랫폼으로 기능할 것으로 예상된다.

26. Q: 본문은 무엇에 관한 것인가?

(a) 여성들의 고통을 보여주는 공연

(b) 전 세계의 전쟁에 반대하는 시위

(c) 다양한 지역에 파견된 군인들 사이의 갈등

(d) 일반 여성들이 직면하는 다양한 어려움들

27. Q: 본문에서 추론할 수 있는 것은?

(a) 그 댄스 공연은 군인들의 트라우마를 치료하기 위해 만들어졌다.

(b) 전쟁의 실상은 언론매체에 의해 공개되어 왔다.

(c) 그 공연은 미국에서만 진행될 것이다.

(d) "어머니들의 고통"과 같은 공연들은 때때로 사람들의 내면세계를 대변한다.

26. "어머니들의 고통"이라는 댄스 공연에 대해 쓴 글이며, "ordinary women are facing different challenges while living in a period of aggression and militarization"라는 문장을 통해 여성들의 고통에 대해 다룬 공연이므로, 정답은 (a)이다.

27. 댄스 공연이 여성들의 고통에 대해 다루고 있으며, "It is expected to function as a platform for all mothers to tell their own

inner stories and their children's"라는 문장을 통해 댄스 공연이 사람들의 내면세계를 다루는 대상이 될 수 있다는 것을 알 수 있으므로, 정답은 (d)이다.

agony 고통 conceal 감추다, 숨기다 misery 비참, 불행, 고통 disastrous 비참한, 불행한 irreparable 치료할 수 없는 destruction 파괴 traumatic 외상성의, 충격이 큰 take a toll on ~에 타격을 입히다 tackle 다루다, 해결하다 dispatch 파견하다, 파병하다 conflict 갈등 premiere 초연 aggression 공격 militarization 군사화 represent 보여주다, 대변하다 demonstration 시위 remedy 치료하다

28-29

구인 : 아동교육가

– 헌신적인 아동교사 –

살렘 유치원은 아동교육에서 50년의 우수함을 자랑하는 수상경력이 있는 유치원입니다. 우리는 내년 1월부터 시작할 수 있는 유치원 교사를 찾고 있습니다. 우리 학교에 대한 더 많은 정보를 원하신다면, www.salemprep.or.us를 방문해 주세요.

자격요건:

– 아동교육 자격증

– 유효한 응급 처치 자격증

– 범죄경력 증명서

– 유치원 근무 경력 우대

– 고용 전 수업 시연

복리후생:

– 높은 임금

– 1년 2주의 유급 휴가

– 유급 전문 연수

– 유급 병가

– 초과 근무 없음 (부모님들과의 상담은 수업시간에 진행)

– 때때로 주말 업무 필요

28. Q: 구인광고에서 어떤 자격요건이 언급되어 있는가?

(a) 응급 수술 자격증

(b) 범죄경력 증명서

(c) 유치원 경력 필수

(d) 고용 이후 시연 수업

29. Q: 본문에서 광고된 직업에 대해 옳은 것은?

(a) 고용된 교사는 연말까지 일을 시작해야 한다.

(b) 아동들과의 몇 년간의 훈련이 필수이다.

(c) 고용된 교사에게는 많은 월급이 보장되어 있다.

(d) 새로운 교사는 때때로 필요하다면 초과근무를 해야 한다.

28. 유치원 교사를 구인하는 광고지문이며, 여러 가지 자격요건으로 언급한 것 중에서, "Criminal Record Check"은 범죄경력 증명서이므로, 정답은 (b)이다.

29. 구인광고에서 여러 가지 복리후생제도에 대해 언급하고 있으며, "Competitive remuneration"은 다른 직장보다 더 나은 월급을 보장한다는 내용이므로, 고용된 교사에게 더 많은 월급이 보장되어 있다는 것을 알 수 있으므로, 정답은 (c)이다.

dedicated 헌신적인　award-winning 수상 경력이 있는　celebrate 기념하다, 축하하다　qualification 자격요건　certificate 자격증　valid 유효한, 타당한　first aid 응급 처치　criminal 범죄의　tryout 시연, 시험 benefits 복리후생제도　competitive 경쟁력 있는, 뛰어난 remuneration 보수, 급료　overtime 초과시간　emergency surgery 응급수술　mandatory 의무적인　preliminary 예비적인　generous 후한, 넉넉한

editorial 사설　solution 해결책　impact 영향, 충격　total 총계가 ~이다 equivalent 동등한, 대등한　come up with 떠올리다, 생각해 내다　a profusion of 수많은　curtail 억제시키다　trigger 유발하다, 발생시키다 edible 먹을 수 있는　keep up with 뒤처지지 않다, 따라가다　take action 조치를 취하다　implement 실행하다, 수행하다　discard 버리다 impose 부과하다, 부여하다

30-31

국내 〉 사회　　　　　　　　　　　　　　　　위클리 뉴스

사설: 식료품점 음식물 쓰레기에 대한 해결책들

매리 패터슨 | 8월 20일

기사 전문 읽기 ▼

식료품점들에서 음식물 쓰레기의 경제적 영향은 주요한 문제가 되었다. 왜냐하면 국립 식량 및 영양 센터가 작성한 보고서에 따르면, 농산물의 45%가 먹지도 않은 상태에서 매립지로 가고 있다고 평가되기 때문이다. 그것 중의 일부가 소비자들에 의해 버려지기도 하지만, 일부는 소매업자들에 의해 버려지고 있다. 농산물 손실은 지난해에 약 380억 파운드였으며, 이것은 소매 수준에서 국가 전체의 음식물 공급의 12%와 유사하다.

미국 주들 중 일부는 식료품점들에 의해 유발되는 농산물 쓰레기를 억제하기 위해 수많은 해결책들을 찾기 위해 노력해왔으나 허사였다. 그러나 작년 유럽의 일부 국가들은 식료품점들이 팔지 않은 식용 가능한 농산물을 버리는 것을 금지하는 법안을 통과시켰다. 그들과 보조를 맞추기 위해, 몇몇 주들은 더 엄격한 제한을 가함으로써 조치를 취할 계획을 세워야 한다. 그 주들은 식료품점들이 사용가능한 농산물을 기부하거나 다른 목적으로 사용하도록 촉구할 필요가 있다.

30. Q: 사설의 주요 목적은 무엇인가?
(a) 주 정부들이 식료품점들의 수를 억제하도록 요구하기 위해
(b) 소매업자들이 수많은 판매되지 않은 농산물을 버리는 이유를 설명하기 위해
(c) 식료품점들이 먹을 수 있는 음식을 자선단체들에 기부하도록 조언하기 위해
(d) 주 정부들이 음식물 쓰레기를 줄이기 위해 계획을 수립하도록 촉구하기 위해

31. Q: 사설에 따르면 옳은 것은?
(a) 음식물 쓰레기는 미국에서 가장 심각한 문제이다.
(b) 대부분의 먹을 수 있는 농산물은 소매업자들에 의해 버려지고 있다.
(c) 몇몇 미국 주들은 음식물 쓰레기를 줄일 수 있는 방법을 찾지 못했다.
(d) 몇몇 미국 주들은 이미 법률적 통제를 하기 위한 조치를 취하고 있다.

30. 식료품점 등에서 버리는 음식물 쓰레기의 문제점을 지적하면서, "To keep up with them, several states should plan to take action by implementing stricter restrictions"라는 문장을 통해 각 주에서 대책을 수립할 것을 촉구하고 있으므로, 정답은 (d)이다.

31. 미국의 몇몇 주들의 해결책을 찾기 위한 노력을 언급하면서, "Some U.S. states have unsuccessfully sought to come up with a profusion of solutions"를 언급하고 있으므로, 실제로는 노력이 허사였다는 것을 알 수 있으므로, 정답은 (c)이다.

32-33

오레건 일간 신문

지방 소식

포틀랜드 시장, 2,000만 달러 법인세 인상을 제안하다

시 정부에 따르면, 포틀랜드 시장인 팀 타일러는 도시의 법인세와 관련하여 2,000만 달러 증가를 제안할 예정이다. 그러한 급증은 도시의 예산을 강화해 줄 것으로 여겨지며, 세수 증가에도 불구하고 적자였던 상황이었다. 그러한 규모의 세금 인상은 약 12%의 증가를 나타낼 것이며, 그것은 특히 도시의 수익성이 높은 회사들에게 영향을 주게 될 것이다.

도시의 세무 공무원들은 그 법인세가 경찰, 소방관 그리고 공원 관리를 위해 지불해야 할 불균형적인 예산을 위해 이용되기를 기대하고 있다. 왜냐하면 그들을 위한 비용은 놀라운 속도로 증가해왔기 때문이다. 또한, 세금 인상에서 발생한 수익은 홈리스들을 위해 특정한 추가적인 서비스에 자금을 지원할 것이다. 공무원들은 그 증가가 그 도시의 가장 주요한 문제들 중의 하나인 노숙인 위기 상태를 더 잘 해결하도록 돕기를 희망한다.

그럼에도 불구하고, 그 제안은 여전히 몇 가지 어려움들을 극복해야 한다. 이전 시장인 찰스 맥도날드는 5년 전에 법인세를 인상하려고 시도했으나, 대중들의 반대에 직면하게 되었다. 대부분의 시민들은 제안된 세금 인상이 불필요한 것이라고 여겼다. 그의 계획은 시의회의 지원을 받지 못했기 때문에 비현실적인 것으로 입증되었다.

32. Q: 세금 인상으로 재정지원을 받지 못하는 것은 무엇인가?
(a) 경찰관
(b) 소방관
(c) 노숙인
(d) 도시 공무원

33. Q: 신문 기사에서 추론할 수 있는 것은?
(a) 증가하는 세금 수익은 도시의 예산 적자를 해결해 왔다.
(b) 제안된 세금 증가는 내년도 예산에 배정될 것으로 예상된다.
(c) 팀 타일러의 제안은 시의회에 의해 지지를 받지 못한다면 실패할 가능성이 높다.
(d) 노숙인 위기 상태는 도시 공무원들 사이에 가장 심각한 문제였다.

32. 법인세 인상을 통해 세수 부족을 메우고, 특정 업무에 대해 지원을 강화할 계획을 말하면서, "police officers, firefighters"와 "the homeless crisis"를 언급하고 있으므로, 도시 공무원은 해당되지 않는다. 따라서 정답은 (d)이다.

33. 팀 타일러 이전 시장의 계획도 실패로 돌아갔는데, 그 이유로 "His plan turned out to be impractical since he didn't earn the city council's support"라는 문장을 제시하고 있으며, 이를 통해 시의회의 지원이 있어야 성공 가능성이 높아진다는 것을 알 수 있으므로, 정답은 (c)이다.

tax hike 세금 인상 be expected to ~하기로 되어 있다, ~할 예정이다
business tax 법인세 upsurge 급증, 증가 solidify 강화하다 deficit
결함, 결핍 revenue 수익 approximately 대략, 약 gross 수익을 내다
discretionary 임의의, 자유재량의 upkeep 유지비, 보존비 top
priority 최우선순위 gratuitous 무료의, 불필요한, 여분의 allot 할당하다,
배당하다

34-35

파블로 피카소의 "게르니카"

1937년 게르니카라는 스페인 마을에 대한 독일 비행기들의 폭격에 영감
을 받은 파블로 피카소의 "게르니카"는 그의 가장 강력한 정치적 주장이
라고 여겨진다. 전쟁의 비극 그리고 그것이 무고한 시민들에게 가하는 고
통을 다루고 있는 이 작품은 반전의 상징으로서 영원한 위상을 얻게 되었
다. 완성하자마자, 그 작품은 전 세계의 수많은 미술관에서 전시되었으며,
유명해지고 널리 호평을 받았다. 그 전시들은 스페인 내전의 비참한 상황
을 세계의 이목이 집중되도록 했다.

그러나 수년 동안에 걸쳐, "게르니카"에 대한 해석은 매우 다양했으며, 서
로 대조적이기도 했다. 예를 들어, 그 그림의 두 가지 주요한 요소들인 소
와 말은 논쟁적인 것이었다. 몇몇 비평가들은 피카소는 분명히 그것들이
스페인 문화에서 중요한 동물이기 때문에 그의 경력 전반에 걸쳐서 몇
가지 다른 역할들을 수행하는 이 요소들을 이용했다고 지적했다. 그러나
다른 비평가들은 소는 아마도 파시즘의 학살을 의미하며, 말은 게르니카
의 무고한 시민들을 상징한다고 주장한다.

34. Q: 본문의 주요 논점은 무엇인가?
(a) 왜 "게르니카"가 스페인 사람들 사이에서 인기를 얻게 되었는가
(b) 피카소는 어떻게 "게르니카"를 그렸으며, 논란을 유발했는가
(c) 스페인 내전이 어떻게 예술적 업적에 해를 끼쳤는가
(d) 비평가들이 왜 처음에 피카소의 작품을 호평하지 않았는가

35. Q: "게르니카"에 대해 추론할 수 있는 것은 무엇인가?
(a) 그것은 전쟁의 실상을 감추기 위해 전쟁의 비극성을 최소화했다.
(b) 그것은 다른 나라들이 스페인 내전에 참전하도록 하는 중요한 동력을
만들었다.
(c) 작품 속 동물들은 공감을 얻기 위해 다른 문화들로부터 가져온 것이다.
(d) 작품 속 소와 말은 다양한 의미를 가지고 있다.

34. 파블로 피카소의 "게르니카"를 설명하는 글이며, 그 작품이 그려진 이유
그리고 그 작품을 둘러싼 논쟁에 대해 다루고 있으므로, 정답은 (b)이다.

35. 파블로 피카소의 "게르니카"에는 소와 말이 등장하며, 마지막 두 문장
을 통해 소와 말을 인식하는 비평가들의 비평이 다르고 다양한 의미
를 나타낸다는 것을 알 수 있으므로, 정답은 (d)이다.

inspire 영감을 불어넣다 tragedy 비극 anguish 고통 inflict 고통을
가하다 perpetual 영구적인 a throng of 많은 acclaim 칭찬하다,
환호하다 interpretation 해석 contradict 반박하다 dominant 지배적인
controversial 대조적인 onslaught 맹공격, 맹습 popularity 인기
artistic establishment 예술계 deny 거부하다, 부인하다
momentum 힘, 기세, 역동성 multifaceted 다면적인

ACTUAL TEST 2 p.154

Part I
1 (b) 2 (c) 3 (a) 4 (b) 5 (c)
6 (b) 7 (a) 8 (c) 9 (c) 10 (a)

Part II
11 (c) 12 (c)

Part III
13 (a) 14 (b) 15 (d) 16 (c) 17 (d)
18 (b) 19 (d) 20 (a) 21 (b) 22 (a)
23 (d) 24 (c) 25 (c)

Part IV
26 (a) 27 (c) 28 (d) 29 (c) 30 (a)
31 (a) 32 (b) 33 (d) 34 (b) 35 (c)

Part I

1

조울증은 몇 분만에 우울함에서 행복함으로 또는 그 반대로 기분의 두드
러진 변화를 야기할 수 있는 질환이다. 다행히 식습관과 관련하여 이 장
애로부터 지킬 수 있는 간단한 방법이 있다. 첫째, 흔히 양배추에 함유된
엽산의 섭취를 늘리는 것이 문제에 도움이 될 수 있다. 둘째, 생선과 가금
류와 같은 저지방 단백질 음식은 필수적인데 단백질이 기분을 나아지게
하기 때문이다. 적당량의 신선한 과일을 매일 섭취하고 사람들이 일반적
으로 먹는 모든 포화 지방은 올리브 오일이나 생선 기름과 같은 건강한
지방으로 대체되어야 한다. 이 장애를 고치는 데 필요한 필수 영양소의
일일 섭취량을 늘리는 것을 명심해야 한다.

(a) 다양한 영양소의 일일 섭취량을 제한하다
(b) 필수 영양소의 일일 섭취량을 늘리다
(c) 권장된 양만큼의 약을 복용하다
(d) 다양한 종류의 건강에 좋은 과일과 채소를 섭취하다

식이 요법을 통해 조울증을 치료할 수 있는 방법을 소개하고 있다. 그렇
기 때문에 마지막 문장에서는 조울증과 싸우기 위해 좋은 식이 요법이 필
요하다는 내용이 필요하므로 정답은 (b)이다.

bipolar disorder 조울증 mood swing 기분의 두드러진 변화
depression 우울 elation 크게 기뻐함 vice-versa 반대로
a matter of 겨우 intake 섭취 folic acid 엽산 poultry 가금(류)

2

크리스마스는 더블린에서!

올해 크리스마스 기간 동안 놀라움으로 가득한 도시 더블린에서 휴식을 가지세요. 더블린에서 황홀한 크리스마스 쇼핑 경험을 할 수 있는 곳은 도크랜즈 크리스마스 마켓입니다. 진정한 독일풍 크리스마스 마법을 제공하는 한 독일 회사가 이 시장을 아일랜드의 수도로 가져올 것입니다. 놓칠 수 없는 아름다운 장식과 샬레, 수공예품을 생각해 보세요! 긴 쇼핑을 마친 후에는 아일랜드의 수도에서 크리스마스 쇼핑을 하고 싶어 하는 누구에게나 놀라운 편안함을 제공해 주는 많은 훌륭한 더블린의 호텔 중 한 곳에서 휴식을 취하십시오. 별 세 개짜리 베스트 셀던 파크 호텔은 더블린의 도심에서 겨우 15분 거리에 있습니다. 그러니 뭘 망설이십니까. **지금 휴가를 예약하십시오!**

(a) 지금 자신에게 휴가를 주세요
(b) 지금 오랫동안 기다렸던 휴가를 즐기세요
(c) 지금 휴가를 예약하세요
(d) 지금 그것을 위해 중단하세요

크리스마스에 더블린을 방문하라는 광고이다. 따라서 마지막에는 빨리 오라고 하는 이야기와 가장 비슷한 답이 되어야 하므로 (c)가 가장 적절하다. (a)는 자기 자신에게 좀 여유를 주라는 뜻이며 (d)는 지금 빨리 중단하라는 뜻이라서 어색하다.

enchanting 황홀한 **authentic** 진정한 **chalet** 샬레, 스위스풍 농가
arts and crafts 공예 **make a break** 중단하다

3

카메라는 발명 이래로 **큰 진보를 겪었다.** 19세기 카메라는 크고 매우 원시적인 기술에 기반을 두었다. 예를 들어, 당시 카메라는 사진 건판과 장시간 노출이 필요했다. 인물 사진의 대상은 몇 분 동안 앉아 있어야 했다. 현재는 많은 사진작가들이 디지털 카메라로 가능해진 새로운 성능을 탐구하기 시작했다. 디지털 사진술의 가장 흥미로운 부분은 사람들이 어디에 있든지 웹에 연결된 컴퓨터 앞에만 있으면 사진을 보여줄 수 있다는 개념이다. 카메라의 진화는 놀라웠고 계속되는 발달은 기회, 관찰, 기억의 완벽한 융합을 이루어 낼 것이다.

(a) 큰 진보를 겪다
(b) 발달하면서 많은 어려움을 인내했다
(c) 쓸모가 없어지기 시작했다
(d) 개발이 늦춰졌다

마지막 문장을 보면 카메라가 진화하고 발전하면서 더욱 멋진 작품이 가능해질 것이라고 한다. 그렇다면 첫 문장은 카메라가 진화했다는 내용이 자연스러우므로 정답은 (a)이다. (b)는 발전에 대해서 언급을 하지만 어려움을 극복한 후라고 했기 때문에 오답이다.

primitive 원시적인 **photographic plate** 사진 건판 **exposure** 노출
portrait 인물 사진 **compelling** 흥미진진한 **confluence** 융합
hardship 어려움 **obsolete** 쓸모없게 된

4

실직자를 위한 대출은 담보 대출과 무담보 대출 이렇게 두 가지로 나뉜다. 담보 대출은 대출에 대해 가치 있는 자산을 저당 잡힐 수 있으면 받을 수 있다. 이런 대출을 통하면 낮은 이율로 큰 대출금을 받을 수 있다. 그러나 무담보 대출은 대출에 대해 저당 잡힐 필요는 없지만 담보 대출보다 적은 금액을 받는다. 무담보인 특징 때문에 비교적 더 높은 이자를 내야 할 것이다. 두 가지 대출의 도움으로 실직자들은 **재정 자금 신청을** 더 이상 망설일 필요가 없다.

(a) 새로운 직업을 찾는다
(b) 재정 자금을 신청한다
(c) 복지 수당을 신청한다
(d) 재정 조언을 요청한다

실직자들을 위한 두 가지 종류의 대출을 소개하며 그 차이점을 이야기하고 있다. 마지막 문장에서는 대출의 도움으로 직업이 없는 사람들은 더 이상 주저할 필요가 없다고 하는데 이것은 금전적인 도움을 요청하는 데 주저할 필요가 없다고 하는 것이 가장 논리적이기 때문에 정답은 (b)이다.

secured loan 담보 대출 **asset** 자산 **collateral** 담보물 **interest rate** 이율 **nature** 특징 **welfare** 복지 **benefit** 수당

5

태초부터 존재한다는 것은 생존한다는 것을 의미했다. 고대인은 물, 불, 주거지와 음식인 네 가지 생존에 필요한 기본적인 것을 획득해야 했다. 첫째, 식수를 확보하기 위해 고대인은 수원지를 찾아야 했다. 불은 사기를 높이고, 소독뿐만 아니라 취사하는 방법은 물론이고, 잠재적인 포식 동물로부터의 훌륭한 방어책이 되었다. 주거지에 대해서는 초기 인간들은 잠재적인 포식 동물과 악천후로부터 보호를 받을 의도로 높은 동굴 안에 안식처를 찾았을 것이다. 창과 조잡한 생존용 칼은 초기 인간들에게 사냥감을 제공했고, 인간은 결국 덫을 놓는 기술을 습득했다. 모든 것은 **야생에서의 생존을 보장하기 위해** 주로 이 네 가지 요소에 기반을 두었다.

(a) 무인도에서 살아남기 위해
(b) 기상 악조건으로부터 보호하기 위해
(c) 야생에서의 생존을 보장하기 위해
(d) 포식 동물과 싸우기 위해

원시인이 살아남기 위해 필요했던 네 가지를 소개한다. 그래서 마지막 문장에서는 모든 것이 살아남기 위해 이 네 가지에 근거를 두고 있다는 얘기가 나와야 한다. 따라서 정답은 (c)이다. (a)는 무인도에만 한정을 둬 틀리다.

secure 확보하다 **source** 수원지 **predator** 포식 동물 **disinfect** 소독하다 **haven** 안식처 **elevated** 높은 **cavern** 동굴 **crude** 조잡한
game 사냥감 **trap** 덫을 놓다 **adverse** 불리한

6

울프 씨께

새로 나온 소프트이지 텍스트 편집 프로그램이 준비되었다는 것을 알려 드리게 되어 기쁩니다. 자사 사이트 www.softex.com에서 아무 조건 없이 무료로 **문서 편집 프로그램을 다운로드 받으시고** 30일 동안 시험해 보실 수 있습니다. 만약 성능에 만족하지 않으시다면 그냥 프로그램을 삭제하면 되며 2-3분 걸릴 것입니다. 새로 나온 편집 프로그램은 인보이스 3.0, 어드레시스 2.0과 호환되기 때문에 송장과 주소록을 빠르고 편리하게 수정하실 수 있습니다. 이제는 상용 편지와 우편물 수신자 명단을 아무 실수 없이 쉽게 만들 수 있습니다. 더 도움이 필요하시면 언제든지 연락주세요. 감사합니다.

마크 오웬

(a) 백신 프로그램을 설치하다
(b) 문서 편집 프로그램을 다운로드하다
(c) 편집 프로그램을 삭제하다
(d) 워드 프로세서를 업로드하다

소프트이지라는 문서 편집 프로그램을 소개하는 편지로 30일 동안 시험해 볼 수 있고, 마음에 들지 않으면 삭제할 수 있다고 하므로 (b)가 정답이다.

uninstall 삭제하다 **compatible** 호환이 되는 **invoice** 송장 **revise** 수정하다

7

이중 언어를 할 수 있다는 것의 가장 기본적인 장점 중 하나는 순전히 언어적인 것인데 사람들은 그로 인해 **독자적이고 자립적일 수** 있다. 이중 언어를 할 수 있는 사람들은 더 많은 사람들과 의사소통을 할 수 있다. 그들은 그들 자신의 언어를 알기 위해서 다른 사람에게 의존하거나 자신의 메시지를 전달하기 위해서 통역자에게 의지할 필요가 없다. 그들의 메시지는 다른 사람의 도움 없이 전달되고 이해될 수 있다. 대조적으로, 단일 언어 구사자들은 의사소통을 위해서 반드시 전적으로 다른 사람에게 의지해야 한다. 사실, 1개 이상의 언어를 구사하는 것에 대한 단점은 없으며, 더 많은 사람들이 다른 언어를 배우는 데 노력을 기울여야 한다.

(a) 독자적이고 자립적이다
(b) 사교적이고 거침없이 말한다
(c) 믿을 수 있고 의사를 잘 전달한다
(d) 언어적이고 의존적이다

2개 국어를 할 수 있다면 자신의 메시지를 전달하기 위해서 통역 등 타인의 도움 없이도 더 많은 사람들과 의사소통을 할 수 있다는 내용이 빈칸 뒤에 나오므로 문맥상 (a)가 적절하다.

bilingual 두 개 언어를 할 수 있는 **linguistic** 언어적인 **resort to** ~에 의지하다 **get across** 이해[전달]되다 **with the aid of** ~의 도움으로 **monolingual** 1개 언어를 하는 **put the effort** 노력하다

8

목 근육에 매달린 것으로 밝혀진 설골은 인간에게만 있는 것으로 **사람들에게 말할 수 있는 능력을 준다**. 편자 모양의 이 작은 뼈는 신체상의 위치 때문에 후두 및 혀와 협력해서 인간에게 복잡한 소리를 형성하는 능력을 주는 기능을 수행한다. 설골의 존재외에, 말을 하기 위해서 또 다른 중요한 발달이 필요한데, 그것은 후두가 내려가는 것이다. 유아의 후두는 비강 안에 높게 위치하기 때문에 아기들은 동시에 마시고 호흡을 할 수 있지만 말을 하는데 방해를 받는다. 생후 3개월 정도가 되면, 후두가 목구멍에서 훨씬 아래로 내려가서 말하기가 가능한 적절한 위치에 놓인다.

(a) 말의 골격에서 발견된 것과 동일한 형태이다
(b) 소리를 내는 대부분의 동물들에서 볼 수 있다
(c) 사람들에게 말할 능력을 준다
(d) 태어나서 단지 몇 달 후에 형성된다

뒤이어 오는 larynx and tongue(후두와 혀)에 주목하자. 후두와 혀는 설골과 함께 말하는 데 필요한 기관이다. 이러한 세 기관이 상호 관계에서 어떤 기능을 해야 하는지 생각해 본다면 정답은 (c)임을 알 수 있다.

hyoid bone 설골 **exclusive to** ~에게 국한된 **horseshoe-shaped** 편자 모양의 **in conjunction with** ~와 협력하여 **larynx** 후두 **infant** 유아 **nasal cavity** 비강

9

브리티시컬럼비아 주에서는 모든 지역에서 모닥불과 산림용의 불은 허용이 되지만 모든 해안과 내륙 지역 열린 장소에서의 불은 제약을 둔다. **그밖에** 대초원 위험이 높은 몇몇 지역에서는 예방 공문과 규제가 계속 시행 중이다. 마지막으로 노스웨스트 주의 노스슬레이브 지역은 여전히 위험할 정도로 건조하다고 평해져서 관계자만이 통제된 불을 놓도록 허용된다.

(a) ~임에도 불구하고
(b) 결과적으로
(c) 그밖에
(d) 현격히 대조적으로

캐나다의 불에 대한 규제를 계속 나열하고 있는데 첫 문장에서 언급한 지역에의 다른 지역에 대해 계속 이야기를 하고 있으므로 (c)가 빈칸에 가장 적절하다.

restriction 제한, 규제 **in place** 제자리에, 가동 중인 **coastal** 해안의 **interior** 내부, 내륙 **prairie** 대초원 **in effect** 사실상, 시행중인

10

사업 개발은 어느 조직에서나 중요하고, 최적의 개발을 하기 위해서는 조직이 반드시 지니고 있어야 할 몇몇 중요 특징이 있다. 훌륭한 의사소통은 어떤 사업에서나 요구되는 필수 능력이다. 게다가 회사의 성향에 가장 적합한 경영 방식은 회사가 얼마큼 성장할 것인가를 결정한다. **예를 들어**, 주간 생산성 목표 달성을 요구하는 공장과 기업은 지시가 경영자에게서 오기 때문에 독재적인 방식을 택하는 것이 더 나을 수 있다. 반면에 광고 회사와 같은 조직은 보다 민주적인 경영 방식이 더 나을지도 모른다. 이런 점은 번창하는 기업을 설립하기 위해 고려해야 할 두어 가지 필수 변수일 뿐이다.

(a) 예를 들어
(b) 게다가
(c) 물론
(d) 그럼에도 불구하고

빈칸 전 문장을 보면 회사의 성격에 가장 적합한 경영 스타일이 성공을 좌우한다는 내용이며 빈칸 뒤에는 공장 같은 곳에서는 독재적인 스타일이 어울린다고 한다. 빈칸 뒤에 오는 내용은 하나의 예를 보여주는 것이므로 정답은 (a)이다.

productivity 생산성 **autocratic** 독재적인 **fare** 일이 되어가다
democratic 민주적인 **prosperous** 번창한

Part II

11

사시나무는 다양한 용도로 쓰이는 목재로 가치를 인정받는다. (a) 한 가지 주목할 만한 용도는 성냥 제조이며 나무의 낮은 가연성이 다른 나무에 비해 불을 더 쉽게 끌 수 있게 해준다. (b) 잘게 조각난 사시나무는 동물에게 호흡기 질환을 일으키는 것으로 알려진 자연 화학 물질인 페놀이 없기 때문에 동물의 잠자리 짚을 만드는 데 많이 사용된다. (c) 반면에 페놀은 소나무와 향나무에서 다량 발견되어 가구 목재로 선택하기에 덜 적합하다. (d) 사시나무로 만든 가구는 여러 가정에 많은 특징을 더해주는데 그 이유는 일상생활에 친환경적 요소를 더해주기 때문이다.

사시나무의 다양한 용도를 소개하고 있다. 그러나 (c)는 페놀이 소나무와 향나무에 다량 발견되는 요소를 설명하고 있으므로 어색하다.

flammability 가연성 **bedding** 잠자리 짚 **respiratory ailment**
호흡기 질환 **juniper** 향나무

12

과학자들은 지능이라는 주제를 수년간 연구했으며 다양한 형태의 지능이 있다고 주장한다. (a) 강한 언어 지능을 가진 사람들은 언어의 구조와 소리에 깊이 있게 반응할 것이다. (b) 논리적인 수학 지능을 가진 사람들은 성공적인 수학자, 컴퓨터 프로그래머, 과학자가 될 수 있다. (c) 다른 형태의 지능은 신체적 운동 지능, 사회적인 사교 지능과 개인 내의 지능을 포함한다. (d) 음악적 지능은 배경 소음뿐만 아니라 멜로디와 짜임새, 리듬의 상호 작용으로부터 오는 깊은 의미를 얻을 수 있는 음악을 이해하고 음악에 반응하는 능력이다.

지능을 종류별로 소개하고 있는데 (c)는 홀로 여러 가지 지능을 한 문장 안에 다 소개한다. 주로 설명이 끝나고 마지막에 와야 자연스러운데 설명이 끝나기 전 중간에 나오기 때문에 어색하다.

profound 깊은 **kinetic** 운동의 **interpersonal** 대인 관계의

Part III

13

현명하게 쇼핑을 하려면 소비자들은 생분해성과 퇴비로 만들 수 있다는 용어는 다르다는 점을 알 필요가 있다. 퇴비로 사용될 수 있는 물품은 세 가지 특징을 지녀야 한다. 그것은 생분해성, 분해, 환경 독성이다. 생분해성은 퇴비화 시설에 두었을 때 180일 안에 제품의 60에서 90퍼센트가 분해된다는 것을 의미한다. 분해된다는 것은 제품의 90퍼센트가 지름 2mm이하인 작은 조각으로 분해된다는 것을 의미한다. 환경 독성은 제품이 산업 시설에서 분해될 때 다량의 유독성 금속을 남기지 않을 것이라는 것을 가리킨다. 그 반면 생분해성이라는 단어는 제품이 자연적인 현상으로 어느 기간 동안 분해된다는 의미인데 이것은 수천 년을 의미할 수도 있다.

Q: 주로 무엇에 관한 글인가?
(a) 생분해성이 있는 제품과 퇴비로 만들 수 있는 제품의 차이점
(b) 생분해성이 있는 제품과 퇴비로 만들 수 있는 제품의 위험한 특징
(c) 퇴비로 만들 수 있는 제품 대신 생분해성이 있는 제품을 써야 하는 이유
(d) 퇴비로 만들 수 있는 제품 사용의 환경적인 혜택

이 지문은 친환경 소비에 있어서 biodegradable과 compostable이라는 단어의 차이를 알려 준다. 따라서 가장 적절한 정답은 (a)이다.

biodegradable 생물 분해성이 있는 **compostable** 퇴비로 사용할 수 있는
disintegration 분해 **toxicity** 독성 **diameter** 지름

14

조각 예술은 미술 세계에서 중요하게 간주되었고, 오늘날의 모습을 갖추기까지 많은 변화를 겪었다. 조각품을 통해 고대 과거를 엿볼 수 있다. 예를 들어, 고대 유적에서 발견된 유물은 고대 그리스 문명 시대의 삶을 묘사한다. 이런 조각품은 시대를 걸친 미술의 발전을 이해하는 데 도움을 준다. 고전적인 그리스 역사 시대를 시작으로 조각품은 로맨틱 스타일과 오늘날 선호하는 추상적인 스타일까지도 발달했다. 전통적으로 예술의 형태로 여겨졌기 때문에 조각품은 표현의 수단으로써 그 기능과 유효성을 잃지 않을 것이다.

Q: 지문의 주제로 가장 알맞은 것은?
(a) 역사상 유명한 조각가
(b) 조각 예술의 발전
(c) 조각의 예술적 가치
(d) 현대 조각 기술

조각이 예술로 과거에 어떻게 변해왔는지 이야기하고 있으므로 핵심 단어는 '변화'가 되겠다. 따라서 정답은 development(발전)라는 단어가 있는 (b)가 가장 적절하다.

sculpting 조각 **witness** 증인 **relic** 유물 **medium** 매체

15

맥도웰 앤 더글러스

회사 브랜드는 쉽게 눈에 띄고 많은 사람들의 관심을 끌도록 시각적으로 흥미를 끌어야 합니다. 그렇기 때문에 여기 맥도웰 앤 더글러스에서는 귀사의 제품이 팔리도록 뛰어난 그래픽과 브랜드 디자인을 제공하기 위해 전념하고 있습니다. 저희 디자인 회사는 고객이 귀사가 판매하는 상품을 구입하도록 고무하는 사업이 될 수 있도록 놀라운 콘셉트를 창조합니다. 저희는 사업 예술에 품격 있는 아이디어로 국내외 수백만 사람들의 마음을 지속적으로 사로잡고 있습니다. 저희는 이 사업에 50년 이상 종사했고, 이는 귀사가 두드러지고 사업 목표를 이룰 수 있도록 도움을 주는 충분한 경험과 노하우 그 이상을 의미합니다.

Q: 다음 중 광고의 목적을 가장 잘 설명하는 것은?
(a) 웹디자인 회사를 광고하기 위해
(b) 컨설팅 회사를 광고하기 위해
(c) 브랜드 명명 회사를 광고하기 위해
(d) 브랜드 디자인 회사를 광고하기 위해

광고는 맥도웰 앤 더글러스라는 기업 브랜드를 디자인해주는 회사를 홍보한다. 따라서 정답은 (d)이다. (c)는 브랜드 디자인이 아니라 브랜드 이름을 지어주는 회사라서 오답이다.

stand out 두드러지다 **exceptional** 특별한 **clientele** 고객
seize 사로잡다

16

항생제는 박테리아를 죽이거나 성장을 억제하는 물질이다. 그러나 항생제 과다 처방은 더 이상 항생제에 반응을 보이지 않는 박테리아의 발달을 낳았다. 사람들은 박테리아가 신체에 크게 문제를 일으키지 않아도 항생제를 남용한다. 문제는 그 과정에서 몸에 이로운 박테리아를 손상시킨다는 점이다. 물론 몸에 이로운 박테리아는 저항을 시작하고 항생제로부터 방어하는 방법을 찾아낸다. 이러한 항생제를 견디는 몸에 이로운 박테리아가 항생제를 저항하며 몸에 해로운 박테리아가 되는 것은 시간문제이다. 그 결과는 현재 존재하는 약으로 치료할 수 없는 병을 일으키는 세균이다.

Q: 주로 무엇에 관한 글인가?
(a) 새로운 박테리아를 위한 새로운 항생제의 필요
(b) 박테리아와 싸우는 데 항생제가 주는 이로움
(c) 항생제에 너무 의존했을 때 생기는 위험
(d) 몸에 이롭고 해로운 박테리아의 차이

지문은 항생제를 과다 복용 하면 생기는 문제점을 이야기한다. 따라서 정답은 (c)가 가장 적합하다. (a)는 새로운 항생제의 필요성을 이야기하고, (b)는 항생제의 장점만 초점을 맞춰서 오답이다.

antibiotic 항생제 **substance** 물질 **inhibit** 억제하다
overprescribe 과잉 처방하다 **resistant** 저항하는

17

계절성 정서 장애를 앓는 사람들은 특히 길고 추운 겨울에 급속히 증가하는 것으로 알려졌다. 그렇다면 그 이유는? 물론 햇빛의 부족이다. 그리고 어쩌면 가장 좋은 치료법은 1년 내내 날씨가 좋은 곳으로 겨울을 피하기 위해 여행을 떠나는 것일지도 모른다. 한 인기 있는 목적지는 따뜻한 날씨를 즐기기 위한 멋진 해변이 있는 수천 마일의 해안으로 이루어진 반도인 플로리다이다. 만약 대도시의 밝은 불빛을 선호한다면 세계의 오락수도로 알려진 라스베이거스로 향할 수 있다. 그곳에서는 첫 번째로 많은 카지노와 술집, 호텔을 보게 될 것이다. 다른 따뜻한 목적지로는 바르셀로나와 키프로스와 리스본이 있다.

Q: 다음 중 옳은 것은?
(a) 계절성 정서 장애 환자들은 날씨에 영향을 받지 않는다.
(b) 플로리다는 대도시로 유명하다.
(c) 바르셀로나에는 카지노와 술집이 많다.
(d) 키프로스는 1년 내내 대체로 따뜻하다.

계절성 정서 장애를 치료하기 위해서는 1년 내내 날씨가 따뜻한 곳에 가라고 한다. 그 중 키프로스가 추천되었으므로 키프로스는 1년 내내 날씨가 좋다는 것을 알 수가 있다. 따라서 정답은 (d)이다. (a)는 SAD 환자들이 날씨에 영향을 받기 때문에 오답이다.

embark 배에 타다 **destination** 목적지 **coastline** 해안선
plethora 과다

18

스롤 씨께

고객님의 회원권 갱신 안내서를 못 보고 지나치지 않도록 하고 싶었습니다. 고객님의 하더웨이 헬스클럽 회원이 계속되시길 고대합니다. 다음은 지불 방법입니다.

· 매월 자동 이체: 회원권을 무기한으로 연장해 드립니다. 나중에 취소하고 싶으시면 해당 월의 1일 전에 알려 주세요.
· 현금 할인: 현금 결제 시 제일 저렴한 요금 혜택을 받습니다.
· 마스터 카드와 비자 카드 모두 허용: 모든 신용 카드는 할인을 받을 수 없습니다.

이용해 주셔서 감사드리며, 다시 만나 뵙기를 기대합니다.

데이비드 카루소

Q: 다음 중 옳은 것은?
(a) 비자 카드를 사용하면 할인을 받을 수 있다.
(b) 현금 지불이 회원권을 받는 가장 저렴한 방법이다.
(c) 자동 이체는 1년 중에 취소할 수 없다.
(d) 신용 카드를 사용하면 할부로 낼 수 있다.

편지의 목적은 헬스클럽 회원권을 갱신하는 방법을 알려주기 위한 것이다. 세 가지 지불 방법 중 현찰로 지급하면 가장 낮은 가격에 갱신할 수 있다고 한다. 따라서 정답은 (b)이다. (a)는 신용 카드를 쓰면 할인 혜택이 없다고 했으므로 오답이다. 가입 취소 시 매달 하루 전에 알려 달라고 했기 때문에 1년 중에도 취소가 가능하므로 오답이다.

overlook 못 보고 지나치다 **renewal** 갱신 **withdrawal** 출금
indefinitely 무기한으로 **prior to** ~에 앞서 **patronage** 애용

19

사람들의 재즈에 대한 이해를 돕기 위해 몇몇 재즈 음악 스타일에 대한 간단한 설명을 하겠다. 재즈의 기원 때문에 '뉴올리언스 재즈'로 더 많이 불리는 클래식 재즈는 1800년대 말과 1900년대 초에 관악대가 다양한 악기들을 댄스와 파티에서 공연하면서 생겨났다. 핫 재즈는 루이 암스트롱이 개척했다. 베이스, 드럼, 기타 또는 밴조로 반주되는 감성적이고 강렬한 크레센도로 올라가며 즉석 연주하는 독주곡이 특징이다. 만약 뉴올리언스가 재즈의 근원지라면 시카고는 재즈의 번식지였다. 몇몇 젊고 활발한 연주자들은 시카고 스타일의 재즈를 만들기 위해 고난이도 기술과 하모니가 있는 곡의 결합으로 재즈의 즉석 연주를 크게 발전시켰다.

Q: 다음 중 옳은 것은?
(a) 핫 재즈는 뉴올리언스에서 유래하지 않았다.
(b) 시카고 재즈는 관악대가 만들었다.
(c) 클래식 재즈의 특징은 크레센도이다.
(d) 시카고 재즈는 젊은 음악가들이 즉석 연주했다.

다양한 재즈 음악의 특징을 소개하고 있다. 그중 시카고 재즈의 특징은 젊고 활동적인 연주자들이 새로운 기술과 하모니로 즉석 연주했다는 것이므로 정답은 (d)이다. (a)는 재즈 자체가 뉴올리언스에서 탄생했기 때문에 정답이 될 수 없다.

brass band 관악대 **assortment** 모음 **pioneer** 개척하다
improvise 즉석에서 연주하다 **support** 반주하다 **breeding ground** 번식지 **arrangement** 편곡

20

사우스빌 타임스

음식 〉 현지 식당

베를린 요리는 끊임없이 변화한다. 베를린 호텔 근처에는 손님들이 다소 특이한 경험을 할 수 있는 색다른 음식점이 있다. 독일의 가장 인기 있는 음식점 중 한 곳은 40년 동안 손님들에게 변기를 테마로 한 음식과 음료를 대접했다. 손님들은 독일 전통 소시지와 사워크라우트를 에나멜 유아용 변기에 담아 서빙 받고 맥주는 소변 검사 통에 나온다. 또 하나의 유명 음식점인 녹티 파구스에서 즐거움의 반은 말 그대로 어둠 속에 머무는 경험에서 온다. 그러나 이것은 단순히 속임수가 아니다. 손님들은 시야를 가림으로써 다른 감각이 강화되는 것을 발견했다. 그러므로 손님들은 다른 자극보다 음식 맛에 완전히 몰입할 수 있다.

Q: 다음 중 옳은 것은?
(a) 어둠 속에서 먹으면 미각이 강화된다.
(b) 녹티 파구스에서 손님들은 화장실 테마의 요리를 맛볼 수 있다.
(c) 녹티 파구스에서 손님들은 식사할 때 눈을 가린다.
(d) 화장실이 테마인 음식점에서는 소변을 맥주잔에 넣어서 대접한다.

이 지문은 베를린에 있는 색다른 음식점 두 곳을 소개한다. 녹티 파구스라는 곳에서는 어둠 속에서 식사를 하는데 시야가 어두우면 다른 감각들이 더 살아난다고 하니 미각이 향상된다는 것을 알 수 있다. 따라서 정답은 (a)이다. (c)는 눈을 가려서 어두운 것이 아니라 불을 꺼서 어두운 것이기 때문에 오답이다.

evolve 점진적으로 변화하다 **rather** 다소 **potty** 유아용 변기 **urine** 소변
gimmick 속임수 **diner** 식사하는 손님 **blindfold** ~의 눈을 가리다

21

비닐봉지는 많은 편의를 제공해 주나 또한 장기적인 문제를 일으킨다. 첫째로 비닐봉지는 농작물이 자라는 것을 방해한다. 쓰레기 비닐봉지 제품이 토양과 섞이면 농작물이 영양소와 물을 흡수하는 데 영향을 미칠 것이다. 둘째로 만약 동물이 실수로 비닐 제품을 음식으로 착각해 삼키면 죽을 수 있다. 셋째로 비닐 쓰레기는 처리하기 힘들다. 비닐 쓰레기는 많은 땅을 차지할 뿐 아니라 그것이 버려진 땅은 오랫동안 회복되지 않을 것이다. 비닐 쓰레기가 땅 속에 묻히면 그것이 분해되는 데 200년이 걸릴 것이다. 비닐 봉투 사용으로 생기는 피해를 줄이기 위해서는 비닐을 분해 가능한 다른 재료로 대체하는 것이 매우 시급하다.

Q: 비닐봉지에 관해 옳은 것은?
(a) 비닐봉지는 단지 토양과 농작물에 해를 입힌다.
(b) 비닐 쓰레기는 토양을 오염시킨다.
(c) 비닐 쓰레기는 비교적 빨리 소멸된다.
(d) 비닐 쓰레기는 많은 공간을 차지하지 않는다.

이 지문은 비닐봉지가 어떻게 환경에 해로운지를 설명한다. 그중 하나는 흙과 섞여서 농작물이 영양소와 물을 흡수하는 것을 방해하고 땅 속에 묻혀 부패해 없어지는 데 200년이 걸린다고 했으므로 정답은 (b)이다. (a)는 비닐봉지가 땅과 농작물에게만 피해를 주는 것이 아니라 동물들에게도 피해를 주기 때문에 오답이다.

hinder 방해하다 **absorption** 흡수 **crop** 농작물 **swallow** 삼키다
dispose 처리하다 **take up** 차지하다 **occupy** 사용하다
degradation 분해 **replacement** 대체 **urgent** 시급한

22

최근 몇 년 동안 사람들은 건설에 대리석과 화강암과 같은 자연석을 사용하는 추세를 주목해왔다. 그렇다면 이런 돌이 무엇이 그렇게 특별할까? 대리석은 특히 입구에 있는 홀과 베란다에 우아함을 더해 준다. 한눈에 반할만한 대리석은 매우 많다. 대리석은 주로 집이나 사무실에 꾸밈없는 아름다움을 더하면서 잘 어울린다. 화강암은 자연이 주는 가장 다양한 용도를 가진 훌륭한 광물 중 하나이다. 화강암은 깎아 다듬으면 스크래치, 풍화, 얼룩, 열에 강해진다. 새로운 건물이나 재건축한 건물에 자연석을 사용하는 것에 대한 관심 폭발은 사람들이 대자연이 주는 보물의 아름다움과 다양한 용도를 얼마나 소중히 여기는지 보여 준다.

Q: 다음 중 옳은 것은?
(a) 화강암은 고온을 견딜 수 있다.
(b) 대리석은 긁히지 않는다.
(c) 대리석은 주로 사무실에 사용된다.
(d) 화강암은 아름다움 때문에 인기가 있다.

건설에서 대리석과 화강암의 장점을 소개한다. 그 장점 중 화강암은 고온을 견딜 수 있다는 내용이 나오기 때문에 정답은 (a)이다. (b)는 대리석이 긁히지 않는 것이 아니라 화강암이 긁히지 않기 때문에 오답이다.

marble 대리석 **granite** 화강암 **lanai** 베란다 **multitude** 수많음
versatile 다용도의 **weathering** 풍화 **overwhelming** 압도적인
value 소중히 하다 **mother nature** 대자연

23

많은 이유로 의료 종사자들은 심장에 좋은 지중해식 식습관을 심장혈관계 질병이나 단순히 면역력을 강화하고 싶은 사람들에게 권했다. 지중해식 식단은 올리브유, 채소, 생선이 풍부하고 붉은 고기와 유지방이 적다. 따라서 다른 식단과 비교해서 연어와 같이 기름진 생선이 더 많다. 그 결과 지중해식 식사는 연어 지방에서 발견되는 필수 영양소인 오메가 3 지방산이 많다. 오메가 3 지방산은 심장에만 좋은 것이 아니라 당뇨병 위험을 줄여 주며 면역 체계를 강화시키고 알레르기 반응을 줄이고 근육통 및 관절통을 완화시킨다.

Q: 필자가 가장 동의할 만한 의견은?
(a) 올리브유는 심장병을 가진 사람들에게는 위험하다.
(b) 지중해식 식단에는 치즈가 많이 포함되어 있다.
(c) 오메가 3은 모든 생선 종류에서 발견된다.
(d) 소고기는 지중해 요리에 많이 사용되지 않는다.

지중해식 식단의 특징 중 하나는 붉은 고기를 요리에 잘 사용하지 않는다는 점이다. 따라서 소고기를 많이 쓰지 않는다는 (d)가 정답이다. 유지방이 적다고 했으므로 (b)는 옳지 않다.

health professional 의료 종사자 **Mediterranean** 지중해의
cardiovascular 심혈관의 **fatty acid** 지방산 **fortify** 강화하다
diminish 줄이다 **ease** 완화시키다 **joint** 관절

24

알림: 소중한 모든 고객님들께

재료비 상승으로 인한 압박을 해소하기 위해 저희도 제품 가격을 올릴 수밖에 없게 되었습니다. 그렇게 하는 것을 피하려고 노력했지만, 피할 수 없는 경제적 필요성에 직면했습니다. 동봉된 것은 8월 2일까지 유효한 가격 리스트입니다. 그때까지 진행된 모든 주문은 현재 가격 구조를 따르게 됩니다. 저희에게 베풀어 주시는 변함없는 성원에 다시 한번 감사드리며 저희 상황을 이해해 주시리라 믿습니다. 의문 사항이 있으시면, 주저 말고 연락 주세요.

감사합니다.

제이콥 깁슨

Q: 편지에서 유추할 수 있는 것은?
(a) 상품 가격이 8월 2일 전에 인상될 것이다.
(b) 8월 2일 전에 주문하는 상품은 할인 가격이 적용된다.
(c) 8월 2일 이전에 주문하는 것이 더 저렴하다.
(d) 원자재 가격이 오르면 상품 가격은 떨어진다.

원자재 가격이 올라서 제품의 가격을 인상한다는 내용이다. 그러나 편지를 쓰는 시점에서 8월 2일 사이에 구입을 하면 인상 전 가격으로 구입할 수 있기 때문에 정답은 (c)이다. (b)는 8월 2일 전에 구입하는 것이 저렴하나 모든 상품에 할인 가격이 적용된다는 내용은 없기 때문에 오답이다.

valued 소중한 **incrementally** 증가하여 **pressure** 압박 **stark** 피할 수 없는 **effective** 유효한 **hesitate** 주저하다

25

지구의 양파와 같은 특성을 이야기할 때는 어떤 층이 행성을 구성하는지 아는 것이 중요하다. 첫째로 대륙권은 우리가 살고 있는 암석으로 된 땅이다. 그것은 행성의 지각과 지각 아래에 있는 맨틀로 구성된다. 맨틀은 뜨거운 용해된 암석으로 구성되고, 새로운 지각의 생성지이며, 오래된 지각이 재생되는 지점이다. 핵의 바깥 부분은 지각으로부터 몇 천 마일 아래에 자리 잡고 있다. 행성의 가장 중심부에는 내핵이 있다. 핵의 대부분은 철이고 밀도가 엄청나게 높은 것으로 여겨진다. 중력과 극도로 높은 압력 때문에 내핵은 고체인 것으로 여겨진다.

Q: 필자가 가장 동의할 만한 의견은?
(a) 맨틀은 지구의 핵에서 만들어진다.
(b) 핵은 맨틀과 지각 사이에 있다.
(c) 지각 아래의 맨틀은 액체 상태이다.
(d) 맨틀의 압력은 핵의 압력보다 강하다.

지구의 층을 차례대로 설명하고 있는데 맨틀은 뜨거운 용암으로 구성된다고 네 번째 문장에서 이야기하기 때문에 정답은 (c)이다. 맨틀이 지구의 내핵에서 만들어진다는 이야기는 없기에 (a)는 답이 될 수 없으며, 핵이 맨틀과 지각 사이에 있지 않으므로 (b)도 오답이다.

layer 층 **constitute** ~을 구성하다 **lithosphere** 대륙권 **rocky** 암석으로 된 **crust** 지각 **molten** 용해된 **inner core** 내핵

Part IV

26-27

구인: 홍보과 작가/편집자

공공정보센터에서는 홍보과에서 일할 수 있는 신입 작가/편집자를 찾고 있습니다. 임용자는 회사 내 모든 부서에서 온 내용물을 편집하게 될 것입니다. 업무는 내용물이 주기적으로 업데이트되는지 확인하고, 연구를 수행하고, 다양한 문서들을 만들어내는 것입니다.

업무
이 직업의 주요 업무는 정보와 교육 프로그램을 개발하는 것을 돕고, 과제 자료를 연구하는 직원들을 돕고, 출판 마감일을 유지하고, 출판을 위해 문서를 연구하고 쓰고, 직원들로부터의 자료를 검토하고 분석하고, 배정된 대로 다른 직무 관련 일들을 수행하는 것을 포함한다.

자격요건
이 직업에서 요구하는 자격요건은 출판 과정에 대한 전반적인 지식, 정보 관련 자료들을 개발하기 위한 글쓰기 전략에 대한 상당한 이해, 개인 및 집단과의 효과적인 업무수행 관계, 그리고 개인용 컴퓨터 및 응용 프로그램의 능숙함 등을 포함한다.

학력
커뮤니케이션, 홍보, 경영 혹은 연관 학문분야에서의 학사학위가 필수적이다.

경력
연관된 분야에서의 경력은 우대사항이지만, 관리적 경험은 필수 사항이 아니다.

26. Q: 지원자는 어떤 책임을 갖게 되는가?

(a) 정보 및 교육 프로그램 개발

(b) 출판 과정에서 저작권 유지

(c) 문서를 외부 전문가에게 외주하기

(d) 다른 기관들로부터의 다양한 자료 분석

27. Q: 이 자리에 대한 필수 자격요건으로 언급된 것은?

(a) 경영 지식

(b) 응용프로그램 개발 능숙

(c) 특정 학문분야에서의 학위

(d) 관리직 경력

26. 홍보과의 기자 및 편집자를 구인하는 글이며, 업무 내용 중에서 "developing information and educational programs"이라는 내용이 포함되어 있으므로, 정보 및 교육 프로그램 개발을 제시한 (a)가 정답이다.

27. 자격요건으로 언급된 내용 중에서 학력사항으로 제시한 문장인 "a Bachelor's degree in Communications, Public Relations, Business or related disciplines is required"을 통해 특정 분야에서의 학사학위가 필요하므로, 정답은 (c)이다.

division 부서 **content** 내용물 **responsibility** 책임감 **essential** 기본적인, 본질적인 **coordinate** 대등하게 하다, 통합하다 **analyze** 분석하다 **assign** 배정하다 **requirement** 요구조건 **qualification** 자격요건 **strategy** 전략 **effective** 효과적인 **proficiency** 능숙함 **bachelor's degree** 학사학위 **discipline** 훈육, 교육과정 **supervisory** 관리상의, 감독상의 **maintenance** 유지, 관리 **outsource** 외주화하다

28-29

추가 물자 요청

청구인 : 클라라 해리스, 3학년 수학, 로드 힐 초등학교

수신인 : 마틴 루터, 로드 힐 학군 조달 부서

올해 우리 반은 작년보다 12%나 더 커졌지만, 저는 25명의 학생을 위해 좋은 상태의 12권의 교과서만 받았습니다. 당신은 이미 학생들이 이 교과서를 수업 중 함께 공유할 수 있다고 말했지만, 그들 중 절반은 집에서 공부를 할 수 없습니다. 저는 과제를 위해 추가적인 연습용 교재를 인쇄해 왔으며, 그로 인해 저는 이미 이번 학기 인쇄용지 허용량을 초과했습니다. 저는 스스로 어쩔 수 없이 새로운 교과서들을 구매하거나 더 많은 인쇄용지를 구매해야 하는 상태입니다.

저는 모든 페이지들이 실수 없이 인쇄된다고 할지라도, 이번 학기 나머지 기간 동안 30연(500매 기본 단위)의 인쇄용지가 추가로 필요할 것이라고 계산했습니다. 대량 매입할 경우, 연당 5달러로 계산되었으며, 총 150달러가 필요합니다. 부모님들은 이미 공납금으로 이번 학기에 50달러를 지불했기 때문에, 아이들이 자신의 교과서를 가져야 할 때 인쇄비용으로 지불하라고 요구하는 것은 또 다른 부담이 될 것입니다. 저는 학군에서 이후에 상환을 해 주신다면, 제가 직접 종이를 구매하도록 하겠습니다. 비교를 위해, 몇 군데 업체에서 받은 견적서를 동봉합니다.

28. Q: 편지의 주요한 목적은 무엇인가?

(a) 직무 관련 지급에 대한 상환 수령을 확인하기 위해

(b) 부서에서 모든 학급비용을 지불하도록 요구하기 위해

(c) 학생들을 위해 새로운 교과서를 구매할 수 있는 자금을 요청하기 위해

(d) 학생들을 위한 인쇄용지에 대한 지급을 요청하기 위해

29. Q: 본문에 따르면 옳은 것은?

(a) 학생들의 수는 올해 12%만큼 감소했다.

(b) 선생님은 학생들에게 과제를 내줄 수 없었다.

(c) 선생님은 부모님들에게 인쇄용지에 대한 지불을 요청하는 것을 원하지 않는다.

(d) 선생님은 비용에 대해 상환이 된다면 새로운 교과서를 구매할 것이다.

28. 학생들에게 지급한 교과서가 부족한 상태에서 복사를 통해 추가 자료를 제공해야 하는 상황이며, 이 편지를 쓴 목적으로 "I will purchase the paper myself, provided the school district reimburses me later"라는 문장을 통해 비용에 대한 상환을 요청하고 있으므로, 정답은 (d)이다.

29. 학생들에게 복사본을 제공하는 과정에서 비용과 관련하여 "I think it would be another burden to ask them to pay for copies"라는 내용을 통해 학부모들에게 비용을 부담하도록 요청할 계획이 없다는 것을 알 수 있으므로, 정답은 (c)이다.

request 요청 **procurement** 조달 **squander** 낭비하다, 다 써버리다 **semester** 학기 **allowance** 할당량, 지급량 **calculate** 계산하다 **error-free** 실수가 없는 **bulk rate** 용적률 **quote** 견적을 내다; 견적서 **burden** 부담 **reimburse** 상환하다 **comparison** 비교 **enclose** 동봉하다 **petition for** 요청하다 **advance pay** 선지급금

30-31

최초의 여성 우주비행사: 발렌티나 테레슈코바

소련 우주비행사 발렌티나 테레슈코바는 1963년 6월 16일 우주로 여행한 최초의 여성이 되었으며, 그때까지 다른 어떤 우주비행사들보다 더 많은 시간을 우주에서 보냈다. 22세에 최초의 낙하산 점프를 한 이후에, 그녀는 스카이다이빙에 대한 열정을 소련 우주 프로그램까지 확대했다. 소련 정부는 미국보다 먼저 또 한 번의 "우주 최초"를 달성할 수 있는 수단으로서 여성 비행사를 우주로 보내려고 했다. 결국, 그 운명적인 날에, 테레슈코바가 탔던 우주선 보스톡 6이 우주로 발사되었으며, 그녀는 우주에서 3일을 보낸 이후에 성공적으로 지구로 귀환했다.

그녀가 역사적인 우주 비행을 한 지 3년이 지난 후, 테레슈코바는 소련의 의회인 소련최고의회의 일원이 되었다. 그녀는 세계적으로 유명한 선구자였기 때문에, 그녀는 수많은 국제 여성 단체의 대표자로 활동했다. 그녀가 다시 우주로 가지는 않았지만, 그녀의 선구자적인 업적은 전 세계적으로 다른 가능한 우주비행사 훈련 프로그램에 강하게 영향을 주었는데, 특히 여성에 관련된 것이었다.

30. Q: 발렌티나 테레슈코바에 대해 옳은 것은?

(a) 그녀는 우주비행사가 되기 전에 낙하산 점프를 경험한 적이 있다.

(b) 그녀는 소련 정부의 새로운 프로그램에 합당한 자격을 갖추지 않았다.

(c) 그녀는 비행 직후에 국가 의회의 의원으로 선출되었다.

(d) 그녀는 정치적 활동을 소련의 국내 업무에만 국한했다.

31. Q: 본문에서 발렌티나 테레슈코바에 대해 추론할 수 있는 것은?

(a) 그녀는 우주 프로그램 이외에도 국제 공동체에 대한 영향을 끼쳤다.

(b) 그녀는 최초의 여성 우주비행사가 되기 위해 낙하산 점프를 시도했다.

(c) 그녀는 기술적인 한계 때문에 예상했던 것보다 일찍 지구로 귀환했다.

(d) 비록 그녀의 우주 임무는 성공적이지 않았지만, 그녀는 국가 의회의 일원으로 임명되었다.

30. 최초의 여성 우주비행사였던 발렌티나 테레슈코바에 대해 쓴 글이며, "Having made her first parachute jump at age 22, she extended her enthusiasm for skydiving to the Soviet space program"이라는 문장을 통해 정답이 (a)임을 알 수 있다.

31. 우주비행사로서 성공적인 업적을 달성한 이후, "she served as a representative to a profusion of international women's organizations"라는 문장에서 테레슈코바가 정치적 활동으로서 국제 조직에도 기여했다는 것을 알 수 있으므로, 정답은 (a)이다.

astronaut 우주비행사 **cosmonaut** 우주비행사 **enthusiasm** 열정 **dispatch** 파견하다, 파병하다 **fateful** 운명적인 **spacecraft** 우주선 **parliament** 의회 **pioneer** 선구자 **representative** 대표자, 의원 **a profusion of** 수많은 **qualification** 자격요건 **domestic** 국내의 **obligation** 의무, 책무 **assembly** 의회

32-33

미국의 소득 불균형

마가렛 무어

소득 불균형은 전 세계뿐만 아니라 미국에서 점차 증가하는 문제이다. 기아구호를 위한 옥스퍼드 위원회(옥스팜, Oxfam)에 의해 최근 발표된 보고서에 따르면, 단지 소수의 가장 부유한 사람들이 세계의 전체 부의 거의 80%를 차지하고 있다고 한다. 소득 불균형의 문제는 지역적 수준에서 또한 논의될 수 있다. 미국 인구조사국에 따르면, 미국의 불균형은 각 주의 지니 계수 – 1부터 100까지의 규모로 소득 불균형을 수량화하는 척도 – 에 다르면 주별로 다양하다. 그 문제는 경제 전문가들 사이에 증가하는 문제로 논의 주제가 되고 있다.

이러한 상황에서, 몇몇 경제 지도자들은 그 문제를 완화하기 위해 해결책을 제시해 왔다. 그들 중 일부는 소득보다는 자본에 대한 누진세를 부과할 것을 제안해 왔으며, 그것이 불균형의 확산을 막거나 늦출 수 있을 것 같다. 한편, 몇몇 회사 소유주들은 소비에 대한 누진세에 호의적이다. 그들은 각각의 주가 완전고용 상태로 경제를 되돌리고, 소득 불균형을 줄일 수 있는, 그리고 노동자들에게 구매력을 되돌려 줄 수 있는 정책이 필요하다고 주장했다.

32. Q: 본문의 주요 요점은 무엇인가?

(a) 미국 각 주의 소득 불균형의 다양한 결과들

(b) 소득 불균형을 해결하는 데 있어 누진세의 중요성

(c) 소득 불균형과 제안된 대안들의 문제

(d) 미국에서 증가된 소득 불균형의 결과들

33. Q: 본문에서 소득 불균형에 대해 옳은 것은?

(a) 그것은 미국에서만 심각한 문제이다.

(b) 그것은 지니 계수에 의해 결정된다.

(c) 그것은 미국에서 누진세에 의해 완화되지 않는다.

(d) 그것은 기업 소유주들 사이에서 주요한 문제점들 중의 하나이다.

32. 미국의 소득 불균형의 문제점에 대해 설명하는 글이며, "Some of them have suggested levying a progressive tax on capital rather than income, which is likely to prevent or slow the spread of inequality"라는 문장을 통해 소득 불균형의 문제점을 해결하기 위해 누진세의 중요성을 설명하고 있으므로, 정답은 (b)이다.

33. 소득 불균형이 경제 전반에 걸쳐 영향을 끼친다는 점을 언급하고 있으며, "some business owners are in favor of a progressive tax on consumption"이라는 문장을 통해 기업 소유주들 중 일부는 소득 불균형의 해결이 필요하다고 생각한다는 점을 알 수 있으므로, 정답은 (d)이다.

inequality 불평등, 불균형 **famine** 기근 **Gini coefficient** 지니 계수 **metric** 미터법 **quantify** 수량화하다 **alleviate** 개선하다 **levy** 세금을 부과하다 **progressive tax** 누진세 **in the meantime** 그러는 동안에, 한편으로 **in favor of** ~에 유리한 **income imbalance** 소득불균형 **alternative** 대안 **consequence** 결과

34-35

에너지 타임즈

홈 ∨ 국내 ∨ 국제 ∨ **사설** ∨ 문의

환경 친화적인 에너지원이 필요하다

제임스 렌윅

전기를 생산하는 것은 대기 오염의 주요한 원인이 되었으며, 전 세계적으로 지구 온난화를 유발하는 배출가스의 가장 큰 원인들 중의 하나가 되었다. 연료로서, 석탄은 최악의 범죄자라고 보고되고 있으며, 전체 전력량의 절반 이하만을 생산하지만, 모든 발전소의 탄소 배출가스의 거의 80%를 유발하고 있다.

다행스럽게도, 좋은 소식은 석탄의 이용이 미국에서 감소하고 있다는 점이다. 석탄을 이용하는 많은 발전소들은 점차적으로 줄고 있으며, 어떠한 새로운 석탄 발전소도 미국에서 계획되거나 승인되지 않고 있다.

오히려, 우리는 천연가스를 주로 이용하는 전력 시스템으로 이동하고 있으나, 천연가스에 의존하는 것은 우리의 에너지 수요에 대한 장기적인 해결책은 아니다. 석유 및 석탄과 같이, 그것은 단지 화석 연료에 불과하며, 상당한 지구 온난화를 유발하는 배출가스를 유발할 것이다.

반면에, 과학자들은 우리의 에너지 수요를 충족시키기 위해 더 나은, 더 깨끗한, 더 지속가능한 방법을 찾고 있다. 풍력 및 태양열과 같은 대체 에너지원들은 더 적은 오염과 더 낮은 지구 온난화를 유발하는 배출가스로 전력을 생산할 수 있다.

정부는 재생 가능한 에너지원을 촉진시킬 수 있는 현실적이고 비용효과적인 정책들을 지지해야 한다. 그것들은 신뢰할만하고, 비싸지 않으며, 우리의 건강과 지구에 이로울 수 있다.

34. Q: 기사문의 주요 목적은 무엇인가?

(a) 석탄을 이용하는 발전소의 과도한 이용을 비판하기 위해

(b) 대체 에너지원들을 이용할 필요성을 강조하기 위해

(c) 전력회사들로부터 더 나은 행동을 요구하기 위해

(d) 정부의 대기 오염 정책을 강조하기 위해

35. Q: 글쓴이가 동의할 것 같은 것은?

(a) 석탄은 전력을 생산하는 데 있어 가장 비용 효과적인 것으로 보고된다.

(b) 다른 화석연료들과는 다르게, 천연가스는 대체 에너지원이 될 수 있다.

(c) 정부는 재생 가능한 에너지원을 찾는 것에 대한 책임을 회피해서는 안된다.

(d) 지구 온난화를 유발하는 배출 가스는 환경운동가들 사이에 최근에 나타나는 문제이다.

34. 전기를 생산하는 원료로서 석탄 및 다른 화석 연료들의 문제점을 지적하고 있으며, 대체 에너지원의 개발을 통해 환경에 긍정적인 영향을 줄 수 있다고 주장하는 내용이므로, (b)가 정답이다.

35. 대체 에너지원의 개발의 중요성을 설명하면서, "The government should support practical, cost-effective policies that can promote renewable energy sources"라는 문장을 통해 정부 정책의 필요성을 언급하고 있으므로, (c)가 정답이다.

generate 발생시키다, 유발하다 **emission** 배출가스, 배기가스 **electricity** 전기 **carbon** 탄소 **approve** 승인하다 **dominate** 지배하다, 압도하다 **hinge on** ~에 의존하다 **petroleum** 석유 **trigger** 유발하다 **sustainable** 지속가능한 **alternative** 대안적인 **cost-effective** 비용 효과적인 **promote** 촉진시키다 **renewable** 재생 가능한 **reliable** 믿을 만한 **affordable** 비싸지 않은 **beneficial** 이익이 되는 **highlight** 강조하다 **underline** 강조하다 **initiative** 조치, 계획 **evade** 회피하다

p.174

ACTUAL TEST 3

Part I

| 1 (b) | 2 (b) | 3 (b) | 4 (d) | 5 (c) |
| 6 (a) | 7 (d) | 8 (a) | 9 (a) | 10 (d) |

Part II

| 11 (b) | 12 (c) |

Part III

13 (b)	14 (d)	15 (c)	16 (d)	17 (d)
18 (d)	19 (a)	20 (b)	21 (a)	22 (c)
23 (a)	24 (c)	25 (d)

Part IV

| 26 (c) | 27 (b) | 28 (a) | 29 (d) | 30 (b) |
| 31 (c) | 32 (c) | 33 (c) | 34 (b) | 35 (d) |

Part I

1

1960년대와 1970년대, 한국 정부는 국가의 도덕성에 대해서 훨씬 더 엄격했다. 탱고와 살사와 같은 많은 라틴 춤들에 <u>외설적이라는 딱지가 붙었</u>고 당시 한국에 존속했던 도덕성에 관한 법의 적용을 받았다. 라틴 춤에 대한 열정을 가졌던 사람들은 거슬리는 도덕 경찰로부터 자신의 신분을 보호하기 위해 익명을 사용해서 비밀 클럽에 자주 다녀야 했다. 오늘날 한국은 춤에 대한 이런 한물간 견해에서 벗어났고, 대부분의 주요 도시에는 여러 가지 형태의 라틴 춤을 전문으로 하는 클럽들이 있다. 여러 가지 형태의 춤, 특히 관능적인 라틴 춤에 대한 자신들의 열정을 기념하기 위해 정기적으로 모이는 사교계 춤 클럽들도 있다.

(a) 사회적으로 미숙했다

(b) 외설적이라는 딱지가 붙었다

(c) 별개로써 금지되었다

(d) 억압적으로 선포되었다

한국 정부가 국가의 도덕성에 대해서 매우 엄격했던 시절에 관능적인 라틴 춤에 대해서 어떤 견해를 가지고 있었을까를 생각해 본다면 정답은 (b)가 적절하다.

morality 도덕성 **frequent** 자주 드나들다 **pseudonym** 익명 **antiquated** 한물간 **specialize in** ~을 전문(전공)으로 하는 **sultry** 관능적인 **inept** 미숙한 **discretely** 분리되어 **proclaim** 선포하다

2

지렁이는 흙을 적절한 상태로 유지하는 데 도움을 준다. 지렁이들은 땅속을 기어 돌아다니면서 흙을 느슨하게 만든다. 먹이를 찾는 과정에서 흙의 일부가 지렁이의 입안으로 들어가고 몸통을 곧바로 관통한다. 이런 방식으로 흙이 잘게 부서지고, <u>조밀해지는 것을 방지한다</u>. 공기와 물이 지렁이들이 만든 작은 구멍을 통해서 땅으로 들어가고 지렁이들이 땅속으로 잡아당긴 성긴 나뭇잎과 씨들이 부식되어, 흙을 비옥하게 한다. 토지 1에이커에서 이러한 작업을 하고 있는 수천 마리의 지렁이들은 흙에 매우 유익할 수 있다. 이러한 이유로 지렁이가 많지 않은 장소의 경우 농부들은 지렁이들이 자신의 농토를 비옥하게 해줄 것이라고 기대하면서 지렁이를 구입해서 흙에 놓아준다.

(a) 영양분이 없어진다
(b) 조밀해지지 않게 된다
(c) 수확에 맞추어 준비가 된다
(d) 공기 유통이 막힌다

지렁이들이 땅속을 기어 다니면서 흙이 느슨해지고, 먹이를 찾는 과정에서 흙의 일부가 지렁이 몸을 통해 나오면서 흙이 잘게 부서진다는 내용이 앞에 나온다. 그렇다면, 흙은 어떤 상태가 될 것인지 생각해 보자. 따라서 정답은 (b)이다.

earthworm 지렁이 **crawl about** 기어 돌아다니다 **grind up** 잘게 부수다 **loose** 성긴 **decay** 부식하다 **enrich** 비옥하게 하다 **farmland** 농토 **fortify** 강화하다 **aerate** 공기가 통하게 하다

3

매 2년마다(하계 및 동계 올림픽이 교대로 개최되므로) 전 세계 최고의 선수들이 올림픽 대회에 모이는데, 200개가 넘는 국가에서 11,000명 이상의 선수들이 이 국제적인 시합에서 경쟁하기 위해서 온다. 근대 올림픽 대회는 전 세계 국가 간 평화를 고취하기 위한 노력으로 프랑스 피에르 드 쿠베르탱 남작이 낸 발상이었다. 평화의 협력의 상징으로 올림픽 대회에 대한 쿠베르탱의 비전은 실현되었지만, 최근 과거 중국의 인권 기록으로 인해서 많은 사람들이 베이징 대회 보이콧을 요구했던 것처럼 올림픽 대회는 <u>몇몇 주최국에 저항하기</u> 위해서 이용되고 있다.

(a) 실제 정치적 압력을 보여주다
(b) 몇몇 주최국에 저항하다
(c) 민주주의의 과정을 보여주다
(d) 적국과 협상하다

빈칸 뒤에 이어지는 '과거 중국의 인권 기록으로 인해서 많은 사람들이 베이징 대회 보이콧을 요구했다'는 내용에 주목하자. 이는 주최국에 대해서 무엇을 하기 위한 행동인지 생각해보면 정답은 (b)임을 알 수 있다.

alternate 번갈아 진행되다 **athlete** (운동) 선수 **gather** 모이다 **vie** 경쟁하다 **baron** 남작 **in an effort ~** 하기 위한 노력으로 **cooperation** 협력 **muscle** 압력 **hosting nation** 주최국 **bargain** 합의 **hostile** 적대적인

4

흑사병은 1348년부터 1351년까지 유럽 인구의 25-60%의 <u>생명을 앗아간 것으로 추산되고 있다</u>. 많은 이들은 그것이 사람들이 범한 죄에 대해 신이 내린 벌의 결과라고 생각했다. 지진 혹은 토성과 목성, 화성의 궤도 이탈 등의 천문학적 사건으로부터 방출된 더러운 공기 때문에 생긴 병이라고 믿는 이들도 있었다. 뜨거운 물속에 있는 동안 피부의 구멍이 더 열리기 때문에 목욕 또한 질병을 퍼뜨린다고 믿었다. 중세의 의사들은 긍정적인 태도를 유지하고, 좋은 와인을 마시고, 과일 섭취를 피하고, 가난한 이들을 학대하지 말고, 적당히 먹고 마실 것을 권했다.

(a) 붕괴에 대한 막연한 원인이었다
(b) 운동의 촉매제였다
(c) 보통의 일상생활을 망쳤다
(d) 생명을 앗아간 것으로 추산되고 있다

빈칸 뒤에는 흑사병이 창궐하던 시기와 당시 유럽의 인구가 나오므로 내용의 관련성을 고려했을 때 빈칸에 가장 적절한 것은 (d)이다.

Black Death 흑사병 **sin** 죄 **release** 방출하다 **astronomical** 천문학적인 **misalignment** 어긋남 **Saturn** 토성 **Jupiter** 목성 **Mars** 화성 **medieval** 중세의 **maintain** 유지하다 **abuse** 학대하다 **in moderation** 적당히 **bathing** 목욕 **spread** 퍼뜨리다 **pore** 구멍 **vaguely** 모호하게 **disruption** 붕괴 **catalyst** 촉매제 **plague** 괴롭히다 **claim** (생명을) 앗아가다

5

런던 지하철은 런던 시내를 에섹스와 허트포드셔, 버킹햄셔 같은 교외 지역과 연결해 주는 빠른 교통 시스템이다. 1863년에 첫 구간을 개통한 런던 지하철은 세계 최초의 지하 철도 시스템이었고, 1890년에는 또 최초로 전기 열차로 운행되기 시작했다. 철도망 내에서 가장 깊은 터널 몇몇 곳의 좁은 폭 때문에, '튜브'라고 하는 별칭도 갖고 있다. 런던 지하철은 270개의 역이 있고 선로는 대략 400킬로미터에 이르러 오늘날 세계에서 다섯 번째로 많은 역을 갖고 있으며 선로는 세 번째로 길다. 연간 13억 8천만 명의 승객들이 이용하면서, 파리와 모스크바 다음으로 유럽에서 세 번째로 분주한 지하철 시스템이 되었다. 그러나 노선의 절반 이상이 실제로는 지상에 있어서 '지하철'이라는 <u>이름을 부인하는</u> 셈이다.

(a) 스스로 위장하는
(b) 어떤 추세도 거짓임을 보여주는
(c) 이름을 부인하는
(d) 어떠한 직접적인 혐의도 피하는

런던의 지하철 시스템에 관한 내용으로, 실제로는 노선 대부분이 지상에 있다는 설명으로 보아 지하철이라는 이름에 반한다는 내용이 들어가야 자연스럽다. 따라서 가장 적절한 것은 (c)이다.

rapid 빠른 **transit system** 수송 시스템 **suburban** 교외의 **opening** 개통 **above ground** 지상에 **narrow** 좁은 **breadth** 폭 **retain** 보유하다 **approximately** 대략 **in terms of** ~면에서 **length** 길이 **billion** 10억 **belie** 거짓임을 보여주다 **repudiate** 부인하다 **moniker** 이름, 별명 **circumvent** 면하다

6

모하마드 씨에게

어제 전화 통화로 말씀드린 대로, 더 이상 저희 회사의 이미지에 적합하지 않아 A123 Videx 생산을 중단했다. 공식적으로, 이달 말에 이 제품의 마지막 선적물이 출고될 것입니다. 이 제품을 계속 원하신다면, 합리적인 가격에 **동일한 제품을 제공하는 회사인** 제임슨 보안회사에 연락하실 것을 권합니다. 필요하신 보안 카메라를 지원해드릴 수 있어 늘 기뻤으며 애용해 주셔서 감사드립니다. 귀사에서 그 카메라들을 저희의 신형 B123 Videtron 카메라로 업그레이드하고 싶으시다면, 주저하지 말고 연락 주시면 기꺼이 무료로 설치해 드리겠습니다.

라지 모한

(a) 동일한 제품을 제공하는 회사
(b) 제공을 할 수 있는 중고 보석상
(c) 재고가 있는 보안 회사
(d) 제공되는 전화번호부 서비스

고객에게 더 이상 어떤 제품을 생산하지 않는다는 사실을 알려주며 그 제품을 계속 원할 경우 다른 회사에 연락할 것을 권하고 있는 것으로 보아 빈칸에 들어갈 내용으로 가장 적절한 것은 (a)이다.

as per ~에 따라   **cease** 중단하다   **fit** 맞는   **officially** 공식적으로
shipment 선적   **reasonable price** 합당한 가격   **patronage** 애용
upgrade 개선하다   **free of charge** 무료로   **second-hand** 중고의
jeweller 보석상   **inventory** 재고   **telephone directory**
전화번호부

7

우리 중 많은 이들이 해질녘에 바다의 파도를 보면서 황홀해한 적이 있다. 이들 파도는 수 마일을 이동한 바닷물 때문일 거라고 생각해도 문제가 없었을지도 모른다. 그러나 메건 와츠가 자신의 책 〈해양 생태계〉에서 밝히듯이 바닷물은 실제 짧은 거리를 이동할 뿐이다. 물 분자는 주변 분자와의 접촉을 통해 움직일 수 있다. 또 파도는 장거리를 다닐 수 있음에도 불구하고 물 분자는 단지 앞뒤로만 튈 뿐이다. 바람에 의해 넘실대는 밀밭과 유사한 상황이다. 바람은 **멀리까지 불 수 있고 밀밭에 파도를 만들어내지만** 곡식의 줄기는 뿌리가 박혀있는 그 자리에 있다.

(a) 공기 중에 있고 식물은 땅에 있다
(b) 바다의 파도와 비교하면 상대적으로 빠를지도 모른다
(c) 바다이고 밀은 파도이다
(d) 멀리까지 불 수 있고 들판에 파도를 만들어낸다

파도가 장거리를 다닐 수 있어도 물 분자가 단지 앞뒤로만 튈 뿐이라는 사실과 유사한 것으로 보아 바람도 멀리까지 불 수 있으나 밀밭에 넘실대는 밀은 결국 제자리에서 움직일 뿐이라는 것을 유추할 수 있으므로 정답은 (d)이다.

entrance 황홀하게 만들다   **sunset** 해 질 녘   **ecology** 생태계
molecule 분자   **be subject to** ~에 달려 있다   **surrounding** 주위의
back and forth 앞뒤로   **analogy** 비유; 유사점   **stalk** 줄기

8

샘에게

당신이 새 직장으로 옮기는 것에 대해 **사무실의 우리 모두는 당신이 정말 잘되길 바라요.** 당신과 함께 했던 것은 영광이자 기쁨으로 기억할 거예요. 이제 당신의 공식적인 업무에 대해선 작별을 고해야 할 것 같네요. 수년간 당신이 해냈던 많은 일들을 보면 당신의 빈자리가 클 거예요. 여기서 당신의 일을 누가 맡든 간에 당신의 역할을 감당하려면 무지 노력해야 할 거예요.

당신의 앞날에 좋은 일만 있길 바랍니다. 당신의 새 직장은 전망이 밝은 것 같더군요. 가끔 저희에게 소식을 전해 주시면 좋겠네요.

리자 브레멘

(a) 사무실의 우리 모두는 진심으로 잘되길 바라요
(b) 작별 인사 대신에 이 편지를 써요
(c) 계속해서 이 기회를 이용하고 싶어요
(d) 최고의 작별과 멋진 기억들

수년간 근무하고 회사를 떠나는 동료에게 진심 어린 작별 인사를 하는 편지로 빈칸에 들어갈 적절한 내용은 (a)이다.

head 나아가다   **honor** 영예   **capacity** 공식적인 역할   **presence**
있음, 존재   **accomplish** 성취하다   **fill one's shoes** ~를 대신하여 일을
해내다   **in lieu of** ~대신에   **extend** 연장하다

9

14세기 유럽에서는 메디치 가문이 사업을 통해서 번 재물을 **통해서** 이태리 플로렌스에서 권세를 얻었다. 당시 장인들은 부유한 누군가에 의해서 후원을 받아야만 살아남을 수 있었다. 메디치 가문은 문화를 진흥시키는 데 열렬한 관심이 있었고 (미켈란젤로, 라파엘, 브루넬레스키, 다빈치, 갈릴레오 그리고 보티첼리와 같은) 당시의 위대한 지성들에 의한 작업을 의뢰함으로써 예술, 과학 및 문화에 있어서 엄청난 작품들의 제작을 가능케 했다. 그들의 노력은 플로렌스 시를 유럽 전역으로 퍼져나간 르네상스의 최전방으로 밀어붙였고, 서방 세계를 암흑시대로부터 끌어냈다.

(a) ~을 통해
(b) ~하는 동안
(c) ~위에
(d) ~이기 때문에

14세기 유럽에서 장인들은 부자들의 후원으로 살아갈 수 있었는데 사업을 통해서 부를 축적한 메디치 가문이 당시의 위대한 지성들의 생계를 도운 내용이므로 빈칸에 가장 적절한 것은 (a)이다.

rise to power 권세를 얻다   **artisan** 장인   **sponsor** 후원하다
someone of wealth 부유한 누군가   **mind** 지성   **colossal** 엄청난
forefront 최전방   **Dark Ages** 암흑시대 (유럽 역사에서 로마시대 말기부터
서기 1000년경까지 기간)

10

바티칸은 세계에서 가장 작은 독립된 도시 국가로, 800명의 인구가 44 헥타르의 땅에 살고 있다. 도시는 로마로 완전히 둘러싸인 소수 민족 거주지로, 교황청과 바티칸 시티 두 구역으로 나뉜다. 두 구역의 주민들에게는 다른 형태의 여권이 발행되는데, 교황청에 거주하는 이들에게는 외교와 일반 여권이 발행된다. 교황청 밖이지만 여전히 바티칸 시티에서는 일반 바티칸 여권이 발행된다. **게다가** 바티칸에는 자체 경호단원과 약 450대의 자동차 번호판, 고유의 국가(교황 찬가) 그리고 마지막으로 유럽 연합 전역에서 통용되는 자체 법정 통화도 있다. 교황에 의해 임명한 추기경들은 입법과 사법적 목적에 행사할 권한을 갖고 있지만 교황에게는 절대적인 권력이 있다.

(a) 그렇더라도
(b) 따라서
(c) 마찬가지로
(d) 게다가

두 구역으로 나뉘어져 있는 독립된 도시 국가인 바티칸의 구조를 얘기하고 다른 종류의 여권 발행을 언급하며 다음에 바티칸의 다른 특징들을 나열하고 있으므로 빈칸에 가장 적절한 것은 (d)이다.

city-state 도시 국가 **enclave** 소수 민족 거주지 **surround** 둘러싸다 **Holy See** 교황청 **issue** 발행하다 **resident** 거주민 **diplomatic** 외교의 **regular** 표준적인 **automotive license plate** 자동차 번호판 **national anthem** 국가 **pontifical** 교황의 **hymn** 찬가, 찬송가 **legal tender** 법정 통화 **cardinal** 추기경 **pope** 교황 **authority** 권한 **legislative** 입법의 **judicial** 사법의

Part II

11

미국의 제9대 대통령인 윌리엄 헨리 해리슨은 눈에 띄는 많은 행동을 한 인물이다. (a) 그는 의대를 마치지 못했지만 의사가 되려고 공부했던 유일한 대통령이었다. (b) 그는 일곱 형제 중 막내였고 대통령이 되기 전에 군대에서도 복무했다. (c) 1841년 3월 4일, 그는 어떤 대통령보다 긴 취임 연설을 했다. (d) 며칠 후, 그는 감기에 걸렸고, 감기는 폐렴으로 악화되었으며, 1841년 4월 4일, 그는 어떤 대통령보다 짧은 임기를 수행한 후 현직에서 사망한 최초의 대통령이 되었다.

미국의 제9대 대통령인 윌리엄 헨리 해리슨에 관한 내용인데 '많은 놀랄만한 행동'을 한 인물이라는 것에 주목해야 한다. (a), (c), (d)는 모두 미국 대통령 중 유일하거나 특이했던 이력이라고 볼 수 있으나 일곱 형제 중 막내라는 것과 군대 복무 이력은 주목할 만한 것은 아니므로 정답은 (b)이다.

medical school 의과대학 **serve in the army** 군대에서 복무하다 **inaugural speech** 취임연설 **catch a cold** 감기에 걸리다 **pneumonia** 폐렴 **in office** 현직의 **term** 임기

12

전 세계 고등학생에 관한 조사에 의하면 미국 고등학생들은 세계지리에 대해 잘 알지 못한다. (a) 놀라울 정도로 많은 미국 학생들은 자신들의 살고 있는 주의 수도를 몰랐다. (b) 멕시코가 미국과 국경을 접하는 2개국 중 하나로, 나머지 한쪽은 캐나다인데 많은 학생들이 지도에서 멕시코를 찾지 못했다. (c) 캐나다 학생들은 지리적인 인접국에 대해 더 모르고 있었다. (d) 몇몇 교육자들은 이러한 지리 지식의 부족을 최근 미국 학교에서 있었던 '자료 암기식 공부의 중단' 탓으로 돌리고 있다.

(a)와 (b)는 미국 학생들은 지리학에 대한 지식이 별로 없다는 사실의 예이며 (d)는 학생들의 지리 실력이 떨어진 이유이다. (c)는 미국 학생들의 지리 실력에 대한 이해도가 떨어지는 상황과 직접적인 관련이 없으므로 정답은 (c)이다.

geography 지리 **capital** 수도 **border** 국경을 접하다 **educator** 교육자 **blame on** ~탓으로 돌리다 **memorization** 암기

Part III

13

환경 보호 지역 안에서 통제할 수 없이 발생하는 화재는 벼락, 화산, 심지어 암석이 떨어지면서 일으킨 불꽃 등에서 시작될 수 있다. 어떤 의미에서 이러한 화재는 자연 환경의 필연적인 부분으로 여겨질 수도 있다. 그러나 이렇게 자연에서 불가피한 것을 인간은 통제하려고 노력한다. 사람들은 자연 화재를 다스리기 위해 헬리콥터나 비행기로 물을 뿌린다. 때로는 말 그대로 불로 불에 맞서기도 한다. 일부 지역을 소규모의 통제된 불로 계획적으로 태워서 불의 연료가 되는 것을 제거함으로써 화재가 번지는 것을 막는다. 이렇게 계획된 맞불 자체가 화재가 되어 버릴 수 있으므로 세심한 주의가 필요한 작업이다.

Q: 글의 요점은 무엇인가?
(a) 자연 화재를 끄기 위해 맞불을 놓아서는 안 된다.
(b) 사람들은 산불을 통제하기 위해 최선의 노력을 한다.
(c) 자연 화재는 알아서 타도록 내버려 두어야 한다.
(d) 자연 화재에 물을 뿌리는 것은 맞불을 놓는 것보다 안전하다.

자연 화재를 자연 환경의 필연적인 부분으로 보고 그냥 방치하기보다는 이를 통제하려는 인간들의 여러 수단을 설명하고 있으므로 (b)가 가장 적절하다.

wilderness area 환경 보호 지역, 자연 보호 구역 **lightning** 벼락, 번갯불 **in a sense** 어떤 의미에서는 **inevitable** 필연적인 **ecology** 자연 환경 **literally** 문자 그대로 **deliberately** 계획적으로 **deprive of** ~에게서 빼앗다[박탈하다] **delicate** 세심한 주의가 필요한 **prescribed** 미리 정해진

14

일 년에 두 차례, 두 가지 천문학적 현상인 지점(하지, 동지)과 분점(춘분, 추분)이 일정한 간격을 두고 나타난다. 지점은 태양이 움직임을 멈추고 경로를 바꾸려는 듯 보이는 천구상의 위치에 도달했을 때 나타난다. 예를 들어, 북미에서 1년 중 낮이 가장 긴 하지는 6월 21일이다. 반면에, 12월 22일, 동지에 북미에서는 낮이 가장 짧다. 분점(춘분, 추분)은 태양이 적도를 지나 낮과 밤의 길이가 같을 때 나타난다. 3월 21일에 나타나는 춘분이 있고, 9월 22일은 추분이라 한다.

Q: 이 글의 요점은 무엇인가?

(a) 지점과 분점을 볼 수 있는 곳

(b) 밤낮 주기의 예측

(c) 태양과 일조량

(d) 매년 지점과 분점의 발생

일 년에 두 차례 나타나는 지점(하지, 동지)과 분점(춘분, 추분)에 관한 내용으로, 북미에서의 하지와 동지, 춘분과 추분을 예로 들어 설명하고 있다. 따라서 지문에서 말하고자 전체적인 내용을 포괄하는 요점으로 가장 적절한 것은 (d)이다.

astronomical phenomenon 천문학적 현상 **solstice** 지점(하지와 동지) **equinox** 분점(춘분과 추분) **at regular intervals** 일정한 간격을 두고 **reverse** 바꾸다 **in contrast** 대조적으로 **equator** 적도 **vernal** 봄의 **autumnal** 가을의 **occurrence** 발생, 존재

15

중국의 어촌에서 여전히 고대 기술이 사용되는 걸 볼 수 있다. 소주 지방의 마을에서 어부들이 채비를 할 때 새를 한 마리 가져간다. 물론 이 새는 친구 삼아 데리고 가는 애완용이 아니다. 이것은 일하는 새이며 정확히 말하면 가마우지이다. 이 목이 긴 새는 어부가 매일 물고기를 잡으러 다니는 데 도움이 된다. 그러나 어떻게 가능할까 궁금할지 모르겠다. 간단히 말하자면 새들은 그렇게 하도록 훈련 받았다. 물고기를 낚아채는 이들의 본능을 활용해서 어부들은 말 그대로 새들에게 세를 놓는다. 게다가 목에 있는 금속 고리는 가마우지가 삼킨 물고기가 여전히 어부가 가져갈 수 있도록 해준다. 가마우지한테 불공평하다고? 일이 끝나면 가마우지도 잡은 물고기 몇 마리를 가진다고 한다.

Q: 이 글은 주로 무엇에 관한 것인가?

(a) 동물을 길들이는 예

(b) 고대 어부의 의식

(c) 훈련받은 동물을 이용한 어업

(d) 소멸되는 한 생활 방식

중국 어촌에서는 가마우지의 본능을 이용해서 물고기를 잡는 데 이용하고 있다는 내용이다. 따라서 정답은 (c)이다.

company 함께 있음 **cormorant** 가마우지 **harness** 이용하다 **swoop up** 낚아채다 **literally** 말 그대로 **lease** 임대차 계약 **ensure** 확실하게 하다 **domestication** 가축화 **rite** 의식 **vanish** 사라지다

16

사람들은 의도적으로 우연히 말의 자음들을 뒤바꾸는데 이를 '두음 전환' 혹은 '매로스키'라고 한다. 이 두 가지 명칭은 옥스퍼드, 뉴 칼리지의 윌리엄 아치볼드 스푸너 목사와 폴란드의 백작 매로스키 두 사람의 이름에서 따온 것이다. 이들은 모든 자음을 섞은 어구를 발음해서 종종 재미있는 말을 만들어내는 것으로 널리 알려져 있다. 이러한 말 유형의 예로 'Tale of Two cities'를 'sale of two titties'라고 하거나 'Doing the chores'를 'Chewing the doors'라고 말하는 것이 있다. 많은 코미디언들이 술 취한 연기를 할 때 일련의 동작으로 이런 유형의 말장난을 이용해 왔다. 부적절한 소리도 고유의 의미를 지닌다는 것을 관객들이 이해할 때 유머가 된다.

Q: 이 글의 주제는 무엇인가?

(a) 스푸너와 매로스키는 새로운 농담을 고안했다.

(b) 어구들은 말로 하기 어렵다.

(c) 코미디언들은 말하면서 많은 실수를 저지른다.

(d) 자음은 두음 전환에서 바뀐다.

짧은 문구에 들어있는 자음들의 순서를 뒤바꿔서 말의 의미를 달라지게 하는 두음 전환을 하는 말장난에 관한 내용으로, 그런 명칭이 붙게 된 연유와 관련 예를 들어 설명하고 있다. 따라서 지문의 주된 주제로 가장 적절한 것은 (d)이다.

deliberately 의도적으로 **consonant** 자음 **spoonerism** 두음 전환 **Polish** 폴란드의 **count** 백작 **utterance** 발언 **chores** 허드렛일

17

담당자께

저는 프랭크 아론을 화학 공학 박사 과정 입학을 전폭적으로 추천하고자 합니다. 제가 2년간 컬맨 대학에서 프랭크의 지도교수였는데 그가 이 분야의 박사 과정을 할 준비가 되어 있고 그럴 만한 인물이라는 확신이 있습니다. 프랭크는 최고의 노력과 뛰어난 자질로 자신의 공부를 해냈던 매우 성실한 대학원생이었습니다. 저를 만나기 전 우수한 학부생이었고 몇 년간 우등생이었습니다.

프랭크는 박사 학위를 따낼 학생입니다. 귀하가 프랭크의 지난 업적을 살펴보시고 장래 박사 과정에서 뛰어난 자질을 보일 학생으로 인정하셨으면 합니다.

테런스 웰링턴 박사

Q: 지문에 의하면 다음 중 옳은 내용은?

(a) 학생이 교수님과 함께 연구하고자 신청하고 있다.

(b) 편지에서 학생이 박사 과정을 따기를 권하고 있다.

(c) 컬맨 대학에는 대학원이 없다.

(d) 교수님은 2년간 학생을 지도했다.

다른 학교 박사 과정에 지원하는 제자를 위해서 2년간 지도해준 교수님이 추천 편지를 쓰고 있는 내용이다. 따라서 옳은 내용은 (d)이다.

verify 확인하다 **wholeheartedly** 전폭적으로 **conscientious** 성실한, 양심적인 **utmost** 최고의 **outstanding** 뛰어난 **undergraduate** 학부생 **Dean's List** 우등생 명단

18

도시가 세워지기 전에 사람들은 혼자서 모든 생활필수품을 공급함으로써 자급자족하는 방법을 배워야 했다. 곧 사람들은 하나 또는 몇 가지 상품 생산에 집중하고, 과잉 상품을 자신의 생활에 필요한 다른 마을 사람들의 다른 품목과 교환하는 것이 더 쉽다는 것을 알았다. 사람들은 다른 사람들과 상품을 교환하기 위해서 더 멀리 이동하는 것을 꺼리지 않았고, 이런 방식으로 '교역'은 탐험과 문화 간 상호 작용의 촉매가 되었다. 전역에서 상인들이 시장으로 모이면서 '교역'은 또한 많은 도시의 부와 권력의 성장을 초래했다. 이로 인해서 상품을 장거리로 운반하기 위한 개선안에 대한 요구가 증가했다.

Q: 글에 의하면 다음 중 옳은 것은?
(a) 상인들은 그들의 근거지에서 멀리 여행하기를 꺼렸다.
(b) 사람들은 생존에 필요한 모든 것을 생산해야 했다.
(c) 문화를 배우기 위해서 탐험이 시작되었다.
(d) 상업의 요구에 부응하여 운송이 발전했다.

이 글은 자급자족 시대에서 교역의 시대로 넘어가는 과정을 기술하고 있으며, 교역을 위해서 장거리 운송수단에 대한 수요가 증가했다는 내용이므로 정답은 (d)이다.

establish 세우다 **self-sufficient** 자급자족 **necessities of life** 생활필수품 **trade** 교환하다 **be willing to** ~하기를 꺼리지 않는 **catalyst** 촉매 **cross-cultural interaction** 문화 간 상호 작용 **flock** 모이다 **expedition** 탐험 **initiate** 개시하다 **accommodate** (요구 등에) 부응하다

19

피부 가꾸는 법

당신의 안색이 항상 아름다울 수 있도록 피부를 가꿔라. 그러면 당신은 완벽한 피부뿐만 아니라 더 오랫동안 젊은 피부를 유지할 것이다.

· 당신은 햇빛에 너무 많이 노출되는 것을 피해야 한다. 피부암, 빠른 노화, 주름을 일으킬 수 있기 때문이다.

· 흡연자라면 담배를 줄여라. 담배는 혈액 순환을 떨어뜨려 건강한 피부에 없어서는 안 될 산소와 비타민 A를 빼앗기 때문이다.

· 매일 뜨거운 샤워나 목욕을 하면 피부에 중요한 기름기를 없앨 수 있기 때문에 목욕 시간을 줄이고 목욕물 온도를 낮춰라.

· 향이 매우 강한 비누를 사용하지 말고 그 대신 순한 무향 세안제를 써라.

Q: 좋은 피부를 위해 권장되는 것은?
(a) 매일 샤워를 하지 않는 것
(b) 향이 있는 세안제를 쓰는 것
(c) 햇빛에 나가 있는 것
(d) 목욕을 더 오래 하는 것

피부 관리를 위한 몇 가지 팁을 소개한다. 그중 매일 샤워나 목욕을 하면 피부에 좋은 기름이 씻겨 없어지기 때문에 권장되지 않는다고 하니 정답은 (a)이다.

complexion 안색 **wrinkle** 주름 **deprive** 빼앗다 **utilize** 이용하다 **scented** 향기가 나는

20

한반도에서 발견된 뿔공룡 최초의 유해인 공룡 화석이 최근 발견되었다. 백악기 초기 후반에 나타났고 트리케라톱스와 관련된 파충류인 코리아케라톱스 화성엔시스는 길이가 2m이고 중량이 27-45kg인 비교적 작은 공룡이었다. 앵무새와 같은 부리는 이 공룡이 초식 동물이었다는 가능성을 시사하고 뒷다리에 대한 조사 결과 두 발로 빠르게 움직이는 동물이었다는 증거가 나왔다. 꼬리는 다른 공룡에 비해서 짧다는 점에서 독특하며, 이 공룡이 의사소통을 위해서 사용했을 것 같은 거대한 주름 구조의 토대인 대못 형태의 뼈가 꼬리 안에 들어 있었다.

Q: 글에 의하면 다음 중 옳은 것은?
(a) 다른 공룡과 구분이 되는 유일한 특징은 꼬리 위에 있는 대못 형태의 뼈이다.
(b) 이 공룡이 나타나기 전에 한국에 트리케라톱스와 같은 공룡이 있었다는 것이 알려지지 않았다.
(c) 전반적인 출현은 대형 조류의 등장과 아주 많이 비슷하다.
(d) 속도를 이용해서 다른 작은 동물을 잡아먹었다.

한반도에서 처음 발견된 코리아케라톱스 화성엔시스는 트리케라톱스와 관련된 초식 파충류라고 했으므로 정답은 (b)이다.

fossil 화석 **remains** 유해 **peninsula** 반도 **reptile** 파충류 **Early Cretaceous** 백악기 초기 **point to** 시사하다 **likelihood** 가능성 **herbivore** 초식동물 **bipedal** 두 발로 걷는 **in comparison to** ~와 비교하여 **column** 기둥 모양 **spike** 대못

21

많은 팬들과 스포츠 기자들은 야구 월드 시리즈가 미국과 캐나다의 팀들로만 구성되기는 하지만 '실질적으로' 세계적인 스포츠 시합의 하나로 생각하고 있다. 북아메리카에서 월드 시리즈의 인기는 이러한 대회를 지원할 수 있을 만큼 많은 관중들을 끌어 모으고 있다. 메이저리그 야구팀은 아메리칸 리그와 내셔널 리그, 두 리그로 나뉜다. 플레이오프에서는 상위 3팀과 와일드카드 팀이 5판 3선승제로 각 리그에 한 팀만 남을 때까지 서로 경기를 펼친다. 이 최종 두 팀은 우승 팀의 각 선수와 팀 매니지먼트에게 반지와 함께 주어지는 협회 회장의 트로피를 놓고 서로 겨루게 된다.

Q: 글에 의하면 다음 중 옳은 것은?
(a) 많은 이들은 월드 시리즈를 세계 최고의 야구 경기라고 생각한다.
(b) 플레이오프에서는 각 팀이 서로 한 게임씩 펼쳐 패자를 가려낸다.
(c) 내셔널 리그 팀들은 아메리칸 리그 팀들과 한 팀만 남을 때까지 경기한다.
(d) 각 리그의 우승 팀은 우승 트로피와 반지를 받는다.

야구 월드 시리즈에 관한 내용으로, 북아메리카의 미국과 캐나다팀들만이 경기를 펼친다는 것, 메이저리그 야구팀은 두 부로 나누어진다는 것, 플레이오프가 진행되는 방식에 관한 것, 우승 팀은 트로피와 반지를 받는 것 등을 설명하고 있다. 따라서 지문의 내용으로 옳은 것은 (a)이다. 플레이오프는 5전 3승제이므로 (c)는 옳지 않고, 한 팀이 남을 때까지 경기하는 것은 상위 3팀과 와일드카드 팀이므로 (b)도 옳지 않다. 리그가 아니라 전체 우승 팀이 받는 것이 반지와 트로피이므로 (d) 역시 답이 될 수 없다.

de facto 사실상의, 실질적인 **athletic** 체육의 **popularity** 인기 **wild card** 와일드카드(일반적으로 자격이 없지만 기회를 갖게 된 팀) **best-of-five** 5전 3선승제 **division** 부 **commissioner** 협회 회장

22

파리에서 잊을 수 없는 휴가를!

파리에서 낭만적인 휴가를 보내는 여러 가지 방법이 있다. 많은 여행객들은 죽 늘어선 고급 상점을 쇼핑하며 웅장한 샹젤리제를 한가로이 거닌다. 만약 쇼핑을 건너뛰고 싶다면 도시 안의 많은 공원 중 하나를 방문할 수도 있다. 만약 배를 타고 싶으면 센 강과 센 강의 여러 무수한 명소가 있다. 물랭 루주에 가서 카바레, 옛날 음악과 춤을 맛보는 건 어떨까? 사실 많은 커플들은 살면서 적어도 한 번은 파리에 가보고 싶어 한다. 그러니 당신도 한번 방문해서 그 이유를 알아보는 것이 어떨까?

Q: 다음 중 옳은 것은?
(a) 물랭 루주는 파리에 없다.
(b) 파리는 쇼핑 장소로 추천되지 않는다.
(c) 샹젤리제는 고급 상점으로 유명하다.
(d) 센 강은 파리 주변을 흐른다.

이 지문은 파리를 홍보하는 내용이다. 파리의 명소 중 샹젤리제 거리에서 고급 상점 쇼핑을 한다고 했으므로 정답은 (c)이다. (d)는 지문만 보고 센 강이 파리를 가로지르는지 파리 주변을 도는지 알 수 없으므로 오답이다.

stroll 산책하듯이 걷다 **array** 배열 **high-end** 고급의 **innumerable** 셀 수 없이 많은

23

학자들은 수백 년 넘게 파이가 세상에서 가장 정평 있고 무엇보다 흥미로운 수학적 상수라고 생각하곤 했다. 원의 지름에 대한 둘레의 비합리적인 비율로 정의된다. 가장 초기에 알려진 파이에 관한 기록 중 하나는 BC 1650년에 아메스라고 하는 이집트인 서기가 쓴 것으로, 현재는 린드파피루스로 알려져 있다. 그의 계산은 오늘날의 근사치인 3.141592와 1%도 차이가 나지 않았다. 린드파피루스는 최초로 원 안에 정사각형을 그려서 원의 지름을 측정해 '원의 면적과 같은 정사각형을 작도'하는 방식으로 파이 값을 계산하고자 시도했다.

Q: 글로부터 유추할 수 있는 것은?
(a) 파이의 값은 기하학을 이용해 측정할 수 있다.
(b) 오늘날 수학자들은 파이의 정확한 숫자를 갖고 있다.
(c) 고대 서기는 파이의 신비를 완전히 풀어냈다.
(d) 이 상수는 파피루스 덕분에 널리 알려졌다.

가장 정평 있고 흥미로운 수학적 상수로 인정 받아온 파이에 관한 이야기로, 원 안에 정사각형을 그려서 지름을 측정한 다음 파이의 값을 계산하려고 시도한 예로 보아 (a)를 유추할 수 있다.

scholar 학자 **recognized** 정평 있는 **intriguing** 아주 흥미로운 **constant** 상수 **irrational** 비합리적인 **ratio** 비율 **circumference** 원의 둘레 **scribe** 서기 **calculation** 계산, 산출 **by less than** ~ 이하의 **approximation** 근사치 **attempt** 시도 **measure** 측정하다 **geometry** 기하학

24

건축은 수천 년 넘게 발전되어 오면서 수학과 과학, 미술, 역사, 정치, 철학의 개념을 받아들여 포용해 왔다. 건축적인 디자인을 창조해 실행하기 위해, 건축가들은 예술성과 실용주의 사이에 용인되는 균형을 유지해야만 한다. 예를 들어, 무엇보다 아름다운 몇몇 디자인들이 물리 법칙에 희생양이 되어 엔지니어링 측면에서 실현이 불가능한 경우가 있다. 정치적 이유로 거부당하는 디자인들도 있다. 경제 공황 시기 동안에는 예술적이지만 비용이 많이 드는 컨벤션 센터 건립은 정치적으로 위험한 결정이 되어 대부분 거부당했을 것이다.

Q: 글로부터 유추할 수 있는 것은?
(a) 정치가는 가능성 있는 건축 사업을 잘 검토하기 위해 물리학을 알아야 한다.
(b) 공학적인 고려 사항들은 건물의 디자인 예술보다 덜 제한적이다.
(c) 건축가들이 자신의 디자인을 성공시키려면 창의적이면서 실용적이어야 한다.
(d) 건축할 대상은 당시에 어느 정당이 권력을 쥐고 있는가와 관련이 있다.

다양한 분야를 수용해 발전해온 건축에 관한 이야기로, 본문에서 건축가들은 예술성과 실용주의 사이에 균형을 유지해야 한다고 주장하고 있으므로 지문의 내용으로부터 유추할 수 있는 것은 (c)이다.

architecture 건축 **embrace** 받아들이다 **implement** 시행하다 **architect** 건축가 **strike a balance** 균형을 유지하다 **acceptable** 용인되는 **artistry** 예술성 **pragmatism** 실용주의 **feasible** 실현 가능한 **fall victim** ~에 희생이 되다 **laws of physics** 물리학의 법칙 **ground** 이유 **risky** 위험한 **restrictive** 제한적인

25

남위도 맨 끝에 간다면, 세계에서 그 지역에만 기이한 하늘의 빛을 찾아보라. 그 남극의 오로라 즉 남극광은 남반구에서 북극의 오로라 즉 북극광과 동일하게 나타나는 것이다. 남극이든 북극이든, 이런 오로라가 발생하는 원인은 하나이다. 태양에서 발산된 전자들의 흐름인 소위 태양풍이 대기권 안에서 지구 자기장에 부딪히게 된다. 그 자기장이 극지방의 대기권 내에 있기 때문에 결과적으로 그곳에서 오로라를 볼 수 있는 것이다.

Q: 다음 중 유추할 수 있는 것은?
(a) 남극광은 러시아에서만 볼 수 있다.
(b) 북극광의 원인과 남극광의 원인은 다르다.
(c) 오로라는 남반구에서 흰색이 아니다.
(d) 지구의 자기장이 부분적으로 오로라 발생의 원인이 된다.

북극광과 남극광에 대한 설명이다. 오로라는 태양풍이 지구의 자기장과 반응해서 생기는 결과라고 했으므로 정답은 (d)이다.

extreme 맨 끝의 **latitude** 위도 **peculiar** 특유한, 기이한 **aurora australis** 남극광 **aurora borealis** 북극광 **cause** 원인 **solar wind** 태양풍 **electron** 전자 **magnetic field** 자기장 **atmosphere** 대기 **consequently** 그 결과로 **partially** 부분적으로 **responsible for** ~의 원인이 된다

Part IV

26-27

가드너 씨께,

이 편지는 최근 위내시경 검사 치료에 대한 보상을 거절한 스피릿 보험사의 결정에 대한 항의입니다. 당신이 그 위내시경 검사는 암세포가 없을 경우 일 년에 한 번 이상 승인되지 않기 때문에 그 상환이 거부되었다고 알려주셨습니다. 그러나 저는 작년 말에 위암이 발병했다고 진단받았으며, 위절제술을 받았습니다. 최근 위내시경 검사 치료는 현재 상태를 확인하기 위해 시행된 것이며, 리차드 도널드슨 박사가 추천한 것이었습니다.

저는 당신이 최초의 검토를 할 때 모든 필요한 정보를 갖지 못했다고 생각합니다. 오레건 메디컬 센터의 도널드슨 박사님의 추가권유장을 첨부합니다. 그는 제 수술을 담당했으며, 그의 분야에서 최고의 전문가들 중의 한 명입니다. 그의 편지는 왜 그 치료과정이 필요했는지, 그리고 불가피했는지 상세하게 설명해 주고 있습니다. 또한 제 의료 기록도 첨부합니다. 그것은 추가적인 치료가 왜 필요했는지 설명해 주고 있습니다. 그 정보에 근거하여, 저는 당신의 회사가 제 위내시경 검사 치료를 보상해주기를 요구합니다.

진심으로,
스텔라 스미스
보험증서 번호 : 878230 – 987632

26. Q: 편지의 주요 목적은 무엇인가?
(a) 보험에 가입하라는 제안을 거부하기 위해
(b) 보험 회사에게 글쓴이의 위내시경 검사 치료를 알리기 위해
(c) 보험 회사에게 글쓴이의 의료비를 지급해달라고 요청하기 위해
(d) 의료센터로부터 온 진단서를 검토하기 위해

27. Q: 편지에 따르면 옳은 것은?
(a) 보험사는 위내시경 검사 치료에 대해 결코 비용을 지불하지 않는다.
(b) 글쓴이는 작년 말에 위암 수술을 받았다.
(c) 보험사는 처음에 도널드슨 박사의 편지를 검토했다.
(d) 글쓴이는 도널드슨 박사의 과잉진료에 화가 나 있다.

26. 보험료 청구 거절에 대해 쓴 편지글이며, "I am requesting that your company cover my gastroscopy procedure"라는 내용을 통해 보험료 청구를 요청하고 있으므로, 정답은 (c)이다.

27. 보험료 청구에 대한 재검토를 요청하면서, "I was diagnosed as developing gastric cancer at the end of last year and underwent a resection of my stomach"라는 문장에서 암수술을 받았다는 것을 밝히고 있으므로, 정답은 (b)이다.

insurance 보험 **appeal** 간청, 탄원 **coverage** 보상 **gastroscopy** 위내시경 검사(법) **procedure** 수술, 치료, 절차 **deny** 거부하다 **cancerous** 암의 **diagnose** 진단하다 **gastric** 위의 **undergo** 경험하다, 겪다 **resection** 절제 **initial** 최초의 **follow-up letter** 추가권유장 **be in charge of** ~을 책임지다 **inevitable** 불가피한 **subscribe to** 정기가입하다 **notify** 공지하다, 알리다 **medical expense** 의료비 **reimburse** 상환하다 **overtreatment** 과잉진료

28-29

http://www.madisongames.co.kr/recruitment

회사소개 ∨ 뉴스 ∨ 제품 ∨ **지원하기** ∨ 문의하기

구인: 온라인 마케터

매디슨 게임즈사는 고객들에게 비디오 게임 산업에서 다양한 언어로 최신 기술과 도구를 제공하고 있습니다. 우리 회사의 기업 문화는 평등한 관계를 특징으로 하며, 새롭고 흥미로운 기술과 게임을 추구하는 전 세계 출신의 젊고 유능한 노동력에 의해 확립된 것입니다.

자격요건

당신은 국제 비즈니스, 마케팅, 커뮤니케이션, 디지털 미디어, 혹은 연관된 분야에서 최소 학사 학위 이상을 가지고 있어야 합니다. 당신은 당신의 미디어 기술을 시장에서 실천할 수 있고, 다양한 소셜 미디어 플랫폼에 분석적이고 영감을 주는 에세이를 쓸 수 있는 창의적 사고의 소유자이어야 합니다. 당신은 또한 완벽한 영어 글쓰기 능력을 가진 뛰어난 소통가가 되어야 합니다.

업무

우리는 본사 마케팅 팀에서 일할 뛰어난 작가들을 찾고 있습니다. 당신은 주로 우리의 온라인 게임을 모니터하고, 분석하고, 평가하며, 홍보하는 업무를 담당하게 될 것입니다. 게다가, 당신은 소셜 미디어에서 우리 계정을 운영하고, 블로그에서 에세이를 쓰고, 고객들의 성공 스토리를 출판하는 데 있어 중요한 역할을 담당하게 될 것입니다. 또한, 당신은 새로운 고객들에게 홍보물을 제작하고 전달하는 데 있어 팀 구성원들을 도와주어야 합니다.

급료

당신은 시장 기준에 따라 고액의 월급을 받게 될 것입니다.

28. Q: 이 직위에 대해 의무적인 자격요건으로 언급되지 않은 것은?
(a) 마케팅 분야의 석사 학위
(b) 커뮤니케이션의 학위
(c) 창의적인 사고 능력
(d) 뛰어난 글쓰기 능력

29. Q: 광고에 따르면 옳은 것은?
(a) 회사는 고객들에게 영어로만 게임 분석글을 제공한다.
(b) 회사는 일반적으로 국내에서 신입직원들을 모집한다.
(c) 고용된 직원은 새로운 소셜 미디어를 개발하는 데 참여할 것이다.
(d) 고객들의 성공 스토리를 보도하는 것은 그 직책의 책임들 중의 하나이다.

28. 온라인 마케터를 구하는 구인광고이며, 자격요건으로 "a bachelor's or college degree", "a creative thinker", "impeccable written English skills"라는 요건들이 제시되어 있으나, "마케팅 분야의 석사 학위"는 언급되어 있지 않으므로, 정답은 (a)이다.

29. 온라인 마케터의 업무 영역 중에서 "publishing customers' success stories"가 제시되어 있으므로, 고객들의 성공 스토리 보도가 업무 중의 하나라는 것을 알 수 있다. 정답은 (d)이다.

a wide range of 다양한   corporate 기업의   feature ~을 특징으로 하다   flat hierarchy 평등한 관계   hail from ~출신이다   in pursuit of ~을 추구하는   put into practice 실천하다   analytical 분석적인   inspiring 영감을 주는   competent 능력 있는   impeccable 흠잡을 데 없는, 뛰어난   competitive 경쟁력 있는, 훌륭한   mandatory 의무적인   proficiency 능숙함   domestically 국내

30-31

열정적인 페미니스트: 엘리너 루스벨트

전 대통령 프랭클린 루스벨트의 아내로 유명한, 엘리너 루스벨트는 작가, 대중연설가 그리고 정치 활동가로 활동하면서 인권 및 여성의 권익을 향상시키는 데 기여했다. 그녀는 20세기 가장 널리 존경받는 사람들 중 한 명으로 평가되는 열정적인 정치적 인물이었다. 그녀는 또한 비정부기구인 '프리덤 하우스'를 설립하고 UN의 안정화를 지지하는 데 중요한 역할을 수행했던 영향력 있는 인물이었다.

루스벨트가 1933년 32번째 대통령으로 선출되었을 때, 그녀는 자신의 정치적 역할을 발전시킬 수 없을 것이라는 생각 때문에 일시적으로 좌절감을 느꼈다. 그러나 이후 그녀는 에세이를 쓰고 대중 연설을 함으로써 정치적 영향력을 계속해서 확대했다. 그녀는 또한 언론 인터뷰에 자주 등장했으며, 인권에 대해 이야기했다. 또한, 그녀는 많은 열정을 린치를 반대하는 캠페인과 소수인종을 위한 공정 주택을 위해 헌신했다. 그녀는 전통적인 퍼스트레이디가 되는 것보다 훨씬 더 높은 위치로 올라갔으며, 시민권의 뛰어난 옹호자로 여겨졌다.

30. Q: 엘리너 루스벨트에 대해 옳은 것은?
(a) 그녀의 대부분의 글들은 여성의 권리에 관한 것이었다.
(b) 그녀는 국제 조직을 발전시키기 위해 노력했다.
(c) 그녀는 프랭클린 D. 루스벨트가 대통령이 되었을 때 만족했다.
(d) 그녀는 시민권 활동가로서 전통적인 역할에 충실하려고 노력했다.

31. Q: 본문에서 엘리너 루스벨트에 대해 추론할 수 있는 것은?
(a) 그녀는 정치학 분야에서 가장 존경받는 사람이었다.
(b) 그녀는 자신을 다른 여성 정치인들과 차별화하지 못했다.
(c) 그녀의 삶은 다른 퍼스트레이디들의 삶과는 매우 달랐다.
(d) 그녀는 개인적인 성격 때문에 기자들을 만나는 것을 거부했다.

30. 엘리너 루스벨트의 정치적 역할에 대해 설명하는 글이며, "endorsing the stabilization of the United Nations"라는 문장을 통해 국제 조직의 발전에 기여했다는 것을 알 수 있으므로, 정답은 (b)이다.

31. 엘리너 루스벨트의 역할 중에서, 퍼스트레이디로서의 삶을 지적하면서 "She rose even higher than just being the conventional First Lady"라는 문장을 통해 다른 영부인들과의 삶이 달랐다는 것을 알 수 있으므로, 정답은 (c)이다.

feminist 페미니스트, 여성 운동가   contribute to ~에 공헌하다   empowerment 권한이양   fervent 열심인, 열렬한   figure 인물   venerate 존경하다   significant 중요한, 의미 있는   endorse 후원하다, 지지하다   stabilization 안정화   temporarily 일시적으로   press conference 기자회견   dedicate 헌신하다   lynch (죄가 있다고 여겨지는 사람을) 재판을 거치지 않고 불법적으로 죽이다   conventional 전통적인   prominent 뛰어난, 눈에 띄는   advocate 옹호자   faithful 충실한, 신뢰할 수 있는   revere 존경하다   be reluctant to ~을 거부하다, 꺼리다

32-33

텔레비전 프로그램 및 영화와 같은 대중매체에서 간접광고에 대한 생각은 실제 브랜드와 제품들을 보여줌으로써 영화의 현실감을 증진시키기 위해 영화 제작자들과 감독들의 노력에서 유래했다. 그러나 마케팅 전문가들이 놀랍게도, 영화에서 간접광고는 판매 증가로 이어졌다. 간접광고의 효과성을 깨닫게 된 이후에, 수많은 회사들이 다양한 간접광고 활동에 관여하기 시작했다. 다른 마케팅 전략들과 비교하여, 각각의 제품은 특정한 맥락에서 그리고 환경에서 드러나거나 이용될 수 있다.

마케팅 전문가들은 간접광고를 통해 통합된 마케팅 전달에 의해 유발된 시너지 효과를 입증해왔다. 그들의 연구에서 증명된 대로, 시각 효과와 제품에 대한 구어적 설명의 결합은 가장 비싼 것 중에서 한 가지 방식이지만, 가장 효과적인 광고 방식이다. 대중매체에서의 간접광고는 광고되는 각 제품의 브랜드와 친숙함과 유대감을 증가시킨다. 또한, 제품광고의 수명도 다른 광고 전략들에 비교할 때 상당히 더 길다.

32. Q: 본문의 주요 논점은 무엇인가?
(a) 영화와 TV 프로그램에서 현실감을 촉진시키는 혁신적인 방법
(b) 시너지를 유발하기 위한 다양한 광고들에 대한 연구
(c) 간접광고를 통한 광고의 효과적인 방법
(d) 마케팅 분야에서 간접광고의 장점과 단점

33. Q: 본문에 따르면 간접광고에 대해 옳은 것은?
(a) 그것은 각 영화와 텔레비전 프로그램에서 현실성을 저하시킨다.
(b) 그것은 한 번의 광고로 다양한 고객들을 목표로 한다.
(c) 그것은 브랜드 및 제품에 대한 고객들의 친밀감을 촉진시킨다.
(d) 그것은 고객들의 기억 속에서 각 제품의 수명을 줄인다.

32. 영화 등의 대중 매체를 통해 진행되는 간접광고의 효과에 대해 설명하고 있으므로, 정답은 (c)이다.

33. 간접광고의 다양한 효과를 제시하면서, "Product placement in mass media develops familiarity and a sense of being associated with the brand of each product displayed"라는 문장을 통해 대중들 사이의 친밀감을 키운다는 것을 알 수 있으므로, 정답은 (c)이다.

product placement 간접광고   originate 일어나다, 기원이 되다   feature 보여주다, 특징을 나타내다   efficiency 효과성, 능률   a profusion of 수많은   strategy 전략   context 맥락   verify 증명하다, 확인하다   synergy 공동작용, 상승작용   integrated 통합된, 조직화된   evidence 입증하다   combination 결합, 조합   visual effect 시각효과   verbal 언어의, 언어적인   reference 언급, 참조   albeit ~임에도 불구하고   lifespan 수명   familiarity 친밀성   pros and cons 장단점

34-35

https://www.openforum.org/economy/unemployment

심각한 실업률

크리스 윌리엄스

프랑코 몬티엘의 기사 "노령층을 위한 더 많은 기회들"의 역설적인 제목은 잃어버린 세대를 가진 미국의 증가하는 우려를 잘 묘사하는 것 같다. 절망에 빠진 회사들이 젊은 직원들을 먼저 해고하고 연공서열에 근거하여 법에서 정한 해고보상금을 지급하기를 거절하게 되면서 젊은 세대의 실업은 점차적으로 증가했다. 그들이 새로운 직원들을 고용할 때에도, 그들은 경력직 직원들을 찾고 있으며, 따라서 젊은 사람들은 줄의 뒤쪽에 위치하며, 그들의 경력을 늘릴 수 있는 기회를 갖지 못하고 있다.

미국에서 평균적인 청년 실업률은 약 21%이며, 성인 노동자들의 약 2배이다. 물론, 청년 실업률은 젊은이들의 노동 시장을 평가하는 최고의 지표는 아니다. 왜냐하면 그들 중 많은 사람들은 교육 제도에 등록된 상태이기 때문이다. 그러나 수십만 명의 실업 상태의 젊은이들은 많은 도시에서 준비한 직업 박람회에 방문하지만, 그들 중 많은 사람들은 고용되지 못하고 있다. 오히려, 높은 실업률은 경기 침체를 촉진시키고 있으며, 노동시장을 악화시키면서, 결국에는 그 국가의 노동시장의 유연성을 가속화시키고 있다.

34. Q: 신문기사의 주요 목적은 무엇인가?
(a) 노동 시장에서 기회 상실을 설명하는 신문기사를 비판하기 위하여
(b) 젊은 사람들의 실업률의 심각성을 알리기 위해
(c) 미국에서 발견되는 유연한 노동시장을 지지하기 위해
(d) 많은 도시들에서 젊은 구직자들을 위한 직업 박람회를 광고하기 위해

35. Q: 글쓴이가 동의할 것 같은 것은?
(a) 경력직 노동자들이 일반적으로 불리한 조건에서 일하고 있다.
(b) 젊은 직원들은 유연한 노동 시장에서 더 많은 경력을 쌓을 수 있다.
(c) 실업률은 경제 상황을 보여주는 좋은 지표이다.
(d) 직업 박람회를 조직하는 것은 신입 지원자들에게 도움이 되지 않는다.

34. 미국 내에서 발생하고 있는 실업률 증가의 심각성을 지적하는 글이며, "younger people are placed at the back of the queue and don't have the opportunity to augment their own career"등의 문장을 통해 특히 청년층의 실업률의 문제점을 제시하고 있으므로, 정답은 (b)이다.

35. "while hundreds of thousands of unemployed young people visit job fairs organized in many cities, many of them don't get recruited"라는 문장을 통해 대학 등 여러 기관이 직업 박람회 등을 통해 청년 실업률을 해결하기 위한 노력을 하고 있으나, 실제 고용으로 연결되지 않고 있다는 것을 알 수 있으므로, 정답은 (d)이다.

unemployment 실업 paradoxical 역설적인 in distress 괴로운, 궁핍한 release 해고하다 statutory 법률적인 redundancy payment 해고보상금 queue 줄 augment 늘리다, 증대하다 admittedly 사실, 인정하듯이 indicator 지표 precipitate 촉진시키다 recession 후퇴, 불경기 devastate 악화시키다 accelerate 가속화시키다 flexibility 유연성 endorse 후원하다, 지지하다 in adverse condition 불리한 조건에 있는 conducive to ~에 도움이 되는

ACTUAL TEST 4   p.194

Part I

| 1 (d) | 2 (b) | 3 (c) | 4 (d) | 5 (b) |
| 6 (b) | 7 (b) | 8 (a) | 9 (b) | 10 (d) |

Part II

| 11 (c) | 12 (c) |

Part III

13 (d)	14 (c)	15 (b)	16 (c)	17 (b)
18 (b)	19 (b)	20 (a)	21 (a)	22 (b)
23 (b)	24 (d)	25 (b)

Part IV

| 26 (b) | 27 (b) | 28 (c) | 29 (a) | 30 (c) |
| 31 (a) | 32 (a) | 33 (d) | 34 (c) | 35 (b) |

Part I

1

근로자의 직업 만족도는 **본인이 가치 있는 일을 찾는지 아닌지에** 따라 부분적으로 영향을 받을 수 있다. 구직 시장에서 사람들은 주로 자신의 재능에 딱 맞고 돈도 많이 주는 탄탄한 회사와의 일거리를 찾고 있다. 그래서 월급과 근무 조건은 분명 만족도에 가장 많은 영향을 미친다. 그러나 근로자가 임금을 낮게 받거나 과도하게 일을 해야 할 때, 그들이 사회에 이로운 일을 하고 있다고 생각함으로써 적은 월급이나 긴 근무 시간을 더 쉽게 받아들일 수 있다. 하지만 불행하게도, 흔히 의료 서비스업이나 사회 복지 사업, 교육 분야에 있는 근로자들만이 자신들이 타인을 돕는다고 생각한다.

(a) 본인의 의료 혜택의 질
(b) 일하면서 얼마나 많은 돈을 버는지
(c) 본인이 동료와 얼마나 잘 어울리는지
(d) 본인이 가치 있는 일을 찾는지 아닌지

이 글의 핵심은 후반부에 있다. 임금이 적거나 업무량이 많아도 사회에 이로운 일을 한다는 생각이 직업의 만족도를 높일 수 있다는 것이다. 따라서 직업에 대한 만족이 근로자 본인이 가치 있는 일을 찾는지의 여부에 달려있다는 (d)가 적절하다.

satisfaction 만족 depend on ~에 의존하다 primarily 주로 talent 재능 underpay 저임금을 주다 overwork 과도하게 일을 시키다 beneficial 유익한 paycheck 급료 health care 의료 social service 사회 복지 사업 benefits (회사의) 특전, 복지 valuable 가치 있는

2

영국의 오크니 섬에 있는 광대하고 복잡한 구조물의 발견은 **영향력이 큰 문명에 대한 새로운 이해를 제공한다.** 이 구조물은 섬의 수 마일의 크기이며, 이집트의 피라미드나 스톤헨지보다 앞서 5천 년도 더 이전에 지어졌다. 현장의 공예품을 보건대, 뚜렷한 건물 양식과 도자기를 만드는 것과 같은 물질적인 설계는 오크니 섬에 기원을 두고 영국의 다른 지역으로 퍼진 것이 분명하다. 그 지역을 세세히 연구하는 사람들은 그곳이 당시 새로운 사상의 중심지였다고 한다.

(a) 영국이 어떻게 한 국가로서 권력을 장악했는지를 설명한다
(b) 영향력이 큰 문명에 대한 새로운 이해를 제공한다
(c) 영국 종교의 기원에 대한 새로운 이론을 드러낸다
(d) 과학적, 문화적 이론의 초기의 발전을 보여 준다

글 후반부에 오크니 섬의 문명이 다른 지역으로 퍼져나갔고, 그곳이 새로운 사상의 중심지였다고 하므로 이 구조물의 발견은 영향력이 컸던 문명에 대한 새로운 정보를 준다는 내용의 (b)가 적절하다. 이론의 발전이 아니라 문명 자체에 대한 발견이므로 (d)는 알맞지 않다.

vast 광대한 **structure** 구조물 **construct** 건설하다 **artifact** 공예품 **distinctive** 독특한 **material** 물질적인 **originate** 시작하다 **insight** 통찰력 **influential** 영향력이 큰 **reveal** 드러내다 **advancement** 발전

3

민주주의 국가에서 법원은 종종 **개인의 자유와 공공의 안전 사이의 경계에 대해** 논쟁한다. 예를 들어, 어떤 사람이 북적거리는 극장에서 거짓으로 "불이야"하고 외친다면, 이것은 자유 발언일까? 공황에 빠진 관객들이 건물을 탈출하려 하기 때문에 이러한 행동은 해가 될 수 있다. 유사하게, 자유 국가의 시민들은 자신들이 부당하게 싫어하는 집단에 대해 공공연하게 증오의 발언을 하도록 두어야 할까? 즉각적인 위험 요소는 없을지 모르지만, 정부는 이런 발언이 폭력으로 이어질 가능성이 있음을 상당히 걱정할지도 모른다.

(a) 사회의 어느 단체가 발언하도록 허락받아야 하는지를
(b) 폭력적인 행동에 대한 적정한 처벌의 수준에 대해
(c) 개인의 자유와 공공의 안전 사이의 경계에 대해
(d) 솔직하게 의견을 나누는 시민들의 영향에 대해

빈칸 이후에는 개인의 발언의 자유와 공공의 안전이 서로 충돌하는 예가 이어지고 있다. 따라서 논쟁의 내용은 개인의 자유와 공공의 안전에 대한 것임을 알 수 있으므로 (c)가 적절하다. 누가 발언할 수 있는가가 초점이 아니므로 (a)는 적절하지 않다.

democratic 민주주의의 **court** 법원 **debate** 논쟁하다 **falsely** 가짜로 **yell** 소리치다 **free speech** 자유 발언 **in public** 공개적으로 **immediate** 즉시의 **reasonably** 상당히, 꽤 **potentially** 잠재적으로 **lead to** ~로 이어지다 **proper** 적절한 **punishment** 처벌

4

2010년 건조(建造)된 역사에 남을 만한 배 한 척이 **환경 공학에 대해 생각하는** 방식을 변화시켰다. 이 배의 이름은 플라스티키이다. 이 배는 데이비드 드 로스차일드가 디자인했는데, 그는 후에 태평양을 건너 8천 마일을 항해했다. 플라스티키의 내부 구조는 재활용이 가능한 플라스틱으로 만들어졌으며, 배를 물에 계속 뜨게 하는 플라스틱 병 수천 개가 한데 묶여 있다. 드 로스차일드는 캐슈와 설탕으로 만든 접착제를 발명하기도 했는데, 이에 반하여 대부분의 해양용 접착제는 유해한 화학 물질을 사용한다. 플라스티키는 석유나 전기를 사용하지 않고 태양 전지판을 장착하고 있다.

(a) 바다를 건너 먼 거리를 여행하는
(b) 우리가 매일 사용하는 플라스틱을 재활용하는
(c) 해양 오염의 원인을 이해하는
(d) 환경 공학에 대해 생각하는

재활용할 수 있는 플라스틱 병과 천연 접착제를 이용해 만든 배인 플라스티키에 대해 설명하고 있다. 이 배는 환경오염을 일으키지 않는 태양열을 연료로 사용하는 등, 환경을 생각한 기술로 볼 수 있으므로 (d)가 가장 알맞다.

watercraft 배 **sail** 항해하다 **inner** 내부의 **recyclable** 재활용이 가능한 **afloat** 물에 떠서 **toxic** 유해한 **chemical** 화학 물질 **electricity** 전기 **be equipped with** ~을 갖추고 있다 **solar panel** 태양 전지판

5

무인 승용차가 앞으로 몇 년 내로 시장에 소개될 테지만, 그 인기를 예측하기는 어렵다. 전자 센서와 GPS 내비게이션은 수년 간 있어 왔고, 고급 승용차는 이미 주차용 카메라 보기를 제공한다. 이 모든 것을 차량 조종 장치에 장착하는 것은 알아서 주행하는 차량을 위한 다음 단계이다. 하지만 알아서 주차하는 차는 인기를 끄는 데 더뎠다. 고객은 그런 차량이 필요한가에 대해 의구심을 갖는다. 아마도 무인 차량 역시 **운전자들의 외면과 함께 비슷한 반응에 직면할** 것이다.

(a) 미숙한 운전자들에게 더 많은 이점을 줄
(b) 운전자들의 외면과 함께 비슷한 반응에 직면할
(c) 큰 찬사를 받았던 똑같은 기술을 가질
(d) 현재 고객과 잠재 고객 모두에게서 충성심을 얻을

첫 문장부터 무인 승용차에 대해 회의적인 견해를 보이고 있다. 빈칸 앞에 있는 also로부터 스스로 주차하는 차량의 인기가 더뎠던 것과 유사한 내용이 이어지는 것이 알맞다. 따라서 (b)가 적절하다.

popularity 인기 **predict** 예측하다 **electronic sensor** 전자 센서 **steering** 조종 장치 **park** 주차하다 **catch on** 유행하다, 인기를 얻다 **doubt** 의심 **inexperienced** 미숙한 **turn away** 외면하다 **praise** 칭찬하다 **loyalty** 충성, 성실 **existing** 현재의 **potential** 잠재적인

6

미국의 성인들이 40년 전보다 당분을 2배나 더 섭취하고 있다는 것을 아십니까? 우리는 단것을 너무 많이 먹으면 건강에 좋지 않다고 알고 있습니다. 하지만 새로운 연구에 의하면 당분은 유독할 수 있다고 합니다. 과학자들은 쥐를 실험 대상으로 하여, 식단에 당분이 증가하면 조기 사망에 이를 수 있다는 사실을 발견했습니다. 쥐들에게 25프로의 당분을 더 투여했을 때 자신의 영역을 지키거나 새끼를 낳을 가능성이 더 낮아졌습니다. 이것은 동물들이 <u>스스로를 돌볼 능력을</u> 잃었다는 신호였습니다.

(a) 불어났던 추가 체중
(b) 스스로를 돌볼 능력
(c) 다른 음식 재료에 대한 내성
(d) 문제 해결을 위한 사고력

당분이 유독할 수 있다는 증거로 쥐에게 당분을 더 투여하면 자기 영역을 지키거나 번식할 가능성이 낮아졌다고 하므로 동물들이 잃은 것은 스스로를 챙길 능력이라고 볼 수 있다. 따라서 (b)가 적절하다.

sweet 단것 **test subject** 실험 대상 **early death** 조기 사망 **territory** 영역 **weight** 무게, 체중 **gain** 얻다, 증가하다 **care for** 돌보다 **tolerance** 내성, 저항력 **food source** 음식 재료 **thinking skill** 사고력

7

아이들은 3살이 되면 유치원이나 운동장에서 또래 아이들과 더 적극적으로 어울리기 시작한다. 좀 더 발달이 빠른 친구들을 보면서 아이들은 뭔가 새로운 것을 하려는 용기와 영감을 갖게 된다. 동시에, 싹트기 시작하는 자아로 소유욕이 강해지고 타인의 행동에 민감하게 되어, 종종 울거나 감정을 다치게 된다. 이때가 아이들이 <u>자신감을 표현하고 감정을 조절하는</u> 법을 배워야 하는 힘든 성장의 시기이다.

(a) 친구들과 더 효율적으로 의사소통하는
(b) 자신감을 표현하고 감정을 조절하는
(c) 한계를 시험하고 자신에게 새로운 기술을 연습하는
(d) 더 두드러진 방식으로 가족들에게 헌신하는

유아기에 또래들과 어울리면서 용기와 영감을 얻게 된다고 한다. 자아가 발달하면서 감정적 상처를 받을 때 아이들이 성장하면서 배워야 하는 것은 자신감을 표현하고 감정을 조절할 수 있는 법이라는 내용인 (b)가 적절하다.

actively 활발히 **peer** 또래 **advanced** 상급의 **courage** 용기 **budding** 싹트기 시작하는 **ego** 자아 **possessive** 소유욕이 강한 **sensitive** 민감한, 예민한 **toddler** 걸음마를 배우는 아이 **channel** (생각, 느낌 등을) 행동으로 표현하다 **confidence** 확신, 자신 **mood** 기분, 감정 **contribute to** ~에 헌신하다 **noticeable** 뚜렷한

8

영화 리뷰

영화 〈엘리시움〉은 100년도 더 되는 미래를 배경으로 한다. 지구는 황무지가 되었고 빈민층은 살아남기 위해 고군분투한다. 지구의 부유층은 엘리시움이라는 호화로운 우주 정거장으로 이주했고, 그곳에서 편안하게 살며 최고의 건강관리의 기술을 누린다. 영화의 줄거리는 지구에 있는 고통 받는 사람들이 부유층의 세계에 밀고 들어가 더 나은 삶을 살려고 하면서 전개된다. 하지만 부자들은 지구 거주인들이 진입하는 것을 막기 위해 돈을 쓴다. 결론은 이 영화는 <u>인간이 계급의 차이에 어떻게 반응하는가를 탐구하는</u> 영화라는 것이다.

(a) 인간이 계급의 차이에 어떻게 반응하는가를 탐구하는
(b) 발전된 특수 효과를 곁들여 긴박한 상황을 만들어 낸
(c) 미래의 삶에 대해 일반적인 묘사를 보여 주는
(d) 현대 사회의 실제 경험을 상세히 설명하는

이 영화는 미래 사회에서 자본 계급에 의한 삶의 차이를 보여 주면서, 상황을 전복하려는 빈민층과 그들을 막으려는 부유층 간의 이야기라고 한다. 따라서 이 영화는 사람들이 각자의 처지에서 계급의 차이에 대해 반응하는 모습을 보여 준다고 할 수 있으므로 빈칸에는 (a)가 적절하다.

wasteland 황무지 **space station** 우주 정거장 **health care** 건강관리 **unfold** (이야기가) 펼쳐지다 **force one's way** 밀고 나아가다 **class** 계급적인 **high drama** 긴박한 상황

9

미국 작가 트루먼 카포트는 작가로서 초기에는 뉴욕의 상류 사회에 대한 묘사로 유명했다. <u>이후,</u> 카포트는 좀 더 무거운 주제들을 다루고 싶어 했다. 그는 다음 책을 쓰기 위해 캔자스의 작은 마을로 갔는데, 〈인 콜드 블러드〉라는 이 소설은 무고한 가족의 잔혹한 살인뿐만 아니라 그 범죄를 저지른 이들에 관한 실화를 바탕으로 한다. 허구와 사실의 획기적인 조합인 그 소설은 바로 다 팔렸고, 여전히 현대 고전으로 남아 있다.

(a) 그렇다 하더라도
(b) 이후
(c) 그러므로
(d) 정말로

빈칸 뒤는 작가가 초기에 뉴욕 상류 사회 묘사로 유명세를 쌓은 이후에 대한 설명이므로 정답은 (b)이다.

portrait 묘사 **high society** 상류 사회 **tackle** 다루다 **weightier** 무거운 **innocent** 무고한 **brutal** 잔혹한 **commit a crime** 범죄를 저지르다 **groundbreaking** 획기적인 **blend** 혼합 **modern classic** 근대 고전 **increasingly** 점점 더 **intensely** 심하게 **hungry for** ~을 갈망하는

10

도서 리뷰

말라 존슨의 신작 판타지 소설은 뱀파이어가 대도시에 자기들만의 공동체를 형성한다면 어떤 일이 일어날지 상상한다. 그녀의 소설에서 인간은 피에 굶주린 뱀파이어를 그들이 해를 미치지 않을 분리된 지역에 강제로 거주하게끔 한다. **그럼에도 불구하고** 뱀파이어들은 성공적인 사업을 일구고 TV에 방영되는 사치스러운 파티를 여는 데 돈을 쓴다. 인간들은 이를 지켜보면서 뱀파이어들의 생활 방식을 점점 질투하게 된다. 결과적으로 서로 다른 무리들 간의 복잡한 관계가 흥미롭고 훌륭하게 그려진다.

(a) 게다가
(b) 그렇지 않으면
(c) 마찬가지로
(d) 그럼에도 불구하고

빈칸 앞뒤 관계를 보면, 뱀파이어가 성공적으로 사업을 일군 것은 뱀파이어를 격리시킨 조치를 했음에도 불구하고 일어난 일이므로 정답은 (d)이다.

establish 설립하다 **neighborhood** 지역, 지방 **extravagant** 사치스러운 **broadcast** 방송하다 **look on** 지켜보다 **fascinating** 대단히 흥미로운 **celebrity** 유명인 **demonstrate** 입증하다 **obsessed** 집착하는

Part II

11

비밀 감시의 범위에 관한 최근 보도들이 또 다시 사생활 대 안보에 대한 논쟁을 부채질하고 있다. (a) 9/11 테러는 필요한 거의 모든 수단을 동원해 테러에 맞서도록 대통령에게 폭넓은 권한을 주는 동기가 되었다. (b) 여기에는 군사 행동과 무인 공습, 정보 수집이 포함될 수 있다. (c) 위키리크스는 2006년에 기밀 정보를 폭로하는 문서와 동영상들을 대중에 공개하기 시작했다. (d) 한 컴퓨터 분석가는 자신이 몸담았던 미국 국가 보안국이 불법으로 일반 시민들을 감시한다고 주장했다.

9/11 테러 이후 국가의 정보 수집이 도를 넘어 사면서 사생활이냐, 안보냐의 문제로 논쟁이 다시 일었다는 내용이다. (c)는 과거의 한 단체의 기밀 정보 폭로에 대한 이야기로, 언뜻 주제가 어울려 보이지만 전체 맥락에서는 벗어나 있다.

extent 범위 **surveillance** 감시 **privacy** 사생활 **motivation** 동기, 원인 **broad** 폭넓은 **unmanned** 무인의 **air strike** 공습 **intelligence gathering** 정보 수집 **expose** 공개하다 **reveal** 폭로하다 **classifiable** 분류할 수 있는 **analyst** 분석가 **spy on** ~을 감시하다 **unlawful** 불법의

12

유자차는 한국에서 감기를 치료하기 위해 마시는 것으로 인기 있는 허브차다. (a) 전통적으로 유자차는 유자 조각을 꿀에 절여서 준비한다. (b) 이 방법으로 과실의 시고 쓴 맛을 없애고 겨울 동안 썩지 않게 저장할 수 있다. (c) 유자청 한 스푼은 차가운 물보다 뜨거운 물에 더 쉽게 잘 녹는다. (d) 이것은 대부분의 사람들이 매년 겪는 질병에 대한 믿을 수 있는 자연식 치료법으로 간주된다.

감기에 효력이 있는 유자차의 특징에 관한 글이다. (a)와 (b)가 긴밀하게 연결되어 있고, (d)는 첫 문장의 감기 치료라는 내용과 연결된다. (c)도 유자차가 소재지만, 글의 전체적인 맥락에서 가장 벗어나 있다.

citron 시트론, 유자 **remedy** 치료 **marinate** 절이다 **get rid of** ~을 제거하다 **preserve** 보존하다 **dissolve** 녹다 **reliable** 믿을 수 있는

Part III

13

사우스빌 타임스

과학 〉 기술

과학자들은 이제 원격 장치를 이용해 바퀴벌레를 조종할 수 있다. 바퀴벌레의 더듬이에 작은 장치를 연결함으로써, 인간이 컴퓨터를 이용해 벌레의 움직임을 지시할 수 있다. 이런 '바퀴벌레 로봇'은 생명을 구할 수도 있다. 예를 들어, 곤충의 컴퓨터 배낭에 작은 마이크나 카메라를 붙일 수 있다. 그러면 그 작은 생물체는 지진이 일어난 후 파괴된 건물의 잔해 속으로 투입될 수 있다. 시청각 장치가 재난 후 갇힌 사람들의 도움을 구하는 외침을 감지할 수 있다.

Q: 뉴스 보도는 주로 무엇에 관한 것인가?
(a) 인간의 일을 하도록 곤충 훈련시키기
(b) 바퀴벌레처럼 행동하는 새로운 로봇들
(c) 해충들을 없애는 미세한 기술
(d) 구조에 나설 컴퓨터화된 벌레들

원격 장치로 바퀴벌레를 조정하여 무너진 건물의 잔해 속에서 사람들을 구하는 데 투입하여 이용할 수 있다고 하므로, 적절한 정답은 (d)이다. 곤충을 훈련시키는 것이 아니라, 컴퓨터를 부착해 조종하는 것이므로 (a)는 알맞지 않다.

control 제어하다 **cockroach** 바퀴벌레 **remote device** 원격 장치 **connect** 연결하다 **antennae** (곤충의) 더듬이 **direct** 지시하다 **rubble** 잔해 **earthquake** 지진 **detect** 감지하다 **trapped** 갇힌 **disaster** 재난, 참사 **eliminate** 제거하다 **pest** 해충 **computerize** 컴퓨터화하다 **rescue** 구출

14

기본 구조는 간단하다. 각 숫자는 0과 1에서 시작해 이전 숫자 두 개를 더한 결과이다. 비슷한 발상은 이미 고대 인도에서 두 숫자의 모든 가능한 조합을 계산할 때 존재했다. 하지만 오늘날 우리는 레오나르도 피보나치가 만들었던 중세 시대의 형태로 이 기법을 알고 있다. 이 수열은 그 부분의 합보다 진정으로 위대하다. 이 수열의 매력은 나뭇가지나 조개껍데기에서 발견되는 패턴도 면밀히 묘사한다는 점이다.

Q: 이 글의 주제는?
(a) 한 수학 공식의 문화적 의의
(b) 어떤 발상이 국가에서 국가로 번지는 방법
(c) 자연의 특징을 묘사할 수 있는 수열
(d) 현재의 문제점에 과거의 방법 적용하기

피보나치수열의 개념에 대해 설명하면서, 이 수열이 자연의 모습을 설명할 수 있다는 데 진정한 위대함이 있다는 내용이다. 나뭇가지나 조개껍데기의 패턴도 묘사한다고 하므로 자연의 모습을 묘사할 수 있는 수열에 관한 글로 볼 수 있다. 따라서 (c)가 적절하다.

combination 조합 medieval 중세의 sum 합 branch 나뭇가지
significance 중요성, 의의 seashell 조개껍데기 formula 공식
sequence 연속적인 것들, 수열 characterize ~의 특징을 묘사하다
method 방법

15

만약 진지하게 지역에서 일자리를 구하고 있다면, 어디를 찾아 봐야 할지
알면 구직이 쉽다는 것을 알아라. 인기 있는 검색 장소는 구직 센터이다.
구직 센터는 다양한 직업의 수많은 일자리 정보를 제공한다. 지역 신문과
국내 신문도 현재 나와 있는 구인 광고를 제공한다. 또한 모든 산업은 잡
지와 신문을 발간하고 있고 대부분의 고용주들은 전문가를 채용하기 위
해 이러한 출판물을 본다. 당신의 지역에서 일자리를 찾기 위한 가장 비
용 효율이 높은 방법은 인터넷을 통해서 찾는 것이다. 원하는 일자리를
구하는 것은 도전일 수 있지만 구직을 위한 올바른 방법을 찾는 것은 일
자리를 구할 가능성을 높일 것이다.

Q: 글의 주요 내용은?
(a) 적절한 직원들을 고용하는 것
(b) 구직을 위한 효과적인 방법
(c) 일자리를 찾는 어려움
(d) 구직 광고를 올리는 다양한 방법

일자리를 쉽게 알아볼 수 있는 다양한 방법들을 소개하는 지문이다. 따라
서 가장 적절한 주제는 (b)가 된다. 일자리를 찾는 데 겪는 어려움이나, 구
직 광고를 내는 내용은 아니기 때문에 (c)와 (d)는 오답이다.

numerous 수많은 vacancy 빈자리 publication 출판물 cost-
effective 비용 효율이 높은 challenge 도전 channel 방법
land 획득하다

16

이안 조인트 박사에 따르면 대기 중에 이산화탄소의 증가가 전 세계 바다
의 산성도를 약화시켜 해양 생물과 산소 수준에 영향을 미치고 있다고 한
다. 게다가, 해양 생물에 미치는 영향은 인류의 주된 식량원의 손실을 가
져올 만큼 중대한 것일 수 있다. 지구를 비옥하게 만들며 바닷속에 독소
의 양이 줄어들도록 돕는 일을 도맡아 하고 있는 수백만 종의 박테리아들
이 바다의 산성화로 인해 나타나는 불균형 때문에 죽어가는 위험에 처해
있다. 산소의 경우, 바다의 식물 물질인 미생물들이 전 세계 산소의 거의
절반을 생성하고 있다. 미생물들을 위험에 처하게 하는 것은 인류를 위험
에 처하게 하는 것이다.

Q: 이 글의 요점은 무엇인가?
(a) 해양 생태계 내 산소의 정도
(b) 동물에게 해로운 해양 박테리아
(c) 해양 미생물을 죽이는 바다의 산성화
(d) 온실가스로 인해 늦춰진 산성화

바다의 산성화로 인해 바닷속 독소의 양을 줄이는 역할을 담당하고 있는
박테리아가 죽어갈 수 있다고 했으므로 정답은 (c)이다.

carbon dioxide 이산화탄소 atmosphere 대기 marine life 해양
생물 significant 중요한 humankind 인류, 인간 fertile 비옥한
toxin 독소 imbalance 불균형 acidification 산성화 microbial
미생물의 globally 세계적으로 at risk 위험에 처한

17

코를 고는 여섯 명 중 한 사람은 심한 폐쇄성 수면 무호흡증(OSA)을 앓
고 있다. 혀와 목구멍 뒷부분의 근육이 기도를 막는 지점까지 이완되어
호흡하기가 곤란해질 때 이 증상이 초래된다. 이러한 증상이 일어나면 하
룻밤에 수백 번 잠깐 잠을 깨기 때문에 숙면을 취하기가 불가능해진다.
이러한 장애가 건강에 미치는 영향은 매우 심각해서, 지속적인 피로감,
체중 증가, 혈압 상승, 심부전이나 심장 발작까지도 초래한다. 환자들은
수술이나 코골이를 방지하는 수면 도구를 사용해서 코골이를 치료해야
한다.

Q: 폐쇄성 수면 호흡증에 대한 내용으로 옳은 것은?
(a) 폐쇄성 수면 무호흡증이 있는 사람은 밤에 깨서 다시 잠들지 못한다.
(b) 폐쇄성 수면 무호흡증은 심장 기능에 영향을 준다.
(c) 코골이를 하는 거의 모든 사람이 심각한 건강 장애를 앓고 있다.
(d) 수면 무호흡증 환자의 목구멍 근육은 수축된다.

코를 고는 사람 6명 중 1명꼴로, 혀와 목구멍 뒷부분의 근육이 기도를 막
는 지점까지 이완되어 수면 무호흡증이 초래되고, 밤에도 수백 번 잠깐씩
깨며, 심장 질환을 일으킬 수 있다는 내용이므로 정답은 (b)이다.

snore 코를 곯다 Obstructive Sleep Apnea (OSA) 폐쇄성 수면
무호흡증 disorder 장애 constantly 끊임없이 heart failure 심부전
stroke 심장 발작 sufferer 환자

18

미국 이민 사회의 한 보고서에 의하면 농업과 어업의 전체 노동 인구의
45.8%가 이주민들로 구성되었다. 그것은 그 분야 노동자 1,250만 명 중
약 5,725,000명에 해당한다. 이는 미국의 총 노동 인구 1억 2,800만 명에
서 이민자들이 차지하는 16%의 비율보다 더 높다. 스펙트럼의 반대편 끝
에 있는 미국 전체 변호사와 법률 전문직 종사자의 약 5.8%가 이주민들
이다.

Q: 이 글에 의하면 다음 중 옳은 것은?
(a) 많은 이민자들이 변호사다.
(b) 이주 노동자들은 미국 전체 노동자의 16%에 해당한다.
(c) 미국에는 대략 1,200만 명의 이주 노동자가 있다.
(d) 전체 이민자의 거의 절반이 농업과 어업에 종사한다.

미국의 총 노동 인구 1억 2,800만 명에서 이주민이 차지하는 16%라고 설
명했으므로 (b)가 적절하다. 이주민들 중 높은 비율은 농업과 어업에 종
사하므로 (a)는 적절하지 않고, 미국 내 어업과 농업의 노동자 중에 이주
민이 절반가량인 것이지 이주민의 절반가량이 종사한다는 내용은 아니므
로 (d) 또한 적절하지 않다.

immigration 이민 labor force 노동력 agriculture 농업 fishing
어업 be comprised of ~로 구성되다 immigrant 이주민
approximately 대략 sector 부문 spectrum 스펙트럼, 영역 legal
professional 법률 전문직 percentage 비율 roughly 대략

19

로켓 과학은 대개 수준이 높은 과학자들과 관련이 있다. 하지만 고대 역사를 보면 기본적인 로켓 연료, 즉 화약은 우연히 개발된 것일 수 있다. 로켓의 정의에 들어맞는 최초의 장치는 중국에서 발명되었다. 많지 않은 자료에 근거하여, 역사가들은 중국 화학자들이 영원히 살 수 있는 약을 만들기 위해 애쓰는 중에 불꽃놀이용 화약을 발견했다고 본다. 다른 물질들을 결합해 시험하던 중에 마침내 물체를 공중으로 쏘아 올릴 수 있는 발상을 알아냈다.

Q: 로켓 과학에 관해 다음 중 옳은 것은?
(a) 고대 중국의 의학적 치료였다.
(b) 그 역사가 완벽하게 문서로 기록되어 있지 않다.
(c) 무기 제작을 위해 빠르게 발전되었다.
(d) 계획된 실험의 산물이었다.

많지 않은 자료에 근거하여 역사가들이 중국 화학자들이 화약을 발견했다고 생각한다고 하므로 (b)가 가장 적절하다. 불로초를 찾기 위해 실험하던 중 우연히 발견된 것이므로 (d)는 적절하지 않다.

associate 연관 짓다　**rocket fuel** 로켓 연료　**gunpowder** 화약
accidentally 뜻하지 않게　**definition** 정의　**collection** 수집
historian 역사가　**chemist** 화학자, 약사　**firework** 불꽃놀이
substance 물질　**uncover** 알아내다, 폭로하다　**launch** 발사하다
treatment 치료　**document** (상세한 내용을) 기록하다　**evolve**
발달[진화]하다　**weapon** 무기　**experiment** 실험

20

더치커피라고 알려진 것은 사실 우연히 발견되었다. 17세기 네덜란드 상인들은 인도네시아에서 이국적인 물건들을 싣고 고향으로 돌아오기 위해 출항했다. 이러한 선박 중 한 척이 커피를 싣고 가던 중, 높은 파도에 찬물에 푹 젖어 버렸다. 남은 커피는 독특하지만 좋은 맛이 났다. 오늘날 카페에서 차가운 물에 더치커피를 만드는 일은 몇 시간이 걸리는데, 끓는 물을 이용할 때보다 빠른 원두에서 색다른 맛을 뽑아낸다. 원두에서 더 적은 산도와 카페인이 추출되어 마시기에 더 부드럽다.

Q: 더치커피에 관해 다음 중 옳은 것은?
(a) 뜨거운 물로 만든 커피보다 맛이 더 풍부하고 부드럽다.
(b) 네덜란드인들은 커피를 내리는 대체 방법을 고안할 생각이었다.
(c) 시간이 걸리는 제조 과정으로 인해 가격이 비싸다.
(d) 주로 인도네시아에서 자란 커피 원두로 만든다.

끓는 물로 내릴 때보다 색다른 맛이 나고, 더 적은 산도와 카페인이 추출되어 마시기에 더 부드럽다고 하므로 (a)가 적절하다. 우연히 발견된 것이므로 발명의 의도가 있었던 것은 아니므로 (b)는 옳지 않다. 인도네시아는 네덜란드 배의 출항지로 언급되었을 뿐, 더치커피 원두의 원산지라는 내용은 없으므로 (d) 또한 적절하지 않다.

by chance 우연히　**sail from** ~에서 출항하다　**exotic** 이국적인
soak 흠뻑 젖다　**brew** (차를) 끓이다. 우러나다　**ground** 빻은　**acid** 산.
신맛이 나는 것　**time-consuming** 시간이 걸리는　**manufacturing**
procedure 제조 과정

21

넓은 의미에서 암은 몸에 위험한 종양들을 형성하는 모든 유형의 통제 불능의 세포 성장이다. 여러 가지 요소가 개입될 수 있기 때문에 대부분의 암이 발병하는 원인은 알기 힘들다. 유전은 낮은 비율을 차지할 뿐이고 대다수의 경우가 생활 방식의 요인들 때문으로 본다. 어떤 나라로 간 이주민들이 그 새로운 환경에서 흔한 질병에 걸린다는 사실은 질병에 영향을 주는 생활 방식의 중요성을 나타낸다.

Q: 이 글에 의하면 다음 중 옳은 것은?
(a) 이주민들의 건강은 새로운 환경에 영향을 받는다.
(b) 대부분의 암의 기원은 환자를 연구함으로써 알 수 있다.
(c) 유전은 의사들이 생각했던 것보다 더 큰 영향을 미칠 수 있다.
(d) 대부분의 치명적인 종양들은 공기와 물의 오염 탓이다.

암의 원인이 주로 생활 방식에 기인하며 다른 나라로 간 이주민들이 종종 그곳의 흔한 질병에 걸린다는 것은 새로운 환경이 건강에 영향을 미치는 것으로 볼 수 있다. 따라서 (a)가 정답이다.

broad 폭넓은　**uncontrolled** 통제 불능의　**tumor** 종양　**outbreak** 발발
factor 요소, 원인　**be involved** 연루되다, 개입되다　**genetics** 유전학,
유전적 특징　**develop** (병을) 발병시키다　**disease** 병　**surrounding**
주변 환경　**origin** 발단, 기원　**pollution** 오염　**blame** ~을 탓하다
deadly 치명적인

22

남아프리카공화국의 인카운터 페스티벌은 아프리카 대륙에서 다큐멘터리 영화만을 위한 가장 큰 영화제다. 1999년에 시작한 이래로 영화제는 다큐멘터리 장르에 관심을 이끄는 데 도움이 되었고, 새로운 제작을 촉진했으며, 아프리카에 국제적인 영화를 들여왔다. 영화제는 신인 영화 제작자들을 고무시키는 데에도 지도된 노력을 한다. 신인 감독들은 경험이 많은 전문가 팀에 프로젝트를 제안할 수 있는데, 최고의 프로젝트들이 제작을 위한 자금을 따낸다. 영화제가 시작된 후로 거의 1,500편의 신작 다큐멘터리를 지원했다.

Q: 영화제에 관해 다음 중 옳은 것은?
(a) 다양한 종류의 영화를 소개한다.
(b) 모든 경력 수준의 영화 제작자들을 기린다.
(c) 다큐멘터리 영화계에 영향력이 거의 없다.
(d) 영화를 다른 국가에 보이기 위해 세계 투어를 한다.

신인 감독들이 경력이 많은 전문가들에게 프로젝트를 제안한다고 하므로 다양한 수준의 경력을 가진 제작자들이 이 행사에 참여하고 있는 것을 알 수 있다. 따라서 (b)가 정답이다. 다큐멘터리 영화만을 위한 축제라고 하므로 (a)는 알맞지 않다.

continent 대륙　**dedicate** 헌신하다　**first-time** (무엇을) 처음으로 해 보는
production 제작　**impact** 영향

23

전 직원에게:

개발팀에서 회사의 새로운 로고와 브랜드 이미지를 발표합니다. 변화하는 기업 환경에 발맞춰 우리 회사의 이미지를 바꾸기 위해 개발팀에서 애써 주었습니다. 웹 페이지와 회사 문서, 문구류, 명함 등 모든 매체에 적용할 새 표준 가이드를 배포하고 있습니다. 회사 웹 사이트에서 최신 템플릿을 받으시고, 교육을 통해 여러분께 변환 과정을 차례로 보여 줄 것입니다. 우리 회사의 최신 로고를 선보이게 되면 우리 브랜드를 차별화하는 데 큰 도움이 될 것입니다.

Q: 안내문으로부터 회사에 관해 유추할 수 있는 것은?
(a) 사람들이 새 로고와 옛 로고를 둘 다 보기를 원한다.
(b) 시장에 적응하기 위해 노력하고 있다.
(c) 새 로고는 주로 온라인에서의 노출을 바꿀 것이다.
(d) 직원들은 새 로고에 관해 제안을 할 수 있다.

변화하는 기업 환경에 발맞춰 자사의 이미지를 바꾸기 위해 새롭게 회사의 로고와 브랜드 이미지를 내놓았다고 하므로 이 회사는 시장에 적응하기 위해 노력하고 있음을 알 수 있다. 따라서 (b)가 정답이다. 온라인을 비롯해 회사의 문서나 명함 등 모든 매체의 모습을 바꿀 것이므로 (c)는 알맞지 않다.

development team 개발팀 transform 바꿔 놓다 distribute 배포하다 stationery 문구류 business card 명함 instruction 교육 switching 전환 up-to-date 최신의 go a long way to ~에 크게 도움이 되다 distinguish 차별화하다 alter 바꾸다 adapt to ~에 적응하다

24

오스트레일리아 건국 기념일은 1788년 오스트레일리아 섬에 온 영국 정착민의 도착을 기념하는 연례 기념일이다. 이 날은 1800년대 초에 처음으로 기념되었다. 이후, 1900년대에 오스트레일리아 섬에 수 세기 동안 거주했던 원주민들은 항의의 의미로 그들만의 기념일을 만들었다. 그들은 이 날을 애도의 날이라고 부르고, 영토 찬탈과 원주민 아이들을 가정에서 빼앗아 영국 학교로 보낸 것 등 영국인들이 행한 수년의 잔인한 처사에 반대하며 거리를 행진했다. 토착민들은 평등한 권리를 요구했고, 영국식 '진보'에는 희생이 따랐다고 주장했다.

Q: 이 글로부터 유추할 수 있는 것은?
(a) 두 반대 세력이 마침내 화해할 수 있었다.
(b) 식민지적 전통이 긍정적인 시위로 대체되었다.
(c) 두 개의 기념일을 열어 문화적 경험을 풍부하게 했다.
(d) 이 나라를 세우기 위한 행동이 전적으로 공정한 것은 아니었다.

오스트레일리아 건국 기념일이 영국의 정착을 기념하는 반면, 원주민들은 영국의 잔인한 처사에 항의하는 의미로 애도의 날을 지정하여, 영국식 진보라는 것이 원주민들의 희생을 치르고 이루어진 것이라고 주장했다는 내용으로 보아 유추할 수 있는 것으로 (d)가 적절하다.

celebration 기념행사 aborigine 원주민 found 설립하다 in protest 항의하여 object to ~에 반대하다 cruel 잔인한 takeover 탈취, 장악 removal 제거, 이동 opposing 맞서는 make peace 화해하다 colonial 식민지의 protest 항의, 시위 enrich 풍성하게 하다 entirely 완전히 just 공정한

25

다음 이색 여행은 기프트 오브 트래블과 함께 계획하세요!

저희는 휴식하고 관광할 충분한 시간을 드리지만, 여러분은 환경 문제를 다루고 있는 지역 단체들과 함께할 것입니다.

· 미얀마의 해변을 방문해서 그곳의 해안 지대의 침식을 막는 프로젝트를 도울 수 있습니다.
· 아니면 브라질로 여행을 떠나 그곳의 열대 우림 복원을 도우며 음식과 아름다운 풍경을 즐길 수 있습니다.
· 남아프리카로 떠나면 그곳의 역사적 건축물들을 보며 코뿔소 개체 복원 노력에도 참여합니다.

Q: 지문의 여행 프로그램에 대해 추론할 수 있는 것은?
(a) 브라질의 현지인들을 크게 돕고 있다.
(b) 환경 문제 명분을 위해 만들어졌다.
(c) 아프리카의 코뿔소 개체 수에 큰 영향을 미쳤다.
(d) 많은 여행객들에게 인기가 높다.

여행 프로그램 하나하나가 해안 지대 침식을 막고, 열대우림 복원을 돕고, 코뿔소 개체 복원 노력에 참여하는 등 환경 보존 활동을 포함하고 있으므로 정답은 (b)이다.

exotic 이색적인 ample 충분한 address 다루다 assist with ~을 돕다 erosion 침식 coastline 해안선 cuisine 요리 restore 복구하다 rainforest 열대 우림 historical monument 역사적 기념비 rhino 코뿔소

Part IV

26-27

글락소클라인 프로바이오틱스+ 비타민 D

건강보조식품으로서, 글락소클라인 프로바이오틱스+ 비타민 D는 당신의 위장관에서 "좋은" 박테리아로 기능하며, 당신의 신체 내에서 일반적인 건강과 행복을 보장해 줍니다. 당신의 위장에서 박테리아의 건강한 균형을 유지하는 것은 당신의 소화 건강을 최적화된 상태로 만들어줍니다.

여러분 모두 잘 알고 계시듯이, 비타민 D의 인기는 소화 및 면역 체계에서의 향상과 같은 수많은 건강상의 이점 때문에 급증했으며, 당신의 정서적 건강뿐만 아니라 뼈의 건강에도 영향을 끼치고 있습니다.

글락소클라인 프로바이오틱스+ 비타민 D는 소화 건강과 관련하여 가장 자주 연구된 박테리아들 중의 하나인 락토바실러스 아시도필러스를 특징적으로 보여 줍니다. 이 건강 보조 식품은 추가적인 면역 지원을 위해 60 마이크로그램 이상의 비타민 D를 포함하고 있으며, 편리한 캡슐형으로 건강상의 이점을 제공하고 있습니다.

냉장 보관은 필수적인 것은 아니지만, 일단 개봉하면 최고의 효능을 보장하기 위해 냉장을 하셔야 합니다. 자연적인 변색이 묶음에 따라 일어날 수도 있습니다. 하루에 하나의 캡슐씩 물과 함께 드세요. 그러나 당신이 임신한 상태이거나 임신할 계획이 있다면 이용 전에 의사와 상의하세요.

26. Q: 광고에서 이익으로 언급되지 않은 것은?
(a) 소화계 건강
(b) 혈액 순환
(c) 뼈 건강
(d) 면역 체계

27. Q: 광고에 따르면 글락소클라인 프로바이오틱스+ 비타민 D에 대해 옳은 것은?
(a) 그것은 위장관 질환의 효과적인 치료제이다.
(b) 그것은 연구자들에 의해 자주 연구된 박테리아를 특징적으로 보여준다.
(c) 그것은 변색을 막기 위해 냉장이 되어야 한다.
(d) 그것은 임신한 여성들의 건강을 개선하는 데 이롭다.

26. 글락소클라인 프로바이오틱스+ 비타민 D의 장점과 단점에 대해 알리는 글이며, "digestive", "immune systems", 그리고 "bone health" 등이 언급되어 있지만, 혈액순환은 제시되어 있지 않다. 정답은 (b)이다.

27. 글락소클라인 프로바이오틱스+ 비타민 D의 여러 가지 특징 중에서 "lactobacillus acidophilus, one of the most frequently researched bacteria"라는 내용을 통해 이 제품은 자주 연구된 박테리아 중의 하나를 포함하고 있다는 것을 알 수 있으므로, 정답은 (b)이다.

probiotics 활생균, 프로바이오틱스   supplement 보충제   gastrointestinal tract 위장관   gut 내장, 창자   digestive 소화의   optimum 최적조건   surge 급증하다   a myriad of 수많은   immune system 면역체계   lactobacillus acidophilus 락토바실러스 아시도필루스 (유산간균의 일종)   formula 공식, 조제법   nutritional 영양의   refrigeration 냉각, 냉장   refrigerate 냉각시키다, 냉장하다   potency 효능, 효력   variation 변화, 변이   batch 한 묶음   conceive 임신하다, 생각해내다   discoloration 변색, 퇴색

28-29

관계자님께,

올해 4월 15일에, 저는 다리 통증 때문에 당신의 응급실에서 치료를 받았습니다. 저는 스티브 로한 박사님께 X-레이를 찍고 검사를 받을 때까지 극심한 고통 속에서 한 시간 이상을 기다렸습니다. 검사 이후에, 저는 어떠한 심각한 문제도 제 다리에서 발견되지 않았기 들었으며, 단지 진통제만을 처방받았습니다.

그러나 참을 수 없는 고통이 2일이나 더 지속되었기 때문에, 저는 앨라배마 대학병원에 갔으며, 거기에서 찍은 X-레이는 제 다리가 골절되었다는 것을 보여주었습니다. 불필요한 고통을 겪었기 때문에, 저는 이러한 오진과 근무태만에 대하여 그 의사가 징계를 받기를 원합니다. 제가 당신 병원에서 받았던 처방전 사본과 영수증뿐만 아니라 2차 검진 X-레이 사본과 문서들을 동봉합니다. 비록 저는 응급실이 붐비는 현상에 대해 이해하지만, 저는 전문적이고 정확한 진단을 예상하고 있었습니다. 제가 이러한 경우에 취할 수 있는 조치가 무엇일지 알려주시기 바랍니다.

진심으로,
엘리 허드슨

28. Q: 편지의 주요 목적은 무엇인가?
(a) 글쓴이가 지불했던 의료비용에 대한 상환을 요청하기 위하여
(b) 병원이 글쓴이의 골절된 다리를 재검사해 줄 것을 요구하기 위하여
(c) 글쓴이가 오진에 대해 취할 수 있는 조치에 대해 묻기 위하여
(d) 응급실이 붐비는 현상에 대해 불평하기 위해

29. Q: 본문에 따르면 옳은 것은?
(a) 한 시간 정도 지나서야, 엘리는 의사에게 검사를 받을 수 있었다.
(b) 응급실에서 찍은 X-레이에서 엘리의 다리의 문제점들을 발견했다.
(c) 엘리는 앨라배마 주립 병원에서 2차 검진을 받았다.
(d) 엘리는 앨라배마 주립병원에서 처방전 혹은 영수증을 받지 못했다.

28. 병원에서 진단과 치료를 받았으나, 다른 병원에서의 재진 결과 오진으로 밝혀진 사항에 대해 항의를 하고 있으며, "Please let me know what, if any, measure I should take in this case"라는 문장을 통해 추가 조치에 대해 묻고 있으므로, 정답은 (c)이다.

29. 진단 및 치료를 받는 과정에 대해 언급하면서, "I waited for more than one hour"라는 내용을 언급하고 있으며, 이를 통해 그녀가 한 시간 이상 동안 대기하고 있었다는 것을 알 수 있으므로, 정답은 (a)이다.

emergency 응급   extreme 극단적인, 심한   prescribe 처방하다   excruciating 심한 고통을 주는   fracture 골절시키다   reprimand 질책하다   misdiagnosis 오진   negligence 근무태만   receipt 영수증   crowdedness 혼잡함   petition for 청원하다, 요청하다   reimbursement 상환   a second opinion 제2차 검진

30-31

www.politicaljournal.ca/policy/registration

〈사설〉 유권자 등록: 효과와 논란

많은 정치 전문가들은 유권자 등록 요건이 많은 사람들, 특히 가난한 사람들이 투표할 권리를 행사하는 것을 막고 있으며, 더 낮은 투표자수를 유발한다고 주장해왔다. 유권자 등록은 사람이 투표를 허락받기 전에 투표인 명부에 등록해야 하는 것을 의미한다. 등록은 대부분의 연방, 주, 그리고 지방 선거에서 적용된다. 많은 주들은 유권자 등록을 위해 그들 자체적인 마감일을 정하고 있으며, 선거 전 2주에서 4주까지를 의미한다.

그러나 등록이 각 개인의 책임인 몇몇 지역의 많은 개혁가들은 투표자수를 극대화하기 위해 등록하는 쉬운 절차를 제안해 왔다. 그들은 그러한 혁신적인 등록 시스템이 자동화 되어야 하며, 선거일에 적용이 되어야 한다고 주장한다. 그에 따라서 정부 기관이 유권자 등록 정보를 업데이트하기 위해 정부 기관이 정보를 선거담당기구에 정보를 제공한다면 유권자들은 자동으로 투표권을 얻을 수 있다.

30. Q: 본문에 따르면 옳은 것은?
(a) 현재 등록 시스템은 투표 과정을 용이하게 한다.
(b) 유권자 등록 규정은 지방 선거에는 적용되지 않는다.
(c) 몇몇 지역들은 등록의 책임을 개인들에게 돌리고 있다.
(d) 정부 기관은 유권자들의 정보를 공개하는 것을 거부해왔다.

31. Q: 본문에 따르면 추론할 수 있는 것은?
(a) 자동 등록 절차는 투표자수를 증가시킬 수 있다.
(b) 대부분의 주들은 선거 전에 동일한 마감일을 설정하고 있다.
(c) 유권자 등록 요건은 부에 따라 차별적이다.
(d) 많은 유권자들은 정보를 기밀로 하기 위해 등록하지 않기를 선택할 것이다.

30. 미국 선거 제도의 문제점들 중 하나인 등록제도에 대해 설명하는 글이며, "registration is each individual's accountability"라는 내용을 통해 등록의 책임이 개인에게 있다는 것을 알 수 있으므로, 정답은 (c)이다.

31. 현재의 등록 시스템을 비판하면서, 자동화된 등록 시스템이 도입되어야 한다고 주장하고 있는데, 시스템 혁신의 목적은 투표자수 증가에 있으므로, 정답은 (a)이다.

registration 등록 **controversy** 논란, 논쟁 **pundit** 전문가 **assert** 주장하다 **destitute** 가난한 **turnout** 참석자수 **enrollment** 등록 **electoral roll** 선거인명부 **accountability** 책임 **innovative** 혁신적인 **automatic** 자동적인 **electoral agency** 선거 담당기구 **facilitate** 용이하게 하다, 촉진시키다 **reluctant** 꺼려하는 **discriminatory** 차별적인 **confidential** 기밀의

32-33

사키 원숭이들은 남아메리카 북부 및 중부에 살고 있는 몇몇 신대륙 원숭이들 중 하나이다. 그것들은 검은색, 회색 혹은 적갈색의 털이 있는 피부와 길고, 털이 무성한 꼬리를 가진 상대적으로 더 작은 원숭이이다. 비록 그것들의 머리는 털로 덮여 있기는 하지만, 그들의 얼굴은 털이 없다. 강한 뒷다리는 그들이 점프를 하도록 해주며, 긴 꼬리는 2킬로그램까지 무게를 견디도록 하기 때문에, 그들의 신체는 나무에서의 생활에 맞춰져 있다. 열대 우림의 나무에서 살고 있는 그들은 때때로 지상으로 내려가기도 한다.

사키 원숭이들은 부모와 새끼들로 구성된 가족 집단으로 공동체의 삶을 살아간다. 그들은 영역 중심 동물로서 나무에서 나무로 이동을 하고 다른 가족들로부터 그들의 서식지를 지킨다. 그들은 또한 가족 구성원들 사이에 연계 수단으로서 높고 날카로운 울음소리 또는 새와 같은 소리를 통해, 그리고 다른 동물들에 대한 경고로서 큰 소리를 통해 그들의 가족에 속한 다른 원숭이들과 의사소통을 한다. 잡식동물로서, 그들은 과일, 곤충, 그리고 작은 척추동물을 포함하여 다양한 음식을 먹는다.

32. Q: 본문의 주요 논점은 무엇인가?
(a) 사키 원숭이들의 외모와 삶
(b) 사키 원숭이 종들 사이의 차이
(c) 사키 원숭이들의 신체적 특징들
(d) 독특한 원숭이 종의 공동생활

33. Q: 본문에서 사키 원숭이들에 대해 옳은 것은?
(a) 그들 종의 대부분은 남미 전역에 걸쳐 살고 있다.
(b) 그들의 꼬리는 나무에 그들의 몸을 유지할 정도로 강하지는 않다.
(c) 그들은 그들의 서식지에서 다른 가족들과 조화롭게 살아간다.
(d) 그들은 몇 가지 목적에 따라 독특한 소리를 이용한다.

32. 남아메리카에 서식하는 사키 원숭이에 대해 설명하는 글이며, 외형적 모습과 공동체의 삶에 대해 설명하고 있으므로, 정답은 (a)이다.

33. 사키 원숭이들의 공동체 삶 중에서 중요한 것은 의사소통이며, "They also communicate with other monkeys in their family through shrill cries or bird–like twitter as a means of connection among family members and a loud roar as a warning against other animals"라는 문장을 통해 다양한 소리를 통해 의사소통을 하고 있다는 것을 알 수 있다. 정답은 (d)이다.

relatively 상대적으로, 비교적 **furry** 털이 무성한 **bushy** 덥수룩한 **hind leg** 뒷다리 **communal** 공동체의 **offspring** 후손, 자손 **territorial** 영토의, 지역적인 **habitat** 서식지 **shrill** 높고 날카로운 **twitter** 지저귀는 소리, 킬킬거리는 소리 **roar** 소리, 울부짖음 **omnivore** 잡식동물 **vertebrate** 척추동물 **attribute** 특성, 특징 **cohabitation** 동거 **distinct** 다른, 구별되는

34-35

전기 자동차: 대기 오염의 대안은 아니다

공무원들은 최근에 대기오염을 줄일 수 있는 계획을 수립하라는 강요를 받아왔으나, 끔찍하게도 잘못된 결과를 낳았을 뿐이다. 전기 모터들은 환경에 대한 깨끗하고 안전한 대안을 제공한다고 오랫동안 알려져 왔다. 대부분의 사람들은 전기 자동차를 운전하는 것이 배기가스에서 나오는 해로운 대기 오염을 줄일 수 있다고 믿는다. 전기 자동차를 재충전하기 위해 이용된 재생 가능한 에너지는 온실가스 배출을 훨씬 더 줄여줄 것이라고 여겨져 왔다. 이러한 줄어든 해로운 배기가스는 우리 건강에 좋은 소식처럼 보인다. 더 나은 대기 질은 더 적은 건강 문제를 이끌어 내고 대기 오염에 의해 유발된 비용을 낮출 것으로 예상되고 있다.

그러나 공무원들에게 놀랍게도, 새로운 연구는 오염을 줄이기 위한 소위 깨끗하고 비용 효과적인 조치는 실제로는 더러운 차들이 시내 중심으로 들어오게 촉구하고 있음을 보여주었다. 몇몇 전문가들에 따르면, 전기 자동차들이 어떠한 배기가스도 배출하지는 않지만, 브레이크와 타이어에서 많은 양의 미세 오염 물질을 유발한다. 따라서 도시 주변에서 안전하고 효율적인 운동들 중의 한 가지는 더 깨끗하고 더 확대된 대중교통 시스템을 이용하여 달성될 수 있을 뿐이다. 지속적으로 깨끗하고, 값싸고, 신뢰할만한 자동차들이 대기 오염에 대한 궁극적인 대안이 될 수 있을 것이다.

34. Q: 신문기사의 주요 목적은 무엇인가?
(a) 전통적인 자동차들의 해로운 결과를 보여주기 위해
(b) 도시 주변의 해로운 온실가스를 줄이기 위해
(c) 대안 자동차의 해결하지 못한 문제를 지적하기 위해
(d) 운전자들이 도로에서 전기 자동차를 이용하는 것을 막기 위해

35. Q: 글쓴이가 동의할 것 같은 말은 무엇인가?
(a) 전기 자동차들을 재충전하는 것은 많은 양의 에너지를 요구하지 않는다.
(b) 전기 자동차들은 부당하게도 긍정적인 평가를 받아왔다.
(c) 대기 오염은 자동차들이 유발하는 가장 심각한 문제이다.
(d) 정부는 대기 오염을 줄이기 위해 아무 일도 하지 않는다.

34. 현행 자동차의 문제점을 극복하기 위한 대안으로 제시된 전기 자동차의 한계성을 지적하는 지문이므로, (c)가 정답이다.

35. 전기 자동차의 신화에 대해 비판하는 내용이며, "Most people believe that driving an electric vehicle could reduce harmful air pollution from exhaust emissions"를 통해서 사람들이 오해하고 있다는 것을 알 수 있으므로, 정답은 (b)이다.

electric 전기의 **generate** 유발하다, 발생시키다 **woefully** 비참하게 **inadequate** 부정확한 **exhaust emission** 배기가스 **renewable** 재생 가능한 **recharge** 재충전하다 **cost-effective** 비용 효과적인 **measure** 조치, 계획 **urge** 촉구하다 **fume** 가스, 냄새 **particle** 입자, 분자 **efficient** 효율적인 **mass transit** 대중교통 **consistently** 지속적으로 **reliable** 신뢰할만한 **ultimate** 궁극적인 **compromising** 해로운 **abate** 줄이다, 경감시키다 **unsettled** 해결되지 않은

ACTUAL TEST 5

p.214

Part I

1 (c)	2 (a)	3 (d)	4 (a)	5 (d)
6 (a)	7 (b)	8 (c)	9 (d)	10 (c)

Part II

11 (b)   12 (c)

Part III

13 (c)	14 (c)	15 (b)	16 (b)	17 (d)
18 (c)	19 (c)	20 (b)	21 (d)	22 (a)
23 (d)	24 (d)	25 (d)		

Part IV

26 (b)	27 (d)	28 (c)	29 (c)	30 (a)
31 (c)	32 (b)	33 (c)	34 (b)	35 (c)

Part I

1

갠지스 강은 인도의 고대 베다 전통에 있어서 중요한 상징이다. 강가 여신은 천국은 물론 지상과 지하 저승 세계를 다닌다고 한다. 결과적으로 그녀의 이름을 딴 이 신성한 강은 신앙인들이 몸과 영혼을 정화하고 심지어 내세로 여행하기 위한 장소이다. 많은 사람들이 목욕과 화장을 위해 강을 사용하면서, 안타까운 결과로 오염의 수위가 높아지고 있다. 그럼에도 수백만 명의 사람들이 영적인 공간으로써 강을 계속 찾고 있어, 그 때문에 **환경 문제의 원인이 되고 있다.**

(a) 간과되었던 관행을 되살리고 있다
(b) 주요한 종교적 신념 체계를 퍼뜨리고 있다
(c) 환경 문제의 원인이 되고 있다
(d) 명소에 대한 관심을 불러일으키고 있다

초반에는 갠지스 강의 의미와 의의에 관해 설명하고 있지만, 결과적으로 많은 사람들이 영적인 공간이 된 강을 찾아와 오염이 되고 있다는 문제를 제기하고 있으므로 (c)가 적절하다.

underground 지하의   **holy** 신성한   **name after** ~의 이름을 따서 짓다
the faithful 신앙인   **purify** 정화하다   **afterlife** 사후 세계   **cremation**
화장(火葬)   **consequence** 결과   **pollution** 오염   **spiritual** 영적인
revive 소생하게 하다   **practice** 관행   **spread** 퍼뜨리다   **belief** 신념
contribute ~의 한 원인이 되다   **environmental problem** 환경 문제
spark interest in ~에 관심을 불러일으키다

2

정부가 사회 기반 시설 건설에 개입할 때는 **몇몇 영역에서 경제를 강화하도록 모색하는** 재정 정책을 시행할 것이다. 이러한 노력은 경기 침체기에 활기를 북돋우거나 일개 회사가 처리하기에는 너무 크고 복잡한 프로젝트를 수행하는 데 도움을 줄 수 있다. 어느 쪽이든 사회 기반 시설은 필요한 것으로 여겨지며, 따라서 정부에 의해 공공의 자금이 동원된다. 사회 기반 시설 자체가 사회에 유용할 뿐만 아니라 작업을 완료하기 위해 고용된 노동자들 역시 그 일로 인해 혜택을 입는다.

(a) 몇몇 영역에서 경제를 강화하도록 모색하는
(b) 기업들이 벌어들이는 수익을 나누도록 허용하는
(c) 필요한 천연 자원을 적소에 제공하는
(d) 근로자들을 자기 일자리에서 새로운 프로젝트에 투입하는

정부가 사회 기반 시설 건설에 재정적으로 개입함으로 인해 사회적인 필요를 충족시키고 노동자 개인에게도 도움을 주어 경기 침체기에 활기를 북돋울 수 있다고 하므로 여러 영역에서 경제를 강화하는 재정 정책이라는 내용이 적절하다. 따라서 (a)가 정답이다. 천연 자원과는 거리가 먼 이야기이므로 (c)는 알맞지 않고, 정부의 이러한 정책이 새로운 일자리 창출로 노동자들에게 이익이 된다는 내용이므로 (d)도 적절하지 않다.

step in 개입하다   **infrastructure** 사회 기반 시설   **set in motion**
~에 시동을 걸다   **fiscal** 국가 재정의   **slump** 불황   **public fund** 공금
mobilize 동원하다   **front** (특정) 영역, 일선

3

가장 초기 모델의 물리적인 버튼에서 벗어나 터치스크린이 무선 기기를 점령했다. 최초의 화면 키보드는 화면에 가하는 물리적인 압력이 필요했다. 예를 들어, 많은 휴대 전화가 펜처럼 생긴 스타일러스를 제공했는데, 이 펜으로 화면을 터치하고 자판을 칠 수 있었다. 오늘날의 휴대 전화 키보드는 모든 압력 신호 없이, 오로지 인간의 몸에서 방출하는 작은 전기 신호에만 의존한다. 이러한 디자인 형태가 시장을 차지하면서 최신 휴대 전화는 **디지털 기기와 사용자 간의 상호 작용을 간소화한다.**

(a) 화면에 눈에 보이는 아이콘으로 버튼을 나타낸다
(b) 기계 장치의 메뉴를 탐색하기 위해 더 작은 스타일러스를 사용한다
(c) 작동을 위해 터치 및 목소리 인식을 사용한다
(d) 디지털 기기와 사용자 간의 상호 작용을 간소화한다

휴대 전화의 입력 체계가 과거 압력 신호에서 이제는 인간의 미세한 전기 신호에 의존한다고 하므로, 사용자가 기기를 사용하는 것이 점차 간소화되는 것으로 정리할 수 있다. 따라서 (d)가 적절하다.

take over 차지하다   **mobile device** 무선 기기   **on-screen** 화면의
stylus 스타일러스(펜처럼 생긴 모바일 기구용 필기구)   **signal** 신호
solely 온전히   **radiate** 방출하다   **navigate** 탐색하다   **gadget** 장치
recognition 인식   **operation** 작동   **simplify** 간소화하다
interaction 상호 작용

4

고대에는 **정신적 특성을 신체적 외모 탓으로 돌리는** 일이 흔했다. 그리스 로마 시대의 현자들은 인간의 특성을 그에 상응하는 동물에 비교하곤 했었다. 여기에는 얼굴형 및 체형의 비교가 포함되었다. 이러한 것들은 인간의 행동에 대해 예측하는 데 사용되었다. 중세 시대에는 선호도가 떨어졌지만, 이런 부류의 것은 다윈설의 결과로 부활했다. 이 현대적 버전은 어떤 의미에서 고대의 이론들보다 더 공격적이었다. 대신에 인종적 차이, 우생학, 범죄 행동이 주요 초점이 되었다.

(a) 정신적 특성을 신체적 외모 탓으로 돌리는
(b) 사람과 동물의 겉모습의 차이를 확인하는
(c) 인간을 신이 창조한 유일한 이성적인 창조물로 정의하는
(d) 각 인종이 다른 조상과 관련이 있다고 간주하는

고대에는 인간의 특성을 동물에 비교하여 외모를 비교하거나 인간 행동 예측하였다고 한다. 즉, 외형적 특성에 기반을 두어 인간의 행동을 예측한다는 것은 심리적, 정신적 자질과 신체적 외양을 연관 지어 생각하는 것이므로 (a)가 알맞다.

feature 특성, 특징 **corresponding** 상응하는 **prediction** 예측 **based on** ~에 기반을 둔 **outward** 표면상의 **trait** 특성 **revival** 재생, 회복 **come about** 발생하다 **in the wake of** ~의 결과로서 **aggressive** 공격적 **racial** 인종의 **eugenics** 우생학 **assign** ~의 탓으로 하다 **psychological** 정신[심리]의 **attribute** 자질, 속성 **rational** 이성이 있는 **connection** 관련성

5

전 세계는 히로시마 폭격에 의한 파괴를 알지만, 많은 사람들이 생존자들이 신체적 장애뿐만 아니라 고통스러운 사회적 어려움을 직면했다는 것은 모른다. 폭탄에 영향을 받은 사람들을 '폭격의 영향을 받은 사람들'이라는 의미의 '히바쿠샤'라고 한다. '히바쿠샤'는 일본 정부로부터 보조금을 받기는 했지만, 이웃들은 방사능 질환이 퍼질 수도 있다는 두려움에 그들을 고용하지 않았다. 같은 이유로 그들은 좀처럼 결혼을 하거나 아이를 가질 수 없었다. 그렇게 전 세계 최악의 사건 중 하나를 겪은 후 **그들은 자국민에게 거부당했다.**

(a) 정부는 그들을 묵살하고 잊었다
(b) '히바쿠샤'는 고통스러운 기억을 극복했다
(c) 미국은 이민을 허가해 주었다
(d) 그들은 자국민에게 거부당했다

히로시마 폭격의 영향을 받은 사람들은 정부의 지원을 받았지만 사람들은 방사능에 대한 걱정 때문에 고용하지 않았고 결혼을 하거나 자식을 갖기도 어려웠다고 하므로, 폭격 사건 후에 자국민들로부터 거부당했다는 결론이 적절하다. 따라서 (d)가 정답이다. 정부가 그들에게 보조금을 주었다고 하므로 (a)는 적절하지 않고, 히바쿠샤들이 극복해 냈다는 내용은 문맥에 맞지 않으므로 (b) 또한 적절하지 않다.

devastation 황폐, 파괴 **bombing** 폭격 **survivor** 생존자 **explosion** 폭발 **hire** 고용하다 **radiation sickness** 방사능 숙취(병) **spread** 퍼지다 **live through** 겪고 지내다 **ignore** 묵살하다 **permit** 허가하다 **immigration** 이민 **reject** 거절하다

6

어린이 학습은 개인의 가치를 정하고 그에 의해 결정을 내리는 방식에 거의 중점을 두고 있지 않다. 학교는 수학과 과학 같은 학업 영역만 강조하는 반면, 어린아이들이 자신에게 무엇이 중요한지, 타인에게 어떻게 대해야 하는지에 대해 초기부터 배우도록 도와주는 수업은 회피한다. 결과적으로, 많은 어른들이 그런 상황에 대해 연습을 거의 하지 않았기 때문에 자신의 진가를 그대로 나타내지 않는 결정을 하게 된다. 하지만 학교가 교수 접근법의 영역을 넓힐 수 있다면 **아이들은 보다 완벽한 교육을 받게 될 것이다.**

(a) 아이들은 보다 완벽한 교육을 받게 될 것이다
(b) 선생님들은 그들의 수업에 보다 만족하게 될 것이다
(c) 우리의 아이들은 보다 많은 학습 도구를 만들 수 있다
(d) 어려운 과목의 교육이 더 쉬워질 것이다

학교가 학업의 영역만 강조할 게 아니라 가치 판단을 배우는 인성적인 부분까지 교수 접근법의 영역을 넓힌다면, 아이들이 커서 자신의 진가를 나타낼 수 있다는 내용이다. 따라서 (a)가 가장 적절하다. 학습 도구를 만드는 것과는 별개의 내용이므로 (c)는 알맞지 않다.

determine 결정[확정]하다 **accordingly** 그에 맞춰 **matter** 중요하다 **treat** 대하다 **reflect** 반영하다 **true value** 진가, 진정한 가치 **practice** 연습 **broaden** 넓히다 **instruction** 교수 **subject** 과목

7

비즈니스 뉴스

자전거와 버스에 주로 의존하는 대도시 거주자들을 위한 새로운 사업이 **의지할 만한 교통수단이 없는 사람들에게** 도움을 준다. 이는 집카라고 불리며, 도시 곳곳의 주차장에 차를 비치해 둔다. 특별한 날에 운전을 해야 하는 사람들은 미리 또는 이용 직전에 온라인이나 전화로 차를 예약할 수 있다. 서비스에 가입해서 1년 치 요금을 내야 하지만, 예약된 시간 동안은 차를 열 수 있는 출입 카드를 받게 된다.

(a) 구입하고 싶은 차를 사람들이 시험하는 데
(b) 의지할 만한 교통수단이 없는 사람들에게
(c) 새로운 유형의 자동차를 홍보하는 데
(d) 시에서 증가하는 온라인 접속량을 줄이는 데

자가용이 없지만 필요할 때 예약해서 쓸 수 있는 차량 서비스업에 관한 글이다. 이 서비스는 차가 없는 사람들에게 도움이 될 것이므로 (b)가 적절하다. 차를 구입하는 게 아니라 빌려 쓰는 것이므로 (a)는 적절하지 않으며, 온라인 문제를 언급하고 있지 않으므로 (d)는 문맥에 맞지 않다.

dweller 거주자 **rely on** ~에 의존하다 **place** 놓다 **occasion** 특별한 일 **reserve** 예약하다 **in advance** 미리 **subscribe** 가입하다 **access** 접근 **unlock** 열다 **reliable** 믿을 만한 **transportation** 교통수단 **automobile** 자동차

8

도시 지역은 전통적으로 한 국가의 사람들이 모여서 소통하는 곳이다. 도시 지역 안에서도 어떤 곳은 이런 목적을 위해 공간적으로 지정되었다. 고대 그리스의 거의 모든 도시에는 시민들이 상품을 구입하고 거래할 뿐 아니라 정치, 과학, 철학에 대한 생각을 교환했던 만남의 장소가 있었다. 이 회합 장소('아고라'라 칭함)들은 보통 도시의 중심이었고 **다양한 직종의 사람들이** 방문했다. 지역 사회 지도자, 과학자, 정부 행정가, 상인, 철학자, 귀족 그리고 범법자 및 노예들까지 아고라에 모여서 (민주주의의 개념과 같은) 역사상 가장 위대한 몇몇 사상을 토론하고 발전시켰다. 소크라테스, 플라톤, 아리스토텔레스, 히포크라테스, 피타고라스와 같은 사람들이 생각을 나눴던 곳이 그리스의 이 아고라였다.

(a) 최고의 사회계층 사람들만이
(b) 정부에 불만을 느끼는 사람들이
(c) 다양한 직종의 사람들이
(d) 오로지 상품 거래를 원했던 사람들이

아고라에서 시민들이 상품을 구입하고 거래했을 뿐 아니라, 지역 사회 지도자, 과학자, 정부 행정가, 상인, 철학자, 귀족, 범법자 및 노예들이 생각과 사상을 토론하고 발전시켰다는 내용이다. 즉, 다양한 직종의 사람들이 모였다는 것을 알 수 있으므로 정답은 (c)이다.

congregate 모이다 **designate** 지정하다 **citizen** 시민 **goods** 상품 **exchange** 교환하다 **politics** 정치 **philosophy** 철학 **focal** 중심의 **town** 도시 (city보다 작은 규모) **community** 지역 사회 **outlaw** 범법자 **democracy** 민주주의

9

건강 뉴스

많은 사람들이 풍미를 높이기 위해 음식에 흔히 사용하는 재료인 MSG가 술이나 흡연보다 훨씬 더 위험하다고 생각한다. **특히** 미국의 식품에서는 크래커나 샐러드드레싱 같은 엄청나게 많은 종류의 통조림 식품과 포장 식품에 MSG를 쓴다. 많은 사람들은 자신이 MSG를 많이 먹고 있다는 것을 자각하지 못할 뿐만 아니라, 그것의 안 좋은 점도 알아차리지 못한다. MSG는 해를 입는 정도까지 몸 안의 세포를 자극한다. 이것은 대부분 뇌와 신경계에 영향을 미쳐 학습 장애나 파킨슨병을 유발할 수 있다.

(a) 이것에도 불구하고
(b) 대조적으로
(c) 게다가
(d) 특히

첫 문장에서 음식에 흔히 첨가되는 MSG의 위험성에 언급한 뒤, MSG가 많이 첨가되는 음식 중 대표적인 예가 될 수 있는 크래커, 샐러드드레싱 등이 언급되고 있다. 따라서 문맥상 적절한 연결어는 (d)이다.

ingredient 성분 **enhance** 높이다 **flavor** 맛, 풍미 **canned** 통조림을 한 **packaged food** 포장 식품 **aware** 알아차리고, 깨닫고 **downside** 안 좋은 점, 단점 **excite** 자극하다 **nervous system** 신경계 **learning disability** 학습 장애 **Parkinson's disease** 파킨슨병

10

많은 사람들은 감기가 올 것 같을 때 닭고기 수프나 오렌지 주스에 의존한다. 하지만 식물 화학 물질이 포함된 다른 음식들이 병을 퇴치하는 데 실로 도움이 될 수 있다. 이 화합물들은 당근과 피망 같은 식물에서 자연적으로 난다. 이것들은 필수 영양소로 간주되지는 않는다. 그보다 면역 체계를 강화시키고 박테리아와 바이러스의 공격을 늦추며, 세포 회복을 높일 수 있는 강한 생물학적 특성을 갖고 있다. 아플 때만 식물 화학 물질이 들어 있는 식물을 먹는 것으로 갑자기 병을 낫게 하지는 않을 것이다. **대신**, 규칙적으로 식단에 이것들을 포함시키는 것이 중요하다.

(a) 정말로
(b) 결국
(c) 대신
(d) 다른 말로

식물 화학 물질이 섞인 식품은 아플 때만 먹는 대신 규칙적으로 식단에 포함시키라는 문맥으로 이해될 수 있으므로 정답은 (c)이다.

phytochemical 식물 화학 물질 **fight off** 퇴치하다 **compound** 화합물 **bell pepper** 피망 **nutrient** 영양소 **biological** 생물학적 **property** 특성, 성질 **immune system** 면역 체계 **viral** 바이러스성 **repair** 수리, 회복 **consume** 먹다, 섭취하다 **symptom** 징후, 증상 **recreate** 재생성하다, 다시 만들다 **laboratory** 실험실

Part II

11

특히 감염성이 높은 바이러스인 메가버그가 온 지구에 1년 안에 퍼지기 위해서는 특정한 조건이 충족되어야 한다. (a) 첫째로는 특히 추운 날씨에 널리 퍼지는 독감 바이러스 종류여야 한다. (b) 안타깝게도 끊임없는 연구가 있었지만 독감 바이러스를 죽일 백신은 없다. (c) 그것은 기도에 영향을 미치기 때문에 재채기와 기침은 3피트 반경 안에 있는 사람은 누구든지 쉽게 감염시킬 수 있다. (d) 마지막으로 바이러스는 대륙에서 대륙으로 건너갈 수 있게 하기 위해 비행기가 많이 다니는 주요 도시에서 생겨나야 한다.

감염이 매우 빠른 바이러스가 1년 내에 지구 전체를 감염을 시킬 수 있다는 내용과 방법을 이야기하고 있다. 그러나 (b)는 감염 통로를 이야기하지 않고 감기 바이러스를 죽일 백신은 없다고 한다. 따라서 흐름에 어긋나는 내용은 (b)이다.

contagious 전염성의 **strain** 계통 **respiratory tract** 기도 **radius** 반경

12

우리 몸의 뼈는 피부나 다른 신체 부위처럼 살아있다. (a) 뼈에는 혈관이 있고, 키와 몸이 커지면서 뼈가 자란다. (b) 뼈에는 부상에 반응하는 신경이 있으며, 대부분의 신경은 잘 보호되어 있고 심각한 부상이 있을 때만 접촉된다. (c) 신체에서 가장 단단한 뼈는 콘크리트보다 더 강한 넓적다리뼈이다. (d) 나이를 먹으면서 뼈에는 무기질 함량 많아져서 잘 부러지고 깨지기 쉽다.

(a) 뼈가 자라고, (b) 뼈에는 부상에 반응하는 신경이 있으며, (d) 나이가 들면서 뼈에 변화가 일어난다는 것은 뼈가 살아있는 조직이라는 것을 의미한다. 반면, (c)는 단지 넓적다리뼈가 우리 몸에서 가장 단단하다는 사실을 말하고 있으므로 문맥상 어색한 것은 (c)이다.

alive 살아 있는 blood vessel 혈관 nerve 신경 thigh 넓적다리
mineral material 무기질 brittle 잘 부러지는 susceptible to 민감한

Part III

13

19세기 초반 스페인은 군주제가 재건되고 있었고, 러시아는 알래스카와 아메리카 대륙의 서부 해안을 따라 확장하고 있었다. 당시 미국의 외교 정책은 그 시점 이후로 유럽과 미국이 정치적으로 분리된다는 것이었다. 후에 먼로주의라고 알려진 원칙에서 미국 정부는 아메리카 대륙에 새롭게 건국된 나라들은 더 이상 유럽 식민 세력의 간섭에 있지 않다고 선언했다.

Q: 이 글의 주제는?
(a) 미국에 대한 유럽의 위협
(b) 미국이 서양을 차지한 방법
(c) 아메리카 대륙의 독립
(d) 제임스 먼로, 제5대 대통령

아메리카 대륙에 대한 유럽의 불간섭주의를 선언한 미국의 외교 정책인 먼로주의에 관한 글이다. 유럽과 미국의 정치적 분리와 유럽의 식민 세력으로부터의 자유를 선언했다고 하므로 (c)가 가장 적절하다.

monarchy 군주제 restore 복구하다 sphere 영역 politically 정치적으로 Monroe Doctrine 먼로주의 declare 선언하다 Western Hemisphere 서반구 interference 간섭, 방해 threat 위협 independence 독립

14

영화 리뷰

디즈니의 애니메이션 영화 〈겨울왕국〉의 흥행 대성공의 이면에 그 인기를 설명하는 데 사실상 도움이 될 수 있는 조금의 놀라운 스토리 요소가 있었다. 처음에는 기존의 동화의 구성처럼 보이는 것이 전형성을 거스르는 테마를 포함하는 것으로 드러난다. 악당이 사회로부터 소외당하고 고립 속에 살아가는 것이 아이들의 이야기책에서 일반적인 반면, 여기에서 엘사 공주는 그녀의 고독 속에서 역량을 강화시키는 동정심을 불러일으키는 여주인공이다. 자연적인 본능을 부정하는 것을 강조한 그녀의 양육은 이 사회로부터 그녀 스스로를 유배시키는 것으로 끝났고, 아마도 양육의 실패로 보일 것이다.

Q: 이 글의 요지는?
(a) 줄거리 반전이 지겨운 이야기를 더 재미있게 만든다.
(b) 옛날식 동화는 악당을 동정심이 가게 만든다.
(c) 전통적인 것을 깨는 것이 이야기의 매력을 더한다.
(d) 유배되어 고립되는 것은 이야기 캐릭터의 몰락이다.

전형적인 것을 거스르는 테마를 포함한 영화 〈겨울왕국〉이 대성공했다는 이야기를 하고 있으므로 정답으로는 (c)가 타당하다.

box office success 흥행의 대성공 plot 구성 conventional 전통적인, 종래의 counter to ~을 거스르다 stereotype 고정 관념, 정형화된 생각 villain 악당 be shunned 소외되다 sympathetic 동정적인, 동정어린 heroine 여주인공 empowerment 역량 강화 upbringing 양육, 교육 natural instinct 자연 본능 exile 유배시키다 inconsistency 불일치, 모순 enliven 더 재미있게 만들다 tired 지겨운 old-fashioned 구식의 exile 망명, 유배 downfall 몰락

15

펑크는 70, 80년대 유행했던 시끄럽고 빠르며 과격한 록음악의 한 종류로 정의된다. 펑크 록은 음악계에 충격을 주었던 빠르고 신랄하며 솔직한 노래가 미국, 영국, 호주에 도입된 70년대 중반에 부상했다. 펑크는 개러지 록 장르에서 발전했고 당시 글램 로큰롤과 디스코와는 철저하게 대조적이었던 빠르고 예리한 신랄함을 보여주기 위해 노래의 복잡한 특징을 없앴다. 펑크는 매우 격렬한 강도로 등장했지만, 펑크의 무질서하고 격렬한 분노가 희박해지고 그 특징을 잃었기 때문에 불가피하게 생명이 짧았다. 펑크 밴드는 많은 돈을 버는 데에는 제 일을 했지만, 짧은 기간 동안만이었다.

Q: 이 글의 주제는 무엇인가?
(a) 펑크 이면에 숨겨진 이유
(b) 펑크의 흥망성쇠
(c) 펑크 패션의 역사
(d) 펑크 음악의 기원

이 지문은 펑크 음악의 등장과 마지막을 소개한다. 따라서 가장 적절한 정답은 (b)이다.

surface 부상하다 edgy 신랄한 anarchic 무질서의 rage 격노 diluted 희박화 된

16

중독은 현대 사회가 직면한 가장 큰 문제 중 하나이다. 주변의 중독자들을 돕기 위해서는 중독에 어떤 종류가 있는지, 그리고 그것들이 어떻게 발생하는지를 알 필요가 있다. 중독에는 두 종류가 있다. 약물 중독 (예를 들어 알코올 중독과 약물 남용, 흡연)과 행위 중독 (예를 들어 게임, 도박, 컴퓨터, 쇼핑, 식사)이 그것이다. 그러면 우리는 어떻게 중독되는가? 뇌의 특정 부위에서 도파민이 분비되면 즐거움이나 만족감을 준다. 이런 만족감을 바라게 되고 이 만족감에 대한 바람이 더 커진다. 이런 바람을 충족시키기 위해 도파민을 분비하는 행동을 반복하게 되고 반복은 중독이 된다.

Q: 이 글의 목적은 무엇인가?
(a) 중독을 방지하는 법을 알려주기 위해
(b) 인간이 어떻게 중독되는지 설명하기 위해
(c) 중독의 증상에 관해 교육시키기 위해
(d) 주변의 중독자들을 돕는 법을 가르치기 위해

두 종류의 중독과 중독이 되는 이유를 소개하고 있으므로 정답은 (b)이다. 나머지 정답은 중독이 되는 이유와는 거리가 멀기 때문에 오답이다.

addict 중독자 substance 약물 dopamine 도파민 repetition 반복 symptom 증상

17

영어에서 대개는 친척끼리 서로 많이 닮았다는 뜻으로 '빼닮았다'고 말하는 것을 들을 수 있다. 어떤 사람의 외모와 '내뱉다'라는 말을 연결 짓는 것은 이상하게 보일 수 있지만, 이 말은 수백 년 동안 영어에 있었다. 예를 들어, "그는 자기 아버지의 입에서 내뱉어진 것 같아"라는 식이다. 이런 발상은 두 사람이 너무 닮아서 한 명이 다른 한 명의 몸에서 만들어졌을 거라는 생각이다. 번식의 법칙에 의하면 이런 관용구는 상당 부분 진실을 품고 있다.

Q: 이 글에 나온 관용구에 관해 다음 중 옳은 것은?
(a) 현재는 원래 형태를 잃어버렸다.
(b) 친척들 사이에 어떻게 같은 성격을 갖는지를 설명한다.
(c) 큰 차이점이 있는 사람들의 유사점을 보여 준다.
(d) 거의 똑같이 보이는 사람들을 가리킨다.

사람들끼리 서로 많이 닮았다는 걸 의미하는 표현이므로 (d)가 적절하다.

spit (침을) 뱉다 **resemble** 닮다 **relative** 친척 **in connection with** ~와 관련되어 **look alike** 같아 보이다 **reproduction** 생식, 번식 **idiom** 관용구 **personality** 성격 **identical** 동일한

18

이제 졸업률이 〈유에스 뉴스 & 월드 리포트〉에서 발표하는 연례 학교 순위에서 가장 중요한 요소가 될 것이다. 매년 입학하는 신입생의 수를 세는 다른 카테고리는 덜 중요해질 것이다. 이 새로운 방식은 고등 교육의 실증적인 결과를 좀 더 보는 최근의 추세와 사고방식을 반영한다. 최고 학교들은 상위권에 남아 있지만 몇몇 대학은 순위가 껑충 뛰어 오를 것이다. 교육부는 사회적으로 혜택을 받지 못하는 학생을 돕는 데 중점을 두기 위해 등급제 역시 조정하고 있다.

Q: 이 글에 의하면 대학 순위에 관해 옳은 것은?
(a) 정부는 잡지들에게 초점을 바꿀 것을 요청하고 있다.
(b) 현재 빈곤한 신입생 비율이 증가하고 있다.
(c) 교육에 관한 관점과 가치가 변화하고 있다.
(d) 새로운 시스템 하에서 최고 순위가 바뀌었다.

학교의 순위를 매기는 데 신입생의 수를 세는 것은 덜 중요해질 것이고 이제는 졸업률이 중요한 요소가 되며, 이것은 교육에 대한 최근 변화된 추세를 반영한 것이라고 하므로 (c)가 적절하다. 새로운 시스템에도 최고 순위의 학교는 그대로 남아 있다고 하므로 (d)는 알맞지 않다.

school ranking 학교 순위 **reflect** 반영하다 **attitude** 사고방식 **practical** 실용적인 **adjust** 조절하다 **disadvantaged** 사회적으로 혜택을 받지 못한 **perspective** 관점 **shift** 이동하다

19

그랜빌 타임스
사회)교육

오늘날 대학생들은 졸업 후에 갚아야 하는 상당 금액의 대출을 받는다. 하지만 어려운 경제 상황에서 보수가 많은 일자리는 거의 없고, 졸업생들은 빚더미에서 벗어나기 위해 수십 년을 고생한다. 새로운 방침은 그 부담을 줄여 줄 것이다. 이 방식은 학생들의 등록금을 선불로 내준다. 졸업 후에 대출자들은 돈을 얼마나 버는지에 상관없이 매년 소득의 고정된 비율을 낼 것이다. 현재 체계와 비슷하게 들리지만, 경제적으로 어려운 시대에 저임금을 받는 학생들의 숨통을 트이게 해 줄 것이다.

Q: 이 글에 의하면 제안된 방침에 대해 다음 중 옳은 것은?
(a) 대학이 등록금을 낮추도록 할 것이다.
(b) 학업적으로 최고의 성적을 보이는 학생들에게 수여한다.
(c) 대출자의 졸업 후 소득을 고려한다.
(d) 대학이 덜 소비하고 더 저축하도록 하도록 독려한다.

대학생들 대출의 문제는 졸업 후 보수가 좋지 않아도 대출금을 갚느라 고생한다는 것이다. 이를 해결하기 수입에 상관없이 자기 소득의 고정 비율을 내게끔 하는 것이므로 (c)가 가장 적절하다.

decade 10년 **debt** 빚 **lessen** 덜어 주다 **tuition** 등록금 **up front** 선불로 **borrower** 빌리는 사람 **income** 소득 **spare** 면하게 하다, 할애하다 **wage** 임금 **financial** 재정적인 **reward** 상을 주다

20

흔히 생명체는 수십억 년 전 지구상에 존재했던 유일한 화학 물질의 조합으로 형성된 것이라고 알려져 있다. 하지만 지구 화학자 스티븐 베너는 현재의 지구 생명체에 관한 이론이 사실 틀렸으며, 적어도 부분적으로 옳지 않다고 믿고 있다. 베너는 우리 지구에는 어떤 핵심적인 요소가 빠져 있었다고 말한다. 그는 이 필수 광물이 운석에 의해 화성으로부터 왔을 것이라고 생각한다. 이 광물을 몰리브덴이라고 부르는데, 이것이 없으면 대부분의 유기체가 탄소의 끈적한 혼합물인 타르로 변한다. 공교롭게도 수십억 년 전 화성에는 몰리브덴이 풍부했다.

Q: 이 글에 의하면 스티븐 베너에 관해 다음 중 옳은 것은?
(a) 운석의 광물 구성에 대해 연구하고 기록한다.
(b) 화성이 없었더라면 지구에 생명체가 없었을 거라고 생각한다.
(c) 태양계의 다른 행성에서 생명체의 징후를 찾는다.
(d) 유기체가 지구에서 기인했다고 생각한다.

그는 지구에 빠져 있던 핵심 물질이 화성에서 온 몰리브덴이며, 이것이 없다면 유기체는 타르로 변할 거라고 생각한다. 따라서 (b)가 가장 적절하다.

form out of ~로 만들다 **combination** 결합 **geochemist** 지구화학자 **mineral** 광물질 **meteorite** 운석 **organic matter** 유기물 **sticky** 끈적끈적한 **mixture** 혼합물 **as it happens** 마침, 공교롭게도 **rich** ~이 풍부한 **solar system** 태양계 **organic** 유기체의 **neighboring** 인근의

21

대체로 젊은 사람들이 환경에 매우 잘 적응한다는 데 동의한다. 요즘 이런 얘기는 기술적으로 풍부한 시대에도 들어맞는데, 아이들이 오랜 시간을 컴퓨터와 휴대폰을 들여다보기 때문에 일반 국민들의 염려가 커지고 있다. 이런 경향은 '디지털 치매'라고 부르는데 아이들의 주의력이 집중되는 기간, 기억력, 감정 상태에 영향을 주기 때문이다. 이런 상황들은 영구적이지 않지만 젊은이들이 전자 기기에 많은 세월을 보낼 때 노인성 치매와 마찬가지로 그 영향력은 오래 간다.

Q: 이 글에 의하면 디지털 치매에 관해 다음 중 옳은 것은?
(a) 노인성 치매와 매우 유사하다.
(b) 10대들의 학습 능력에 미미한 위험이 있다.
(c) 디지털 미디어 이용자들에게 매우 잘 적응한다.
(d) 오래 방치하면 영향력은 평생 갈 것이다.

디지털 치매는 오래 되면 영향력이 오래 간다고 하므로 (d)가 적절하다. 아이들의 주의력이 집중되는 시간, 기억력, 감정 상태에 영향을 주기 때문에 학습 능력에 많은 영향을 끼친다고 볼 수 있으므로 (b)는 적절하지 않다.

adaptable 적응할 수 있는 **surroundings** 주변, 환경 **stare** 응시하다, 빤히 보다 **dementia** 치매 **span** 기간 **permanent** 영구적인 **persist** 계속되다 **endure** 지속되다

22

감정에 대한 호소인 파토스는 설득력이 있는 주장에 대한 아리스토텔레스의 이론에서 핵심적인 세 가지 요소 중 하나다. 각각 윤리와 논리를 의미하는 에토스와 로고스가 나머지 두 요소이다. 아리스토텔레스는 최고의 효과를 내기 위해서는 이 세 가지 기술이 모두 사용되어야 한다고 말했지만, 사람의 판단을 변화시키는 데 있어서 생각이나 이론에 대한 청자의 감정적인 반응이 결정적이라고 생각했다. 후대의 철학자들은 수사적 기교의 형태로서 파토스에 등을 돌리고 거의 전적으로 논리만을 강조했다. 그들은 사람의 마음을 변화시키려 할 때 파토스는 부당한 접근이라고 여겼다.

Q: 이 글에 의하면 파토스에 대해 다음 중 옳은 것은?
(a) 좀 더 현대적인 환경에서는 덜 강조되었다.
(b) 타인이 행동하도록 설득하기 위해 논리에 의존한다.
(c) 생각을 정당화하기 위한 핑계로 사용된다.
(d) 다른 두 구성 요소와 모순되는 개념이다.

아리스토텔레스의 설득의 세 요소 중 하나인 파토스를 후대의 철학자들은 외면했다고 하므로 가장 옳은 것은 (a)이다. 파토스가 에토스나 로고스를 부정하는 개념이라는 언급은 없으므로 (d)는 옳지 않다.

appeal 호소 **component** 구성 요소 **persuasive** 설득력 있는 **ethics** 윤리 **logic** 논리 **crucial** 중대한, 결정적인 **judgment** 판단 **philosopher** 철학자 **rhetoric** 수사법, 웅변술 **emphasize** 강조하다 **exclusively** 오로지 **unfair** 불공평한 **context** 정황, 배경 **contradict** 부정하다, 모순되다

23

신입생들에게 알립니다!

교육부에 따르면 내년 모든 9학년 학생들은 새로운 학업 기준을 충족시켜야 합니다.

· 전 학생들은 미술 수업을 4시간 대신 6시간 이수해야 합니다. 우등으로 졸업하고 싶은 학생들은 미적분학 I과 미적분학 II를 통과해야 합니다.

· 체육 교육이 필요하다면 이제 헬스장이나 학교 이외의 체육 수업에 참석하는 것을 허가합니다.

· 전 학생들은 총 30시간 중 6시간 이상 인증된 자원봉사 활동을 수행해야 합니다.

그에 맞춰 계획을 짜고 졸업에 필요한 모든 것을 확실히 하기 위해 학교 상담 교사와 이야기하세요.

Q: 이 글로부터 유추할 수 있는 것은?
(a) 학생들은 미적분 I, II를 이수하면 졸업할 수 있다.
(b) 학생들이 들어야 하는 미술 수업은 줄어들었다.
(c) 학생들은 교실 밖에서 제공되는 어떤 수업도 들을 수 없다.
(d) 학생들이 충족시켜야 하는 일부 조건들이 강화되었다.

의무적으로 이수해야 하는 미술 수업 시간은 4시간에서 6시간으로 늘어나고, 봉사활동 시간은 6시간 더 해야 하므로 일부 조건들이 강화되었음을 알 수 있다. 따라서 정답은 (d)이다.

calculus 미적분학 **requirement** 필수 **physical education** 체육 **certificated** 인증된 **ensure** 확실히 하다 **refine** 개선하다 **tactic** 전략 **slip in** 알아채지 않게 들어가다 **physical** 신체적인

24

온라인 쇼핑몰은 오프라인 몰과 거의 똑같이 작용한다. 웹 사이트 하나만으로 소비자들은 주택 개조 용품들, 의류, 서적, 액세서리 등을 구매하며 여러 다양한 상점에서 쇼핑을 할 수 있다. 사이트들은 온라인 구매 경험을 더욱 편리하게 만듦으로써 쇼핑객들을 매료시키려 노력한다. 몇몇 회사들은 소비자의 후기를 온라인 쇼핑몰 콘셉트로 포함시키기 시작하고 있다. 예를 들어, 쇼핑몰은 각각 다른 상점 물건이더라도 최상위 순위에 오른 겨울 재킷들을 알아낼 수 있고, 소비자들이 자신에게 가장 잘 맞는 상품을 더 쉽게 찾을 수 있도록 도울 수 있는 것이다.

Q: 이 글로부터 온라인 쇼핑몰에 관해 유추할 수 있는 것은?
(a) 소비자들이 요구한 상품만을 주문하고 있다.
(b) 사업 모델이 오프라인 몰의 사업 모델을 변화시켰다.
(c) 온라인 쇼핑몰의 성공으로 오프라인 몰이 망하고 있다.
(d) 쇼핑을 향상시킬 수 있는 서비스를 결합하고 있다.

웹 사이트 하나만으로 오프라인에서 쇼핑하는 것처럼 여러 가지 다양한 상점에서 쇼핑을 할 수 있다는 점을 강조하고 있고, 소비자들이 더 잘 선택할 수 있도록 순위를 보여 준다고 했으므로 (d)가 가장 적절하다.

function 작용하다 **physical** 물질의, 물리적인 **home improvement product** 주택 개조 용품 **incorporate** 포함하다 **suit** 어울리다 **order** 주문하다 **out of business** 파산한

25

현재의 레바논 근처인 페니키아 도시 국가의 성장은 기원전 약 1200년경 뱃사람들의 침략 후에 이루어졌다. 상세히 기록된 것은 아니지만, 북쪽에서 온 이 공격은 이집트와 히타이트 제국을 상당히 약화시켰다. 이런 권력의 공백으로 인해 페니키아인들은 지중해 동쪽 끝에 자신들의 무역 제국을 건설했다. 그들은 도심지를 조직하고 믿을 만한 배를 건조하는 능력으로 빠르게 유명해졌다. 기원전 539년 키루스 대왕의 페르시아의 통치 하에 놓이자, 그들의 몰락이 시작되었다.

Q: 이 글로부터 페니키아인에 관해 유추할 수 있는 것은?
(a) 그들은 움직이면서 절대 한 곳에서 오래 살지 않았다.
(b) 바다의 침략자들이 공격해 오자 배로 도망쳤다.
(c) 그들의 종교적인 믿음은 이웃 나라들과 달랐다.
(d) 그들은 도시와 상업을 건설하는 데 유능했다.

도시를 구성하고 배를 건조하는 능력이 있는 등 무역 제국을 건설했다고 하므로 (d)가 가장 적절하다.

Phoenician 페니키아의 **come along** 생기다 **invasion** 침략 **weaken** 약화시키다 **vacuum** 진공, 공백 **distinguish** 두드러지게 하다 **reliable** 믿을 수 있는 **invader** 침략군 **belief** (종교·정치상의) 신조, 교의 **effective** 유능한, 인상적인 **commerce** 상업, 교역

Part IV

26-27

◀ 제니퍼

〈나〉

안녕, 제니퍼. 어떻게 지냈어? 너와 네 가족들이 건강하게 지내기를 바라. 나는 최근에 플로리다(우편번호 32805), 올란도, 7 콘라드 가, 343호의 새 아파트로 이사를 했다는 것을 알려주고 싶어. 그래서 나는 4월 20일에 집들이 파티를 열고 싶어. 네가 함께 해 준다면 매우 기쁠 것 같아. 그 파티는 저녁 7시 정각에 시작할 예정이고, 저녁과 함께 술과 간단한 디저트가 제공 될거야. 파티에서 네가 함께 해 주기를 기다리고 있을게. 그때까지 잘 지내.

〈제니퍼〉

너의 집들이 파티에 나를 초대해주어 고마워. 하지만 유감스럽게도 너의 특별한 날에 가지 못할 것 같아. 나는 선약 때문에 다른 중요한 행사에 참석하러 다른 곳에 갈 예정이야. 너에게 많은 사랑과 행운을 빌어주고 싶어. 돌아오자마자 너의 행복을 직접 축하해 줄게. 안녕.

26. Q: 집들이에서 제공되는 것은 무엇인가?
(a) 국수
(b) 알코올음료
(c) 과일 주스
(d) 탄산음료

27. Q: 메시지들에 따르면 옳은 것은 무엇인가?
(a) 토마스는 다음 주에 새로운 아파트로 이사 갈 예정이다.
(b) 토마스는 그의 집들이 파티에 모든 친구들을 초대할 것이다.
(c) 제니퍼는 토마스의 집들이 파티에 참석할 예정이다.
(d) 제니퍼는 선약에서 돌아온 이후에 토마스를 만날 것이다.

26. 토마스가 집들이에 초대하는 내용에서 "dinner", "dessert" 그리고 "liquor"를 제공하겠다고 했으므로 알코올음료가 제공된다는 것을 알 수 있다. 정답은 (b)이다.

27. 제니퍼는 선약 때문에 참석하지 못하지만, "I'll celebrate your happiness in person"이라는 문장을 통해 직접 만나서 축하하겠다는 것을 알 수 있다. 정답은 (d)이다.

host 열다, 개최하다 **house warming party** 집들이 **presence** 참석, 존재 **delight** 기쁨 **sharp** 정각 **liquor** 술, 알코올음료 **prior** 사전의 **celebrate** 축하하다 **arrangement** 약속

28-29

의료 기록 요청서

발신자: 폴 스미스 (환자 번호: 289423)
수신자: 휴스턴 시립 병원 고객서비스 담당자
복사 부수: 2

이 편지는 당신 병원이 가지고 있는 제 의료기록의 복사본을 요청하기 위한 것입니다. 저는 건강관리 및 보험법에 따라서 환자들이 그들의 의료기록의 복사본을 가질 권한이 있다는 것을 알고 있습니다.

저는 3월 23일부터 4월 2일까지 당신의 병원에서 치료를 받고 입원했었습니다. 저는 혈액 검사 결과, 영상 분석, 수술 보고서, 의사들의 기록, 전문가들과의 상담 기록, 그리고 의료 파일에 있는 모든 기록 등을 포함하여 제 의료기록의 모든 것의 복사본을 받고 싶습니다.

저는 당신이 기록물을 복사하고 병원에 가지고 있는 제 주소로 보내주는 것에 대해 합당한 수수료를 청구하는 것을 이해합니다. 저는 당신이 이 요청서를 받은 이후에 30일 이내에 위에서 언급한 기록물을 받기를 바라고 지연되는 경우에는 사유를 설명하는 편지를 받기를 바랍니다.

질문이 있으시다면, 222-555-4652로 전화를 주시거나, paulsmith@gmail.com으로 연락을 주세요.

28. Q: 양식의 주요 목적은 무엇인가?
(a) 환자의 의료 기록에 있는 실수를 교정해 달라고 병원에 요구하기 위해
(b) 재검진을 받기 위해 대한 의사로부터의 기록을 요청하기 위해
(c) 병원에게 환자의 의료 기록을 보내달라고 요청하기 위해
(d) 병원에서 청구된 과도한 수수료에 대해 불만을 제기하기 위해

29. Q: 양식에서 옳은 것은 무엇인가?
(a) 환자들은 특별한 경우에만 그들의 의료 기록 복사본을 요청할 수 있다.
(b) 폴은 외래 환자로서 10일 동안 병원에서 치료를 받았다.
(c) 폴은 자신의 질병을 치료하기 위해 혈액 검사를 받았다.
(d) 의료 기록들은 일반적으로 이메일로 고객들에게 보내진다.

28. 치료 및 입원 기록을 요청하는 양식이며, "This is a letter to request copies of my medical records your hospital has"를 통해서 의료 기록의 복사본을 요청하고 있으며, 주소로 보내달라고 했으므로, 정답은 (c)이다.

29. 폴 스미스가 진료 받았던 세부 내역을 요청하는 지문이며, 그 중에서 혈액 검사도 포함되어 있으므로, 정답은 (c)이다.

request 요청하다　medical record 의료기록　be entitled to
~할 권한이 있다　be hospitalized 입원하다　consultation 상담, 진찰
reasonable 합리적인, 합당한　excessive 과도한　outpatient 외래환자
conduct 수행하다. 집행하다

30-31

수학적 천재: 에미 뇌터

수학에서 천재로 여겨지는, 유대인 여성이었던 에미 뇌터는 학계에서 성적 차별을 지속적으로 받았었다. 왜냐하면 당시 여성들은 1800년대 후반과 1900년대 초반에 고등교육을 받을 수 없었기 때문이다. 그녀는 "브리태니커 백과사전"에 현대의 가장 창의적인 수학자로 묘사되고 있다. 심지어 알버트 아인슈타인도 공개적으로 그녀를 가장 뛰어난 수학적 천재라고 인정했다.

수학에서 박사학위를 받은 이후에, 그녀는 처음 직함도 없이 그리고 때때로 남성의 가명을 가지고 대학 강사로 일했다. 그녀는 뛰어난 물리학자들 및 수학자들과 함께 일하면서 40편 이상의 학술적 논문을 출판했다.

1933년에, 나치가 독일을 장악하고 모든 유대인 교수들이 학교에서 가르치는 것을 금지시켰다. 그러한 박해 때문에, 뇌터는 미국으로 이주했으며, 그곳에서 그녀는 즉시 학자로 인정받았으며, 수학 및 물리학 이론을 연구했다. 그러나 1930년대 중반에, 그녀는 난소 낭종을 제거하는 수술에서 발생한 합병증 때문에 갑작스럽게 사망했다.

30. Q: 에미 뇌터에 대해 옳은 것은 무엇인가?
(a) 그녀는 학계에서 동등하게 대우받지 못했다.
(b) 그녀는 역사상 가장 창의적인 과학자로 평가받아왔다.
(c) 그녀의 이름으로 제공된 강의들은 학생들 사이에 매우 인기가 있었다.
(d) 그녀는 나치가 그녀를 남겨두려는 시도에도 불구하고 미국으로 이주했다.

31. Q: 본문에서 에미 뇌터에 대해 추론할 수 있는 것은?
(a) 그녀는 유리한 환경에서 고등교육을 받을 수 있었다.
(b) 그녀는 나치의 지지를 받아 40편 이상의 논문을 출판할 수 있었다.
(c) 그녀는 성과 인종 때문에 차별을 받았다.
(d) 그녀는 여전히 새로운 국가에서 성적 차별에 직면했다.

30. 수학 천재였던 에미 뇌터에 대해 설명하는 지문이며, "suffered gender discrimination in academic circles"라는 내용을 통해 성차별을 받았다는 것을 알 수 있으므로, 정답은 (a)이다.

31. 에미 뇌터의 수학자로서의 삶 과정에서, "gender discrimination"과 "banned all Jewish professors from teaching"이라는 내용을 통해서 성적 차별뿐만 아니라 인종적 차별도 겪었다는 것을 알 수 있다. 정답은 (c)이다.

genius 천재　discrimination 차별　contemporary 당대의
describe 묘사하다　pseudonym 가명, 필명　notable 뛰어난, 주목받는
persecution 박해, 학대　immigrate 이민가다　embrace 포용하다,
수용하다　complications 합병증　ovarian cyst 난소 낭종　retain
유지[보유]하다　favorable 호의적인, 유리한　encounter 직면하다

32-33

미국범죄학회지

홈 ∨ **논문** ∨ 학회 소개 ∨ 투고 ∨ 구독 ∨ 최다 인용 논문 ∨ 검색

160만 명 이상의 사람들이 투옥된 상황에서, 미국은 세계에서 두 번째로 가장 높은 투옥률을 가지고 있다. 점점 더 많은 사람들이 이익을 추구하는 사설 회사들에 의해 운영되는 감옥에 투옥되어 있다. 찬성론자들은 이러한 사설 감옥들이 정부 지출을 줄이는 해결책이 될 수 있다고 말한다. 정부 통계에 따르면, 사설 감옥들은 현재 미국에 있는 모든 죄수들 중 10%를 보유하고 있다. 또한, 수십만 명의 비공식적인 불법 이민자들이 매년 때때로 사설로 운영되는 시설에 구금되어 있다.

그러나 최근 학술적 연구에 따르면, 사설로 운영되는 설비들이 비용이 덜 들 수 있지만, 그것들은 때때로 죄수들의 인권을 위반하고 있으며, 도덕적이고 윤리적인 문제들을 제기한다. 몇몇 범죄학자들은 사설 감옥들이 연방 및 주정부에 의해 운영되는 시설들보다 더 위험하고 죄수들을 교화시키는 데 비효과적이라는 점을 우려한다. 따라서 몇몇 반대하는 하원의 원들은 회사들이 정부로부터 자금지원을 받는 것과 법률적 구멍을 이용하는 것을 막는 법안을 제출했다. 그들은 또한 사설 감옥들이 정부가 운영하는 감옥들처럼 동일한 수준의 투명성을 유지하도록 요구한다.

32. Q: 본문의 주요 논점은 무엇인가?
(a) 정부 지출을 절약하기 위해 제안된 해결책
(b) 사설로 운영되는 감옥들의 위상과 논쟁들
(c) 죄수들의 권리를 침해하는 심각성
(d) 사설로 운영되는 시설들의 몇 가지 법률적 구멍들

33. Q: 왜 범죄학자들은 사설로 운영되는 감옥들에 반대하는가?
(a) 사설 감옥들을 유지하기 위해 많은 세금이 쓰이기 때문이다.
(b) 정부가 운영하는 감옥들은 훨씬 더 적은 죄수들을 수용할 수 있기 때문이다.
(c) 사설 감옥을 운영하는 데 있어서 투명성은 종종 의심스럽다고 여겨지기 때문이다.
(d) 사설감옥들은 죄수들을 교화시키는 데 실패했다고 밝혀졌기 때문이다.

32. 미국 내에서 사설 감옥들의 운영 목적과 현황, 그리고 문제점을 지적하는 내용이므로, 정답은 (b)이다.

33. 사설 감옥의 경영에 대해 반대하는 사람들의 논리 중, "require private prisons to maintain the same level of transparency"라는 내용을 통해, 반대론의 이유들 중 한 가지는 투명성의 문제이므로, 정답은 (c)이다.

behind bars 감옥에 갇힌　incarceration 투옥, 구금　be held in
prison 감옥에 갇히다　proponent 찬성론자　expenditure 지출, 비용
inmate 죄수　undocumented 공식기록이 없는　detain 구금하다
facility 설비, 시설　criminologist 범죄학자　rehabilitate 교화시키다
opponent 반대론자　transparency 투명성　controversy 논쟁, 논란
loophole 구멍, 틈　dubious 의심스러운, 모호한

34-35

뉴질랜드의 남섬의 산악 지역 태생인 케아 앵무새들은 포유동물들에 의한 포식과 인간 활동에 의한 영향 때문에 고통 받고 있다. 고양이들은 주요한 포식동물들 중의 하나로 알려져 있는데, 특히 고양이들이 케아 앵무새들의 서식지에 침입할 때 그러하다. 주머니쥐들 또한 케아 앵무새들을 잡아먹으며, 그들의 서식지를 파괴하는데 그들의 위협이 족제비들보다 심각한 것은 아니다. 그들의 둥지는 특히나 취약한데, 그것들은 땅 속에 있는 구멍에 불과하여 발견하고 침입하기 쉽기 때문이다.

연구에 따르면, 취식 지역에 있는 케아 앵무새들은 건물과 자동차와 같은 인공적인 물건들에 의한 사고로부터 위험에 처해 있다. 납으로 만든 못으로 만들어진 건물들은 납이 그들에게 단맛을 제공하며, 납 중독을 유발하기 때문에 케아 앵무새들에게 위협을 주고 있다. 그들은 또한 자동차의 와이퍼와 앞 유리창 고무를 노리며 자동차에 해를 끼치는 경향이 있다. 그것들은 또한 캠핑장과 주차장 주변의 부지에 해를 끼치고 있으며, 케아 앵무새들과 인간들 사이에 갈등을 유발한다. 따라서 비록 불법이기는 하지만, 인간들은 케아 앵무새들을 쏘아 죽이고 있다.

34. Q: 본문의 주요 논점은 무엇인가?
(a) 케아 앵무새들의 취약한 지하 서식지
(b) 케아 앵무새 개체수를 위협하는 몇 가지 요인들
(c) 케아 앵무새들을 끌어들이는 해로운 인공물들
(d) 인간과 케아 앵무새들 사이의 갈등을 유발하는 원인들

35. Q: 본문에서 케아 앵무새들에 대해 추론할 수 있는 것은?
(a) 그들의 서식지는 지하에 구멍처럼 꼼꼼하게 그리고 안전하게 위장되어 있다.
(b) 주머니쥐들은 침입자로서 그들에게 가장 위험한 포식동물이다.
(c) 그들은 특정 물질에 대한 특별한 기호 때문에 종종 위험에 처한다.
(d) 대부분의 인간들은 그들의 개체수를 보호하기 위해 노력하고 있다.

34. 뉴질랜드에 고유한 케아 앵무새에 대해 설명하는 내용이며, 포식동물, 습성에 의해 발생하는 문제들, 그리고 인간과의 갈등 등을 언급하고 있으므로, (b)가 정답임을 알 수 있다.

35. 케아 앵무새의 여러 가지 습성들을 언급하는 과정에서, "posing a threat to kea parrots since lead has a sweet taste to them, resulting in lead poisoning"을 지적하고 있으며, 이를 통해서 특이한 기호가 위험이 되고 있다는 것을 알 수 있으므로, 정답은 (c)이다.

kea parrot 케아 앵무새   **predation** 포식, 약탈   **invasion** 침입, 침해   **opossum** 주머니쥐   **prey on** 잡아먹다, 포식하다   **disturb** 방해하다, 폐를 끼치다   **stoat** 족제비   **vulnerable** 상하기 쉬운, 약점이 있는   **windshield** 자동차 앞 유리   **compromise** 손상시키다   **property** 특징, 특성   **albeit** ~임에도 불구하고   **illegal** 불법적인   **meticulously** 세심하게, 조심스럽게   **disguise** 위장하다

TEPS Test of English Proficiency developed by Seoul National University

독해 Reading Comprehension

Actual Test 1

1	a	b	c	d	26	a	b	c	d
2	a	b	c	d	27	a	b	c	d
3	a	b	c	d	28	a	b	c	d
4	a	b	c	d	29	a	b	c	d
5	a	b	c	d	30	a	b	c	d
6	a	b	c	d	31	a	b	c	d
7	a	b	c	d	32	a	b	c	d
8	a	b	c	d	33	a	b	c	d
9	a	b	c	d	34	a	b	c	d
10	a	b	c	d	35	a	b	c	d
11	a	b	c	d					
12	a	b	c	d					
13	a	b	c	d					
14	a	b	c	d					
15	a	b	c	d					
16	a	b	c	d					
17	a	b	c	d					
18	a	b	c	d					
19	a	b	c	d					
20	a	b	c	d					
21	a	b	c	d					
22	a	b	c	d					
23	a	b	c	d					
24	a	b	c	d					
25	a	b	c	d					

Actual Test 2

1	a	b	c	d	26	a	b	c	d
2	a	b	c	d	27	a	b	c	d
3	a	b	c	d	28	a	b	c	d
4	a	b	c	d	29	a	b	c	d
5	a	b	c	d	30	a	b	c	d
6	a	b	c	d	31	a	b	c	d
7	a	b	c	d	32	a	b	c	d
8	a	b	c	d	33	a	b	c	d
9	a	b	c	d	34	a	b	c	d
10	a	b	c	d	35	a	b	c	d
11	a	b	c	d					
12	a	b	c	d					
13	a	b	c	d					
14	a	b	c	d					
15	a	b	c	d					
16	a	b	c	d					
17	a	b	c	d					
18	a	b	c	d					
19	a	b	c	d					
20	a	b	c	d					
21	a	b	c	d					
22	a	b	c	d					
23	a	b	c	d					
24	a	b	c	d					
25	a	b	c	d					

Actual Test 3

1	a	b	c	d	26	a	b	c	d
2	a	b	c	d	27	a	b	c	d
3	a	b	c	d	28	a	b	c	d
4	a	b	c	d	29	a	b	c	d
5	a	b	c	d	30	a	b	c	d
6	a	b	c	d	31	a	b	c	d
7	a	b	c	d	32	a	b	c	d
8	a	b	c	d	33	a	b	c	d
9	a	b	c	d	34	a	b	c	d
10	a	b	c	d	35	a	b	c	d
11	a	b	c	d					
12	a	b	c	d					
13	a	b	c	d					
14	a	b	c	d					
15	a	b	c	d					
16	a	b	c	d					
17	a	b	c	d					
18	a	b	c	d					
19	a	b	c	d					
20	a	b	c	d					
21	a	b	c	d					
22	a	b	c	d					
23	a	b	c	d					
24	a	b	c	d					
25	a	b	c	d					

Actual Test 4

1	a	b	c	d	26	a	b	c	d
2	a	b	c	d	27	a	b	c	d
3	a	b	c	d	28	a	b	c	d
4	a	b	c	d	29	a	b	c	d
5	a	b	c	d	30	a	b	c	d
6	a	b	c	d	31	a	b	c	d
7	a	b	c	d	32	a	b	c	d
8	a	b	c	d	33	a	b	c	d
9	a	b	c	d	34	a	b	c	d
10	a	b	c	d	35	a	b	c	d
11	a	b	c	d					
12	a	b	c	d					
13	a	b	c	d					
14	a	b	c	d					
15	a	b	c	d					
16	a	b	c	d					
17	a	b	c	d					
18	a	b	c	d					
19	a	b	c	d					
20	a	b	c	d					
21	a	b	c	d					
22	a	b	c	d					
23	a	b	c	d					
24	a	b	c	d					
25	a	b	c	d					

Actual Test 5

1	a	b	c	d	26	a	b	c	d
2	a	b	c	d	27	a	b	c	d
3	a	b	c	d	28	a	b	c	d
4	a	b	c	d	29	a	b	c	d
5	a	b	c	d	30	a	b	c	d
6	a	b	c	d	31	a	b	c	d
7	a	b	c	d	32	a	b	c	d
8	a	b	c	d	33	a	b	c	d
9	a	b	c	d	34	a	b	c	d
10	a	b	c	d	35	a	b	c	d
11	a	b	c	d					
12	a	b	c	d					
13	a	b	c	d					
14	a	b	c	d					
15	a	b	c	d					
16	a	b	c	d					
17	a	b	c	d					
18	a	b	c	d					
19	a	b	c	d					
20	a	b	c	d					
21	a	b	c	d					
22	a	b	c	d					
23	a	b	c	d					
24	a	b	c	d					
25	a	b	c	d					

기본부터 실천까지, 가장 빠르게!

NEW TEPS 실력편 독해

뉴텝스 400+ 목표 대비

- 서울대텝스관리위원회 NEW TEPS 경향 완벽 반영
- 뉴텝스 400점 이상 목표 달성을 위한 최적의 기본서
- 올바른 독해를 위한 문장 구조 이해 중심의 문법 수록
- 신유형을 포함한 뉴텝스 독해의 파트별 문제풀이 공략법
- 뉴텝스 독해의 배경지식을 넓히는 주제별 독해 훈련 제공
- 뉴텝스 실전 완벽 대비 Actual Test 5회분 수록
- 고득점의 감을 확실하게 잡아 주는 상세한 해설 제공
- 모바일 단어장 및 보카 테스트 등 다양한 부가자료 제공

Reading